Christian Colleges & Universities

Profiles of Leading Colleges That Emphasize Academic Quality and Spiritual Growth

The Official Guide to
Member Institutions
of the Council for
Christian Colleges
& Universities

Council for Christian
Colleges & Universities

7th edition

PETERSON'S
★
THOMSON LEARNING ™

Australia • Canada • Mexico • Singapore • Spain • United Kingdom • United States

About Peterson's

Founded in 1966, Peterson's, a division of Thomson Learning, is the nation's largest and most respected provider of lifelong learning online resources, software, reference guides, and books. The Education Supersite^{SM} at petersons.com—the Web's most heavily traveled education resource—has searchable databases and interactive tools for contacting U.S.-accredited institutions and programs. CollegeQuest^{SM} (CollegeQuest.com) offers a complete solution for every step of the college decision-making process. GradAdvantage^{TM} (GradAdvantage.org), developed with Educational Testing Service, is the only electronic admissions service capable of sending official graduate test score reports with a candidate's online application. Peterson's serves more than 55 million education consumers annually.

Thomson Learning is among the world's leading providers of lifelong learning, serving the needs of individuals, learning institutions, and corporations with products and services for both traditional classrooms and for online learning. For more information about the products and services offered by Thomson Learning, please visit www.thomsonlearning.com. Headquartered in Stamford, Connecticut, with offices worldwide, Thomson Learning is part of The Thomson Corporation (www.thomson.com), a leading e-information and solutions company in the business, professional, and education marketplaces. The Corporation's common shares are listed on the Toronto and London stock exchanges.

For more information, contact Peterson's, 2000 Lenox Drive, Lawrenceville, NJ 08648; 800-338-3282; or find us on the World Wide Web at: www.petersons.com/about

ISSN 1521-9070
ISBN 0-7689-0586-9

Printed in Canada

10 9 8 7 6 5 4 3 2 1   02 01 00

Contents

MAP OF CHRISTIAN COLLEGES AND UNIVERSITIES (CANADA AND THE UNITED STATES)

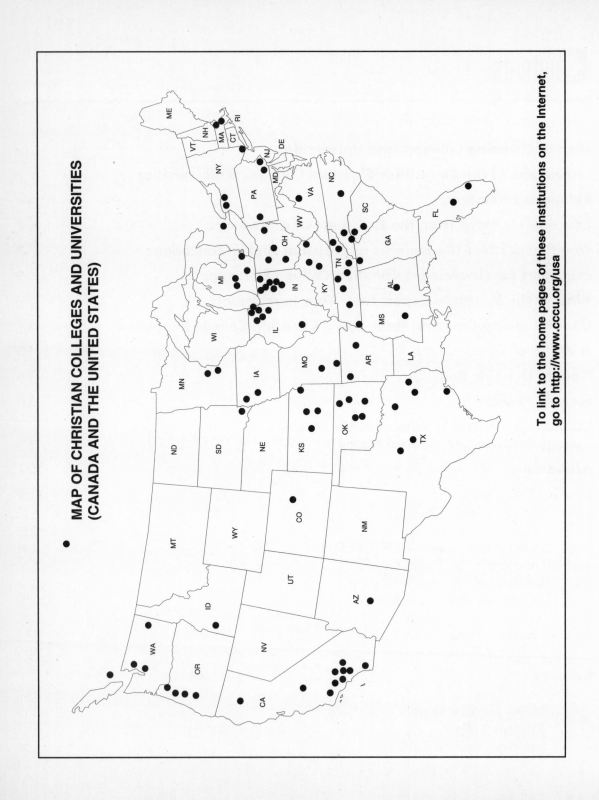

To link to the home pages of these institutions on the Internet, go to http://www.cccu.org/usa

Institutions of the Council for Christian Colleges & Universities

Religious Affiliations

ASSEMBLIES OF GOD
Evangel University
Northwest College
Vanguard University of Southern California

BAPTIST DENOMINATIONS

American Baptist
Eastern College
Judson College (IL)
University of Sioux Falls

Baptist
Cornerstone University
Dallas Baptist University
Western Baptist College

Baptist General Conference
Bethel College (MN)

General Association of Regular Baptist Churches
Cedarville University

Southern Baptist
California Baptist University
Campbell University
Campbellsville University
East Texas Baptist University
Howard Payne University
Judson College (AL)
North Greenville College
Oklahoma Baptist University
Southwest Baptist University
Union University
Williams Baptist College

The Christian and Missionary Alliance
Nyack College
Simpson College

CHRISTIAN CHURCH
Hope International University
Northwest Christian College

CHRISTIAN CHURCH (DISCIPLES OF CHRIST) AND CHRISTIAN CHURCHES/CHURCHES OF CHRIST
Northwest Christian College

CHRISTIAN CHURCHES/CHURCHES OF CHRIST
Kentucky Christian College
Milligan College

CHURCH OF CHRIST
Abilene Christian University
Lipscomb University
Oklahoma Christian University

CHURCH OF GOD (Anderson, IN)
Anderson University
Warner Pacific College
Warner Southern College

CHURCH OF GOD (Cleveland, TN)
Lee University

CHURCH OF THE NAZARENE
Eastern Nazarene College
MidAmerica Nazarene University
Mount Vernon Nazarene College
Northwest Nazarene University
Olivet Nazarene University
Point Loma Nazarene University

Southern Nazarene University
Trevecca Nazarene University

BRETHREN AND MENNONITE DENOMINATIONS
Church of the United Brethren in Christ
Huntington College
Fellowship of Grace Brethren Churches
Grace College & Seminary
Mennonite Brethren Church
Fresno Pacific University
Tabor College
General Conference Mennonite Church
Bethel College (KS)
Bluffton College
Mennonite Church
Eastern Mennonite University
Goshen College

EVANGELICAL COVENANT
North Park University

EVANGELICAL FREE CHURCH
Trinity Western University

EVANGELICAL FREE CHURCH OF AMERICA
Trinity International University

FRIENDS DENOMINATIONS
Evangelical Friends
George Fox University
Evangelical Friends Church, Eastern Region
Malone College

FREE METHODIST
Greenville College
Roberts Wesleyan College
Seattle Pacific University
Spring Arbor College

FUNDAMENTAL, NONDENOMINATIONAL
The Master's College & Seminary

MISSIONARY CHURCH
Bethel College (IN)

PRESBYTERIAN DENOMINATIONS
Associate Reformed Presbyterian
Erskine College
Presbyterian Church
Belhaven College
King College
Presbyterian Church (USA)
College of the Ozarks
Montreat College
Sterling College
Whitworth College
Presbyterian Church in America
Covenant College
Reformed Presbyterian Church N.A.
Geneva College

REFORMED DENOMINATIONS
Christian Reformed Church
Calvin College
Dordt College
Reformed Church in America
Northwestern College (IA)

WESLEYAN CHURCH
Bartlesville Wesleyan College
Houghton College
Indiana Wesleyan University
Southern Wesleyan University

INDEPENDENT
Grand Canyon University
Houston Baptist University

INTERDENOMINATIONAL
Messiah College
Westmont College
William Tyndale College

INTER/DENOMINATIONAL
Gordon College

INTER/NONDENOMINATIONAL
Asbury College
Azusa Pacific University
Biola University
Bryan College

Colorado Christian University
John Brown University
The King's University College
LeTourneau University
Palm Beach Atlantic College
Redeemer University College
Taylor University
Trinity Christian College
Wheaton College

NONDENOMINATIONAL
Northwestern College (MN)
Oral Roberts University

Education Is More Than the Exchange of Knowledge

■ Choosing a college is one of life's most important decisions. It represents not only a significant financial investment, but also influences so much of who we become in all areas of life—our philosophy, values, intellectual and emotional preparedness for careers, long-term friendships, and a commitment to serving others.

The array of choices is overwhelming, even for students and families desiring a "Christian" college education. For example, some colleges are church-related only in the sense of being historically linked to a particular denomination. Then there are all the choices among locations, academic offerings, available financial aid, and more.

Of the 3,600 colleges and universities in the United States, only 700 maintain some tie to a specific church denomination or religious tradition. Among these, a smaller number are referred to as "Christ-centered." One hundred of these colleges and universities are members of the Council for Christian Colleges & Universities, an association of regionally accredited four-year colleges and universities rooted in the liberal arts and professional studies. These are the institutions featured in this guide.

On the surface, most small colleges look a lot alike. They promise a strong academic program, varied co-curricular offerings, a pleasant campus, and a friendly faculty. What sets Christ-centered colleges apart is the way in which faith, learning, and life come together.

Faculty members play a key role in making Christian colleges and universities truly Christ-centered. Faculty members at Christian colleges are hired for their academic credentials as well as their mature faith. Classroom instruction is first-rate. Professors are not afraid to pose tough questions and challenge young scholars to think deeply about their faith. These professors are willing to reveal their own imperfections as humans and recognize the complexity even for Christians, freeing students to ask honest questions about anything. For many students, faculty members become much more than teachers—they are role models, mentors, and lifelong friends.

Academically

- Find all the advantages expected from a smaller, private college.
- Choose from more than 300 majors and 90 graduate programs.
- Be taught by real professors, not graduate students.
- Be sought after by graduate programs.
- Interact with challenging classmates.
- Expand your world through study-abroad experiences.

Spiritually

- Be strengthened and encouraged to live a vibrant Christian faith, equipping you to face life's challenges.
- Work with professors committed to their faith.

- Learn to witness God's hand in all subjects—from accounting to history to dance.
- Broaden your faith through student-led worship services, prayer, and Bible study groups.

Personally

- Be challenged to think critically
- Live in a community that values your character development as much as knowledge development.
- Actively seek out your gifts and God's purpose for your life.
- Take on leadership responsibilities through on-campus activities and outreach ministries.

Relationally

- Receive one-on-one attention from professors.

- Meet friends who share your views, understand what makes you tick, and challenge you.
- Be matched to mentors in your academic field.

Professionally

- Be in demand. Major employers seek out CCCU graduates because of their competence and values.
- Stand beside alumni who are national leaders in medicine, science, business, law, religion, education, and many other fields.
- Build a powerful resume through excellent internships with recognized companies.
- Get connected through campus career centers.
- Be involved in a wide array of clubs and student-run organizations.

One Perspective: The Benefits of Christian Higher Education

by James C. Dobson, Ph.D.

■ You have much to think about and many education options. As you consider the array of choices before you, you should include one or more Christian colleges and universities—for the range and depth of their academic quality, their reasonable costs, and for their adherence to traditional Christian principles.

In an age in which higher education is increasingly dominated by "political correctness" and moral relativism, the real question is why you would want to attend any other kind of college.

Christian colleges are wonderful places to live and study—great places to learn, to grow, to prepare for graduate school or a career and to enrich your faith. And we should thank God that He works through them to nurture new generations of students to become responsible, mature, productive Christian members of our society.

_____

James C. Dobson is president of Focus on the Family in Colorado Springs, Colorado. Focus on the Family is a 21-year old, nonprofit organization dedicated to strengthening the home. The ministry produces several radio programs and magazines, as well as family-oriented books, films, videos, and audiocassettes, all from a Christian perspective.

(Reprinted with permission from Christian Colleges & Universities, an edition of Private Colleges & Universities, Carnegie Communications, Inc.)

Principles for Financing a Christian College Education

by Larry Burkett

■   The lasting value of a Christian education makes it one of the most important investments a parent can make. After all, who can put a price tag on your young adult's character being influenced by a biblical worldview? And how do you measure parents' peace of mind as their sons or daughters leave home for the first time, headed for the campus of a Christian college?

Since the cost of a college education—Christian or secular—has risen rapidly over the past decade, a more conscientious effort toward both savings and financial planning is required to help students through college. But meeting the challenge is not impossible, and it's never too late to start. You may find it helpful to have frank conversations with your student regarding mutual sacrifices that can be made in order to make ends meet. Of course, one of the greatest contributions the student can make is maintaining good grades in high school that could translate into scholarships or grants.

Over the years, I have had the opportunity to visit with hundreds of parents about financing their son or daughter's education. From those experiences, the following are principles that you may find helpful.

1. Explore possible support from your extended family, your home church, scholarships and grants, part-time work, co-op programs, and summer employment. Grandparents may desire to contribute to this critical period of their grandchildren's training.

2. Teach your child to live on a budget. A budget will help him or her track monthly expenses, plan for future bills, and limit excessive spending.

3. Contact the schools' financial aid officer early in the admissions process. Resources available today may evaporate by next month.

4. Investigate cost-reducing steps such as living at home and commuting to class, purchasing used textbooks, and preparing meals instead of eating out. If your son or daughter lives on campus, he or she may consider riding a bike instead of driving a car.

5. Make borrowing a last resort, not the first choice. Many college graduates find themselves disqualified from Christian ministry opportunities because of indebtedness, which also can burden a person when entering the workplace.

When it comes to the wisdom of investing in a Christian education, the apostle Paul said it succinctly in Galatians 6:7: "For whatever a man sows, this he will also reap." Providing a Christian education for your son or daughter will yield eternal dividends that cannot be measured in earthly terms.

Dr. Larry Burkett is president and founder of Christian Financial Concepts. Dr. Burkett has published 47 books on finances. His daily radio broadcasts, "Money Matters" and "How to Manage Your Money," are carried on over 1,000 outlets worldwide.

What Is the Return to Expect from Your Investment?

Any private college is a big investment. However, many thousands of families have found a Christian college education well worth the price. Parents and alumni alike agree that it is impossible to place a dollar value on the lifelong benefits of a Christ-centered undergraduate experience.

It is no accident that most graduates of Christian colleges have little trouble finding a first job or gaining admittance to graduate or professional schools. These colleges and universities work hard at providing students with a broad array of resources and at helping alumni succeed in life after college. The individual stories of Christian college alumni illustrates their faithfulness to the cause of Christ. Evangelist Billy Graham; president of Youth for Christ/USA Roger Cross; former NFL running back Christian Okoye; U.S. Senator Dan Coates; and award-winning author of books for young people Katherine Paterson are all graduates of Christian colleges and universities. Their lives stand as a testimony to the lifelong impact and value of a Christian college education.

To assist families in meeting educational costs, most Christian colleges and universities provide generous aid packages to financially and/or academically qualified students. At many Christian colleges about two thirds of all students receive some form of institutional aid. Financial aid officers are eager to work with families to structure financial aid packages to meet individual situations. At some colleges, more aid is available for students who apply and are accepted early, so an early conversation with an admis-

sions officer is wise. A majority of students receive a financial aid package of grants, work study and loans that each college determines for its students. Students may also be able to graduate in less time at a private Christian college than at other public universities. This will mean fewer years of tuition, room and board and an earlier transition into the job market or graduate studies.

We hope this guide helps you narrow your options to several Christian colleges and universities from which you can request additional information. You will find their admissions offices to be friendly and anxious to be of service to you. Nothing will help you make a better decision than visiting campus. When you are on campus, spend time visiting with students and professors to get a feel for what life is like at the college. Through the Internet you can learn more about Christian colleges at http://www.christiancollegesearch.com.

Understanding Cost and Financing a Christian College Education

by Ron Blue

■ If you are serious about attending a Christian college or university, you are probably already aware that your education is apt to cost significantly more than it would at a public state-supported school. What you may not know is that, in general, a Christian college costs less than the average private school, according to statistics provided annually to the federal government.

But actual numbers can become somewhat staggering when you stop to consider the total cost of going to college—public or private. These days, some experts tell young parents to set aside upwards of $500 per month to prepare for a toddler's future education! Gone are the days when you could realistically expect to totally "work your way" through school. Today, almost everyone has to borrow at least a little money by the time they finish their fourth year.

For most Christians, this prospect is unpleasant. For some it may even be unthinkable. Yet the Bible does not prohibit borrowing; rather, Scripture discourages it by pointing out the dangers associated with going into debt (see, for example, Proverbs 22:7). While we must keep these admonitions in mind, we must also recognize that there are some cases in which borrowing may make sense. One common example is purchasing a home. Another is financing a college education.

As I've counseled clients over the years about borrowing, I have asked them to keep two principles in mind. First, do not go into debt without a carefully considered repayment plan. Borrowing itself is not a sin—but as Psalm 37:21 warns, "The wicked borrow and do not repay." Instead of presuming on the future, parents and students must get together and map out a strategy whereby a college loan will be repaid on time.

Second, go into debt only when the return outweighs the cost. Borrowing money to pay for college is not like borrowing money to buy a car. A new car may make you feel good, but it does not add value to your life. By contrast, a college education increases your career options and your earning power. Whether from savings, earnings or borrowing, you will find the benefit and value you get from attending a Christian college or university will be well worth the cost.

Ron Blue is managing partner of Ronald Blue & Co. He is the author of six books on personal finance, including Master Your Money, *a best-seller first published in 1986 and now in its twenty-first printing,* The Master Your Money Workbook, *and* Taming the Money Monster. *He has appeared on numerous radio and television programs, including* Prime Time America *and* Moody Radio Open Line.

A World of Opportunity

■   The heart of this book is detailed profiles of the 100 member institutions of the Council for Christian Colleges & Universities, containing data supplied by each of them. Each one provides information on things like enrollment, academic offerings, costs, athletic programs, admission procedures, and financial aid. Familiarizing yourself with the format of the profiles will help you review them and compare schools easily.

A special note from each school appears at the beginning of each profile. These notes include information about the school's mission, special programs and curricular emphases, and campus life.

Off-Campus Opportunities Available to All Students

The Council makes available seven student programs around the world. These specialized programs are open to application from all students of member institutions. These programs provide opportunities for off-campus study in China, Washington, D.C., Costa Rica, Hollywood, Egypt, Russia and an honours programme in Oxford, England. The Council also offers summer programs in Oxford, England and a journalism institute in Washington, DC. These programs allow you to make the world your classroom!

Christian College and University Graduates...

- gain a solid biblical foundation through coursework and community life.

- attend leading graduate schools.
- have developed marketable skills for the world of work.
- are prepared for life after college through valuable networks of professors and alumni.
- are involved in their communities through volunteer service.

How To Use This Book

■ It is likely you are reading this book because you are a student or care about a student who is thinking seriously about going to college and wondering how to select a school that will best allow you to get everything you want out of your college years. If you believe that a college with an active Christian orientation might be what you're looking for, this book can help you by providing information on 100 colleges and universities that combine academically challenging programs in the liberal arts and sciences with a Christ-centered campus life.

The Introduction: Choose a Christian College

The introductory essays can help you determine whether a Christian college or university is the best choice for you. It provides a rich overview of what you can expect from a Christian liberal arts institution, compared to other approaches to higher education.

The College Profiles

The heart of this book is detailed profiles of the 100 member campuses of the Council for Christian Colleges & Universities, each containing data supplied by the colleges and universities themselves. The profiles provide information on things like enrollment, academic offerings, costs, athletic programs, admission procedures, international admissions, and financial aid.

Familiarizing yourself with the format of the profiles will help you review them and compare schools easily.

Programs Sponsored by the Council for Christian Colleges & Universities

The Council makes available seven semester-long student programs. These programs provide opportunities for off-campus study in Washington, D.C., Costa Rica, Hollywood, Egypt, Russia, Oxford, England, and China. The Council also offers summer programs in Oxford, England and a journalism institute in Washington, D.C. Consider these programs when choosing a college since they can not only round out your studies but also provide a rich setting for personal growth.

The Indexes

We've provided indexes at the back of the book to assist you in picking out the profiles you wish to review, based on three criteria: academic majors, intercollegiate athletics, and graduate programs. In addition, to make it easy to pick out the schools that are in a particular geographical area, we've provided a geographical listing and map, which appear at the front of this book immediately following the contents page.

About the Council for Christian Colleges & Universities

The Council for Christian Colleges & Universities, a Washington, D.C.-based association of

100 colleges and universities of the liberal arts and sciences, is North America's primary organization devoted specifically to serving and strengthening Christian higher education. Council institutions meet eight criteria for membership: an institutional commitment to the centrality of Jesus Christ to all campus life, integration of biblical faith with academics and student life,

hiring practices that require a personal Christian commitment from each full-time faculty member and administrator, accreditation and primary orientation as a four-year liberal arts college, fund-raising activities consistent with the standards set by the Evangelical Council for Financial Accountability, a commitment to participating Council programs, cooperation with and sup-

Sample Profile

Special Note from the College
In a brief statement, each institution presents key information about itself that prospective students should know.

Academics
Tells the types and level of degrees, special programs, most popular majors, number of faculty, percent with terminal degrees, and student-faculty ratio.

Campus Resources
Provides details about campus computerization and library resources.

The Statistical Snapshot
Provides a quick reference portrait of the school in numbers and percentages related to admission difficulty, aspects of the freshman class and student body, costs, financial aid, and outcomes for graduates.

GENEVA COLLEGE
Beaver Falls, Pennsylvania

http://www.geneva.edu/

Founded in 1848, Geneva College is one of the oldest evangelical Christian colleges in the nation, the second oldest in the Coalition of Christian Colleges & Universities. It offers an education that articulates the implications of Christ's sovereignty over all his creation. Geneva is one of 14 model sites chosen for the Coalition Racial and Ethnic Diversity Project. Students of color are encouraged to explore educational opportunities at Geneva. Majors include engineering, speech pathology, and cardiovascular technology. Through a cooperative program, students can combine degrees in aviation, air traffic control, or aerospace management with our business degree. All students complete a core program, which integrates courses in history, music, art, literature, and culture with biblical Christianity. Cocurricular activities include intercollegiate programs in all major sports, theater, choir, an FM radio station, and marching and concert bands. Although Geneva seeks students with a biblical world and life view, all students are welcome.

Academics
Geneva offers a Christian liberal arts and sciences curriculum and core academic program; a few graduate courses are open to undergraduates. It awards associate, bachelor's, and master's **degrees.** Challenging opportunities include advanced placement, accelerated degree programs, student-designed majors, tutorials, freshman honors college, an honors program, double majors, independent study, and a senior project. **Special programs** include cooperative education, internships, summer session for credit, off-campus study, and study-abroad.
The most popular **majors** include elementary education, business administration, and biology. A complete listing of majors at Geneva appears in the Majors Index beginning on page
The **faculty** at Geneva has 60 full-time undergraduate teachers, 72% with terminal degrees. The student-faculty ratio is 18:1, and the average **class size** in required courses is 35.

Campus Resources
Students are not required to have a computer. 150 **computers** available in the computer center, computer labs, classrooms, the library, and the student center provide access to on-campus e-mail addresses, off-campus e-mail addresses, and the Internet. Staffed computer lab on campus provides training in the use of computers, software, and the Internet.

The 5 **libraries** have 158,045 books and 855 subscriptions.

Career Services
The career planning and placement office has 3 full-time staff members. Services include job fairs, resume preparation, interview workshops, resume referral, career/interest testing, career counseling, careers library, job bank (available online), and job interviews.

Campus Life
There are 25 active organizations on campus, including a drama/theater group and student-run newspaper and radio station. 80% of students participate in student government elections. No national or local **fraternities** or **sororities.** Student **safety services** include late night transport/escort service, 24-hour emergency telephone alarm devices, 24-hour patrols by trained security personnel, and electronically operated dormitory entrances.
Geneva is a member of the NAIA and NCCAA. **Intercollegiate sports** (some offering scholarships) include baseball (m), basketball (m,w), cross-country running (m,w), football (m), soccer (m,w), softball (w), tennis (m,w), track and field (m,w), volleyball (m,w).

International Students
For fall 1997, 63 international students applied, 32 were accepted, and 25 enrolled. Students can start in fall, spring, and summer. The **admissions test** required for entrance is TOEFL (minimum score: 550; recommended is SAT I or ACT. Application deadline is rolling. On-campus **housing** is guaranteed, also available during summer. Services include an international student adviser on campus.

Applying
Geneva requires an essay, SAT I or ACT, a high school transcript, recommendations, 4 years of high school English, 2 years of high school math, 1 year of high school science, 2 years of high school foreign language, 3 years of high school social studies, 4 years of high school academic electives, and a minimum high school GPA of 2.0, and in some cases an interview. It recommends a minimum high school GPA of 3.0. Application deadline: rolling admissions; 4/15 priority date for financial aid. Early and deferred entrance are possible. **Contact:** Mr. David Layton, Director of Admissions, 3200 College Avenue, Beaver Falls, PA 15010-3599, 724-847-6500 or toll-free 800-847-8255 (out-of-state); fax 724-847-6776; e-mail admissions@geneva.edu.

GETTING IN LAST YEAR	From 36 states and territories,	Average percent of need met 75%
875 applied	15 other countries	Average amount received per student $9000
54% were accepted	80% from Pennsylvania	
13% from top tenth of their h.s. class	53.2% women, 46.9% men	**AFTER FRESHMAN YEAR**
21% had SAT verbal scores over 600	2.3% international students	78% returned for sophomore year
22% had SAT math scores over 600		
65% had ACT scores over 24	**COSTS AND FINANCIAL INFORMATION**	**AFTER GRADUATION**
1 National Merit Scholars	1997–98 tuition and fees $11,534	15% pursued further study (6% arts and
5 valedictorians	1997–98 room and board $4750	sciences, 4% medicine, 3% education)
		74% had job offers within 6 months
THE STUDENT BODY		35 organizations recruited on campus
Total 1,956, of whom 1,763		
are undergraduates		

Career Services
Tells the extent of and kinds of career planning and placement help available to students and graduates.

Campus Life
Provides a picture of extracurricular life, student participation in student participation in student government, campus safety services, and intercollegiate athletic programs.

Applying
This section shows all basic application requirements, deadlines for admission and financial aid applications, and the appropriate admissions contact name, postal address, phone, fax, and e-mail information.

port of other Council colleges, and responsible financial operation. The Council also includes a growing number of nonmember affiliates. Affiliate institutions may include institutions that do not meet member curriculum or hiring criteria, are not primarily four-year undergraduate colleges, or are outside North America.

To conduct searches on Council institutions go to http://www.christiancollegesearch. com. For information on the Council for Christian Colleges & Universities at 321 Eighth Street NE, Washington, D.C., 20002; telephone 202-546-8713; e-mail council@cccu.org. Visit the Council Web site at www.cccu.org.

Council for Christian Colleges & Universities College Profiles and Special Notes

■ This section contains detailed factual profiles of the member campuses of the Council for Christian Colleges & Universities, covering such items as background facts, enrollment figures, number of faculty members, academic programs, majors, expenses, financial aid, campus life, athletics, admission procedures, and whom to contact for more information. In addition, there is a special note from each college describing the institution's distinctive features.

The data in each of these profiles, collected from fall 1999 to spring 2000, come primarily from Peterson's Annual Survey of Undergraduate Institutions, which was sent to deans or admission officers at each institution.

ABILENE CHRISTIAN UNIVERSITY

Abilene, Texas

http://www.acu.edu/

Abilene Christian University emphasizes high quality academics in a distinctively Christian environment. Christian education at ACU is a total integration of faith and hands-on learning represented in every facet of campus life. Located about 180 miles west of Dallas, it is one of the largest private universities in the Southwest. The university offers 117 bachelor programs through its three colleges: Arts and Sciences, Biblical and Business Administration, and the School of Nursing. As a teaching institution, ACU emphasizes a dynamic personal relationship between professors and their students. Qualified faculty members teach underclassmen, and when professors do research, undergraduates work with them. On ACU's state-of-the-art campus, each student has many opportunities to become technologically proficient with easy access to about 400 computers during daytime and evening hours. Students have access to E-mail and the Internet through ACU's network and multiple labs on campus.

Academics

ACU awards associate, bachelor's, master's, doctoral, and first-professional **degrees**. Challenging opportunities include advanced placement, accelerated degree programs, student-designed majors, an honors program, double majors, independent study, and a senior project. **Special programs** include cooperative education, internships, summer session for credit, off-campus study, and study-abroad. The most frequently chosen **baccalaureate** fields are business/marketing, education, and interdisciplinary studies. A complete listing of majors at ACU appears in the Majors Index beginning on page 147. The **faculty** at ACU has 207 full-time members, 72% with terminal degrees. The student-faculty ratio is 18:1.

Students of ACU

The student body totals 4,650, of whom 4,078 are undergraduates. 54.6% are women and 45.4% are men. Students come from 47 states and territories and 61 other countries. 77% are from Texas. 4.2% are international students. 73% returned for their sophomore year.

Career Services

The career planning and placement office has 2 full-time, 1 part-time staff members. Services include job fairs, resume preparation, resume referral, career counseling, careers library, job bank, and job interviews.

Campus Life

There are 104 active organizations on campus, including a drama/theater group, newspaper, radio station, television station, choral group, and marching band. 22% of eligible men and 23% of eligible women are members of local **fraternities** and local **sororities**. ACU is a member of the NCAA (Division II). **Intercollegiate sports** (some offering scholarships) include baseball (m), basketball, cross-country running, football (m), golf (m), soccer, softball (w), tennis, track and field, volleyball (w).

Campus Safety

Student safety services include late-night transport/escort service, 24-hour emergency telephone alarm devices, and 24-hour patrols by trained security personnel.

Applying

ACU requires SAT I or ACT, a high school transcript, and 2 recommendations. It recommends an interview and a minimum high school GPA of 2.0. Application deadline: 8/1; 3/1 priority date for financial aid. Deferred admission is possible. **Contact:** Mr. Tim Johnston, Director of Admissions, ACU Box 29100, Abilene, TX 79699-9100, 915-674-2650 or toll-free 800-460-6228 ext. 2650; e-mail info@admissions.acu.edu.

GETTING IN LAST YEAR
2,292 applied
79% were accepted
924 enrolled (51%)
24% from top tenth of their h.s. class
3.4 average high school GPA
29% had SAT verbal scores over 600
31% had SAT math scores over 600
42% had ACT scores over 24

5% had SAT verbal scores over 700
6% had SAT math scores over 700
9% had ACT scores over 30
5 National Merit Scholars
21 valedictorians

COSTS AND FINANCIAL INFORMATION
$10,290 tuition and fees (1999–2000)
$4190 room and board
92% average percent of need met

$10,694 average financial aid amount
    received per undergraduate (1998–99)

AFTER GRADUATION
27% graduated in 4 years
18% graduated in 5 years
5% graduated in 6 years
30% pursued further study
70% had job offers within 6 months
150 organizations recruited on campus

ANDERSON UNIVERSITY

Anderson, Indiana

http://www.anderson.edu/

Anderson University is a community of Christian higher education where high-quality learning and Christian service come alive. Believing that scholarship and scholars should serve a purpose, Anderson University is a mission-minded school that offers students a strong liberal arts foundation on which to build career credentials. Business, computer science, education, music, religious studies, social work, and sociology are among the most popular of the 60 majors and programs offered. The Tri-S program (study, serve, and share) is probably most representative of the spirit of the University. Through this program, more than 500 students volunteer each year for 50 different cross-cultural work projects throughout the world. Bill and Gloria Gaither and Sandi Patti are a few of the nearly 25,000 loyal alumni who make up the University's international alumni association and whose strength is not only in their numbers but also in their belief.

Academics

Anderson University awards associate, bachelor's, master's, doctoral, and first-professional **degrees**. Challenging opportunities include advanced placement, accelerated degree programs, student-designed majors, and a senior project. **Special programs** include cooperative education, internships, and summer session for credit. The most frequently chosen **baccalaureate** fields are education, business/marketing, and philosophy. A complete listing of majors at Anderson University appears in the Majors Index beginning on page 147. The **faculty** at Anderson University has 139 full-time members, 60% with terminal degrees. The student-faculty ratio is 14:1.

Students of Anderson University

The student body totals 2,251, of whom 1,988 are undergraduates. 59.1% are women and 40.9% are men. Students come from 43 states and territories and 12 other countries. 65% are from Indiana. 1.3% are international students. 76% returned for their sophomore year.

Facilities and Resources

The **library** has 280,575 books and 928 subscriptions.

Career Services

The career planning and placement office has 3 full-time staff members. Services include job fairs, resume preparation, career/interest testing, career counseling, careers library, and job interviews.

Campus Life

There are 33 active organizations on campus, including a drama/theater group, newspaper, radio station, and choral group. No national or local **fraternities** or **sororities**. Anderson University is a member of the NCAA (Division III). **Intercollegiate sports** include baseball (m), basketball, cross-country running, football (m), golf, soccer, softball (w), tennis, track and field, volleyball (w).

Campus Safety

Student safety services include 24-hour crimeline, late-night transport/escort service, 24-hour emergency telephone alarm devices, 24-hour patrols by trained security personnel, and student patrols.

Applying

Anderson University requires SAT I or ACT, a high school transcript, 2 recommendations, lifestyle statement, and a minimum high school GPA of 2.0, and in some cases an interview. It recommends an essay. Application deadline: 8/25; 3/1 priority date for financial aid. Deferred admission is possible. **Contact:** Mr. Jim King, Director of Admissions, 1100 East Fifth Street, Anderson, IN 46012-3495, 765-641-4080 or toll-free 800-421-3014 (in-state), 800-428-6414 (out-of-state); fax 765-641-3851; e-mail info@anderson.edu.

GETTING IN LAST YEAR
1,595 applied
80% were accepted
506 enrolled (40%)
29% from top tenth of their h.s. class
3.39 average high school GPA
25% had SAT verbal scores over 600
27% had SAT math scores over 600
55% had ACT scores over 24

4% had SAT verbal scores over 700
3% had SAT math scores over 700
7% had ACT scores over 30
24 valedictorians

COSTS AND FINANCIAL INFORMATION
$14,680 tuition and fees (2000–2001 estimated)
$4750 room and board
95% average percent of need met

$13,530 average financial aid amount received per undergraduate (1999–2000)

AFTER GRADUATION
31% graduated in 4 years
17% graduated in 5 years
1% graduated in 6 years
21% pursued further study
46 organizations recruited on campus

ASBURY COLLEGE
Wilmore, Kentucky

http://www.asbury.edu/

Asbury College is a fully-accredited, independent, Christian, liberal arts institution located in Wilmore, Kentucky. Offering more than 45 majors and areas of study, Asbury annually enrolls a student body of approximately 1,300 scholars and offers a distinctly Christ-centered education. Ranked among the top 10 regional liberal arts colleges in the south by *U.S. News & World Report* in 1999 and 2000, Asbury is also listed as a character-building institution in The Templeton Guide. Coming from approximately 45 states and 20 countries, students live and study on a red-bricked campus just 20 minutes from Lexington, the second-largest city in the state.

Academics
Asbury College awards bachelor's **degrees**. Challenging opportunities include advanced placement, double majors, independent study, and a senior project. **Special programs** include internships, summer session for credit, study-abroad, and Army and Air Force ROTC. The most frequently chosen **baccalaureate** fields are philosophy, education, and English. A complete listing of majors at Asbury College appears in the Majors Index beginning on page 147. The **faculty** at Asbury College has 87 full-time members, 77% with terminal degrees. The student-faculty ratio is 13:1.

Students of Asbury College
The student body is made up of 1,317 undergraduates. 58.3% are women and 41.7% are men. Students come from 43 states and territories and 20 other countries. 27% are from Kentucky. 2.1% are international students. 84% returned for their sophomore year.

Facilities and Resources
The **library** has 123,351 books and 575 subscriptions.

Career Services
The career planning and placement office has 1 full-time staff member. Services include job fairs, resume preparation, interview workshops, resume referral, career/interest testing, career counseling, careers library, job bank, and job interviews.

Campus Life
There are 35 active organizations on campus, including a drama/theater group, newspaper, radio station, television station, and choral group. No national or local **fraternities** or **sororities**. Asbury College is a member of the NAIA and NCCAA. **Intercollegiate sports** include baseball (m), basketball, cross-country running, soccer (m), softball (w), swimming, tennis, volleyball (w).

Campus Safety
Student safety services include late night security personnel, late-night transport/escort service, 24-hour emergency telephone alarm devices, and electronically operated dormitory entrances.

Applying
Asbury College requires an essay, SAT I or ACT, a high school transcript, 3 recommendations, and a minimum high school GPA of 2.5, and in some cases ACT and an interview. Application deadline: rolling admissions; 3/1 priority date for financial aid. Early and deferred admission are possible. **Contact:** Mr. Stan F. Wiggam, Dean of Admissions, 1 Macklem Drive, Wilmore, KY 40390, 606-858-3511 ext. 2142 or toll-free 800-888-1818; fax 859-858-3921; e-mail admissions@asbury.edu.

GETTING IN LAST YEAR
838 applied
87% were accepted
328 enrolled (45%)
34% from top tenth of their h.s. class
3.51 average high school GPA
42% had SAT verbal scores over 600
38% had SAT math scores over 600
62% had ACT scores over 24

11% had SAT verbal scores over 700
8% had SAT math scores over 700
11% had ACT scores over 30
9 National Merit Scholars
18 valedictorians

COSTS AND FINANCIAL INFORMATION
$13,784 tuition and fees (2000–2001)
$3566 room and board
83% average percent of need met

$10,010 average financial aid amount received per undergraduate (1999–2000)

AFTER GRADUATION
35% graduated in 4 years
14% graduated in 5 years
1% graduated in 6 years
20 organizations recruited on campus

AZUSA PACIFIC UNIVERSITY

Azusa, California

http://www.apu.edu/

At APU, students participate in exceptional academic programs in 40 fields, dynamic leadership and music projects, innovative service opportunities, and on strong athletic teams. They train alongside Olympic athletes; gain acceptance to America's most prestigious graduate schools (Harvard, Stanford, Georgetown); participate in Bridges, a San Francisco outreach to homeless people and AIDS patients, and Walk-About, an intense, nine-day wilderness excursion that hones leadership skills and deepens faith; and minister in Haiti, Guatemala, Laos, Mexico, Romania, and Russia. Whether in the classroom, in athletics, or on the mission field, Azusa Pacific students learn that serving others is the cornerstone of Christian servant leadership.

Academics
APU awards bachelor's, master's, doctoral, and first-professional **degrees**. Challenging opportunities include advanced placement, accelerated degree programs, freshman honors college, an honors program, double majors, and a senior project. **Special programs** include cooperative education, internships, summer session for credit, off-campus study, study-abroad, and Army ROTC. The most frequently chosen **baccalaureate** fields are business/marketing, liberal arts/general studies, and health professions and related sciences. A complete listing of majors at APU appears in the Majors Index beginning on page 147. The **faculty** at APU has 190 full-time members. The student-faculty ratio is 15:1.

Students of APU
The student body totals 5,982, of whom 3,092 are undergraduates. 63.2% are women and 36.8% are men. 74% are from California. 3.5% are international students.

Facilities and Resources
The 3 **libraries** have 147,377 books and 1,411 subscriptions.

Career Services
The career planning and placement office has 3 full-time, 3 part-time staff members. Services include job fairs, resume preparation, career counseling, careers library, and job interviews.

Campus Life
Active organizations on campus include a drama/theater group, newspaper, and choral group. No national or local **fraternities** or **sororities**. APU is a member of the NAIA. **Intercollegiate sports** (some offering scholarships) include baseball (m), basketball, cross-country running, football (m), golf (m), soccer, softball (w), tennis (m), track and field, volleyball.

Campus Safety
Student safety services include late-night transport/escort service, 24-hour emergency telephone alarm devices, 24-hour patrols by trained security personnel, student patrols, and electronically operated dormitory entrances.

Applying
APU requires an essay, SAT I or ACT, a high school transcript, 2 recommendations, and a minimum high school GPA of 2.5, and in some cases an interview. Application deadline: 7/1; 8/1 for financial aid, with a 3/2 priority date. Deferred admission is possible. **Contact:** Mrs. Deana Porterfield, Dean of Admissions, 901 East Alosta Avenue, PO Box 7000, Azusa, CA 91702-7000, 626-812-3016 or toll-free 800-TALK-APU; e-mail admissions@apu.edu.

GETTING IN LAST YEAR
1,967 applied
80% were accepted
680 enrolled (43%)
3.57 average high school GPA
22% had SAT verbal scores over 600
18% had SAT math scores over 600
46% had ACT scores over 24

3% had SAT verbal scores over 700
3% had SAT math scores over 700
7% had ACT scores over 30

COSTS AND FINANCIAL INFORMATION
$14,727 tuition and fees (1999–2000)
$4880 room and board
74% average percent of need met

$6859 average financial aid amount received
  per undergraduate (1998–99)

AFTER GRADUATION
31% graduated in 4 years
15% graduated in 5 years
6% graduated in 6 years
150 organizations recruited on campus

BARTLESVILLE WESLEYAN COLLEGE

Bartlesville, Oklahoma

http://www.bwc.edu/

Bartlesville Wesleyan College is a distinctive Christian college. The campus community strongly believes in providing a Christ-centered educational experience that will produce lifelong results. It is located in the south-central part of the United States, 45 miles north of suburban Tulsa. Bartlesville is a cosmopolitan city of 40,000 and is the world headquarters for Phillips Petroleum Company. Local cultural opportunities include a choral society, a civic ballet, a theater guild, a symphony orchestra, and an annual International OK Mozart festival. The focal point of the 27-acre campus is an elegant 60-year-old, 32-room, Spanish-style mansion overlooking a beautiful lake.

Academics

BWC awards associate and bachelor's **degrees**. Challenging opportunities include advanced placement, student-designed majors, independent study, and a senior project. **Special programs** include cooperative education, internships, summer session for credit, and off-campus study. A complete listing of majors at BWC appears in the Majors Index beginning on page 147.

Students of BWC

The student body is made up of 603 undergraduates. Students come from 28 states and territories and 7 other countries. 54% are from Oklahoma. 70% returned for their sophomore year.

Facilities and Resources

The **library** has 124,722 books and 300 subscriptions.

Career Services

The career planning and placement office has 2 full-time, 3 part-time staff members. Services include resume preparation, career counseling, careers library, and job bank.

Campus Life

There are 10 active organizations on campus, including a newspaper and choral group. No national or local **fraternities** or **sororities**. BWC is a member of the NAIA and NCCAA. **Intercollegiate sports** (some offering scholarships) include baseball (m), basketball, golf (m), soccer, softball (w), volleyball (w).

Campus Safety

Student safety services include 24-hour emergency telephone alarm devices, 24-hour patrols by trained security personnel, and electronically operated dormitory entrances.

Applying

BWC requires SAT I or ACT, a high school transcript, and recommendations. It recommends a minimum high school GPA of 2.0. Application deadline: rolling admissions; 3/31 priority date for financial aid. Early and deferred admission are possible. **Contact:** Mr. Marty Carver, Director of Enrollment Services, 2201 Silver Lake Road, Bartlesville, OK 74006-6299, 918-335-6219 or toll-free 800-468-6292 (in-state); fax 918-335-6229; e-mail admissions@bwc.edu.

GETTING IN LAST YEAR
489 applied
66% were accepted
30% from top tenth of their h.s. class
3.59 average high school GPA
32% had SAT verbal scores over 600
19% had SAT math scores over 600

38% had ACT scores over 24
2% had SAT verbal scores over 700
4% had SAT math scores over 700
3% had ACT scores over 30
1 National Merit Scholar

COSTS AND FINANCIAL INFORMATION
$9700 tuition and fees (2000–2001)

$4100 room and board
55% average percent of need met
$6466 average financial aid amount received
per undergraduate (1999–2000 estimated)

AFTER GRADUATION
10% pursued further study (6% theology, 2% arts and sciences, 1% business)

BELHAVEN COLLEGE

Jackson, Mississippi

http://www.belhaven.edu/

Founded in 1883, Belhaven College is a four-year, coeducational Christian liberal arts college, serving 1,500 students from across the United States and 20 countries. The 42-acre campus features traditional southern architecture and is located within the historic Belhaven residential neighborhood of Jackson, Mississippi, the state's political, economic, and educational capital. The stated mission of Belhaven is to prepare students to serve Christ Jesus in their relationships, their careers, and in the world of ideas. To that end, the college offers an academic program that unifies faith and learning and integrates the rigor of scholarship with the passion of Christian ministry.

Academics

Belhaven awards bachelor's and master's **degrees**. Challenging opportunities include advanced placement, accelerated degree programs, an honors program, double majors, independent study, and a senior project. **Special programs** include internships, summer session for credit, off-campus study, and study-abroad. The most frequently chosen **baccalaureate** fields are business/marketing, education, and psychology. A complete listing of majors at Belhaven appears in the Majors Index beginning on page 147. The **faculty** at Belhaven has 50 full-time members, 78% with terminal degrees. The student-faculty ratio is 16:1.

Students of Belhaven

The student body totals 1,415, of whom 1,317 are undergraduates. 61.6% are women and 38.4% are men. Students come from 30 states and territories. 74% are from Mississippi. 0.2% are international students. 56% returned for their sophomore year.

Facilities and Resources

The **library** has 84,662 books and 498 subscriptions.

Career Services

The career planning and placement office has 1 part-time staff member. Services include job fairs, resume preparation, resume referral, career/interest testing, career counseling, careers library, job bank, and job interviews.

Campus Life

There are 20 active organizations on campus, including a drama/theater group, newspaper, and choral group. 1% of eligible women are members of local **sororities**. Belhaven is a member of the NAIA. **Intercollegiate sports** (some offering scholarships) include baseball (m), basketball, cross-country running, football (m), golf, soccer, softball (w), tennis, volleyball (w).

Campus Safety

Student safety services include late-night transport/escort service, 24-hour emergency telephone alarm devices, 24-hour patrols by trained security personnel, and electronically operated dormitory entrances.

Applying

Belhaven requires SAT I or ACT, a high school transcript, 1 recommendation, 1 academic reference, and a minimum high school GPA of 2.0, and in some cases an essay and an interview. Application deadline: rolling admissions; 4/1 priority date for financial aid. Early and deferred admission are possible. **Contact:** Dr. Stephen Livesay, Vice President for Advancement, 150 Peachtree Street, Jackson, MS 39202, 601-968-5940 or toll-free 800-960-5940; fax 601-968-9998; e-mail admissions@belhaven.edu.

GETTING IN LAST YEAR
518 applied
64% were accepted
147 enrolled (44%)
16% from top tenth of their h.s. class
3.23 average high school GPA
38% had SAT verbal scores over 600
34% had SAT math scores over 600
50% had ACT scores over 24

23% had SAT verbal scores over 700
8% had SAT math scores over 700
9% had ACT scores over 30
1 National Merit Scholar
4 valedictorians

COSTS AND FINANCIAL INFORMATION
$10,340 tuition and fees (1999–2000)
$3850 room and board
66% average percent of need met

$10,875 average financial aid amount
  received per undergraduate (1999–2000)

AFTER GRADUATION
25% graduated in 4 years
6% graduated in 5 years
3% graduated in 6 years
72% had job offers within 6 months
28 organizations recruited on campus

BETHEL COLLEGE
Mishawaka, Indiana

http://www.bethel-in.edu/

Bethel College is located in northern Indiana on a beautiful 70-acre wooded campus. Bethel is the College of the Missionary Church, an evangelical denomination with roots in Methodist and Mennonite traditions. Since its founding in 1947, the hallmark of the College has been an emphasis on excellent teaching and warm student-faculty relationships. Bethel College provides programs to challenge the mind, to enlarge the vision, and to equip the whole person for lifelong service. Bethel is a college with a deep Christian commitment. There is an open and joyful emphasis on the Christian life. Chapel meets 3 times a week and is the center of the campus culture. "With Christ at the helm" is more than a motto—it is the purpose and intent of living and studying together.

Academics
Bethel awards associate, bachelor's, and master's **degrees**. Challenging opportunities include advanced placement, accelerated degree programs, freshman honors college, an honors program, double majors, independent study, and a senior project. **Special programs** include internships, summer session for credit, off-campus study, study-abroad, and Army and Air Force ROTC. A complete listing of majors at Bethel appears in the Majors Index beginning on page 147. The **faculty** at Bethel has 69 full-time members, 75% with terminal degrees. The student-faculty ratio is 18:1.

Students of Bethel
The student body totals 1,640, of whom 1,552 are undergraduates. 65.8% are women and 34.2% are men. Students come from 29 states and territories and 13 other countries. 72% are from Indiana. 2.3% are international students. 80% returned for their sophomore year.

Facilities and Resources
The **library** has 90,450 books and 456 subscriptions.

Career Services
The career planning and placement office has 1 full-time, 1 part-time staff members. Services include job fairs, resume preparation, resume referral, career counseling, careers library, job bank, and job interviews.

Campus Life
There are 23 active organizations on campus, including a drama/theater group, newspaper, radio station, and choral group. No national or local **fraternities** or **sororities**. Bethel is a member of the NAIA and NCCAA. **Intercollegiate sports** (some offering scholarships) include baseball (m), basketball, cross-country running, golf (m), soccer, softball (w), tennis, track and field, volleyball (w).

Campus Safety
Student safety services include 24-hour patrols by trained security personnel, student patrols, and electronically operated dormitory entrances.

Applying
Bethel requires SAT I or ACT, a high school transcript, and 1 recommendation, and in some cases an essay. It recommends an interview and a minimum high school GPA of 2.3. Application deadline: 8/1; 3/1 priority date for financial aid. Early and deferred admission are possible. **Contact:** Ms. Andrea M. Helmuth, Director of Admissions, 1001 West McKinley Avenue, Mishawaka, IN 46545-5591, 219-257-3319 or toll-free 800-422-4101; fax 219-257-3326; e-mail admissions@bethel-in.edu.

GETTING IN LAST YEAR
704 applied
72% were accepted
277 enrolled (55%)
23% from top tenth of their h.s. class
3.34 average high school GPA
24% had SAT verbal scores over 600
24% had SAT math scores over 600

52% had ACT scores over 24
3% had SAT verbal scores over 700
4% had SAT math scores over 700
6% had ACT scores over 30
9 valedictorians

COSTS AND FINANCIAL INFORMATION
$11,950 tuition and fees (1999–2000)
$3950 room and board

90% average percent of need met
$9514 average financial aid amount received per undergraduate (1999–2000 estimated)

AFTER GRADUATION
10% pursued further study (4% business, 3% theology, 2% arts and sciences)
82% had job offers within 6 months
34 organizations recruited on campus

BETHEL COLLEGE
North Newton, Kansas

http://www.bethelks.edu/

We are a small college. We welcome students of every religious and ethnic heritage. Live and study with us at Bethel College and prepare for lifelong learning and for flexible, changing career roles. Explore your creative potential. Develop skills that are necessary in an information society. Value your spiritual, physical, and psychological well-being. Discover a sense of vocation that gives meaningful direction to life. Join a learning and worshipping Christian community informed by the service-oriented and peace-loving ethos of the Mennonite Church. Respond to the redemptive love of God by cultivating a personal faith, loving others, and working for reconciliation. You are welcome. Please join us.

Academics
Bethel awards bachelor's **degrees**. Challenging opportunities include advanced placement, double majors, independent study, and a senior project. **Special programs** include cooperative education, internships, summer session for credit, off-campus study, and study-abroad. The most frequently chosen **baccalaureate** fields are health professions and related sciences, business/marketing, and visual/performing arts. A complete listing of majors at Bethel appears in the Majors Index beginning on page 147. The **faculty** at Bethel has 39 full-time members, 95% with terminal degrees. The student-faculty ratio is 10:1.

Students of Bethel
The student body is made up of 477 undergraduates. 51.4% are women and 48.6% are men. Students come from 24 states and territories and 13 other countries. 69% are from Kansas. 67% returned for their sophomore year.

Facilities and Resources
The 2 **libraries** have 128,039 books and 625 subscriptions.

Career Services
The career planning and placement office has 1 full-time staff member. Services include job fairs, resume preparation, interview workshops, resume referral, career/interest testing, career counseling, careers library, job bank, and job interviews.

Campus Life
There are 30 active organizations on campus, including a drama/theater group, newspaper, radio station, and choral group. No national or local **fraternities** or **sororities**. Bethel is a member of the NAIA. **Intercollegiate sports** (some offering scholarships) include baseball (m), basketball, football (m), soccer, tennis, track and field, volleyball (w).

Campus Safety
Student safety services include community police patrols, 24-hour emergency telephone alarm devices, and student patrols.

Applying
Bethel requires SAT I or ACT, a high school transcript, and a minimum high school GPA of 2.5, and in some cases an essay and 2 recommendations. It recommends an interview. Application deadline: 8/15; 3/1 priority date for financial aid. Deferred admission is possible. **Contact:** Dr. Shirley King, Dean of Enrollment Services, 300 East 27th Street, North Newton, KS 67117, 316-283-2500 ext. 230 or toll-free 800-522-1887; fax 316-284-5286; e-mail admissions@bethelks.edu.

GETTING IN LAST YEAR
303 applied
84% were accepted
120 enrolled (47%)
17% from top tenth of their h.s. class
3.38 average high school GPA
51% had ACT scores over 24
12% had ACT scores over 30

8 valedictorians

COSTS AND FINANCIAL INFORMATION
$11,800 tuition and fees (2000–2001)
$4700 room and board
97% average percent of need met
$12,777 average financial aid amount received per undergraduate (1999–2000 estimated)

AFTER GRADUATION
42% graduated in 4 years
10% graduated in 5 years
11% pursued further study
67% had job offers within 6 months
35 organizations recruited on campus

BETHEL COLLEGE
St. Paul, Minnesota

http://www.bethel.edu/

There are a couple of ways to look at college: As preparation for a career, or as preparation for life. Bethel College does both. Bethel offers academic programs that compete with the best. In fact, Bethel was recently named among the top teaching schools in the nation and ranked eighth among colleges in the Midwest by *U.S. News & World Report*. What that means for students is classes taught by outstanding faculty members like Weldon Jones, Harvard-trained professor of biological sciences and 1995 Minnesota Professor of the Year. At Bethel, education is something you do. Some 250 students a year spend a semester studying abroad, making Bethel nineteenth in the nation among schools offering study-abroad options. Students participate in numerous service-learning projects and volunteer hundreds of hours on a host of community outreach teams. Our voluntary chapel services are packed, and upwards of 3,000 gather each Sunday night for student-led Vespers services. A Bethel education means experiences for a lifetime and a faith that's put into action!

Academics
Bethel awards associate, bachelor's, and master's **degrees**. Challenging opportunities include advanced placement, student-designed majors, freshman honors college, an honors program, double majors, independent study, and a senior project. **Special programs** include internships, summer session for credit, off-campus study, study-abroad, and Army, Navy and Air Force ROTC. The most frequently chosen **baccalaureate** fields are health professions and related sciences, business/marketing, and interdisciplinary studies. A complete listing of majors at Bethel appears in the Majors Index beginning on page 147. The **faculty** at Bethel has 134 full-time members, 72% with terminal degrees. The student-faculty ratio is 16:1.

Students of Bethel
The student body totals 2,983, of whom 2,721 are undergraduates. 63.4% are women and 36.6% are men. Students come from 38 states and territories. 72% are from Minnesota. 83% returned for their sophomore year.

Facilities and Resources
The **library** has 150,203 books and 3,449 subscriptions.

Career Services
The career planning and placement office has 3 full-time, 1 part-time staff members. Services include job fairs, resume preparation, interview workshops, resume referral, career/interest testing, career counseling, careers library, job bank, and job interviews.

Campus Life
Active organizations on campus include a drama/theater group, newspaper, radio station, television station, and choral group. No national or local **fraternities** or **sororities**. Bethel is a member of the NCAA (Division III). **Intercollegiate sports** include baseball (m), basketball, cross-country running, football (m), golf (m), ice hockey, soccer, softball (w), tennis, track and field, volleyball.

Campus Safety
Student safety services include late-night transport/escort service, 24-hour emergency telephone alarm devices, 24-hour patrols by trained security personnel, student patrols, and electronically operated dormitory entrances.

Applying
Bethel requires an essay, SAT I, ACT or PSAT, a high school transcript, and 2 recommendations, and in some cases an interview. It recommends an interview. Application deadline: 6/1; 4/15 priority date for financial aid. Deferred admission is possible.
Contact: Mr. John C. Lassen, Director of Admissions, 3900 Bethel Drive, St. Paul, MN 55112, 651-638-6436 or toll-free 800-255-8706 ext. 6242; e-mail bcoll-admit@bethel.edu.

GETTING IN LAST YEAR	6% had SAT verbal scores over 700	$12,726 average financial aid amount received per undergraduate (1999–2000 estimated)
1,526 applied	8% had SAT math scores over 700	
81% were accepted	7% had ACT scores over 30	
519 enrolled (42%)		
30% from top tenth of their h.s. class	**COSTS AND FINANCIAL INFORMATION**	**AFTER GRADUATION**
44% had SAT verbal scores over 600	$15,335 tuition and fees (1999–2000)	65% graduated in 4 years
39% had SAT math scores over 600	$5410 room and board	6% graduated in 5 years
48% had ACT scores over 24	83% average percent of need met	3% graduated in 6 years

BIOLA UNIVERSITY
La Mirada, California

http://www.biola.edu/

BIOLA
UNIVERSITY

Biola University's international reputation as a distinctive Christian institution is prominent. Of the 100 members of the Council for Christian Colleges & Universities, which require faculty members to be Christian, only 17 of those require that their students be Christian: Biola is one of those 17. The University has also been granted *U.S. News & World Report*'s highest ranking, that of a National University, and has been an ongoing member of the John Templeton Foundation Honor Roll for Character-Building Colleges. Requiring 30 units of Bible, Biola's hallmark is a solid biblical foundation to prepare students for all the challenges of life.

Academics
Biola awards bachelor's, master's, and doctoral **degrees**. Challenging opportunities include advanced placement, accelerated degree programs, freshman honors college, an honors program, double majors, independent study, and a senior project. **Special programs** include cooperative education, internships, summer session for credit, off-campus study, study-abroad, and Army, Navy and Air Force ROTC. The most frequently chosen **baccalaureate** fields are communications/communication technologies, business/marketing, and philosophy. A complete listing of majors at Biola appears in the Majors Index beginning on page 147. The **faculty** at Biola has 156 full-time members. The student-faculty ratio is 18:1.

Students of Biola
The student body totals 3,872, of whom 2,564 are undergraduates. 62.6% are women and 37.4% are men. Students come from 41 states and territories and 40 other countries. 79% are from California. 4.8% are international students.

Facilities and Resources
The **library** has 259,285 books and 1,175 subscriptions.

Career Services
The career planning and placement office has 1 full-time, 2 part-time staff members. Services include job fairs, resume preparation, resume referral, career/interest testing, career counseling, careers library, job bank, and job interviews.

Campus Life
There are 33 active organizations on campus, including a drama/theater group, newspaper, radio station, television station, and choral group. No national or local **fraternities** or **sororities**. Biola is a member of the NAIA. **Intercollegiate sports** (some offering scholarships) include baseball (m), basketball, cross-country running, soccer, softball (w), swimming, tennis (w), track and field, volleyball (w).

Campus Safety
Student safety services include access gates to roads through the middle of campus, late-night transport/escort service, 24-hour emergency telephone alarm devices, 24-hour patrols by trained security personnel, student patrols, and electronically operated dormitory entrances.

Applying
Biola requires an essay, SAT I or ACT, a high school transcript, an interview, and 2 recommendations. It recommends a minimum high school GPA of 2.8. Application deadline: 6/1; 3/2 priority date for financial aid. Early and deferred admission are possible. **Contact:** Mr. Greg Vaughan, Director of Enrollment Management, 13800 Biola Avenue, La Mirada, CA 90639-0001, 562-903-4752 or toll-free 800-652-4652; fax 562-903-4709; e-mail admissions@biola.edu.

GETTING IN LAST YEAR
1,501 applied
84% were accepted
565 enrolled (45%)
3.52 average high school GPA
37% had SAT verbal scores over 600
33% had SAT math scores over 600
51% had ACT scores over 24
6% had SAT verbal scores over 700

5% had SAT math scores over 700
4% had ACT scores over 30

COSTS AND FINANCIAL INFORMATION
$15,914 tuition and fees (1999–2000)
$5139 room and board
76% average percent of need met
$12,882 average financial aid amount
    received per undergraduate (1999–2000
    estimated)

AFTER GRADUATION
39% graduated in 4 years
16% graduated in 5 years
1% graduated in 6 years
21% pursued further study
50% had job offers within 6 months
75 organizations recruited on campus

BLUFFTON COLLEGE
Bluffton, Ohio

http://www.bluffton.edu/

Unique to Bluffton College is a seriously Mennonite peace church orientation with genuine openness to students of all racial, ethnic, and denominational backgrounds, including international and American minority students. Within this widely diverse and deeply caring Christian community, faculty and staff members and students seek to apply the insights of both the academic disciplines and the Christian faith to the problems of offender ministries, racial discrimination, oppression and poverty, and violence and war. Academic integrity, broad social concern, a caring community, spiritual nurturing, and a beautiful natural environment are all distinguishing characteristics of Bluffton.

Academics
Bluffton College awards bachelor's and master's **degrees**. Challenging opportunities include advanced placement, accelerated degree programs, student-designed majors, freshman honors college, an honors program, and a senior project. **Special programs** include internships, summer session for credit, off-campus study, and study-abroad. The most frequently chosen **baccalaureate** fields are business/marketing, education, and social sciences and history. A complete listing of majors at Bluffton College appears in the Majors Index beginning on page 147. The **faculty** at Bluffton College has 65 full-time members, 78% with terminal degrees. The student-faculty ratio is 13:1.

Students of Bluffton College
The student body totals 1,014, of whom 999 are undergraduates. 54.3% are women and 45.7% are men. Students come from 14 states and territories and 11 other countries. 92% are from Ohio. 1.5% are international students. 72% returned for their sophomore year.

Facilities and Resources
The **library** has 146,000 books and 1,000 subscriptions.

Career Services
The career planning and placement office has 1 full-time staff member. Services include job fairs, resume preparation, resume referral, career counseling, careers library, and job interviews.

Campus Life
There are 40 active organizations on campus, including a drama/theater group, newspaper, radio station, and choral group. No national or local **fraternities** or **sororities**. Bluffton College is a member of the NCAA (Division III). **Intercollegiate sports** include baseball (m), basketball, cross-country running, football (m), golf (m), soccer, softball (w), tennis, track and field, volleyball (w).

Campus Safety
Student safety services include night security guards, late-night transport/escort service, and electronically operated dormitory entrances.

Applying
Bluffton College requires SAT I or ACT, a high school transcript, 2 recommendations, and rank in upper 50% of high school class or 2.3 high school GPA, and in some cases an essay. It recommends an interview. Application deadline: 5/31; 10/1 for financial aid, with a 5/1 priority date. Early and deferred admission are possible. **Contact:** Mr. Eric Fulcomer, Dean of Admissions, 280 West College Avenue, Bluffton, OH 45817-1196, 419-358-3254 or toll-free 800-488-3257; fax 419-358-3232; e-mail admissions@bluffton.edu.

GETTING IN LAST YEAR
743 applied
86% were accepted
246 enrolled (39%)
16% from top tenth of their h.s. class
3.3 average high school GPA
22% had SAT verbal scores over 600
25% had SAT math scores over 600
44% had ACT scores over 24
4% had SAT verbal scores over 700
2% had SAT math scores over 700
4% had ACT scores over 30

COSTS AND FINANCIAL INFORMATION
$14,306 tuition and fees (2000–2001 estimated)
$5122 room and board
100% average percent of need met
$12,395 average financial aid amount received per undergraduate (1999–2000)

AFTER GRADUATION
51% graduated in 4 years
7% graduated in 5 years
Graduates pursuing further study: 5% arts and sciences, 2% business, 1% dentistry
73% had job offers within 6 months
200 organizations recruited on campus

BRYAN COLLEGE

Dayton, Tennessee

http://www.bryan.edu/

Bryan's motto, "Christ Above All," clarifies its priorities as a Christian liberal arts college. This is a lofty goal, but one that challenges the Bryan community to be exceptional and dynamic in faith and practice. The liberal arts curriculum exposes students to a broad scope of knowledge as well as key skills of communication, interpersonal relations, and critical thinking skills. A major thrust of a Bryan education is biblical world view. Students investigate various world view philosophies, then scrutinize them under the lens of Scripture. The scenic 120-acre campus is located 40 miles north of Chattanooga.

Academics
Bryan awards associate and bachelor's **degrees**. Challenging opportunities include advanced placement, an honors program, double majors, independent study, and a senior project. **Special programs** include internships, summer session for credit, and study-abroad. A complete listing of majors at Bryan appears in the Majors Index beginning on page 147. The **faculty** at Bryan has 31 full-time members.

Students of Bryan
The student body is made up of 521 undergraduates. 56% are women and 44% are men. Students come from 33 states and territories and 15 other countries. 3.9% are international students. 77% returned for their sophomore year.

Facilities and Resources
The **library** has 119,348 books and 949 subscriptions.

Career Services
The career planning and placement office has 1 part-time staff member. Services include job fairs, resume preparation, resume referral, career counseling, careers library, job bank, and job interviews.

Campus Life
There are 7 active organizations on campus, including a drama/theater group, newspaper, and choral group. No national or local **fraternities** or **sororities**. Bryan is a member of the NAIA and NCCAA. **Intercollegiate sports** (some offering scholarships) include basketball, soccer, tennis, volleyball (w).

Campus Safety
Student safety services include police patrols, late-night transport/escort service, student patrols, and electronically operated dormitory entrances.

Applying
Bryan requires an essay, ACT, a high school transcript, 3 recommendations, and a minimum high school GPA of 2.0, and in some cases an interview. It recommends SAT I. Application deadline: rolling admissions; 5/1 priority date for financial aid. Early and deferred admission are possible. **Contact:** Mr. Ronald D. Petitte, Registrar, PO Box 7000, Dayton, TN 37321-7000, 423-775-7237 or toll-free 800-277-9522; fax 423-775-7330; e-mail admiss@bryannet.bryan.edu.

GETTING IN LAST YEAR		
427 applied	49% had ACT scores over 24	69% average percent of need met
74% were accepted	11% had SAT verbal scores over 700	$7457 average financial aid amount received
140 enrolled (44%)	6% had SAT math scores over 700	per undergraduate (1998–99)
21% from top tenth of their h.s. class	7% had ACT scores over 30	
3.4 average high school GPA	4 valedictorians	**AFTER GRADUATION**
31% had SAT verbal scores over 600		37% graduated in 4 years
23% had SAT math scores over 600	**COSTS AND FINANCIAL INFORMATION**	8% graduated in 5 years
	$11,200 tuition and fees (1999–2000)	2% graduated in 6 years
	$4000 room and board	

CALIFORNIA BAPTIST UNIVERSITY
Riverside, California   *http://www.calbaptist.edu/*

California Baptist University is located in Southern California's Inland Empire, which is one of the most rapidly growing areas in the nation. Cal Baptist emphasizes a life of assisting others, whether in service-oriented careers, such as counseling and teaching or in business, which is based on biblical principles. The University is diverse in its ethnicity, denominational affiliation, and the ages of its students, providing students with a global outlook in all areas of campus life. Cal Baptist, with offerings of 20 undergraduate majors and master's degrees in marriage and family therapy, education, and business, provides students with a diverse and challenging academic program and the opportunity for active participation in experiential learning and development. At California Baptist University, knowledge is enhanced through personal experience.

Academics
Cal Baptist awards bachelor's and master's **degrees**. Challenging opportunities include advanced placement, accelerated degree programs, an honors program, double majors, independent study, and a senior project. **Special programs** include cooperative education, internships, summer session for credit, off-campus study, study-abroad, and Army and Air Force ROTC. The most frequently chosen **baccalaureate** fields are education, liberal arts/general studies, and psychology. A complete listing of majors at Cal Baptist appears in the Majors Index beginning on page 147. The **faculty** at Cal Baptist has 79 full-time members, 61% with terminal degrees. The student-faculty ratio is 19:1.

Students of Cal Baptist
The student body totals 2,058, of whom 1,618 are undergraduates. 59.7% are women and 40.3% are men. Students come from 24 states and territories. 72% are from California. 0.1% are international students. 82% returned for their sophomore year.

Facilities and Resources
The **library** has 62,743 books and 434 subscriptions.

Career Services
The career planning and placement office has 1 full-time, 1 part-time staff members. Services include job fairs, resume preparation, interview workshops, resume referral, career/interest testing, career counseling, careers library, job bank, job interviews, and software programs.

Campus Life
There are 14 active organizations on campus, including a drama/theater group, newspaper, and choral group. No national or local **fraternities** or **sororities**. Cal Baptist is a member of the NAIA. **Intercollegiate sports** (some offering scholarships) include baseball (m), basketball, cross-country running, golf (m), soccer, softball (w), swimming, tennis, track and field, volleyball, water polo.

Campus Safety
Student safety services include late-night transport/escort service, 24-hour emergency telephone alarm devices, 24-hour patrols by trained security personnel, student patrols, and electronically operated dormitory entrances.

Applying
Cal Baptist requires an essay, SAT I or ACT, a high school transcript, 2 recommendations, and a minimum high school GPA of 2.5. It recommends an interview. Application deadline: 8/1; 3/2 priority date for financial aid. Early and deferred admission are possible. **Contact:** Mr. Doug Wible, Dean of Admissions, 8432 Magnolia Avenue, Riverside, CA 92504-3206, 909-343-4212 or toll-free 877-228-8866; fax 909-351-1808; e-mail admissions@calbaptist.edu.

GETTING IN LAST YEAR
504 applied
80% were accepted
226 enrolled (56%)
3.30 average high school GPA
5% had SAT verbal scores over 600
5% had SAT math scores over 600
19% had ACT scores over 24

1% had ACT scores over 30
3 National Merit Scholars
2 class presidents
5 valedictorians

COSTS AND FINANCIAL INFORMATION
$10,682 tuition and fees (2000–2001)
$4966 room and board
92% average percent of need met

$9100 average financial aid amount received
    per undergraduate (1999–2000 estimated)

AFTER GRADUATION
44% graduated in 4 years
5% graduated in 5 years
1% graduated in 6 years
15 organizations recruited on campus

CALVIN COLLEGE
Grand Rapids, Michigan

http://www.calvin.edu/

Calvin College is one of the largest, oldest, and most respected of the Council schools. Calvin's modern 400-acre campus provides the setting for 4,200 students and 270 faculty members to explore a broad range of majors and programs. While awarding over half of its degrees in accredited, professional programs such as education, engineering, nursing, social work, and business, Calvin remains committed to a liberal arts approach to learning. Calvin College aims to graduate men and women who have examined their world, their faith, and themselves both critically and discerningly, and who are ready to apply their new understanding and Christ-like compassion in useful service.

Academics
Calvin awards bachelor's and master's **degrees** and post-bachelor's certificates. Challenging opportunities include advanced placement, student-designed majors, an honors program, double majors, independent study, and a senior project. **Special programs** include cooperative education, internships, summer session for credit, off-campus study, study-abroad, and Army ROTC. The most frequently chosen **baccalaureate** fields are business/marketing, education, and social sciences and history. A complete listing of majors at Calvin appears in the Majors Index beginning on page 147. The **faculty** at Calvin has 273 full-time members, 78% with terminal degrees. The student-faculty ratio is 16:1.

Students of Calvin
The student body totals 4,264, of whom 4,218 are undergraduates. 55.4% are women and 44.6% are men. Students come from 44 states and territories and 31 other countries. 57% are from Michigan. 6.9% are international students. 85% returned for their sophomore year.

Facilities and Resources
The **library** has 2,721 subscriptions.

Career Services
The career planning and placement office has 6 full-time, 3 part-time staff members. Services include job fairs, resume preparation, interview workshops, resume referral, career/interest testing, career counseling, careers library, job bank, and job interviews.

Campus Life
There are 40 active organizations on campus, including a drama/theater group, newspaper, radio station, and choral group. No national or local **fraternities** or **sororities**. Calvin is a member of the NCAA (Division III). **Intercollegiate sports** include baseball (m), basketball, cross-country running, golf, ice hockey (m), lacrosse, soccer, softball (w), swimming, tennis, track and field, volleyball.

Campus Safety
Student safety services include crime prevention programs, crime alert bulletins, late-night transport/escort service, 24-hour emergency telephone alarm devices, 24-hour patrols by trained security personnel, student patrols, and electronically operated dormitory entrances.

Applying
Calvin requires an essay, SAT I or ACT, a high school transcript, 1 recommendation, and a minimum high school GPA of 2.5. It recommends ACT. Application deadline: 8/15; 2/15 priority date for financial aid. Deferred admission is possible. **Contact:** Mr. Dale D. Kuiper, Director of Admissions, 3201 Burton Street, SE, Grand Rapids, MI 49546-4388, 616-957-6106 or toll-free 800-668-0122; e-mail admissions@calvin.edu.

GETTING IN LAST YEAR
1,971 applied
99% were accepted
1,061 enrolled (55%)
26% from top tenth of their h.s. class
3.49 average high school GPA
47% had SAT verbal scores over 600
47% had SAT math scores over 600
70% had ACT scores over 24
13% had SAT verbal scores over 700
13% had SAT math scores over 700

15% had ACT scores over 30
20 National Merit Scholars
41 valedictorians

COSTS AND FINANCIAL INFORMATION
$14,040 tuition and fees (2000–2001)
$4890 room and board
86% average percent of need met
$10,350 average financial aid amount received per undergraduate (1999–2000 estimated)

AFTER GRADUATION
46% graduated in 4 years
20% graduated in 5 years
2% graduated in 6 years
Graduates pursuing further study: 7% arts and sciences, 5% education, 2% medicine
72% had job offers within 6 months
154 organizations recruited on campus

CAMPBELLSVILLE UNIVERSITY
Campbellsville, Kentucky

http://www.campbellsvil.edu/

Campbellsville University is a private, comprehensive, graduate/undergraduate (Level III), coeducational university undergirded by a strong liberal arts component. Affiliated with the Kentucky Baptist Convention, Campbellsville is open to students of all denominations. The 75-acre campus is situated in the center of Kentucky, one-half mile from downtown Campbellsville, population 11,000. The university is located 1½ hours from Louisville and Lexington, Kentucky and 2½ hours from Nashville, Tennessee. Enrollment has grown 150% in the past 10 years to approximately 1,600 students. Campbellsville has added a 135-acre educational and research woodland, Clay Hill Memorial Forest, that is being developed as a regional center for environmental education and research. Campbellsville offers new academic programs in sports ministry and Christian social ministries, as well as a Semester in London Program. The music program is an accredited institutional member of the National Association of Schools of Music (NASM). Summer international programs are also available.

Academics
Campbellsville University awards associate, bachelor's, and master's **degrees** and post-bachelor's certificates. Challenging opportunities include advanced placement, accelerated degree programs, an honors program, double majors, and independent study. **Special programs** include internships, summer session for credit, and study-abroad. A complete listing of majors at Campbellsville University appears in the Majors Index beginning on page 147. The **faculty** at Campbellsville University has 74 full-time members. The student-faculty ratio is 16:1.

Students of Campbellsville University
The student body totals 1,608, of whom 1,548 are undergraduates. 60.1% are women and 39.9% are men. Students come from 28 states and territories and 17 other countries. 90% are from Kentucky. 4.5% are international students. 78% returned for their sophomore year.

Facilities and Resources
The **library** has 108,000 books and 500 subscriptions.

Career Services
The career planning and placement office has 1 full-time, 1 part-time staff members. Services include job fairs, resume preparation, resume referral, career counseling, careers library, job bank, and job interviews.

Campus Life
There are 45 active organizations on campus, including a drama/theater group, newspaper, radio station, television station, choral group, and marching band. No national or local **fraternities** or **sororities**. Campbellsville University is a member of the NAIA. **Intercollegiate sports** (some offering scholarships) include baseball (m), basketball, cross-country running, football (m), golf, soccer, softball (w), swimming, tennis, volleyball (w).

Campus Safety
Student safety services include late-night transport/escort service, 24-hour emergency telephone alarm devices, 24-hour patrols by trained security personnel, student patrols, and electronically operated dormitory entrances.

Applying
Campbellsville University requires SAT I or ACT, a high school transcript, and a minimum high school GPA of 2.0. It recommends an essay, an interview, recommendations, and a minimum high school GPA of 3.0. Application deadline: rolling admissions; 3/1 priority date for financial aid. Deferred admission is possible. **Contact:** Mr. R. Trent Argo, Director of Admissions, 1 University Drive, Campbellsville, KY 42718-2799, 270-789-5552 or toll-free 800-264-6014; fax 270-789-5071; e-mail admissions@campbellsvil.edu.

GETTING IN LAST YEAR
786 applied
72% were accepted
308 enrolled (55%)
17% from top tenth of their h.s. class
3.67 average high school GPA
18% had SAT verbal scores over 600
4% had SAT math scores over 600

17% had ACT scores over 24
4% had SAT verbal scores over 700
2% had ACT scores over 30
11 class presidents
7 valedictorians

COSTS AND FINANCIAL INFORMATION
$8240 tuition and fees (1999–2000)
$3990 room and board

59% average percent of need met
$8798 average financial aid amount received
  per undergraduate (1999–2000 estimated)

AFTER GRADUATION
48% pursued further study
60 organizations recruited on campus

CAMPBELL UNIVERSITY
Buies Creek, North Carolina

http://www.campbell.edu/

Campbell University is a private liberal arts institution in southeastern North Carolina, born of a vision over 100 years ago—a vision that lives on today. Campbell's curriculum meets individual needs and interests and offers the range of majors that today's students expect from a high-quality institution, including preprofessional and professional studies. A comprehensive financial aid program helps families meet educational costs. The University has adapted to changing times and needs without losing sight of its heritage and mission to provide educational opportunities in a Christian environment.

Academics
Campbell awards associate, bachelor's, master's, doctoral, and first-professional **degrees**. Challenging opportunities include advanced placement, accelerated degree programs, an honors program, double majors, independent study, and a senior project. **Special programs** include cooperative education, internships, summer session for credit, study-abroad, and Army ROTC. The most frequently chosen **baccalaureate** fields are business/marketing, psychology, and social sciences and history. A complete listing of majors at Campbell appears in the Majors Index beginning on page 147. The **faculty** at Campbell has 181 full-time members, 91% with terminal degrees. The student-faculty ratio is 18:1.

Students of Campbell
The student body totals 3,265, of whom 2,201 are undergraduates. 56.1% are women and 43.9% are men. Students come from 50 states and territories and 46 other countries. 70% are from North Carolina. 3.2% are international students. 71% returned for their sophomore year.

Facilities and Resources
The 3 **libraries** have 189,763 books.

Career Services
The career planning and placement office has 2 full-time staff members. Services include job fairs, resume preparation, resume referral, career counseling, careers library, and job interviews.

Campus Life
There are 50 active organizations on campus, including a drama/theater group, newspaper, radio station, and choral group. No national or local **fraternities** or **sororities**. Campbell is a member of the NCAA (Division I). **Intercollegiate sports** (some offering scholarships) include baseball (m), basketball, cross-country running, golf, soccer, softball (w), tennis, track and field, volleyball (w), wrestling (m).

Campus Safety
Student safety services include late-night transport/escort service, 24-hour emergency telephone alarm devices, 24-hour patrols by trained security personnel, and electronically operated dormitory entrances.

Applying
Campbell requires SAT I or ACT, a high school transcript, and a minimum high school GPA of 2.0, and in some cases 3 recommendations. It recommends an interview. Application deadline: rolling admissions; 3/15 priority date for financial aid. Early and deferred admission are possible. **Contact:** Mrs. Charlotte Bohn, Director of Admissions, PO Box 546, Buies Creek, NC 27506, 910-893-1300 or toll-free 800-334-4111 (out-of-state); fax 910-893-1288; e-mail satterfiel@mailcenter.campbell.edu.

GETTING IN LAST YEAR		
1,902 applied	4% had SAT verbal scores over 700	100% average percent of need met
70% were accepted	4% had SAT math scores over 700	$10,952 average financial aid amount
544 enrolled (41%)	6 National Merit Scholars	received per undergraduate (1999–2000)
16% from top tenth of their h.s. class	19 class presidents	
2.80 average high school GPA	24 valedictorians	**AFTER GRADUATION**
11% had SAT verbal scores over 600		25% pursued further study (8% business, 6%
20% had SAT math scores over 600	**COSTS AND FINANCIAL INFORMATION**	arts and sciences, 4% law)
	$10,997 tuition and fees (1999–2000)	80% had job offers within 6 months
	$3950 room and board	20 organizations recruited on campus

CEDARVILLE UNIVERSITY
Cedarville, Ohio

http://www.cedarville.edu/

Cedarville University's mission is "to offer an education consistent with biblical truth." Commitment and achievement characterize this education. All students and faculty members testify to personal faith in Christ. A Bible minor complements every major. Relevant daily chapels encourage spiritual growth. Over 150 local and worldwide ministries provide avenues for outreach. Cedarville teams consistently finish among top universities in national academic competitions. National, regional, and local employers, as well as graduate schools, recruit students from 100 academic programs. The University attracts national recognition for its campus-wide computer network. Reasonable costs and financial aid make Cedarville affordable.

Academics
Cedarville awards associate and bachelor's **degrees**. Challenging opportunities include advanced placement, accelerated degree programs, an honors program, double majors, independent study, and a senior project. **Special programs** include internships, summer session for credit, study-abroad, and Army and Air Force ROTC. The most frequently chosen **baccalaureate** fields are education, philosophy, and business/marketing. A complete listing of majors at Cedarville appears in the Majors Index beginning on page 147. The **faculty** at Cedarville has 158 full-time members, 63% with terminal degrees. The student-faculty ratio is 17:1.

Students of Cedarville
The student body is made up of 2,762 undergraduates. 54.6% are women and 45.4% are men. Students come from 54 states and territories. 0.4% are international students. 86% returned for their sophomore year.

Facilities and Resources
The **library** has 133,891 books and 2,878 subscriptions.

Career Services
The career planning and placement office has 3 full-time staff members. Services include job fairs, resume preparation, interview workshops, resume referral, career/interest testing, career counseling, careers library, job bank, and job interviews.

Campus Life
There are 55 active organizations on campus, including a drama/theater group, newspaper, radio station, and choral group. No national or local **fraternities** or **sororities**. Cedarville is a member of the NAIA and NCCAA. **Intercollegiate sports** (some offering scholarships) include baseball (m), basketball, cross-country running, golf (m), soccer, softball (w), tennis, track and field, volleyball (w).

Campus Safety
Student safety services include late-night transport/escort service, 24-hour emergency telephone alarm devices, 24-hour patrols by trained security personnel, and student patrols.

Applying
Cedarville requires an essay, SAT I or ACT, a high school transcript, 2 recommendations, and a minimum high school GPA of 3.0, and in some cases an interview. Application deadline: rolling admissions; 3/1 priority date for financial aid. Early and deferred admission are possible. **Contact:** Mr. Roscoe Smith, Director of Admissions, PO Box 601, Cedarville, OH 45314-0601, 937-766-7700 or toll-free 800-CEDARVILLE; fax 937-766-7575; e-mail admiss@cedarville.edu.

GETTING IN LAST YEAR
1,814 applied
74% were accepted
722 enrolled (54%)
36% from top tenth of their h.s. class
3.59 average high school GPA
49% had SAT verbal scores over 600
44% had SAT math scores over 600
68% had ACT scores over 24
10% had SAT verbal scores over 700

9% had SAT math scores over 700
14% had ACT scores over 30
14 National Merit Scholars
85 valedictorians

COSTS AND FINANCIAL INFORMATION
$10,740 tuition and fees (1999–2000)
$4788 room and board
40% average percent of need met
$9452 average financial aid amount received
   per undergraduate (1998–99)

AFTER GRADUATION
59% graduated in 4 years
6% graduated in 5 years
1% graduated in 6 years
Graduates pursuing further study: 4% theology,
   2% medicine, 2% arts and sciences
96% had job offers within 6 months
230 organizations recruited on campus

COLLEGE OF THE OZARKS

Point Lookout, Missouri   *http://www.cofo.edu/*

Called "Hard Work U" by *The Wall Street Journal*, all students at this unique Missouri institution work, rather than pay tuition, for their education. This self-help philosophy is a long-standing tradition and affirms a no-nonsense approach to academics and character education. Students major in a variety of fields, but all must meet a demanding liberal arts core taught by capable faculty. The combination of high academic standards, the work ethic, a pervasive sense of history and values, and a Christian environment creates an atmosphere of high expectations and provides many opportunities for students.

Academics

C of O awards bachelor's **degrees**. Challenging opportunities include advanced placement, accelerated degree programs, student-designed majors, an honors program, and a senior project. **Special programs** include cooperative education, internships, summer session for credit, study-abroad, and Army ROTC. The most frequently chosen **baccalaureate** fields are business/marketing, education, and agriculture. A complete listing of majors at C of O appears in the Majors Index beginning on page 147. The **faculty** at C of O has 89 full-time members. The student-faculty ratio is 14:1.

Students of C of O

The student body is made up of 1,429 undergraduates. 53.3% are women and 46.7% are men. Students come from 34 states and territories and 27 other countries. 66% are from Missouri. 2.6% are international students. 74% returned for their sophomore year.

Facilities and Resources

The 2 **libraries** have 114,549 books.

Career Services

The career planning and placement office has 1 full-time, 6 part-time staff members. Services include job fairs, resume preparation, resume referral, career counseling, careers library, job bank, and job interviews.

Campus Life

There are 49 active organizations on campus, including a drama/theater group, newspaper, radio station, and choral group. No national or local **fraternities** or **sororities**. C of O is a member of the NAIA. **Intercollegiate sports** (some offering scholarships) include baseball (m), basketball, volleyball (w).

Campus Safety

Student safety services include front gate closed 1 a.m. to 6 a.m., gate security 5:30 p.m. to 1 a.m, 24-hour emergency telephone alarm devices, 24-hour patrols by trained security personnel, and electronically operated dormitory entrances.

Applying

C of O requires SAT I or ACT, a high school transcript, an interview, 2 recommendations, and medical history, financial statement. It recommends an essay and a minimum high school GPA of 2.0. Application deadline: 8/15; 3/15 priority date for financial aid. Early admission is possible. **Contact:** Mrs. Janet Miller, Admissions Secretary, Point Lookout, MO 65726, 417-334-6411 ext. 4217 or toll-free 800-222-0525; fax 417-335-2618; e-mail admiss4@cofo.edu.

GETTING IN LAST YEAR	COSTS AND FINANCIAL INFORMATION	AFTER GRADUATION
2,752 applied	2.89 average high school GPA	12% pursued further study (7% arts and sciences, 2% business, 2% education)
18% were accepted	$150 tuition and fees (2000–2001 estimated)	97% had job offers within 6 months
270 enrolled (55%)	$2500 room and board	192 organizations recruited on campus
24% from top tenth of their h.s. class	81% average percent of need met	

COLORADO CHRISTIAN UNIVERSITY
Lakewood, Colorado

http://www.ccu.edu/

Colorado Christian University is located in suburban Denver, one of the most attractive, recreation-centered, major metropolitan regions in the nation. At the foot of the Rockies, the picturesque campus offers students solid academic preparation for opportunities requiring the spiritual, social, and technical skills to compete successfully in today's marketplaces. CCU has established a strong regional reputation for academic quality. The university's graduate, technical, and professional programs are widely recognized in the region for the success of their graduates. Music and theater ensemble opportunities provide interested students with excellent opportunities for participation at a variety of levels. As an NCAA Division II school, CCU stresses achievement and excellence in its athletic programs. On-campus housing is apartment-style living.

Academics
CCU awards associate, bachelor's, and master's **degrees**. Challenging opportunities include advanced placement, accelerated degree programs, student-designed majors, an honors program, double majors, independent study, and a senior project. **Special programs** include cooperative education, internships, summer session for credit, off-campus study, study-abroad, and Army and Air Force ROTC. The most frequently chosen **baccalaureate** fields are business/marketing, education, and philosophy. A complete listing of majors at CCU appears in the Majors Index beginning on page 147. The **faculty** at CCU has 48 full-time members. The student-faculty ratio is 12:1.

Students of CCU
The student body totals 2,026, of whom 1,786 are undergraduates. 55.9% are women and 44.1% are men. Students come from 40 states and territories and 20 other countries. 80% are from Colorado. 1.1% are international students. 53% returned for their sophomore year.

Facilities and Resources
The **library** has 56,000 books and 1,600 subscriptions.

Career Services
The career planning and placement office has 1 full-time staff member. Services include resume preparation, career counseling, careers library, and job bank.

Campus Life
There are 20 active organizations on campus, including a drama/theater group, newspaper, radio station, and choral group. No national or local **fraternities** or **sororities**. CCU is a member of the NCAA (Division II). **Intercollegiate sports** (some offering scholarships) include basketball, cross-country running, golf (m), soccer, tennis, volleyball (w).

Campus Safety
Student safety services include 24-hour emergency telephone alarm devices and 24-hour patrols by trained security personnel.

Applying
CCU requires an essay, SAT I or ACT, a high school transcript, 2 recommendations, and a minimum high school GPA of 2.0, and in some cases an interview and 3 recommendations. Application deadline: rolling admissions; 3/15 priority date for financial aid. Deferred admission is possible. **Contact:** Ms. Kay Myrick, Director of Admissions, 180 South Garrison Street, Lakewood, CO 80226-7499, 303-963-3203 or toll-free 800-44-FAITH; fax 303-238-2191; e-mail admissions@ccu.edu.

GETTING IN LAST YEAR
780 applied
74% were accepted
214 enrolled (37%)
1 National Merit Scholar

COSTS AND FINANCIAL INFORMATION
$10,790 tuition and fees (1999–2000)

$5160 room and board
72% average percent of need met
$9274 average financial aid amount received
    per undergraduate (1999–2000)

AFTER GRADUATION
16% graduated in 4 years
13% graduated in 5 years
1% graduated in 6 years

CORNERSTONE UNIVERSITY
Grand Rapids, Michigan

http://www.cornerstone.edu/

Cornerstone University in Grand Rapids, Michigan, is a four-year, Christ-centered university with traditional and accelerated adult degree completion programs, Grand Rapids Baptist Seminary with master and doctorate programs and Asia extension program (GRBSEP), and a broadcasting ministry. Cornerstone's mission is "to enable individuals to apply unchanging biblical principles in a rapidly changing world." Offered are more than 75 undergraduate academic programs. Incoming freshmen receive a laptop computer to use during their schooling. A practical internship in every undergraduate major prepares students for success in the working world. Record enrollment growth has encouraged the construction of a new residence hall, Corum Student Union, and the $13 million Bernice Hansen Athletic Center. Cornerstone educates its students to apply a Christian worldview in their field of study, utilizing principles from the university's Christian Worldview Institute (CWI). Spiritual formation is emphasized through daily chapel, student ministry involvement, leadership opportunities, and participation in cross-cultural ministry trips. Athletics are used to challenge young people to pursue excellence, developing their leadership skills and character in the heat of battle. Recent accomplishments include the 1999 NAIA Division II National Men's Basketball Championship, 2000 NAIA Region 8 Softball Championship, and All-American finishes in cross country and indoor/outdoor track and field.

Academics

Cornerstone University awards associate and bachelor's **degrees**. Challenging opportunities include advanced placement, accelerated degree programs, double majors, and independent study. **Special programs** include internships, summer session for credit, off-campus study, and Army ROTC. The most frequently chosen **baccalaureate** fields are business/marketing, education, and English. A complete listing of majors at Cornerstone University appears in the Majors Index beginning on page 147. The **faculty** at Cornerstone University has 56 full-time members, 66% with terminal degrees.

Students of Cornerstone University

The student body is made up of 1,508 undergraduates. 60.1% are women and 39.9% are men. Students come from 29 states and territories and 4 other countries. 82% are from Michigan. 0.7% are international students. 67% returned for their sophomore year.

Facilities and Resources

The **library** has 90,444 books.

Career Services

The career planning and placement office has 3 full-time staff members. Services include job fairs, resume preparation, resume referral, career counseling, careers library, job bank, and job interviews.

Campus Life

Active organizations on campus include a drama/theater group, newspaper, and choral group. No national or local **fraternities** or **sororities**. Cornerstone University is a member of the NAIA. **Intercollegiate sports** (some offering scholarships) include basketball, cross-country running, golf (m), soccer, softball (w), tennis (m), volleyball (w).

Campus Safety

Student safety services include late-night transport/escort service, 24-hour emergency telephone alarm devices, 24-hour patrols by trained security personnel, and student patrols.

Applying

Cornerstone University requires an essay, SAT I or ACT, a high school transcript, 1 recommendation, and a minimum high school GPA of 2.25. It recommends an interview. Application deadline: rolling admissions; 3/21 priority date for financial aid. Deferred admission is possible. **Contact:** Mr. Brent Rudin, Director of Enrollment Management, 1001 East Beltline Avenue, NE, Grand Rapids, MI 49325-5597, 616-222-1426 or toll-free 800-968-4722; fax 616-949-0875; e-mail admissions@cornerstone.edu.

GETTING IN LAST YEAR
725 applied
91% were accepted
366 enrolled (56%)
15% from top tenth of their h.s. class
3.42 average high school GPA
35% had ACT scores over 24

5% had ACT scores over 30
7 valedictorians

COSTS AND FINANCIAL INFORMATION
$10,344 tuition and fees (1999–2000)
$4712 room and board

AFTER GRADUATION
12% graduated in 4 years
17% graduated in 5 years
6% graduated in 6 years
14% pursued further study
95% had job offers within 6 months
35 organizations recruited on campus

COVENANT COLLEGE

Lookout Mountain, Georgia   *http://www.covenant.edu/*

Covenant's primary goal is to provide an environment of academic excellence that encourages students to develop a Christian world view. A Covenant education produces skills and values that equip students to serve effectively and live responsibly in a changing world. Covenant is more than a safe enclave for Christian students. It requires a distinctive experience that motivates and enables its young men and women to make an impact on the world for Christ.

Academics

Covenant awards associate, bachelor's, and master's **degrees** (master's degree in education only). Challenging opportunities include advanced placement, student-designed majors, an honors program, double majors, independent study, and a senior project. **Special programs** include internships, summer session for credit, off-campus study, and study-abroad. The most frequently chosen **baccalaureate** fields are business/marketing, social sciences and history, and education. A complete listing of majors at Covenant appears in the Majors Index beginning on page 147. The **faculty** at Covenant has 50 full-time members, 82% with terminal degrees. The student-faculty ratio is 16:1.

Students of Covenant

The student body totals 1,116, of whom 1,049 are undergraduates. 57.9% are women and 42.1% are men. Students come from 46 states and territories and 18 other countries. 22% are from Georgia. 2.5% are international students. 79% returned for their sophomore year.

Facilities and Resources

The **library** has 61,502 books and 554 subscriptions.

Career Services

The career planning and placement office has 2 full-time staff members. Services include job fairs, resume preparation, interview workshops, resume referral, career/interest testing, career counseling, careers library, job bank, and job interviews.

Campus Life

There are 45 active organizations on campus, including a drama/theater group, newspaper, and choral group. No national or local **fraternities** or **sororities**. Covenant is a member of the NAIA. **Intercollegiate sports** (some offering scholarships) include basketball, cross-country running, soccer, volleyball (w).

Campus Safety

Student safety services include night security guards.

Applying

Covenant requires an essay, SAT I or ACT, a high school transcript, an interview, 2 recommendations, and a minimum high school GPA of 2.5. It recommends SAT I. Application deadline: rolling admissions; 3/1 priority date for financial aid. Early and deferred admission are possible. **Contact:** Ms. Leda Goodman, Regional Director, 14049 Scenic Highway, Lookout Mountain, GA 30750, 706-820-1560 ext. 1644 or toll-free 888-451-2683 (in-state); e-mail admissions@covenant.edu.

GETTING IN LAST YEAR
654 applied
78% were accepted
229 enrolled (45%)
26% from top tenth of their h.s. class
3.38 average high school GPA
47% had SAT verbal scores over 600

41% had SAT math scores over 600
65% had ACT scores over 24
14% had SAT verbal scores over 700
4% had SAT math scores over 700
9% had ACT scores over 30

COSTS AND FINANCIAL INFORMATION
$15,960 tuition and fees (2000–2001)

$4450 room and board
87% average percent of need met
$12,633 average financial aid amount received per undergraduate (1999–2000 estimated)

AFTER GRADUATION
100 organizations recruited on campus

CRICHTON COLLEGE

Memphis, Tennessee

http://www.crichton.edu/

A private, four-year, coeducational college, Crichton combines excellence in higher education with evangelical Christian faith and relates education to the needs of individuals in contemporary society. The biblical basis of all programs—a distinctive part of Crichton curriculum—ensures the centrality of Christian principles in the academic programs, philosophy, and life of the college. Crichton offers majors in biblical studies, business, chemistry, communications, psychology, biology, professional education, prenursing, English, liberal studies, prelaw and history. Stressing excellence in teaching in a personalized environment, the faculty encourages students to practice a reasoned and vital faith that will enable them to lead mature and creative lives. The student body represents various churches, races, and social backgrounds.

Academics
Crichton College awards bachelor's **degrees**. Challenging opportunities include advanced placement, accelerated degree programs, student-designed majors, double majors, and independent study. **Special programs** include cooperative education, internships, summer session for credit, and study-abroad. The most frequently chosen **baccalaureate** fields are business/marketing, education, and psychology. A complete listing of majors at Crichton College appears in the Majors Index beginning on page 147. The **faculty** at Crichton College has 26 full-time members, 58% with terminal degrees. The student-faculty ratio is 15:1.

Students of Crichton College
The student body is made up of 896 undergraduates. 58.5% are women and 41.5% are men. Students come from 8 states and territories and 3 other countries. 90% are from Tennessee. 59% returned for their sophomore year.

Facilities and Resources
The **library** has 42,767 books and 435 subscriptions.

Career Services
Services include resume preparation, career counseling, and careers library.

Campus Life
There are 20 active organizations on campus, including a drama/theater group and choral group. No national or local **fraternities** or **sororities**. **Intercollegiate sports** include baseball (m).

Campus Safety
Student safety services include security alarms in campus apartments, 24-hour patrols by trained security personnel, and electronically operated dormitory entrances.

Applying
Crichton College requires SAT I or ACT, a high school transcript, and 3 recommendations, and in some cases an essay. It recommends an interview and a minimum high school GPA of 2.0. Application deadline: 8/31; 3/31 priority date for financial aid. Early and deferred admission are possible. **Contact:** Mr. John G. Smith, Director of Student Recruitment, 6655 Winchester Road, PO Box 757830, Memphis, TN 38175-7830, 901-367-3888 or toll-free 800-960-9777; e-mail jgsmith@crichton.edu.

GETTING IN LAST YEAR
436 applied
67% were accepted
60 enrolled (20%)
2.7 average high school GPA

31% had ACT scores over 24

COSTS AND FINANCIAL INFORMATION
$7152 tuition and fees (1999–2000)
$2800 room only
35% average percent of need met

$4162 average financial aid amount received per undergraduate (1998–99)

AFTER GRADUATION
13% graduated in 4 years
10% graduated in 5 years

DALLAS BAPTIST UNIVERSITY
Dallas, Texas   *http://www.dbu.edu/*

Servant-leadership is at the heart of the Dallas Baptist University educational experience. The academic commitment to the integration of faith and learning, coupled with an attitude of humility and service, provides the foundation for the development of Christian leadership that will extend into the 21st century. DBU's mission is to develop servant-leaders who will impact the world for Christ in their chosen profession. The University relies heavily on the *Intercessory Prayer Ministry* and the prayers of 1,200 senior adults who pray daily for the University to accomplish this mission.

Academics
DBU awards associate, bachelor's, and master's **degrees**. Challenging opportunities include advanced placement, double majors, independent study, and a senior project. **Special programs** include internships, summer session for credit, off-campus study, study-abroad, and Army and Air Force ROTC. The most frequently chosen **baccalaureate** fields are business/marketing, liberal arts/general studies, and education. A complete listing of majors at DBU appears in the Majors Index beginning on page 147. The **faculty** at DBU has 81 full-time members, 79% with terminal degrees. The student-faculty ratio is 20:1.

Students of DBU
The student body totals 3,921, of whom 3,150 are undergraduates. 61.1% are women and 38.9% are men. Students come from 30 states and territories and 37 other countries. 95% are from Texas. 5.1% are international students.

Facilities and Resources
The **library** has 205,724 books and 739 subscriptions.

Career Services
The career planning and placement office has 1 full-time, 1 part-time staff members. Services include job fairs, interview workshops, resume referral, career/interest testing, career counseling, careers library, and job bank.

Campus Life
There are 24 active organizations on campus, including a drama/theater group and choral group. No national or local **fraternities** or **sororities**. DBU is a member of the NAIA. **Intercollegiate sports** (some offering scholarships) include baseball (m), cross-country running, soccer, tennis, track and field, volleyball.

Campus Safety
Student safety services include late-night transport/escort service, 24-hour emergency telephone alarm devices, 24-hour patrols by trained security personnel, and electronically operated dormitory entrances.

Applying
DBU requires an essay, SAT I or ACT, a high school transcript, and rank in upper 50% of high school class or 3.0 high school GPA. It recommends an interview and recommendations. Application deadline: rolling admissions; 3/15 priority date for financial aid. Early and deferred admission are possible. **Contact:** Mr. Jeremy Dutschke, Director of Admissions, 3000 Mountain Creek Parkway, Dallas, TX 75211-9299, 214-333-5360 or toll-free 800-460-1328; fax 214-333-5447; e-mail admiss@dbu.edu.

GETTING IN LAST YEAR
478 applied
55% were accepted
261 enrolled (100%)
15% from top tenth of their h.s. class
3.4 average high school GPA
14% had SAT verbal scores over 600
17% had SAT math scores over 600

25% had ACT scores over 24
3% had SAT verbal scores over 700
3% had SAT math scores over 700
1% had ACT scores over 30
1 valedictorian

COSTS AND FINANCIAL INFORMATION
$8700 tuition and fees (1999–2000)

$3680 room and board
72% average percent of need met
$8905 average financial aid amount received per undergraduate (1998–99)

AFTER GRADUATION
50 organizations recruited on campus

DORDT COLLEGE
Sioux Center, Iowa

http://www.dordt.edu/

Dordt College does not adhere to the traditional distinctions between liberal arts and professional training. The College instead focuses on transmitting "serviceable insight," a biblically based understanding of both the structure of creation and the nature and demands of a wide range of vocations and professions. This is why the College has majors such as agriculture, business, and computer science; why there are accredited programs in social work and engineering; why opportunities for internships and off-campus study abound; and why every course at Dordt will challenge students to think about the real-world applications of their learning.

Academics
Dordt awards associate, bachelor's, and master's **degrees**. Challenging opportunities include advanced placement, student-designed majors, double majors, independent study, and a senior project. **Special programs** include internships, off-campus study, and study-abroad. The most frequently chosen **baccalaureate** fields are education, business/marketing, and engineering/engineering technologies. A complete listing of majors at Dordt appears in the Majors Index beginning on page 147. The **faculty** at Dordt has 78 full-time members, 72% with terminal degrees. The student-faculty ratio is 15:1.

Students of Dordt
The student body is made up of 1,430 undergraduates. 54.9% are women and 45.1% are men. Students come from 35 states and territories and 17 other countries. 46% are from Iowa. 12.3% are international students. 89% returned for their sophomore year.

Facilities and Resources
The 2 **libraries** have 185,000 books and 700 subscriptions.

Career Services
The career planning and placement office has 2 full-time staff members. Services include job fairs, resume preparation, resume referral, career/interest testing, career counseling, careers library, job bank, and job interviews.

Campus Life
There are 40 active organizations on campus, including a drama/theater group, newspaper, radio station, and choral group. No national or local **fraternities** or **sororities**. Dordt is a member of the NAIA. **Intercollegiate sports** (some offering scholarships) include basketball, cross-country running, golf (m), ice hockey (m), soccer, softball (w), tennis, track and field, volleyball (w).

Campus Safety
Student safety services include late-night transport/escort service, 24-hour emergency telephone alarm devices, student patrols, and electronically operated dormitory entrances.

Applying
Dordt requires SAT I or ACT, a high school transcript, minimum ACT composite score of 19 or combined SAT I score of 920, and a minimum high school GPA of 2.25, and in some cases an interview. Application deadline: 8/1; 4/1 priority date for financial aid. Deferred admission is possible. **Contact:** Mr. Quentin Van Essen, Executive Director of Admissions, 498 4th Avenue, NE, Sioux Center, IA 51250-1697, 712-722-6080 or toll-free 800-343-6738; fax 712-722-1967; e-mail admissions@dordt.edu.

GETTING IN LAST YEAR
831 applied
95% were accepted
349 enrolled (44%)
22% from top tenth of their h.s. class
3.35 average high school GPA
39% had SAT verbal scores over 600
36% had SAT math scores over 600
55% had ACT scores over 24
9% had SAT verbal scores over 700

7% had SAT math scores over 700
10% had ACT scores over 30

COSTS AND FINANCIAL INFORMATION
$12,650 tuition and fees (1999–2000)
$3600 room and board
76% average percent of need met
$11,476 average financial aid amount received per undergraduate (1999–2000 estimated)

AFTER GRADUATION
57% graduated in 4 years
8% graduated in 5 years
1% graduated in 6 years
11% pursued further study (5% arts and sciences, 2% business, 2% engineering)
98% had job offers within 6 months
50 organizations recruited on campus

EASTERN COLLEGE
St. Davids, Pennsylvania

http://www.eastern.edu/

Eastern College is known for its innovative academic programs, caring Christian community, commitment to social action, and exceptionally beautiful campus. Class sizes are kept small, and professors are both role models to their students and highly accomplished experts in their fields. In addition to integrating faith and learning, Eastern's creative academic programs encourage students to learn from many disciplines. The campus community is highly diverse, with a multiethnic student body that includes representatives from over 30 countries. A strong campus ministries program and Eastern's proximity to the city of Philadelphia provide many opportunities for Christian service. The life of the Eastern College community is firmly centered in Jesus Christ.

Academics

Eastern awards associate, bachelor's, and master's **degrees**. Challenging opportunities include advanced placement, accelerated degree programs, student-designed majors, an honors program, independent study, and a senior project. **Special programs** include internships, summer session for credit, off-campus study, and Army and Air Force ROTC. The most frequently chosen **baccalaureate** fields are business/marketing, education, and philosophy. A complete listing of majors at Eastern appears in the Majors Index beginning on page 147. The **faculty** at Eastern has 67 full-time members, 75% with terminal degrees. The student-faculty ratio is 14:1.

Students of Eastern

The student body totals 2,757, of whom 1,902 are undergraduates. 66.2% are women and 33.8% are men. Students come from 38 states and territories and 26 other countries. 60% are from Pennsylvania. 1.8% are international students. 79% returned for their sophomore year.

Facilities and Resources

The 2 **libraries** have 143,815 books and 1,215 subscriptions.

Career Services

The career planning and placement office has 2 part-time staff members. Services include job fairs, resume preparation, interview workshops, resume referral, career counseling, careers library, and job bank.

Campus Life

There are 70 active organizations on campus, including a drama/theater group, newspaper, radio station, and choral group. No national or local **fraternities** or **sororities**. Eastern is a member of the NCAA (Division III). **Intercollegiate sports** include baseball (m), basketball, field hockey (w), lacrosse, soccer, softball (w), volleyball (w).

Campus Safety

Student safety services include emergency call boxes, late-night transport/escort service, 24-hour emergency telephone alarm devices, 24-hour patrols by trained security personnel, and electronically operated dormitory entrances.

Applying

Eastern requires an essay, SAT I or ACT, a high school transcript, 1 recommendation, and a minimum high school GPA of 2.0. It recommends an interview, 3 recommendations, and a minimum high school GPA of 3.0. Application deadline: rolling admissions. Early and deferred admission are possible. **Contact:** Mr. Mark Seymour, Executive Director for Enrollment Management, 1300 Eagle Road, St. Davids, PA 19087-3696, 610-341-5967 or toll-free 800-452-0996; fax 610-341-1723; e-mail ugadm@eastern.edu.

GETTING IN LAST YEAR
908 applied
84% were accepted
381 enrolled (50%)
25% from top tenth of their h.s. class
3.39 average high school GPA
32% had SAT verbal scores over 600

26% had SAT math scores over 600
41% had ACT scores over 24
8% had SAT verbal scores over 700
2% had SAT math scores over 700
17 National Merit Scholars

COSTS AND FINANCIAL INFORMATION
$13,728 tuition and fees (1999–2000)

$5878 room and board

AFTER GRADUATION
45% graduated in 4 years
7% graduated in 5 years
3% graduated in 6 years
18% pursued further study
83% had job offers within 6 months

EASTERN MENNONITE UNIVERSITY

Harrisonburg, Virginia

http://www.emu.edu/

EASTERN
MENNONITE
UNIVERSITY
Harrisonburg
VA 22802-8462

EMU students deepen their commitment to being a Christian and a world citizen. EMU's Global Village curriculum integrates the liberal arts and sciences with Christian values and personal contact with people of other cultures. Students spend a semester or summer term in another culture either overseas or stateside or live in Washington, D.C. for a year in a study-service program. Alumni find that they are well-prepared for advanced study and report that their careers are profoundly enriched by a global perspective. Students are encouraged to see life as an opportunity for faithful Christian witness, service, and peacebuilding in a needy world. All of this begins in a friendly campus community in the heart of the scenic Shenandoah Valley of Virginia.

Academics
EMU awards associate, bachelor's, master's, and first-professional **degrees** and post-bachelor's and first-professional certificates. Challenging opportunities include advanced placement, student-designed majors, an honors program, double majors, independent study, and a senior project. **Special programs** include internships, summer session for credit, off-campus study, and study-abroad. The most frequently chosen **baccalaureate** fields are business/marketing, health professions and related sciences, and education. A complete listing of majors at EMU appears in the Majors Index beginning on page 147. The **faculty** at EMU has 76 full-time members, 70% with terminal degrees. The student-faculty ratio is 13:1.

Students of EMU
The student body totals 1,349, of whom 1,099 are undergraduates. 59.9% are women and 40.1% are men. Students come from 35 states and territories and 14 other countries. 40% are from Virginia. 4.7% are international students. 76% returned for their sophomore year.

Facilities and Resources
The **library** has 175,147 books and 1,112 subscriptions.

Career Services
The career planning and placement office has 1 full-time staff member. Services include job fairs, resume preparation, interview workshops, resume referral, career/interest testing, career counseling, careers library, job bank, and job interviews.

Campus Life
There are 26 active organizations on campus, including a drama/theater group, newspaper, radio station, and choral group. No national or local **fraternities** or **sororities**. EMU is a member of the NCAA (Division III). **Intercollegiate sports** include baseball (m), basketball, cross-country running, field hockey (w), soccer, softball (w), tennis, track and field, volleyball.

Campus Safety
Student safety services include night watchman, 24-hour emergency telephone alarm devices, and electronically operated dormitory entrances.

Applying
EMU requires SAT I or ACT, a high school transcript, 1 recommendation, statement of commitment, and a minimum high school GPA of 2.0. It recommends an interview. Application deadline: 8/1; 3/15 priority date for financial aid. Early and deferred admission are possible. **Contact:** Ms. Ellen B. Miller, Director of Admissions, 1200 Park Road, Harrisonburg, VA 22802-2462, 540-432-4118 or toll-free 800-368-2665; fax 540-432-4444; e-mail admiss@emu.edu.

GETTING IN LAST YEAR
619 applied
85% were accepted
219 enrolled (42%)
21% from top tenth of their h.s. class
3.40 average high school GPA
32% had SAT verbal scores over 600
29% had SAT math scores over 600
46% had ACT scores over 24

10% had SAT verbal scores over 700
7% had SAT math scores over 700
18% had ACT scores over 30
2 National Merit Scholars
11 valedictorians

COSTS AND FINANCIAL INFORMATION
$13,480 tuition and fees (1999–2000)
$4950 room and board
82% average percent of need met

$12,247 average financial aid amount received per undergraduate (1999–2000 estimated)

AFTER GRADUATION
10% pursued further study
76% had job offers within 6 months
12 organizations recruited on campus

EASTERN NAZARENE COLLEGE

Quincy, Massachusetts   *http://www.enc.edu/*

Eastern Nazarene College seeks Christian scholars who wish to pursue rigorous academic studies in a small-school, Christian-oriented setting. Located just 6 miles south of Boston, our students are able to culturally, academically, and socially benefit from the city's libraries, universities, conservatories, museums, historic sights, and churches. Sponsored by the Church of the Nazarene, ENC has over 30 denominations represented on campus. ENC seeks to develop in each person a Christian world view and to encourage each person to become God's creative and redemptive agent in today's world.

Academics
ENC awards associate, bachelor's, and master's **degrees**. Challenging opportunities include advanced placement, accelerated degree programs, an honors program, double majors, and a senior project. **Special programs** include internships, summer session for credit, off-campus study, study-abroad, and Army ROTC. The most frequently chosen **baccalaureate** fields are business/marketing, education, and biological/life sciences. A complete listing of majors at ENC appears in the Majors Index beginning on page 147. The **faculty** at ENC has 58 full-time members, 66% with terminal degrees. The student-faculty ratio is 10:1.

Students of ENC
The student body totals 1,558, of whom 1,341 are undergraduates. 58.4% are women and 41.6% are men. Students come from 32 states and territories. 72% are from Massachusetts. 1.8% are international students. 75% returned for their sophomore year.

Facilities and Resources
The **library** has 94,111 books and 3,062 subscriptions.

Career Services
The career planning and placement office has 1 full-time, 1 part-time staff members. Services include resume preparation, career/interest testing, career counseling, and careers library.

Campus Life
There are 26 active organizations on campus, including a drama/theater group, newspaper, radio station, and choral group. No national or local **fraternities** or **sororities**. ENC is a member of the NCAA (Division III). **Intercollegiate sports** include baseball (m), basketball, cross-country running, lacrosse (m), soccer, softball (w), tennis, volleyball.

Campus Safety
Student safety services include late-night transport/escort service, 24-hour emergency telephone alarm devices, 24-hour patrols by trained security personnel, and electronically operated dormitory entrances.

Applying
ENC requires SAT I or ACT, a high school transcript, and 2 recommendations. It recommends an essay and an interview. Application deadline: rolling admissions; 3/1 priority date for financial aid. Early and deferred admission are possible. **Contact:** Mr. James F. Heyward II, Director of Admissions, 23 East Elm Avenue, Quincy, MA 02170, 617-745-3868 or toll-free 800-88-ENC88; fax 617-745-3907; e-mail admissions@enc.edu.

GETTING IN LAST YEAR
546 applied
65% were accepted
179 enrolled (51%)
13% from top tenth of their h.s. class
2.91 average high school GPA
25% had SAT verbal scores over 600
21% had SAT math scores over 600

34% had ACT scores over 24
5% had SAT verbal scores over 700
7% had SAT math scores over 700
17% had ACT scores over 30
4 valedictorians

COSTS AND FINANCIAL INFORMATION
$14,060 tuition and fees (2000–2001 estimated)

$4550 room and board
68% average percent of need met
$9471 average financial aid amount received per undergraduate (1999–2000 estimated)

AFTER GRADUATION
36% graduated in 4 years
10% graduated in 5 years
2% graduated in 6 years

EAST TEXAS BAPTIST UNIVERSITY

Marshall, Texas

http://www.etbu.edu/

East Texas Baptist University is a coeducational institution operated in association with the Baptist General Convention of Texas. The University is committed to fiscal soundness and Christian stewardship and to providing and maintaining an environment conducive to learning. East Texas Baptist University serves students of varied ages and with diverse social, geographic, economic, cultural, and religious backgrounds. We seek students who demonstrate a potential for success in our supportive and challenging environment, and we employ faculty members who are dedicated to teaching, scholarship, advising, and the principles of the Christian faith. Our purpose is the development of intellectual inquiry, social consciousness, wellness, and Christian character, for we believe that these endeavors prepare students to accept the obligations and opportunities of the age in which they live to serve humanity and the Kingdom of God. We affirm that the liberal arts form the surest foundation for education and that the Christian faith provides the surest foundation for life. Our primary focus is baccalaureate studies in the humanities, natural and social sciences, fine arts, and various professional areas. As a Christian University, we are committed to the integration of academic discipline and personal faith in the pursuit of truth.

Academics

ETBU awards associate and bachelor's **degrees**. Challenging opportunities include advanced placement, accelerated degree programs, an honors program, double majors, independent study, and a senior project. **Special programs** include internships, summer session for credit, off-campus study, and study-abroad. The most frequently chosen **baccalaureate** fields are education, business/marketing, and philosophy. A complete listing of majors at ETBU appears in the Majors Index beginning on page 147. The **faculty** at ETBU has 62 full-time members, 63% with terminal degrees. The student-faculty ratio is 15:1.

Students of ETBU

The student body is made up of 1,301 undergraduates. 58.7% are women and 41.3% are men. Students come from 17 states and territories and 23 other countries. 92% are from Texas. 3.4% are international students. 65% returned for their sophomore year.

Facilities and Resources

The **library** has 113,124 books and 672 subscriptions.

Career Services

The career planning and placement office has 1 full-time, 1 part-time staff members. Services include job fairs, resume preparation, career/interest testing, career counseling, careers library, and job bank.

Campus Life

There are 4 active organizations on campus, including a drama/theater group, newspaper, and choral group. 5% of eligible men and 6% of eligible women are members of national **fraternities** and local **sororities**. ETBU is a member of the NCAA (Division III) and NCCAA. **Intercollegiate sports** include baseball (m), basketball, football (m), golf, soccer, softball (w), volleyball (w).

Campus Safety

Student safety services include 24-hour emergency telephone alarm devices and electronically operated dormitory entrances.

Applying

ETBU requires an essay, ACT, a high school transcript, and a minimum high school GPA of 2.0, and in some cases an interview. Application deadline: rolling admissions; 6/1 priority date for financial aid. Deferred admission is possible. **Contact:** Director of Admissions, 1209 North Grove, Marshall, TX 75670-1498, 903-935-7963 ext. 225 or toll-free 800-804-3828; fax 903-938-1705; e-mail mbender@etbu.edu.

GETTING IN LAST YEAR
796 applied
80% were accepted
307 enrolled (48%)
22% from top tenth of their h.s. class
19% had SAT verbal scores over 600
17% had SAT math scores over 600
30% had ACT scores over 24

4% had SAT verbal scores over 700
3% had SAT math scores over 700
2% had ACT scores over 30

COSTS AND FINANCIAL INFORMATION
$8450 tuition and fees (2000–2001)
$3202 room and board
86% average percent of need met

$8246 average financial aid amount received per undergraduate (1999–2000)

AFTER GRADUATION
16% graduated in 4 years
11% graduated in 5 years
3% graduated in 6 years
69 organizations recruited on campus

ERSKINE COLLEGE
Due West, South Carolina

http://www.erskine.edu/

Erskine is the ONLY college in the South that is ranked as a National College (BA1) by the independent Carnegie Foundation and is a member of the Council for Christian Colleges & Universities. Erskine students work alongside a faculty dedicated to helping them grow to their full potential—physically, mentally, and socially. Size is one of our greatest assets. Our 13:1 student-to-faculty ratio allows individual attention that pays huge dividends. Professors know student's names and care about them. At Erskine, our students also serve in the mission field, at home and abroad, during the summers. It is part of Erskine's tradition of Christian commitment. Erskine is not about producing a cookie-cutter product. We provide the opportunity to explore the Christian faith, then live it. As Elizabeth Dole said while addressing our Class of 1999 at commencement, "Everywhere you look, you see Erskine students making a difference." Consider Erskine. We teach. We study. We share our lives. We work hard and we laugh even harder. We expect our students to establish relationships that will last a lifetime, serve with their hearts, and make a difference in the world. Erskine College—looking for a few exceptional students who desire a truly exceptional educational experience.

Academics
Erskine awards bachelor's **degrees**. Challenging opportunities include advanced placement, accelerated degree programs, double majors, independent study, and a senior project. **Special programs** include internships, summer session for credit, off-campus study, and study-abroad. The most frequently chosen **baccalaureate** fields are business/marketing, biological/life sciences, and social sciences and history. A complete listing of majors at Erskine appears in the Majors Index beginning on page 147. The **faculty** at Erskine has 36 full-time members, 81% with terminal degrees. The student-faculty ratio is 13:1.

Students of Erskine
The student body is made up of 519 undergraduates. 58.8% are women and 41.2% are men. Students come from 9 states and territories and 4 other countries. 78% are from South Carolina. 1.4% are international students. 85% returned for their sophomore year.

Facilities and Resources
The 2 **libraries** have 205,799 books and 802 subscriptions.

Career Services
The career planning and placement office has 1 full-time, 1 part-time staff members. Services include job fairs, resume preparation, interview workshops, resume referral, career counseling, careers library, job bank, and job interviews.

Campus Life
There are 39 active organizations on campus, including a drama/theater group, newspaper, radio station, television station, and choral group. 22% of eligible men and 20% of eligible women are members of local **fraternities**, local **sororities**, and Little Sisters. Erskine is a member of the NCAA (Division II). **Intercollegiate sports** (some offering scholarships) include baseball (m), basketball, cross-country running, equestrian sports, soccer, softball (w), tennis.

Campus Safety
Student safety services include late-night transport/escort service, 24-hour patrols by trained security personnel, and electronically operated dormitory entrances.

Applying
Erskine requires SAT I or ACT, a high school transcript, and 1 recommendation, and in some cases an essay, SAT II Subject Tests, and an interview. It recommends an interview. Application deadline: rolling admissions; 6/30 for financial aid, with a 4/1 priority date. **Contact:** Mr. Jeff Craft, Director of Admissions, PO Box 176, Due West, SC 29639, 864-379-8830 or toll-free 800-241-8721; fax 864-379-8759; e-mail admissions@erskine.edu.

GETTING IN LAST YEAR
616 applied
81% were accepted
159 enrolled (32%)
37% from top tenth of their h.s. class
34% had SAT verbal scores over 600
28% had SAT math scores over 600
5% had SAT verbal scores over 700
6% had SAT math scores over 700

2 National Merit Scholars
10 valedictorians

COSTS AND FINANCIAL INFORMATION
$15,229 tuition and fees (1999–2000)
$4769 room and board
92% average percent of need met
$13,100 average financial aid amount received per undergraduate (1999–2000)

AFTER GRADUATION
63% graduated in 4 years
2% graduated in 5 years
2% graduated in 6 years
Graduates pursuing further study: 8% arts and sciences, 2% dentistry, 2% education
76.4% had job offers within 6 months
41 organizations recruited on campus

EVANGEL UNIVERSITY
Springfield, Missouri

http://www.evangel.edu/

As the national college of arts and sciences of the Assemblies of God, Evangel offers more than 80 academic programs which are intended to prepare students for today's professional fields. Campus development in the past three years has brought a massive, new academic building, a state-of-the-art Student Fitness Center, and a new Student Union Complex. Evangel's theme, "Christ is Lord," touches every aspect of campus life—spiritual, intellectual, social, and physical. It is a residential college—80% of its students live on campus in modern residence halls—and draws from all 50 states and several foreign countries. Springfield, Missouri is a medium-sized city with low crime rate and ample employment opportunities. Located in the heart of the Ozark Mountains recreational haven, Evangel is close to numerous lakes, parks, and the highly acclaimed Branson entertainment area.

Academics
Evangel University awards associate, bachelor's, and master's **degrees**. Challenging opportunities include advanced placement and a senior project. **Special programs** include summer session for credit and Army ROTC. The most frequently chosen **baccalaureate** fields are education, business/marketing, and psychology. A complete listing of majors at Evangel University appears in the Majors Index beginning on page 147. The student-faculty ratio is 18:1.

Students of Evangel University
The student body totals 1,564, of whom 1,525 are undergraduates. 57.9% are women and 42.1% are men. Students come from 49 states and territories. 42% are from Missouri. 0.3% are international students. 76% returned for their sophomore year.

Facilities and Resources
The **library** has 96,487 books and 748 subscriptions.

Career Services
The career planning and placement office has 2 full-time staff members. Services include resume preparation, interview workshops, resume referral, career/interest testing, career counseling, careers library, job bank, and job interviews.

Campus Life
Active organizations on campus include a drama/theater group, newspaper, radio station, and choral group. No national or local **fraternities** or **sororities**. Evangel University is a member of the NAIA. **Intercollegiate sports** (some offering scholarships) include baseball (m), basketball, cross-country running, football (m), golf, softball (w), tennis, track and field, volleyball (w), wrestling (w).

Campus Safety
Student safety services include late-night transport/escort service, 24-hour emergency telephone alarm devices, 24-hour patrols by trained security personnel, student patrols, and electronically operated dormitory entrances.

Applying
Evangel University requires SAT I or ACT and a high school transcript. It recommends a minimum high school GPA of 2.0. Application deadline: 8/15; 4/1 priority date for financial aid. Deferred admission is possible. **Contact:** Mr. David I. Schoolfield, Director of Enrollment Management, 1111 North Glenstone, Springfield, MO 65802-2191, 417-865-2811 ext. 7202 or toll-free 800-382-6435 (in-state); fax 417-865-9599; e-mail admissions@mail4.evangel.edu.

GETTING IN LAST YEAR		
641 applied	38% had ACT scores over 24	60% average percent of need met
98% were accepted	8% had ACT scores over 30	$8162 average financial aid amount received
318 enrolled (51%)	7 valedictorians	per undergraduate (1998–99)
19% from top tenth of their h.s. class	**COSTS AND FINANCIAL INFORMATION**	**AFTER GRADUATION**
3.1 average high school GPA	$9720 tuition and fees (2000–2001)	Graduates pursuing further study: 23% arts
	$3770 room and board	and sciences, 6% business, 1% law

FRESNO PACIFIC UNIVERSITY

Fresno, California

http://www.fresno.edu/

Fresno Pacific has been regularly ranked as one of the 10 best regional liberal arts colleges in the West by *U.S. News & World Report*'s "America's Best Colleges." The tree-covered campus is located in the heart of the vast agricultural valley of central California, an hour's drive from the College's retreat center in the High Sierras and 2 hours from Pacific Ocean beaches. Pacific's academic program features a unique core sequence in Christian thinking as well as practical Christian service and professional internships. At Fresno Pacific, special emphasis is placed upon faculty-student mentoring, developing responsible personal freedom, and building strong Christian community. Prospective students should visit campus and meet faculty members and students. People make the difference at Fresno Pacific University.

Academics
Fresno Pacific awards associate, bachelor's, and master's **degrees**. Challenging opportunities include advanced placement, accelerated degree programs, student-designed majors, double majors, independent study, and a senior project. **Special programs** include cooperative education, internships, summer session for credit, off-campus study, and study-abroad. The most frequently chosen **baccalaureate** fields are business/marketing, education, and philosophy. A complete listing of majors at Fresno Pacific appears in the Majors Index beginning on page 147. The **faculty** at Fresno Pacific has 76 full-time members, 50% with terminal degrees. The student-faculty ratio is 15:1.

Students of Fresno Pacific
The student body totals 1,677, of whom 875 are undergraduates. 64.5% are women and 35.5% are men. Students come from 14 states and territories and 12 other countries. 97% are from California. 4.5% are international students. 81% returned for their sophomore year.

Facilities and Resources
The **library** has 148,000 books and 2,000 subscriptions.

Career Services
The career planning and placement office has 1 full-time staff member. Services include resume preparation, interview workshops, resume referral, career/interest testing, career counseling, careers library, job bank, and job interviews.

Campus Life
There are 20 active organizations on campus, including a drama/theater group, newspaper, and choral group. No national or local **fraternities** or **sororities**. Fresno Pacific is a member of the NAIA. **Intercollegiate sports** (some offering scholarships) include basketball, cross-country running, soccer (m), track and field, volleyball (w).

Campus Safety
Student safety services include late-night transport/escort service, 24-hour emergency telephone alarm devices, 24-hour patrols by trained security personnel, student patrols, and electronically operated dormitory entrances.

Applying
Fresno Pacific requires an essay, SAT I or ACT, a high school transcript, and 1 recommendation, and in some cases an interview. Application deadline: rolling admissions; 3/2 priority date for financial aid. Early and deferred admission are possible. **Contact:** Mr. Jon Endicott, Director of Admissions, 1717 South Chestnut Avenue, Fresno, CA 93702-4709, 559-453-2039 or toll-free 800-660-6089 (in-state); fax 559-453-2007; e-mail ugadmis@fresno.edu.

GETTING IN LAST YEAR
400 applied
83% were accepted
168 enrolled (51%)
3.52 average high school GPA
15% had SAT verbal scores over 600
19% had SAT math scores over 600
2% had SAT verbal scores over 700

2% had SAT math scores over 700

COSTS AND FINANCIAL INFORMATION
$14,248 tuition and fees (2000–2001)
$4420 room and board
99% average percent of need met
$15,556 average financial aid amount
   received per undergraduate (1999–2000)

AFTER GRADUATION
49% graduated in 4 years
13% graduated in 5 years
1% graduated in 6 years
30% had job offers within 6 months
7 organizations recruited on campus

GENEVA COLLEGE
Beaver Falls, Pennsylvania

http://www.geneva.edu/

Founded in 1848, Geneva College is one of the oldest evangelical Christian colleges in the nation, the second oldest in the Council for Christian Colleges & Universities. It offers an education that articulates the implications of Christ's sovereignty over all his creation. Geneva is one of 14 model sites chosen for the Coalition Racial and Ethnic Diversity Project. Students of all races are encouraged to explore educational opportunities at Geneva. Majors include engineering, speech pathology, and cardiovascular technology. Through a cooperative program, students can combine degrees in aviation, air traffic control, or aerospace management with our business degree. All students complete a core program, which integrates courses in history, music, art, literature, and culture with biblical Christianity. Cocurricular activities include intercollegiate programs in all major sports, theater, choir, an FM radio station, and marching and concert bands. Although Geneva seeks students with a biblical world and life view, all students are welcome.

Academics
Geneva awards associate, bachelor's, and master's **degrees**. Challenging opportunities include advanced placement, accelerated degree programs, student-designed majors, an honors program, double majors, independent study, and a senior project. **Special programs** include cooperative education, internships, summer session for credit, off-campus study, study-abroad, and Army ROTC. The most frequently chosen **baccalaureate** fields are education, liberal arts/general studies, and business/marketing. A complete listing of majors at Geneva appears in the Majors Index beginning on page 147. The **faculty** at Geneva has 74 full-time members, 95% with terminal degrees. The student-faculty ratio is 18:1.

Students of Geneva
The student body totals 2,127, of whom 1,877 are undergraduates. 54.4% are women and 45.6% are men. Students come from 37 states and territories and 25 other countries. 77% are from Pennsylvania. 2.9% are international students. 80% returned for their sophomore year.

Facilities and Resources
The 6 **libraries** have 160,891 books and 890 subscriptions.

Career Services
The career planning and placement office has 2 full-time, 1 part-time staff members. Services include job fairs, resume preparation, interview workshops, resume referral, career/interest testing, career counseling, careers library, job bank, and job interviews.

Campus Life
There are 50 active organizations on campus, including a drama/theater group, newspaper, radio station, television station, choral group, and marching band. No national or local **fraternities** or **sororities**. Geneva is a member of the NAIA and NCCAA. **Intercollegiate sports** (some offering scholarships) include baseball (m), basketball, cross-country running, football (m), soccer, softball (w), tennis, track and field, volleyball.

Campus Safety
Student safety services include late-night transport/escort service, 24-hour emergency telephone alarm devices, 24-hour patrols by trained security personnel, and electronically operated dormitory entrances.

Applying
Geneva requires an essay, SAT I or ACT, a high school transcript, recommendations, and a minimum high school GPA of 2.0, and in some cases an interview. It recommends an interview and a minimum high school GPA of 3.0. Application deadline: rolling admissions; 4/15 priority date for financial aid. Early and deferred admission are possible. **Contact:** Mr. David Layton, Director of Admissions, 3200 College Avenue, Beaver Falls, PA 15010-3599, 724-847-6500 or toll-free 800-847-8255 (out-of-state); fax 724-847-6687; e-mail admissions@geneva.edu.

GETTING IN LAST YEAR
1,027 applied
78% were accepted
348 enrolled (43%)
15% from top tenth of their h.s. class
3.20 average high school GPA
29% had SAT verbal scores over 600
33% had SAT math scores over 600

51% had ACT scores over 24
4% had SAT verbal scores over 700
3% had SAT math scores over 700
3% had ACT scores over 30

COSTS AND FINANCIAL INFORMATION
$12,650 tuition and fees (1999–2000)
$4952 room and board
75% average percent of need met

$9000 average financial aid amount received per undergraduate (1999–2000)

AFTER GRADUATION
17% pursued further study (6% arts and sciences, 4% medicine, 3% education)
74% had job offers within 6 months
78 organizations recruited on campus

GEORGE FOX UNIVERSITY
Newberg, Oregon

http://www.georgefox.edu/

Freedom or faith. A college decision may seem like a choice between the two: sacrifice your faith or put your mind on the shelf. At George Fox University, academic freedom and Christian faith go hand in hand. Students find faculty members who encourage questions, who value their uniqueness, and who challenge them to explore truth from a foundation of faith. Students find a community of friends who accept them as they are, not as they are "supposed to be." Graduates of George Fox leave with more than a competitive degree from a well-respected school. They leave with the ability to think critically, to express themselves, and to take their faith into today's world. At George Fox University, students have the freedom to think and the freedom to believe.

Academics
George Fox awards bachelor's, master's, doctoral, and first-professional **degrees**. Challenging opportunities include advanced placement, accelerated degree programs, student-designed majors, an honors program, double majors, independent study, and a senior project. **Special programs** include cooperative education, internships, off-campus study, study-abroad, and Air Force ROTC. The most frequently chosen **baccalaureate** fields are business/marketing, education, and social sciences and history. A complete listing of majors at George Fox appears in the Majors Index beginning on page 147. The **faculty** at George Fox has 119 full-time members, 72% with terminal degrees.

Students of George Fox
The student body totals 2,414, of whom 1,677 are undergraduates. 59.9% are women and 40.1% are men. Students come from 27 states and territories and 15 other countries. 65% are from Oregon. 1.3% are international students. 85% returned for their sophomore year.

Facilities and Resources
The 2 **libraries** have 180,272 books and 1,215 subscriptions.

Career Services
The career planning and placement office has 3 full-time staff members. Services include job fairs, resume preparation, interview workshops, career/interest testing, career counseling, careers library, job bank, job interviews, and career courses.

Campus Life
There are 18 active organizations on campus, including a drama/theater group, newspaper, radio station, and choral group. No national or local **fraternities** or **sororities**. George Fox is a member of the NAIA. **Intercollegiate sports** include baseball (m), basketball, cross-country running, soccer, softball (w), tennis, track and field, volleyball (w).

Campus Safety
Student safety services include late-night transport/escort service, 24-hour emergency telephone alarm devices, 24-hour patrols by trained security personnel, student patrols, and electronically operated dormitory entrances.

Applying
George Fox requires an essay, SAT I or ACT, a high school transcript, and 2 recommendations, and in some cases an interview. Application deadline: 6/1; 3/1 priority date for financial aid. Early and deferred admission are possible. **Contact:** Mr. Dale Seipp, Director of Admissions, 414 North Meridian, Newberg, OR 97132-2697, 503-554-2240 or toll-free 800-765-4369; fax 503-554-3830; e-mail admissions@georgefox.edu.

GETTING IN LAST YEAR
780 applied
93% were accepted
287 enrolled (40%)
37% from top tenth of their h.s. class
3.60 average high school GPA
41% had SAT verbal scores over 600
36% had SAT math scores over 600

54% had ACT scores over 24
8% had SAT verbal scores over 700
7% had SAT math scores over 700
11% had ACT scores over 30

COSTS AND FINANCIAL INFORMATION
$17,610 tuition and fees (2000–2001)
$5550 room and board
84% average percent of need met

$14,792 average financial aid amount received per undergraduate (1999–2000 estimated)

AFTER GRADUATION
48% graduated in 4 years
7% graduated in 5 years
64% had job offers within 6 months
200 organizations recruited on campus

GORDON COLLEGE
Wenham, Massachusetts

http://www.gordon.edu/

Gordon College, located two miles from the Atlantic Ocean on Boston's North Shore, is New England's only nondenominational Christian college. Offering 33 majors and nearly two dozen national and international off-campus study programs, Gordon draws students from 40 states and 18 countries. Gordon's undergraduate enrollment is 1,500 and its combined graduate and undergraduate enrollment is 1,600. Students are encouraged to participate in 35 ministry and service activities throughout the year. Gordon College is regularly recognized for its high quality. Edward Fiske lists it in his *Selective Guide to Colleges*. Both Fiske and Barron's rate Gordon as a ''Best Buy'' in education. In 2000, Gordon was named the third safest college in the United States in an independent study done by APB News.

Academics

Gordon awards bachelor's and master's **degrees**. Challenging opportunities include advanced placement, student-designed majors, an honors program, double majors, independent study, and a senior project. **Special programs** include cooperative education, internships, off-campus study, study-abroad, and Army and Air Force ROTC. The most frequently chosen **baccalaureate** fields are social sciences and history, English, and philosophy. A complete listing of majors at Gordon appears in the Majors Index beginning on page 147. The **faculty** at Gordon has 83 full-time members, 88% with terminal degrees. The student-faculty ratio is 14:1.

Students of Gordon

The student body totals 1,549, of whom 1,488 are undergraduates. 64.9% are women and 35.1% are men. Students come from 40 states and territories and 18 other countries. 30% are from Massachusetts. 2.3% are international students. 87% returned for their sophomore year.

Facilities and Resources

The **library** has 169,521 books and 5,751 subscriptions.

Career Services

The career planning and placement office has 3 full-time staff members. Services include job fairs, resume preparation, interview workshops, resume referral, career/interest testing, career counseling, careers library, job bank, and job interviews.

Campus Life

There are 35 active organizations on campus, including a drama/theater group, newspaper, and choral group. No national or local **fraternities** or **sororities**. Gordon is a member of the NCAA (Division III). **Intercollegiate sports** include baseball (m), basketball, cross-country running, field hockey (w), lacrosse, soccer, softball (w), swimming, tennis, volleyball (w).

Campus Safety

Student safety services include late-night transport/escort service, 24-hour emergency telephone alarm devices, and 24-hour patrols by trained security personnel.

Applying

Gordon requires an essay, SAT I or ACT, a high school transcript, an interview, 2 recommendations, and pastoral recommendation, statement of Christian faith. It recommends a minimum high school GPA of 2.5. Application deadline: rolling admissions; 3/1 priority date for financial aid. Early and deferred admission are possible. **Contact:** Mr. Silvio E. Vazquez, Dean of Admissions, 255 Grapevine Road, Wenham, MA 01984-1899, 978-927-2300 ext. 4218 or toll-free 800-343-1379; fax 978-524-3704; e-mail admissions@hope.gordon.edu.

GETTING IN LAST YEAR
963 applied
76% were accepted
385 enrolled (52%)
36% from top tenth of their h.s. class
3.46 average high school GPA
53% had SAT verbal scores over 600
44% had SAT math scores over 600

73% had ACT scores over 24
11% had SAT verbal scores over 700
7% had SAT math scores over 700
5 National Merit Scholars

COSTS AND FINANCIAL INFORMATION
$16,420 tuition and fees (1999–2000)
$5050 room and board
83% average percent of need met

$13,675 average financial aid amount
    received per undergraduate (1999–2000)

AFTER GRADUATION
48% graduated in 4 years
14% graduated in 5 years
3% graduated in 6 years
19% pursued further study
48 organizations recruited on campus

GOSHEN COLLEGE
Goshen, Indiana   *http://www.goshen.edu/*

Goshen College is a national liberal arts school known for leadership in international education, service-learning,and peace and justice issues in the Anabaptist-Mennonite tradition. Recognized for its unique Study-Service Term program and exceptional educational value, GC has 1,000 students from more than 30 states and 35 countries who enjoy opportunities for service and activism, significant internships, exceptional recreation-fitness facilities, and faculty who care about their lives, interests, and ideas. Academic excellence in 70 programs of study has resulted in among the highest percentage of graduates who go on to earn postgraduate degrees among liberal arts colleges. Goshen is one of the only schools in the country offering an undergraduate degree in teaching English as a second language, along with strong new majors in environmental science and peace, justice, and conflict studies. GC has also been recognized for promoting racial harmony and for character-building programs, as well as for innovative technology. GC is one of five private liberal arts colleges tapped for the 1999 Knight Foundation's Presidential Leadership Award Program.

Academics
Goshen awards bachelor's **degrees**. Challenging opportunities include advanced placement, accelerated degree programs, student-designed majors, freshman honors college, an honors program, double majors, independent study, and a senior project. **Special programs** include cooperative education, internships, summer session for credit, off-campus study, and study-abroad. The most frequently chosen **baccalaureate** fields are business/marketing, education, and health professions and related sciences. A complete listing of majors at Goshen appears in the Majors Index beginning on page 147. The **faculty** at Goshen has 73 full-time members. The student-faculty ratio is 12:1.

Students of Goshen
The student body is made up of 1,084 undergraduates. 57% are women and 43% are men. Students come from 38 states and territories and 34 other countries. 52% are from Indiana. 9.5% are international students. 81% returned for their sophomore year.

Facilities and Resources
The 3 **libraries** have 121,500 books and 750 subscriptions.

Career Services
The career planning and placement office has 1 full-time, 1 part-time staff members. Services include job fairs, resume preparation, resume referral, career/interest testing, career counseling, careers library, job bank, and job interviews.

Campus Life
There are 26 active organizations on campus, including a drama/theater group, newspaper, radio station, television station, and choral group. No national or local **fraternities** or **sororities**. Goshen is a member of the NAIA. **Intercollegiate sports** (some offering scholarships) include baseball (m), basketball, cross-country running, golf (m), soccer, softball (w), tennis, track and field, volleyball (w).

Campus Safety
Student safety services include late-night transport/escort service, 24-hour emergency telephone alarm devices, and 24-hour patrols by trained security personnel.

Applying
Goshen requires SAT I or ACT, a high school transcript, an interview, 2 recommendations, rank in upper 50% of high school class, minimum SAT score of 920, and a minimum high school GPA of 2.0. It recommends an essay. Application deadline: rolling admissions; 3/1 priority date for financial aid. Early and deferred admission are possible. **Contact:** Ms. Marty Kelley, Director of Admissions, 1700 South Main Street, Goshen, IN 46526-4794, 219-535-7535 or toll-free 800-348-7422; fax 219-535-7060; e-mail admissions@goshen.edu.

GETTING IN LAST YEAR
574 applied
95% were accepted
226 enrolled (41%)
27% from top tenth of their h.s. class
3.38 average high school GPA
40% had SAT verbal scores over 600
38% had SAT math scores over 600
16% had SAT verbal scores over 700

10% had SAT math scores over 700
8 National Merit Scholars
11 valedictorians

COSTS AND FINANCIAL INFORMATION
$13,140 tuition and fees (2000–2001 estimated)
$4640 room and board
92% average percent of need met
$12,974 average financial aid amount received per undergraduate (1999–2000)

AFTER GRADUATION
39% graduated in 4 years
19% graduated in 5 years
4% graduated in 6 years
40% pursued further study (15% arts and sciences, 11% medicine, 5% business)
40 organizations recruited on campus

GRACE COLLEGE

Winona Lake, Indiana

http://www.grace.edu/

The 160-acre campus of Grace College is located in the heart of historic Winona Lake, Indiana. The mission at Grace is to help students apply biblical values in strengthening character, sharpening competence, and preparing for service. Grace offers more than 40 majors and programs, all designed to equip students to make a positive impact for Christ in whatever career they choose. Outside the classroom, hundreds of Grace students volunteer each year for ministries on campus, in the community, and around the world. In addition, the college has been listed for three years in *America's 100 Best College Buys*.

Academics

Grace awards associate, bachelor's, and master's **degrees**. Challenging opportunities include advanced placement, accelerated degree programs, double majors, independent study, and a senior project. **Special programs** include internships, summer session for credit, off-campus study, and study-abroad. The most frequently chosen **baccalaureate** fields are business/marketing, education, and psychology. A complete listing of majors at Grace appears in the Majors Index beginning on page 147. The **faculty** at Grace has 40 full-time members, 68% with terminal degrees. The student-faculty ratio is 17:1.

Students of Grace

The student body totals 1,045, of whom 923 are undergraduates. 52.4% are women and 47.6% are men. Students come from 35 states and territories and 7 other countries. 60% are from Indiana. 1.7% are international students. 84% returned for their sophomore year.

Facilities and Resources

The **library** has 140,202 books and 350 subscriptions.

Career Services

The career planning and placement office has 1 full-time, 1 part-time staff members. Services include job fairs, resume preparation, interview workshops, resume referral, career/interest testing, career counseling, careers library, job bank, and job interviews.

Campus Life

There are 30 active organizations on campus, including a drama/theater group, newspaper, and choral group. No national or local **fraternities** or **sororities**. Grace is a member of the NAIA and NCCAA. **Intercollegiate sports** (some offering scholarships) include baseball (m), basketball, cross-country running, golf (m), soccer, softball (w), tennis, track and field, volleyball (w).

Campus Safety

Student safety services include evening patrols by trained security personnel, late-night transport/escort service, student patrols, and electronically operated dormitory entrances.

Applying

Grace requires SAT I or ACT, a high school transcript, 2 recommendations, and a minimum high school GPA of 2.0, and in some cases an interview. Application deadline: 8/1; 3/1 priority date for financial aid. Early and deferred admission are possible. **Contact:** Mr. Ron Henry, Dean of Admissions, 200 Seminary Drive, Winona Lake, IN 46590-1294, 219-372-5100 ext. 6006 or toll-free 800-54-GRACE (in-state), 800-54 GRACE (out-of-state); fax 219-372-5265; e-mail enroll@grace.edu.

GETTING IN LAST YEAR
501 applied
87% were accepted
210 enrolled (48%)
24% from top tenth of their h.s. class
3.3 average high school GPA
28% had SAT verbal scores over 600
23% had SAT math scores over 600

45% had ACT scores over 24
4% had SAT verbal scores over 700
3% had SAT math scores over 700
9% had ACT scores over 30

COSTS AND FINANCIAL INFORMATION
$10,500 tuition and fees (1999–2000)
$4600 room and board
90% average percent of need met

$10,490 average financial aid amount
   received per undergraduate (1999–2000)

AFTER GRADUATION
Graduates pursuing further study: 8% arts and
   sciences, 7% theology, 3% medicine
70% had job offers within 6 months
35 organizations recruited on campus

GRAND CANYON UNIVERSITY

Phoenix, Arizona

http://www.grand-canyon.edu/

Grand Canyon University is an institution that seeks the cutting edge in educational opportunities for its students while cherishing the traditional values of a liberal arts community. The University is comprised of the College of Business, the College of Continuing Studies, the College of Education, the College of Liberal Arts, the Samaritan College of Nursing, and the College of Science and Allied Health. Student internships abound in nationally recognized companies, many leading directly to full-time employment upon graduation. Students, faculty, and staff members participate in international exchange programs annually. Every innovative program is founded in a strong Christian heritage which allows each individual to find and utilize his or her God-given talents and abilities.

Academics

Grand Canyon University awards bachelor's and master's **degrees**. Challenging opportunities include advanced placement, accelerated degree programs, freshman honors college, an honors program, double majors, independent study, and a senior project. **Special programs** include internships, summer session for credit, off-campus study, study-abroad, and Army and Air Force ROTC. The most frequently chosen **baccalaureate** fields are biological/life sciences, education, and psychology. A complete listing of majors at Grand Canyon University appears in the Majors Index beginning on page 147. The **faculty** at Grand Canyon University has 94 full-time members, 80% with terminal degrees. The student-faculty ratio is 15:1.

Students of Grand Canyon University

The student body totals 2,991, of whom 1,534 are undergraduates. 65.2% are women and 34.8% are men. Students come from 40 states and territories and 14 other countries. 81% are from Arizona. 3.4% are international students. 73% returned for their sophomore year.

Facilities and Resources

The **library** has 1,256 subscriptions.

Career Services

The career planning and placement office has 1 full-time, 1 part-time staff members. Services include resume referral and job interviews.

Campus Life

Active organizations on campus include a drama/theater group, newspaper, and choral group. No national or local **fraternities** or **sororities**. Grand Canyon University is a member of the NCAA (Division II). **Intercollegiate sports** (some offering scholarships) include baseball (m), basketball, golf (m), soccer, tennis (w), volleyball (w).

Campus Safety

Student safety services include late-night transport/escort service, 24-hour emergency telephone alarm devices, 24-hour patrols by trained security personnel, student patrols, and electronically operated dormitory entrances.

Applying

Grand Canyon University requires SAT I or ACT, a high school transcript, and a minimum high school GPA of 3.0, and in some cases an essay, an interview, and 3 recommendations. It recommends a minimum high school GPA of 3.0. Application deadline: rolling admissions. Early and deferred admission are possible. **Contact:** Mrs. April Chapman, Director of Admissions, 3300 West Camelback Road, PO Box 11097, Phoenix, AZ 86017-3030, 602-589-2855 ext. 2811 or toll-free 800-800-9776 (instate); fax 602-589-2580; e-mail admiss@grand-canyon.edu.

GETTING IN LAST YEAR		
242 enrolled	2% had SAT math scores over 700	$8068 average financial aid amount received per undergraduate (1998–99)
29% from top tenth of their h.s. class	5% had ACT scores over 30	
3.44 average high school GPA	1 National Merit Scholar	**AFTER GRADUATION**
15% had SAT verbal scores over 600	10 valedictorians	23% graduated in 4 years
16% had SAT math scores over 600		21% graduated in 5 years
36% had ACT scores over 24	**COSTS AND FINANCIAL INFORMATION**	5% graduated in 6 years
3% had SAT verbal scores over 700	$8380 tuition and fees (1999–2000)	67% had job offers within 6 months
	$4246 room and board	50 organizations recruited on campus
	64% average percent of need met	

GREENVILLE COLLEGE

Greenville, Illinois

http://www.greenville.edu/

Located in a quaint and friendly rural community, Greenville College offers a nurturing environment for academic, personal, social, and spiritual growth. This quiet setting, however, is just 45 minutes from downtown St. Louis, where students minister to inner-city kids, serve in internships for major corporations, and take advantage of the city's many rich cultural resources. Traditionally strong in the physical sciences, teacher education, music, and business, Greenville offers a wide range of majors. Its faculty are committed to academic excellence within the context of the mission of Greenville College: to transform students for lives of character and service.

Academics

GC awards bachelor's and master's **degrees**. Challenging opportunities include advanced placement, accelerated degree programs, student-designed majors, an honors program, double majors, independent study, and a senior project. **Special programs** include cooperative education, internships, summer session for credit, and off-campus study. The most frequently chosen **baccalaureate** fields are business/marketing, education, and biological/life sciences. A complete listing of majors at GC appears in the Majors Index beginning on page 147. The **faculty** at GC has 56 full-time members, 61% with terminal degrees. The student-faculty ratio is 15:1.

Students of GC

The student body totals 1,081, of whom 1,049 are undergraduates. 54% are women and 46% are men. Students come from 37 states and territories and 14 other countries. 69% are from Illinois. 1.5% are international students. 72% returned for their sophomore year.

Facilities and Resources

The **library** has 126,210 books and 490 subscriptions.

Career Services

The career planning and placement office has 2 full-time staff members. Services include job fairs, resume preparation, interview workshops, career/interest testing, career counseling, careers library, and job interviews.

Campus Life

There are 40 active organizations on campus, including a drama/theater group, newspaper, radio station, and choral group. No national or local **fraternities** or **sororities**. GC is a member of the NCAA (Division III) and NCCAA. **Intercollegiate sports** include baseball (m), basketball, cross-country running, football (m), golf (m), soccer, softball (w), tennis, track and field, volleyball.

Campus Safety

Student safety services include late-night transport/escort service, 24-hour emergency telephone alarm devices, and student patrols.

Applying

GC requires an essay, SAT I or ACT, a high school transcript, 2 recommendations, agreement to code of conduct, and a minimum high school GPA of 2.0, and in some cases an interview. Application deadline: rolling admissions. Early and deferred admission are possible. **Contact:** Mr. Randy Comfort, Dean of Admissions, 315 East College, PO Box 159, Greenville, IL 62246-0159, 618-664-2800 ext. 4401 or toll-free 800-248-2288 (in-state), 800-345-4440 (out-of-state); fax 618-664-9841; e-mail admissions@greenville.edu.

GETTING IN LAST YEAR
541 applied
88% were accepted
215 enrolled (45%)
19% from top tenth of their h.s. class
3.24 average high school GPA
42% had SAT verbal scores over 600
23% had SAT math scores over 600
37% had ACT scores over 24
4% had SAT verbal scores over 700
6% had SAT math scores over 700

5% had ACT scores over 30
4 National Merit Scholars
6 valedictorians

COSTS AND FINANCIAL INFORMATION
$12,586 tuition and fees (1999–2000)
$4850 room and board
89% average percent of need met
$12,608 average financial aid amount received per undergraduate (1999–2000 estimated)

AFTER GRADUATION
41% graduated in 4 years
3% graduated in 5 years
1% graduated in 6 years
Graduates pursuing further study: 18% education, 10% arts and sciences, 8% business
80% had job offers within 6 months
11 organizations recruited on campus

HOPE INTERNATIONAL UNIVERSITY

Fullerton, California   *http://www.hiu.edu/*

Hope International University exists to empower students through higher education to serve the church and impact the world for Christ. The dedicated faculty and staff of Hope International University seek to integrate faith and learning through all of its programs. As such, Hope is committed to high academic standards and servant-leadership development of all students. Located in Southern California, our students are provided with many opportunities to be involved in recreation, service, and outreach projects within our local community, as well as various mission projects throughout Mexico and the world. A formal relationship with California State University-Fullerton, which is adjacent to campus, allows students to study at both institutions.

Academics

Hope International University awards associate, bachelor's, and master's **degrees**. Challenging opportunities include advanced placement, accelerated degree programs, student-designed majors, an honors program, double majors, independent study, and a senior project. **Special programs** include internships, summer session for credit, and off-campus study. A complete listing of majors at Hope International University appears in the Majors Index beginning on page 147. The **faculty** at Hope International University has 25 full-time members, 52% with terminal degrees. The student-faculty ratio is 17:1.

Students of Hope International University

The student body totals 971, of whom 793 are undergraduates. 55.1% are women and 44.9% are men. Students come from 24 states and territories and 24 other countries. 69% are from California. 6.5% are international students. 63% returned for their sophomore year.

Facilities and Resources

The **library** has 72,000 books and 468 subscriptions.

Career Services

The career planning and placement office has 2 part-time staff members. Services include job fairs, resume preparation, and interview workshops.

Campus Life

Active organizations on campus include a drama/theater group, newspaper, and choral group. No national or local **fraternities** or **sororities**. Hope International University is a member of the NAIA. **Intercollegiate sports** (some offering scholarships) include basketball, soccer, softball (w), tennis, volleyball.

Campus Safety

Student safety services include 24-hour emergency telephone alarm devices and student patrols.

Applying

Hope International University requires an essay, SAT I or ACT, a high school transcript, 2 recommendations, and a minimum high school GPA of 2.5, and in some cases an interview. Application deadline: 5/1; 3/2 priority date for financial aid. Early and deferred admission are possible. **Contact:** Ms. Cheryl Lynn Edmond, Assistant Director, Admissions, 2500 East Nutwood Avenue, Fullerton, CA 92831-3138, 714-879-3901 ext. 2225 or toll-free 800-762-1294 ext. 2235; fax 714-526-0231; e-mail twinston@hiu.edu.

GETTING IN LAST YEAR
381 applied
49% were accepted
112 enrolled (60%)
4% from top tenth of their h.s. class
3.07 average high school GPA
21% had SAT verbal scores over 600

22% had SAT math scores over 600
56% had ACT scores over 24
3% had SAT verbal scores over 700
2% had SAT math scores over 700
6% had ACT scores over 30

COSTS AND FINANCIAL INFORMATION
$11,220 tuition and fees (1999–2000)

$4500 room and board

AFTER GRADUATION
40% pursued further study (10% arts and
  sciences, 10% business, 10% education)
30% had job offers within 6 months

HOUGHTON COLLEGE

Houghton, New York

http://www.houghton.edu/

HOUGHTON
A Christian College of Liberal Arts and Sciences

Since 1883, Houghton College has provided an educational experience that integrates high academic quality with the Christian faith. Houghton is selective in admission, attracting a very capable student body from across the country and around the world. The college routinely receives widespread national recognition for the quality of its student profile, faculty, and facilities, as well as affordability. Enrolling 1,200 full-time students, Houghton is located on a scenic 1,300 sq. mile campus in the beautiful countryside of western New York. The college's unique campus includes a 386-acre equestrian center and ski facilities. Houghton's traditional liberal arts curriculum offers 40 diverse majors and programs. Approximately 100 international students and missionary dependents attend Houghton. The First-Year Honors Program offers highly qualified students the opportunity to study in England during the second semester of their first year. All new students receive a laptop computer, with network connections across campus, giving each student access to the Internet and more.

Academics
Houghton awards associate and bachelor's **degrees**. Challenging opportunities include advanced placement, an honors program, double majors, independent study, and a senior project. **Special programs** include internships, summer session for credit, off-campus study, study-abroad, and Army ROTC. The most frequently chosen **baccalaureate** fields are business/marketing, education, and social sciences and history. A complete listing of majors at Houghton appears in the Majors Index beginning on page 147. The **faculty** at Houghton has 78 full-time members, 85% with terminal degrees. The student-faculty ratio is 14:1.

Students of Houghton
The student body is made up of 1,380 undergraduates. 63% are women and 37% are men. Students come from 37 states and territories and 27 other countries. 64% are from New York. 4.6% are international students. 82% returned for their sophomore year.

Facilities and Resources
The **library** has 217,618 books and 3,027 subscriptions.

Career Services
The career planning and placement office has 2 full-time staff members. Services include job fairs, resume preparation, interview workshops, resume referral, career/interest testing, career counseling, careers library, job bank, and job interviews.

Campus Life
There are 50 active organizations on campus, including a drama/theater group, newspaper, radio station, and choral group. No national or local **fraternities** or **sororities**. Houghton is a member of the NAIA. **Intercollegiate sports** (some offering scholarships) include basketball, cross-country running, field hockey (w), soccer, track and field, volleyball (w).

Campus Safety
Student safety services include phone connection to security patrols, late-night transport/escort service, 24-hour patrols by trained security personnel, and electronically operated dormitory entrances.

Applying
Houghton requires an essay, SAT I or ACT, a high school transcript, 1 recommendation, and pastoral recommendation. It recommends an interview and a minimum high school GPA of 2.5. Application deadline: rolling admissions; 3/1 priority date for financial aid. Early and deferred admission are possible. **Contact:** Mr. Timothy Fuller, Vice President for Enrollment, PO Box 128, Houghton, NY 14744, 716-567-9353 or toll-free 800-777-2556; fax 716-567-9522; e-mail admission@houghton.edu.

GETTING IN LAST YEAR
1,030 applied
89% were accepted
294 enrolled (32%)
35% from top tenth of their h.s. class
3.19 average high school GPA
46% had SAT verbal scores over 600
39% had SAT math scores over 600
63% had ACT scores over 24
9% had SAT verbal scores over 700

7% had SAT math scores over 700
13% had ACT scores over 30
8 class presidents
16 valedictorians

COSTS AND FINANCIAL INFORMATION
$15,140 tuition and fees (2000–2001 estimated)
$5400 room and board
76% average percent of need met

$12,340 average financial aid amount received per undergraduate (1998–99)

AFTER GRADUATION
48% graduated in 4 years
15% graduated in 5 years
2% graduated in 6 years
25% pursued further study
69% had job offers within 6 months
26 organizations recruited on campus

HOUSTON BAPTIST UNIVERSITY

Houston, Texas   *http://www.hbu.edu/*

Houston Baptist University is an independent institution of higher learning, related to the Baptist General Convention of Texas, that is committed to fostering academic excellence in the context of Christian faith and teachings, promoting truth in learning, supporting personal and professional growth, and preparing undergraduate and graduate students for service and leadership in a diverse world. The University welcomes and extends its resources to those who strive for academic excellence. The faculty, staff, and administrators are committed to providing a responsive and intellectually stimulating environment that fosters spiritual maturity, strength of character, and moral virtue as the foundation for successful living; develops professional behaviors and personal characteristics for lifelong learning and service to God and to the community; and meets the changing needs of the community and society. The University offers a broad range of programs and services committed to liberal arts education that are designed to promote the growth of the whole person. The integration of scholarship, service, and spirituality essential to liberal arts education is nurtured in an environment of open inquiry. Students are encouraged to think critically, to assess information from a Christian perspective, to arrive at informed and reasoned conclusions, and to become lifelong learners.

Academics
Houston Baptist awards associate, bachelor's, and master's **degrees**. Challenging opportunities include advanced placement and a senior project. **Special programs** include internships, summer session for credit, study-abroad, and Army and Navy ROTC. A complete listing of majors at Houston Baptist appears in the Majors Index beginning on page 147. The **faculty** at Houston Baptist has 122 full-time members.

Students of Houston Baptist
The student body totals 2,362, of whom 1,779 are undergraduates. 69.8% are women and 30.2% are men. Students come from 17 states and territories and 36 other countries. 96% are from Texas. 4.4% are international students. 72% returned for their sophomore year.

Facilities and Resources
The **library** has 188,000 books and 1,025 subscriptions.

Career Services
The career planning and placement office has 1 full-time staff member. Services include job fairs, resume preparation, resume referral, career counseling, careers library, job bank, and job interviews.

Campus Life
There are 57 active organizations on campus, including a drama/theater group, newspaper, and choral group. 15% of eligible men and 20% of eligible women are members of national **fraternities**, national **sororities**, and local fraternities. Houston Baptist is a member of the NAIA. **Intercollegiate sports** (some offering scholarships) include baseball (m), basketball, softball (w), volleyball (w).

Campus Safety
Student safety services include late-night transport/escort service, 24-hour emergency telephone alarm devices, and 24-hour patrols by trained security personnel.

Applying
Houston Baptist requires an essay, SAT I or ACT, a high school transcript, and 1 recommendation. It recommends an interview. Application deadline: rolling admissions; 2/15 priority date for financial aid. Early and deferred admission are possible. **Contact:** Mr. David Melton, Director of Admissions, 7502 Fondren Road, Houston, TX 77074, 281-649-3211 ext. 3208 or toll-free 800-969-3210; fax 281-649-3209; e-mail unadm@hbu.edu.

GETTING IN LAST YEAR		
865 applied	31% had SAT verbal scores over 600	5% had ACT scores over 30
48% were accepted	33% had SAT math scores over 600	
599 enrolled (145%)	40% had ACT scores over 24	**COSTS AND FINANCIAL INFORMATION**
10% from top tenth of their h.s. class	5% had SAT verbal scores over 700	$10,828 tuition and fees (2000–2001)
	6% had SAT math scores over 700	$3900 room and board

HOWARD PAYNE UNIVERSITY

Brownwood, Texas

http://www.hputx.edu/

Founded in 1889, Howard Payne University is a private, coeducational institution affiliated with the Baptist General Convention of Texas. HPU offers liberal arts and preprofessional undergraduate programs in a distinctive residential community. The university is committed to the belief that the total university experience should integrate Christian values to produce servant leaders with a global perspective. The foundation of an HPU education comprises three areas which, when considered collectively, form an educational approach that challenges students to attain academic excellence and encourages development of leadership abilities. These areas are academic excellence, Christian commitment, and servant leadership. Students may choose from more than 50 majors, minors and preprofessional programs within six schools: Business, Christian Studies, Education, Humanities, Music and Fine Arts, and Science and Math. HPU offers several innovative programs, including the nationally recognized Douglas MacArthur Academy of Freedom honors program. At the heart of HPU is a commitment to be a distinctively Christian university. HPU's mission is to do more than transfer information and knowledge; its mission is to teach a value system that comes from a rich Christian heritage. Faculty members are encouraged to integrate their Christian faith in the classroom, and campus-wide programs and activities emphasize the development of Christian character and servant leadership qualities.

Academics

Howard Payne awards bachelor's **degrees**. Challenging opportunities include advanced placement, student-designed majors, an honors program, and a senior project. **Special programs** include internships, summer session for credit, study-abroad, and Army ROTC. The most frequently chosen **baccalaureate** fields are education, business/marketing, and philosophy. A complete listing of majors at Howard Payne appears in the Majors Index beginning on page 147. The **faculty** at Howard Payne has 84 full-time members, 49% with terminal degrees. The student-faculty ratio is 17:1.

Students of Howard Payne

The student body is made up of 1,496 undergraduates. 49.9% are women and 50.1% are men. Students come from 19 states and territories and 10 other countries. 96% are from Texas. 0.6% are international students. 60% returned for their sophomore year.

Facilities and Resources

The **library** has 140,000 books and 2,369 subscriptions.

Career Services

The career planning and placement office has 1 full-time, 1 part-time staff members. Services include job fairs, resume preparation, interview workshops, resume referral, career/interest testing, career counseling, careers library, job bank, and job interviews.

Campus Life

There are 38 active organizations on campus, including a drama/theater group, newspaper, radio station, television station, choral group, and marching band. 15% of eligible men and 20% of eligible women are members of local **fraternities** and local **sororities**. Howard Payne is a member of the NCAA (Division III). **Intercollegiate sports** include baseball (m), basketball, cross-country running, football (m), golf, soccer (m), softball (w), tennis, track and field, volleyball.

Campus Safety

Student safety services include 12-hour patrols by trained security personnel, 24-hour emergency telephone alarm devices, and electronically operated dormitory entrances.

Applying

Howard Payne requires SAT I or ACT, a high school transcript, and a minimum high school GPA of 3.0, and in some cases an interview and recommendations. Application deadline: rolling admissions; 3/15 priority date for financial aid. Early admission is possible. **Contact:** Ms. Cheryl Mangrum, Coordinator of Admission Services, HPU Station Box 828, Brownwood, TX 76801, 915-649-8027 or toll-free 800-880-4478; fax 915-649-8900; e-mail enroll@hputx.edu.

GETTING IN LAST YEAR
530 applied
100% were accepted
364 enrolled (69%)
10% from top tenth of their h.s. class
3.31 average high school GPA
15% had SAT verbal scores over 600
10% had SAT math scores over 600

30% had ACT scores over 24
2% had SAT verbal scores over 700
1% had SAT math scores over 700
2% had ACT scores over 30
7 valedictorians

COSTS AND FINANCIAL INFORMATION
$9000 tuition and fees (1999–2000)

$3830 room and board

AFTER GRADUATION
23% graduated in 4 years
9% graduated in 5 years
4% graduated in 6 years
41% pursued further study (21% theology)
15 organizations recruited on campus

HUNTINGTON COLLEGE

Huntington, Indiana

http://www.huntington.edu/

Huntington College has been honoring Christ through Scholarship and Service since 1897. Huntington is home to the nationally recognized Link Institute for Faithful and Effective Youth Ministry and also features an outstanding theatre arts program. Huntington's campus facilities were described as being "among the finest among liberal arts colleges" by a North Central Association Accreditation Team. The Huntington Plan is a guaranteed tuition program in which students pay a one-time fee equal to 10% of the current year's tuition to lock in tuition at that rate through graduation. Call for a free copy of Huntington's new CD ROM.

Academics

Huntington awards bachelor's and master's **degrees** and post-bachelor's certificates. Challenging opportunities include advanced placement, double majors, independent study, and a senior project. **Special programs** include summer session for credit and off-campus study. The most frequently chosen **baccalaureate** fields are business/marketing, education, and philosophy. A complete listing of majors at Huntington appears in the Majors Index beginning on page 147.

Students of Huntington

The student body totals 904, of whom 857 are undergraduates. 61.7% are women and 38.3% are men. Students come from 22 states and territories. 1.2% are international students.

Facilities and Resources

The **library** has 76,954 books and 553 subscriptions.

Career Services

The career planning and placement office has 1 full-time, 2 part-time staff members. Services include job fairs, resume preparation, resume referral, career counseling, careers library, job bank, and job interviews.

Campus Life

There are 35 active organizations on campus, including a drama/theater group, newspaper, radio station, television station, and choral group. 6% of eligible men and 8% of eligible women are members of national **fraternities** and national **sororities**. Huntington is a member of the NAIA. **Intercollegiate sports** (some offering scholarships) include baseball (m), basketball, cross-country running, golf, soccer (m), softball (w), tennis, track and field, volleyball (w).

Campus Safety

Student safety services include night patrols by trained security personnel, late-night transport/escort service, and 24-hour emergency telephone alarm devices.

Applying

Huntington requires an essay, SAT I or ACT, a high school transcript, and a minimum high school GPA of 2.3. It recommends an interview. Application deadline: 8/15; 3/1 priority date for financial aid. Deferred admission is possible. **Contact:** Mr. Jeff Berggren, Dean of Enrollment, 2303 College Avenue, Huntington, IN 46750-1299, 219-359-4000 ext. 4016 or toll-free 800-642-6493; fax 219-356-9448; e-mail admissions@huntington.edu.

GETTING IN LAST YEAR
630 applied
90% were accepted
222 enrolled (39%)
23% from top tenth of their h.s. class
3.34 average high school GPA
27% had SAT verbal scores over 600
21% had SAT math scores over 600

49% had ACT scores over 24
5% had SAT verbal scores over 700
3% had SAT math scores over 700
12% had ACT scores over 30

COSTS AND FINANCIAL INFORMATION
$14,230 tuition and fees (2000–2001)
$5190 room and board
97% average percent of need met

$11,164 average financial aid amount
   received per undergraduate (1999–2000)

AFTER GRADUATION
52% graduated in 4 years
7% graduated in 5 years
3% graduated in 6 years
15% pursued further study

Indiana Wesleyan University

Marion, Indiana

http://www.indwes.edu/

God has a plan for you. If you seek the challenge and direction of real discovery—about yourself, your faith, the world, and the role you want to play in it—Indiana Wesleyan University is the place for you. IWU is committed to changing the world by developing students in character, scholarship, and leadership. The Center for Life Calling and Leadership Development guides IWU students in finding their purpose or calling in life, including finding the right career. Undergraduate campus enrollment has increased eighty-two percent in the past 10 years to more than 2,000 students. Almost $70 million in new facilities have been added to the campus since 1990. Three of the major facilities built have been the architectural award-winning Performing Arts Center, which includes an auditorium, rehearsal halls, and black box theater, the expansive, well-equipped Wellness and Recreation Center (climbing wall, swimming pool, and fitness center), and the new addition to the Burns Science Hall (nursing hospital lab, specialized biology and chemistry classrooms, and computer labs). The residence halls feature suite-style design with two spacious room that connect with a private bath. Surveys of first-time freshmen indicate that the number one reason for choosing IWU is the spiritual atmosphere. Chapel is held three times a week and freshmen participate in a "World Changers" class in which the fundamentals of the Christian faith are discussed from an evangelical perspective.

Academics
IWU awards associate, bachelor's, and master's **degrees** (also offers adult program with significant enrollment not reflected in profile). Challenging opportunities include advanced placement, accelerated degree programs, student-designed majors, freshman honors college, an honors program, double majors, independent study, and a senior project. **Special programs** include internships, summer session for credit, off-campus study, and study-abroad. The most frequently chosen **baccalaureate** fields are business/marketing, health professions and related sciences, and education. A complete listing of majors at IWU appears in the Majors Index beginning on page 147. The **faculty**

at IWU has 105 full-time members, 51% with terminal degrees. The student-faculty ratio is 17:1.

Students of IWU
The student body totals 6,899, of whom 4,898 are undergraduates. 63% are women and 37% are men. Students come from 44 states and territories and 15 other countries. 53% are from Indiana. 1% are international students. 74% returned for their sophomore year.

Facilities and Resources
The **library** has 99,340 books and 5,341 subscriptions.

Career Services
The career planning and placement office has 1 full-time, 4 part-time staff members. Services include job fairs, resume preparation, interview workshops, career/interest testing, career counseling, careers library, job bank, job interviews, and job newsletter, job search workshop.

Campus Life
There are 35 active organizations on campus, including a drama/theater group, newspaper, radio station, television station, and choral group. No national or local **fraternities** or **sororities**. IWU is a member of the NAIA and NCCAA. **Intercollegiate sports** (some offering scholarships) include baseball (m), basketball, cross-country running, golf (m), soccer, softball (w), tennis, track and field, volleyball (w).

Campus Safety
Student safety services include 12-hour evening patrols by trained security personnel and late-night transport/escort service.

Applying
IWU requires an essay, SAT I or ACT, a high school transcript, 1 recommendation, and a minimum high school GPA of 2.0, and in some cases an interview. It recommends an interview. Application deadline: rolling admissions; 3/1 priority date for financial aid. Early and deferred admission are possible. **Contact:** Ms. Gaytha Holloway, Director of Admissions, 4201 South Washington Street, Marion, IN 46953-4999, 765-677-2138 or toll-free 800-332-6901; fax 765-677-2333; e-mail admissions@indwes.edu.

GETTING IN LAST YEAR
1,722 applied
74% were accepted
822 enrolled (65%)
3.48 average high school GPA
23% had SAT verbal scores over 600

19% had SAT math scores over 600
57% had ACT scores over 24
3% had SAT verbal scores over 700
3% had SAT math scores over 700
9% had ACT scores over 30

COSTS AND FINANCIAL INFORMATION
$11,760 tuition and fees (1999–2000)
$4580 room and board

AFTER GRADUATION
40 organizations recruited on campus

JOHN BROWN UNIVERSITY

Siloam Springs, Arkansas   *http://www.jbu.edu/*

There are two mottos which best describe the mission of John Brown University. The "Christ Over All" motto is demonstrated in our overall mission and purpose under submission to the Lordship of Jesus Christ. Our "Head, Heart, and Hand" motto describes our educational philosophy. We have a balanced approach to academic excellence (Head), spiritual development (Heart), and practical hands-on professional training (Hand). JBU is a diverse Christian community with students from 40 states and 30 countries. With approximately 100 missionary children from third world cultures, JBU offers a global approach to Christian higher education in the beauty of Northwest Arkansas.

Academics

JBU awards associate, bachelor's, and master's **degrees**. Challenging opportunities include advanced placement, freshman honors college, an honors program, double majors, independent study, and a senior project. **Special programs** include internships, study-abroad, and Army ROTC. The most frequently chosen **baccalaureate** fields are business/marketing, education, and philosophy. A complete listing of majors at JBU appears in the Majors Index beginning on page 147. The **faculty** at JBU has 77 full-time members, 68% with terminal degrees. The student-faculty ratio is 16:1.

Students of JBU

The student body totals 1,517, of whom 1,421 are undergraduates. 51.7% are women and 48.3% are men. Students come from 43 states and territories and 33 other countries. 32% are from Arkansas. 8.8% are international students. 80% returned for their sophomore year.

Facilities and Resources

The 5 **libraries** have 93,190 books and 1,580 subscriptions.

Career Services

The career planning and placement office has 2 full-time staff members. Services include job fairs, resume preparation, career counseling, careers library, and job bank.

Campus Life

There are 20 active organizations on campus, including a drama/theater group, newspaper, radio station, television station, and choral group. No national or local **fraternities** or **sororities**. JBU is a member of the NAIA. **Intercollegiate sports** (some offering scholarships) include basketball, soccer (m), swimming, tennis, volleyball (w).

Campus Safety

Student safety services include late-night transport/escort service, 24-hour emergency telephone alarm devices, and 24-hour patrols by trained security personnel.

Applying

JBU requires an essay, SAT I or ACT, a high school transcript, 2 recommendations, and a minimum high school GPA of 3.0. It recommends an interview. Application deadline: 3/1; 3/1 priority date for financial aid. Deferred admission is possible. **Contact:** Ms. Karyn Byrne, Application Coordinator, 200 West University Street, Siloam Springs, AR 72761-2121, 501-524-7454 or toll-free 877-JBU-INFO; fax 501-524-9548; e-mail jbuinfo@acc.jbu.edu.

GETTING IN LAST YEAR
629 applied
80% were accepted
271 enrolled (54%)
24% from top tenth of their h.s. class
3.49 average high school GPA
32% had SAT verbal scores over 600
36% had SAT math scores over 600
51% had ACT scores over 24
9% had SAT verbal scores over 700

8% had SAT math scores over 700
9% had ACT scores over 30
2 National Merit Scholars
11 class presidents
21 valedictorians

COSTS AND FINANCIAL INFORMATION
$11,492 tuition and fees (2000–2001)
$4478 room and board
60% average percent of need met
$9323 average financial aid amount received per undergraduate (1999–2000)

AFTER GRADUATION
31% graduated in 4 years
13% graduated in 5 years
3% graduated in 6 years
28% pursued further study (11% business, 9% education, 2% law)
84% had job offers within 6 months
50 organizations recruited on campus

JUDSON COLLEGE

Marion, Alabama

http://home.judson.edu/

Founded in 1838, Judson College is the sixth oldest women's college in the nation and the only women's college in Alabama. Service, missions, volunteering, worship, Bible study, and Campus Ministries are integral to the College and her relevance to society. Extraordinary leadership positions in honor societies, student government association, dormitory councils, and a host of other clubs and organizations assure women of opportunities to develop communication skills and gain peer recognition. Intercollegiate and intramural sports, a Wellness Center, and activity courses encourage teamwork and fitness. Horseback riding, canoeing, and cycling are activities students enjoy on and around the beautiful 80-acre campus. Resident halls equipped with Internet access provide students the World Wide Web, broadening their research capabilities. With a 10:1 student-to-teacher ratio, and sixty-nine percent of the full-time faculty holding doctorate or terminal degrees in their field, students are offered every advantage to succeed in their course of study. Ninety-five percent of recent graduates have been accepted into graduate programs of their choice or have achieved full-time employment. At Judson College all efforts and facilities are directed toward enabling young women as they strengthen their minds, hearts and souls.

Academics

Judson awards bachelor's **degrees**. Challenging opportunities include advanced placement, accelerated degree programs, student-designed majors, an honors program, double majors, independent study, and a senior project. **Special programs** include internships, summer session for credit, off-campus study, study-abroad, and Army ROTC. The most frequently chosen **baccalaureate** fields are business/marketing, psychology, and education. A complete listing of majors at Judson appears in the Majors Index beginning on page 147. The **faculty** at Judson has 35 full-time members, 69% with terminal degrees. The student-faculty ratio is 10:1.

Students of Judson

The student body is made up of 308 undergraduates. Students come from 19 states and territories and 4 other countries. 88% are from Alabama. 1.6% are international students. 57% returned for their sophomore year.

Facilities and Resources

The **library** has 68,120 books and 397 subscriptions.

Career Services

The career planning and placement office has 1 full-time staff member. Services include job fairs, resume preparation, interview workshops, resume referral, career/interest testing, career counseling, careers library, and job bank.

Campus Life

There are 25 active organizations on campus, including a drama/theater group, newspaper, choral group, and marching band. No national or local **sororities**. Judson is a member of the NCCAA. **Intercollegiate sports** (some offering scholarships) include basketball, equestrian sports, softball, tennis, volleyball.

Campus Safety

Student safety services include late-night transport/escort service, 24-hour emergency telephone alarm devices, 24-hour patrols by trained security personnel, and electronically operated dormitory entrances.

Applying

Judson requires SAT I or ACT, a high school transcript, an interview, 2 recommendations, and a minimum high school GPA of 2.0. Application deadline: rolling admissions; 3/1 priority date for financial aid. Early and deferred admission are possible. **Contact:** Mrs. Charlotte Clements, Director of Admissions, PO Box 120, Marion, AL 36756, 334-683-5110 ext. 110 or toll-free 800-447-9472; fax 334-683-5158; e-mail admissions@future.judson.edu.

GETTING IN LAST YEAR		
243 applied	48% had ACT scores over 24	$8764 average financial aid amount received per undergraduate (1999–2000)
81% were accepted	7% had SAT verbal scores over 700	
79 enrolled (40%)	4% had ACT scores over 30	**AFTER GRADUATION**
22% from top tenth of their h.s. class	2 valedictorians	35% graduated in 4 years
3.14 average high school GPA	**COSTS AND FINANCIAL INFORMATION**	1% graduated in 5 years
43% had SAT verbal scores over 600	$7640 tuition and fees (2000–2001 estimated)	21% pursued further study (13% arts and sciences, 8% education)
14% had SAT math scores over 600	$4600 room and board	72% had job offers within 6 months
	86% average percent of need met	

JUDSON COLLEGE

Elgin, Illinois

http://www.judson-il.edu/

Judson offers students opportunities for practical experience in their fields to ensure they will be strong candidates for jobs or graduate school. Located 40 miles northwest of Chicago and just minutes from the region's Golden Corridor of corporate headquarters, numerous possibilities for internships in business, the visual arts, the sciences, and communications exist. Multiple school districts, social service agencies, and churches provide ample practica options in education, psychology, and ministry. In addition, Judson's faculty members, many of whom have decades of work experience in their fields, are committed to serving as professional and Christian mentors to their students.

Academics

Judson awards bachelor's **degrees**. Challenging opportunities include advanced placement, accelerated degree programs, student-designed majors, an honors program, double majors, independent study, and a senior project. **Special programs** include internships, summer session for credit, off-campus study, study-abroad, and Army ROTC. A complete listing of majors at Judson appears in the Majors Index beginning on page 147.

Students of Judson

The student body is made up of 1,100 undergraduates. 56.6% are women and 43.4% are men. Students come from 21 states and territories and 18 other countries. 2.7% are international students. 74% returned for their sophomore year.

Facilities and Resources

The **library** has 90,000 books and 430 subscriptions.

Career Services

The career planning and placement office has 1 full-time, 1 part-time staff members. Services include job fairs, resume preparation, career counseling, and careers library.

Campus Life

Active organizations on campus include a newspaper and choral group. No national or local **fraternities** or **sororities**. Judson is a member of the NAIA and NCCAA. **Intercollegiate sports** (some offering scholarships) include baseball (m), basketball, cross-country running, soccer, softball (w), tennis, volleyball (w).

Campus Safety

Student safety services include 24-hour emergency telephone alarm devices, 24-hour patrols by trained security personnel, and electronically operated dormitory entrances.

Applying

Judson requires an essay, SAT I or ACT, a high school transcript, and a minimum high school GPA of 2.0, and in some cases an interview and 1 recommendation. It recommends ACT. Application deadline: 8/15; 5/1 priority date for financial aid. Early and deferred admission are possible. **Contact:** Director of Admissions, 1151 North State Street, Elgin, IL 60123-1498, 847-695-2500 ext. 2310 or toll-free 800-879-5376; fax 847-695-0216; e-mail admission@judson-il.edu.

GETTING IN LAST YEAR
576 applied
94% were accepted
223 enrolled (41%)
20% had SAT verbal scores over 600
25% had SAT math scores over 600
41% had ACT scores over 24

2% had SAT verbal scores over 700
2% had SAT math scores over 700
4% had ACT scores over 30

COSTS AND FINANCIAL INFORMATION
$13,890 tuition and fees (1999–2000)
$5360 room and board
85% average percent of need met

$10,092 average financial aid amount received per undergraduate (1999–2000 estimated)

AFTER GRADUATION
79% had job offers within 6 months

KENTUCKY CHRISTIAN COLLEGE

Grayson, Kentucky

http://www.kcc.edu/

Kentucky Christian College, fully accredited by the Southern Association of Colleges and Schools, is the Great Commission College! We are committed to developing you spiritually as a student and as a leader. Every student receives 30 hours of Bible curriculum built into your four year plan, regardless of your chosen field of study. Christian leadership is the focus of everything we do at KCC. You will not only learn the academics of leadership in the classroom, but you'll learn the practice of leadership in many different places. Our students use these skills while building a school for children in Haiti, or performing on the great stage of Carnegie Hall in New York City, or while cutting down the nets after winning the national basketball championship! Our graduates pursue any career they set their sights on. The difference is they take the word of Christ with them into that career, and their time at Kentucky Christian College has made them stronger in their faith. An active student life at KCC, along with a rigorous academic program, will prepare you to face and meet the challenges ahead. Your opportunities are endless at Kentucky Christian College.

Academics
KCC awards associate and bachelor's **degrees**. Challenging opportunities include advanced placement, double majors, independent study, and a senior project. **Special programs** include cooperative education, internships, summer session for credit, and off-campus study. The most frequently chosen **baccalaureate** fields are philosophy, education, and business/marketing. A complete listing of majors at KCC appears in the Majors Index beginning on page 147. The **faculty** at KCC has 29 full-time members, 83% with terminal degrees. The student-faculty ratio is 16:1.

Students of KCC
The student body is made up of 564 undergraduates. 54.1% are women and 45.9% are men. Students come from 27 states and territories and 8 other countries. 28% are from Kentucky. 1.6% are international students. 49% returned for their sophomore year.

Facilities and Resources
The **library** has 447 subscriptions.

Career Services
Services include career counseling.

Campus Life
Active organizations on campus include a drama/theater group, newspaper, and choral group. No national or local **fraternities** or **sororities**. KCC is a member of the NCCAA. **Intercollegiate sports** include basketball, cross-country running, soccer (m), tennis, volleyball (w).

Campus Safety
Student safety services include late night security patrols, late-night transport/escort service, and 24-hour emergency telephone alarm devices.

Applying
KCC requires an essay, SAT I or ACT, a high school transcript, and 3 recommendations, and in some cases an interview. It recommends a minimum high school GPA of 2.0. Application deadline: rolling admissions; 4/1 priority date for financial aid. **Contact:** Mrs. Sandra Deakins, Director of Admissions, 100 Academic Parkway, Grayson, KY 41143-2205, 606-474-3266 or toll-free 800-522-3181; fax 606-474-3155; e-mail knights@email.kcc.edu.

GETTING IN LAST YEAR
272 applied
88% were accepted
157 enrolled (65%)
13% from top tenth of their h.s. class
3.04 average high school GPA
18% had SAT verbal scores over 600
20% had SAT math scores over 600

18% had ACT scores over 24
4% had SAT verbal scores over 700
3% had ACT scores over 30
4 valedictorians

COSTS AND FINANCIAL INFORMATION
$6880 tuition and fees (1999–2000)
$3914 room and board
55% average percent of need met

$8404 average financial aid amount received per undergraduate (1999–2000 estimated)

AFTER GRADUATION
30% graduated in 4 years
7% graduated in 5 years
4% graduated in 6 years

KING COLLEGE

Bristol, Tennessee

http://www.king.edu/

King College educates students in an academically rigorous, collegiate setting, integrating the Christian faith with scholarship, service, and career, leading to meaningful lives of achievement and cultural transformation in Christ. More than 90% of King students are accepted into their first choice of graduate schools, and *U.S. News & World Report* has listed King College as one of America's best colleges for 10 consecutive years. King has also been listed in *Peterson's Top Colleges for Science* and *Peterson's Competitive Colleges*.

Academics

King awards bachelor's **degrees**. Challenging opportunities include advanced placement, accelerated degree programs, an honors program, double majors, independent study, and a senior project. **Special programs** include internships, summer session for credit, off-campus study, study-abroad, and Army ROTC. The most frequently chosen **baccalaureate** fields are social sciences and history, English, and biological/life sciences. A complete listing of majors at King appears in the Majors Index beginning on page 147. The **faculty** at King has 36 full-time members, 69% with terminal degrees. The student-faculty ratio is 10:1.

Students of King

The student body is made up of 587 undergraduates. 59.5% are women and 40.5% are men. Students come from 27 states and territories and 29 other countries. 43% are from Tennessee. 7.5% are international students. 74% returned for their sophomore year.

Facilities and Resources

The **library** has 95,136 books and 605 subscriptions.

Career Services

The career planning and placement office has 1 full-time, 1 part-time staff members. Services include job fairs, resume preparation, interview workshops, resume referral, career/interest testing, career counseling, careers library, job bank, and job interviews.

Campus Life

There are 29 active organizations on campus, including a drama/theater group, newspaper, and choral group. No national or local **fraternities** or **sororities**. King is a member of the NAIA. **Intercollegiate sports** (some offering scholarships) include baseball (m), basketball, golf (m), soccer, tennis, volleyball (w).

Campus Safety

Student safety services include late-night transport/escort service.

Applying

King requires an essay, SAT I or ACT, a high school transcript, and a minimum high school GPA of 2.4, and in some cases an interview and recommendations. It recommends an interview and recommendations. Application deadline: rolling admissions; 3/1 priority date for financial aid. Early and deferred admission are possible. **Contact:** Ms. Mindy Clark, Director of Admissions, 1350 King College Road, Bristol, TN 37620-2699, 423-652-4861 or toll-free 800-362-0014; fax 423-968-4456; e-mail admissions@king.edu.

GETTING IN LAST YEAR
428 applied
79% were accepted
133 enrolled (39%)
34% from top tenth of their h.s. class
3.19 average high school GPA
32% had SAT verbal scores over 600
29% had SAT math scores over 600
39% had ACT scores over 24

9% had SAT verbal scores over 700
8% had SAT math scores over 700
6% had ACT scores over 30

COSTS AND FINANCIAL INFORMATION
$10,750 tuition and fees (1999–2000)
$3850 room and board
77% average percent of need met
$11,005 average financial aid amount
    received per undergraduate (1999–2000)

AFTER GRADUATION
31% graduated in 4 years
8% graduated in 5 years
1% graduated in 6 years
31% pursued further study
65% had job offers within 6 months
15 organizations recruited on campus

THE KING'S UNIVERSITY COLLEGE

THE KING'S UNIVERSITY COLLEGE
Christian University Education

Edmonton, Alberta, Canada

http://www.kingsu.ab.ca/

The King's University College is an independent, degree-granting Christian university college with a strong commitment to the liberal arts, integrating the Christian faith with life and learning. A liberal arts education gives you skills highly valued by employers in today's job market and you will also learn to discover and develop your unique gifts and skills for service. Our programs provide the opportunity for you to explore God's purposes for your life. By studying the broad complexities of life and society, you can come to your chosen area of service with a clearer sense of your God-given purpose for developing new and more responsible ways of living and working. King's degrees are fully accredited and recognized in North America and beyond with many graduates entering master's and doctoral programs in their chosen discipline. Our small size and highly-qualified faculty provide a caring and intellectually stimulating environment for personal and spiritual growth.

Academics
King's awards bachelor's **degrees**. Challenging opportunities include advanced placement, accelerated degree programs, double majors, independent study, and a senior project. **Special programs** include internships, off-campus study, and study-abroad. The most frequently chosen **baccalaureate** fields are social sciences and history, education, and natural resources/environmental science. A complete listing of majors at King's appears in the Majors Index beginning on page 147. The **faculty** at King's has 28 full-time members, 100% with terminal degrees.

Students of King's
The student body is made up of 526 undergraduates. 61.4% are women and 38.6% are men. Students come from 6 states and territories and 6 other countries. 80% are from Alberta. 69% returned for their sophomore year.

Facilities and Resources
The **library** has 62,000 books and 350 subscriptions.

Career Services
The career planning and placement office has 1 full-time staff member. Services include career counseling and careers library.

Campus Life
There are 15 active organizations on campus, including a drama/theater group, newspaper, and choral group. No national or local **fraternities** or **sororities**. **Intercollegiate sports** (some offering scholarships) include basketball, soccer, volleyball.

Campus Safety
Student safety services include 24-hour emergency telephone alarm devices, student patrols, and electronically operated dormitory entrances.

Applying
King's requires a high school transcript and 1 recommendation, and in some cases an essay and an interview. It recommends SAT I and SAT II or ACT. Application deadline: rolling admissions; 3/31 for financial aid. **Contact:** Mr. Glenn J. Keeler, Registrar/Director of Admissions, 9125-50 Street, Edmonton, AB T6B 2H3, Canada, 780-465-8330 or toll-free 800-661-8582; fax 780-465-3534; e-mail registrar@kingsu.ab.ca.

GETTING IN LAST YEAR	COSTS AND FINANCIAL INFORMATION	AFTER GRADUATION
394 applied	$5665 tuition and fees (2000–2001 estimated)	34% graduated in 4 years
70% were accepted	$4883 room and board	3% graduated in 5 years
111 enrolled (40%)		1% graduated in 6 years

LEE UNIVERSITY

Cleveland, Tennessee

http://www.leeuniversity.edu/

The dynamic growth of Lee University—3,250 students today from 1,739 just 10 years ago—marks it as an institution "on the move." Lee's beautiful campus in East Tennessee has doubled in size during that same period with the addition of a 500-seat theater/recital hall, a student recreation/fitness complex, 6 new dorms, and 2 new classroom buildings. Lee offers its own study programs in England, Ukraine, China, Germany, and others. Lee is well-known for the vitality of its student life. More than one third of its students play intramural sports, and 400 of them perform in traveling musical groups. It has ranked at the top of all Council colleges in tuition affordability for more than 5 years.

Academics

Lee awards bachelor's and master's **degrees**. Challenging opportunities include advanced placement, an honors program, independent study, and a senior project. **Special programs** include cooperative education, internships, summer session for credit, and study-abroad. The most frequently chosen **baccalaureate** fields are education, philosophy, and business/marketing. A complete listing of majors at Lee appears in the Majors Index beginning on page 147. The **faculty** at Lee has 113 full-time members, 62% with terminal degrees. The student-faculty ratio is 20:1.

Students of Lee

The student body totals 3,259, of whom 3,155 are undergraduates. 56.3% are women and 43.7% are men. Students come from 46 states and territories and 30 other countries. 37% are from Tennessee. 2% are international students. 67% returned for their sophomore year.

Facilities and Resources

The **library** has 148,179 books and 1,100 subscriptions.

Career Services

The career planning and placement office has 1 part-time staff member. Services include job fairs, career/interest testing, and job bank.

Campus Life

There are 48 active organizations on campus, including a drama/theater group, newspaper, and choral group. 13% of eligible men and 10% of eligible women are members of local **fraternities** and local **sororities**. Lee is a member of the NAIA and NCCAA. **Intercollegiate sports** (some offering scholarships) include basketball, cross-country running, golf (m), soccer, softball (w), tennis, volleyball (w).

Campus Safety

Student safety services include late-night transport/escort service, 24-hour emergency telephone alarm devices, and 24-hour patrols by trained security personnel.

Applying

Lee requires SAT I or ACT, a high school transcript, MMR immunization record, and a minimum high school GPA of 2.0, and in some cases 1 recommendation. It recommends ACT and 3 recommendations. Application deadline: 9/1; 4/15 priority date for financial aid. Early and deferred admission are possible. **Contact:** Admissions Coordinator, PO Box 3450, Cleveland, TN 37311, 423-614-8500 or toll-free 800-LEE-9930; fax 423-614-8533; e-mail admissions@leeuniversity.edu.

GETTING IN LAST YEAR
1,175 applied
90% were accepted
618 enrolled (58%)
20% from top tenth of their h.s. class
2.93 average high school GPA
23% had SAT verbal scores over 600
22% had SAT math scores over 600

40% had ACT scores over 24
3% had SAT verbal scores over 700
2% had SAT math scores over 700
3% had ACT scores over 30

COSTS AND FINANCIAL INFORMATION
$6862 tuition and fees (2000–2001)
$4020 room and board
61% average percent of need met

$6644 average financial aid amount received per undergraduate (1998–99)

AFTER GRADUATION
18% graduated in 4 years
14% graduated in 5 years
4% graduated in 6 years
40 organizations recruited on campus

LeTourneau University

Longview, Texas

http://www.letu.edu/

Set apart by a special "spirit of ingenuity," LeTourneau University continues to build on the excellence and inventive zeal of its heritage. From nationally acclaimed academics in technological fields like engineering, aviation, and computer science to excellent programs in the liberal arts and sciences, the University emphasizes problem-solving, applied knowledge, and analytical thinking. Set in the beautiful pine woods and lakes of East Texas, the spacious contemporary campus is home to innovative students from 48 states and more than 20 nations. At LeTourneau, "Faith brings us together, ingenuity sets us apart."

Academics
LeTourneau awards associate, bachelor's, and master's **degrees**. Challenging opportunities include advanced placement, double majors, independent study, and a senior project. **Special programs** include cooperative education, internships, summer session for credit, and off-campus study. The most frequently chosen **baccalaureate** fields are engineering/engineering technologies, business/marketing, and biological/life sciences. A complete listing of majors at LeTourneau appears in the Majors Index beginning on page 147. The **faculty** at LeTourneau has 59 full-time members, 71% with terminal degrees. The student-faculty ratio is 15:1.

Students of LeTourneau
The student body totals 2,805, of whom 2,523 are undergraduates. 46.8% are women and 53.2% are men. Students come from 49 states and territories and 24 other countries. 50% are from Texas. 1.8% are international students. 79% returned for their sophomore year.

Facilities and Resources
The **library** has 260,000 books and 600 subscriptions.

Career Services
The career planning and placement office has 1 full-time, 2 part-time staff members. Services include job fairs, resume preparation, interview workshops, resume referral, career/interest testing, career counseling, careers library, job bank, and job interviews.

Campus Life
There are 22 active organizations on campus, including a drama/theater group, newspaper, and choral group. 8% of eligible men and 3% of eligible women are members of 3 societies for men, 1 society for women. LeTourneau is a member of the NCAA (Division III) and NCCAA. **Intercollegiate sports** include baseball (m), basketball, cross-country running, golf, soccer, softball (w), tennis, volleyball (w).

Campus Safety
Student safety services include late-night transport/escort service, 24-hour emergency telephone alarm devices, 24-hour patrols by trained security personnel, and electronically operated dormitory entrances.

Applying
LeTourneau requires an essay, SAT I or ACT, a high school transcript, 2 recommendations, and a minimum high school GPA of 2.5, and in some cases an interview. Application deadline: 8/1; 2/15 priority date for financial aid. Early and deferred admission are possible. **Contact:** Mr. Rodney Stanford, Director of Admissions, PO Box 7001, Admissions Office, Longview, TX 75607-7001, 903-233-3400 or toll-free 800-759-8811; fax 903-233-3411; e-mail admissions@letu.edu.

GETTING IN LAST YEAR
953 applied
85% were accepted
263 enrolled (33%)
27% from top tenth of their h.s. class
3.50 average high school GPA
41% had SAT verbal scores over 600
54% had SAT math scores over 600
60% had ACT scores over 24

13% had SAT verbal scores over 700
18% had SAT math scores over 700
14% had ACT scores over 30
6 National Merit Scholars
11 valedictorians

COSTS AND FINANCIAL INFORMATION
$12,240 tuition and fees (2000–2001)
$5250 room and board
84% average percent of need met

$11,748 average financial aid amount received per undergraduate (1999–2000 estimated)

AFTER GRADUATION
32% graduated in 4 years
16% graduated in 5 years
2% graduated in 6 years
91% had job offers within 6 months
60 organizations recruited on campus

LIPSCOMB UNIVERSITY
Nashville, Tennessee

http://www.lipscomb.edu/

Founded in 1891, Lipscomb University is a distinctly Christian university associated with the Churches of Christ. Committed to integrating Christian faith and practice with academic excellence, Lipscomb's residential campus is located in Nashville, Tennessee. With over 2,500 students, the university enrolls students from across the United States and from around the world. There are over 100 undergraduate majors plus graduate programs in Bible, Education, and Business Administration. All faculty members are Christians active in local churches. Daily chapel and Bible classes are a hallmark of a Lipscomb University education. Students and faculty participate in mission trips, inner-city ministry, Habitat for Humanity, and numerous local mission and service projects. The 60-acre campus offers traditional buildings with a high-tech infrastructure including a fiber-optic computer network. The university is moving to NCAA Division I in all sports.

Academics
Lipscomb University awards bachelor's, master's, and first-professional **degrees**. Challenging opportunities include advanced placement, accelerated degree programs, an honors program, double majors, independent study, and a senior project. **Special programs** include internships, summer session for credit, study-abroad, and Army and Air Force ROTC. The most frequently chosen **baccalaureate** fields are business/marketing, education, and communications/communication technologies. A complete listing of majors at Lipscomb University appears in the Majors Index beginning on page 147. The **faculty** at Lipscomb University has 94 full-time members, 85% with terminal degrees.

Students of Lipscomb University
The student body totals 2,504, of whom 2,317 are undergraduates. 56% are women and 44% are men. Students come from 40 states and territories and 38 other countries. 64% are from Tennessee. 1.4% are international students. 79% returned for their sophomore year.

Career Services
The career planning and placement office has 2 full-time staff members. Services include job fairs, resume preparation, resume referral, career/interest testing, career counseling, careers library, job bank, and job interviews.

Campus Life
There are 60 active organizations on campus, including a drama/theater group, newspaper, radio station, and choral group. 15% of eligible men and 20% of eligible women are members of local **fraternities** and local **sororities**. Lipscomb University is a member of the NAIA. **Intercollegiate sports** (some offering scholarships) include baseball (m), basketball, cross-country running, golf, soccer, softball (w), tennis, volleyball (w).

Campus Safety
Student safety services include late-night transport/escort service, 24-hour emergency telephone alarm devices, 24-hour patrols by trained security personnel, and electronically operated dormitory entrances.

Applying
Lipscomb University requires SAT I or ACT, a high school transcript, 2 recommendations, and a minimum high school GPA of 2.25. It recommends an essay and an interview. Application deadline: rolling admissions; 2/28 priority date for financial aid. Early admission is possible. **Contact:** Mr. Scott Gilman, Director of Admissions, 3901 Granny White Pike, Nashville, TN 37204-3951, 615-269-1776 or toll-free 800-333-4358 ext. 1776; fax 615-269-1804; e-mail admissions@dlu.edu.

GETTING IN LAST YEAR
1,598 applied
93% were accepted
598 enrolled (40%)
26% from top tenth of their h.s. class
3.17 average high school GPA
32% had SAT verbal scores over 600
35% had SAT math scores over 600

47% had ACT scores over 24
6% had SAT verbal scores over 700
5% had SAT math scores over 700
10% had ACT scores over 30
1 National Merit Scholar
23 valedictorians

COSTS AND FINANCIAL INFORMATION
$9689 tuition and fees (1999–2000)

$4344 room and board
100% average percent of need met

AFTER GRADUATION
31% graduated in 4 years
16% graduated in 5 years
3% graduated in 6 years
271 organizations recruited on campus

MALONE COLLEGE
Canton, Ohio

http://www.malone.edu/

Malone College is a Christian College for the Arts, Sciences, and Professions. Affiliated with the Evangelical Friends church, Malone is committed to offering an education of the highest quality in an environment that encourages a steadfast devotion to God. Malone students are given the opportunity to develop academically, spiritually, and socially. Through their interaction with Christian faculty members, participation in varsity and intramural athletics, outreach music and drama groups, and mission trips, each student leaves Malone with more than just a diploma. The combination of strong academics, spiritual development, and a "city close, country quiet" campus makes Malone an attractive and challenging opportunity.

Academics
Malone awards bachelor's and master's **degrees** and post-bachelor's certificates. Challenging opportunities include advanced placement, accelerated degree programs, student-designed majors, double majors, independent study, and a senior project. **Special programs** include cooperative education, internships, summer session for credit, off-campus study, and study-abroad. The most frequently chosen **baccalaureate** fields are business/marketing, education, and health professions and related sciences. A complete listing of majors at Malone appears in the Majors Index beginning on page 147. The **faculty** at Malone has 99 full-time members, 58% with terminal degrees. The student-faculty ratio is 15:1.

Students of Malone
The student body totals 2,193, of whom 1,949 are undergraduates. 61% are women and 39% are men. Students come from 20 states and territories and 6 other countries. 91% are from Ohio. 0.6% are international students. 74% returned for their sophomore year.

Facilities and Resources
The **library** has 107,484 books and 1,658 subscriptions.

Career Services
The career planning and placement office has 2 full-time, 1 part-time staff members. Services include job fairs, resume preparation, interview workshops, resume referral, career/interest testing, career counseling, careers library, job bank, and job interviews.

Campus Life
There are 40 active organizations on campus, including a drama/theater group, newspaper, radio station, choral group, and marching band. No national or local **fraternities** or **sororities**. Malone is a member of the NAIA and NCCAA. **Intercollegiate sports** (some offering scholarships) include baseball (m), basketball, cross-country running, football (m), golf, soccer, softball (w), tennis, track and field, volleyball (w).

Campus Safety
Student safety services include late-night transport/escort service, 24-hour emergency telephone alarm devices, and 24-hour patrols by trained security personnel.

Applying
Malone requires an essay, SAT I or ACT, a high school transcript, and a minimum high school GPA of 2.5, and in some cases an interview. Application deadline: 7/1; 3/1 priority date for financial aid. Early and deferred admission are possible. **Contact:** Mr. John Chopka, Dean of Admissions, 515 25th Street, NW, Canton, OH 44709-3897, 330-471-8145 or toll-free 800-521-1146; fax 330-454-6977; e-mail admissions@malone.edu.

GETTING IN LAST YEAR
899 applied
88% were accepted
409 enrolled (51%)
23% from top tenth of their h.s. class
3.28 average high school GPA
22% had SAT verbal scores over 600
22% had SAT math scores over 600
41% had ACT scores over 24
2% had SAT verbal scores over 700

1% had SAT math scores over 700
5% had ACT scores over 30
1 National Merit Scholar
9 valedictorians

COSTS AND FINANCIAL INFORMATION
$12,380 tuition and fees (1999–2000)
$5250 room and board
84% average percent of need met
$10,082 average financial aid amount received per undergraduate (1999–2000)

AFTER GRADUATION
32% graduated in 4 years
14% graduated in 5 years
3% graduated in 6 years
21% pursued further study (8% business, 5% education, 2% arts and sciences)
80% had job offers within 6 months
23 organizations recruited on campus

THE MASTER'S COLLEGE AND SEMINARY

Santa Clarita, California   *http://www.masters.edu/*

The Master's College (TMC) exists to empower Christian students for a life of enduring commitment to Christ, biblical fidelity, moral integrity, intellectual growth, and lasting contribution to the kingdom of God. A dynamic campus community, numerous ministry opportunities, and an outstanding, accessible faculty are key components of this mission. Located on a tree-filled 100-acre campus in the Santa Clarita Valley, TMC offers undergraduate and graduate degrees in over 50 areas of study. Also offered is a wireless computer network and a unique one-semester field study program in Israel.

Academics

Master's awards bachelor's, master's, and first-professional **degrees**. Challenging opportunities include advanced placement, accelerated degree programs, double majors, independent study, and a senior project. **Special programs** include cooperative education, internships, summer session for credit, off-campus study, and study-abroad. A complete listing of majors at Master's appears in the Majors Index beginning on page 147. The **faculty** at Master's has 60 full-time members.

Students of Master's

The student body totals 1,295, of whom 969 are undergraduates. 51.1% are women and 48.9% are men. Students come from 40 states and territories and 8 other countries. 63% are from California. 1% are international students. 67% returned for their sophomore year.

Facilities and Resources

The 2 **libraries** have 106,701 books.

Career Services

The career planning and placement office has 2 full-time, 1 part-time staff members. Services include job fairs, resume preparation, resume referral, career counseling, careers library, and job bank.

Campus Life

Active organizations on campus include a drama/theater group, newspaper, radio station, and choral group. No national or local **fraternities** or **sororities**. Master's is a member of the NAIA and NCCAA. **Intercollegiate sports** (some offering scholarships) include baseball (m), basketball, cross-country running, soccer, volleyball (w).

Campus Safety

Student safety services include 24-hour patrols by trained security personnel.

Applying

Master's requires an essay, SAT I or ACT, a high school transcript, an interview, 2 recommendations, and a minimum high school GPA of 2.5. Application deadline: 3/6; 3/2 priority date for financial aid. Deferred admission is possible. **Contact:** Mr. Yaphet Peterson, Director of Enrollment, 21726 Placerita Canyon Road, Santa Clarita, CA 91321-1200, 805-259-3540 ext. 368 or toll-free 800-568-6248; e-mail enrollment@masters.edu.

GETTING IN LAST YEAR
718 applied
82% were accepted
192 enrolled (32%)
62% from top tenth of their h.s. class
3.58 average high school GPA
41% had SAT verbal scores over 600
37% had SAT math scores over 600

61% had ACT scores over 24
6% had SAT verbal scores over 700
7% had SAT math scores over 700
9% had ACT scores over 30

COSTS AND FINANCIAL INFORMATION
$13,400 tuition and fees (1999–2000)
$5300 room and board
78% average percent of need met

$12,250 average financial aid amount received per undergraduate (1999–2000 estimated)

AFTER GRADUATION
49% graduated in 4 years
13% graduated in 5 years
12% graduated in 6 years
30 organizations recruited on campus

MESSIAH COLLEGE

Grantham, Pennsylvania

http://www.messiah.edu/

Messiah College is a 4-year, private, residential Christian college of the liberal and applied arts and sciences, enrolling 2,700 undergraduate students. The College is committed to an embracing evangelical spirit rooted in the Anabaptist, Pietist, and Wesleyan traditions of the Christian Church. Our mission is to educate students toward maturity of intellect, character, and Christian faith in preparation for lives of service, leadership, and reconciliation in church and society. The College's primary campus of 410 acres is located in suburban, southcentral Pennsylvania. Over 50 majors and 50 minors are available. Opportunities for internships allow students to both gain experience and professional contacts while in college. Numerous study abroad programs provide exciting, cross-cultural experiences. Since 1968, the College has supported a second campus in Philadelphia adjacent to, and in alliance with, Temple University.

Academics

Messiah College awards bachelor's **degrees**. Challenging opportunities include advanced placement, accelerated degree programs, student-designed majors, freshman honors college, an honors program, double majors, independent study, and a senior project. **Special programs** include internships, summer session for credit, off-campus study, and study-abroad. The most frequently chosen **baccalaureate** fields are education, business/marketing, and health professions and related sciences. A complete listing of majors at Messiah College appears in the Majors Index beginning on page 147. The **faculty** at Messiah College has 141 full-time members, 77% with terminal degrees. The student-faculty ratio is 15:1.

Students of Messiah College

The student body is made up of 2,735 undergraduates. 61.6% are women and 38.4% are men. Students come from 39 states and territories and 22 other countries. 51% are from Pennsylvania. 1.7% are international students. 86% returned for their sophomore year.

Facilities and Resources

The **library** has 233,732 books and 1,316 subscriptions.

Career Services

The career planning and placement office has 4 full-time, 1 part-time staff members. Services include job fairs, resume preparation, interview workshops, resume referral, career/interest testing, career counseling, careers library, job bank, and job interviews.

Campus Life

There are 60 active organizations on campus, including a drama/theater group, newspaper, radio station, and choral group. No national or local **fraternities** or **sororities**. Messiah College is a member of the NCAA (Division III). **Intercollegiate sports** include baseball (m), basketball, cross-country running, field hockey (w), golf (m), lacrosse, soccer, softball (w), tennis, track and field, volleyball (w), wrestling (m).

Campus Safety

Student safety services include bicycle patrols, late-night transport/escort service, 24-hour emergency telephone alarm devices, 24-hour patrols by trained security personnel, student patrols, and electronically operated dormitory entrances.

Applying

Messiah College requires an essay, SAT I or ACT, a high school transcript, and 2 recommendations. It recommends an interview and a minimum high school GPA of 3.0. Application deadline: rolling admissions; 4/1 priority date for financial aid. Early and deferred admission are possible. **Contact:** Mr. William G. Strausbaugh, Dean for Enrollment Management, One College Avenue, Grantham, PA 17027-0800, 717-691-6000 or toll-free 800-382-1349 (in-state), 800-233-4220 (out-of-state); fax 717-796-5374; e-mail admiss@messiah.edu.

GETTING IN LAST YEAR
2,088 applied
81% were accepted
678 enrolled (40%)
34% from top tenth of their h.s. class
3.68 average high school GPA
47% had SAT verbal scores over 600
44% had SAT math scores over 600
68% had ACT scores over 24
10% had SAT verbal scores over 700

9% had SAT math scores over 700
20% had ACT scores over 30
13 National Merit Scholars
43 valedictorians

COSTS AND FINANCIAL INFORMATION
$15,096 tuition and fees (1999–2000)
$5580 room and board
75% average percent of need met
$11,909 average financial aid amount
  received per undergraduate (1999–2000)

AFTER GRADUATION
66% graduated in 4 years
4% graduated in 5 years
1% graduated in 6 years
8% pursued further study (5% arts and
  sciences, 2% education, 1% medicine)
89% had job offers within 6 months
453 organizations recruited on campus

MidAmerica Nazarene University

Olathe, Kansas

http://www.mnu.edu/

MidAmerica Nazarene University is a comprehensive liberal arts university in the Wesleyan-Holiness tradition. Sponsored by the Church of the Nazarene, it is a coeducational, career-oriented, liberal arts university offering 6 degree options: Associate of Arts, Bachelor of Arts, Bachelor of Science in Nursing, Master of Education, Master of Business Administration, and Master of Arts in Counseling. The 105-acre campus is 19 miles southwest of Kansas City. MidAmerica has as its purpose the Christian education of individuals in a liberal arts context for personal development, service to God and humanity, and career preparation.

Academics

MNU awards associate, bachelor's, and master's **degrees**. Challenging opportunities include advanced placement, accelerated degree programs, double majors, independent study, and a senior project. **Special programs** include internships, summer session for credit, off-campus study, study-abroad, and Army and Air Force ROTC. The most frequently chosen **baccalaureate** fields are communications/communication technologies, engineering/engineering technologies, and home economics/vocational home economics. A complete listing of majors at MNU appears in the Majors Index beginning on page 147. The **faculty** at MNU has 69 full-time members, 43% with terminal degrees. The student-faculty ratio is 16:1.

Students of MNU

The student body totals 1,559, of whom 1,173 are undergraduates. 54% are women and 46% are men. Students come from 31 states and territories and 8 other countries. 57% are from Kansas. 1.4% are international students. 69% returned for their sophomore year.

Facilities and Resources

The **library** has 80,560 books and 1,025 subscriptions.

Career Services

The career planning and placement office has 2 full-time, 1 part-time staff members. Services include job fairs, resume preparation, interview workshops, career/interest testing, career counseling, careers library, job bank, and job interviews.

Campus Life

There are 28 active organizations on campus, including a drama/theater group, newspaper, radio station, and choral group. No national or local **fraternities** or **sororities**. MNU is a member of the NAIA and NCCAA. **Intercollegiate sports** (some offering scholarships) include baseball (m), basketball, cross-country running, football (m), softball (w), track and field, volleyball (w).

Campus Safety

Student safety services include late-night transport/escort service, 24-hour emergency telephone alarm devices, 24-hour patrols by trained security personnel, student patrols, and electronically operated dormitory entrances.

Applying

MNU requires SAT I or ACT, a high school transcript, 2 recommendations, and a minimum high school GPA of 2.0. Application deadline: 8/1; 3/1 priority date for financial aid. Early and deferred admission are possible. **Contact:** Dr. Daniel Martin, Executive Director of Enrollment Development, 2030 East College Way, Olathe, KS 66062-1899, 913-791-3380 ext. 481 or toll-free 800-800-8887; fax 913-791-3481; e-mail admissions@mnu.edu.

GETTING IN LAST YEAR
449 applied
53% were accepted
222 enrolled (93%)
17% from top tenth of their h.s. class
3.28 average high school GPA
25% had SAT verbal scores over 600
22% had SAT math scores over 600

34% had ACT scores over 24
7% had SAT verbal scores over 700
4% had SAT math scores over 700
7% had ACT scores over 30
1 National Merit Scholar

COSTS AND FINANCIAL INFORMATION
$10,474 tuition and fees (1999–2000)

$5060 room and board

AFTER GRADUATION
20% graduated in 4 years
15% graduated in 5 years
8% graduated in 6 years
40 organizations recruited on campus

MILLIGAN COLLEGE
Milligan College, Tennessee

http://www.milligan.edu/

Milligan College

Milligan College combines the 3 areas of learning: God's world (taught through science), God's man (taught through the humanities), and God Himself (taught through revelation). Christ is central at Milligan College—both in its curriculum and in campus life. Milligan is a Christian liberal arts college dedicated to the integration of faith and learning in all facets of its college program. Milligan's mission is to prepare today's young people for a complicated world, and to do it in a Christian environment. Milligan's motto is "Christian education: the hope of the world!"

Academics
Milligan awards bachelor's and master's **degrees**. Challenging opportunities include advanced placement, accelerated degree programs, double majors, and independent study. **Special programs** include cooperative education, internships, summer session for credit, off-campus study, study-abroad, and Army ROTC. The most frequently chosen **baccalaureate** fields are business/marketing, health professions and related sciences, and education. A complete listing of majors at Milligan appears in the Majors Index beginning on page 147. The **faculty** at Milligan has 67 full-time members, 64% with terminal degrees. The student-faculty ratio is 13:1.

Students of Milligan
The student body totals 914, of whom 796 are undergraduates. 59.2% are women and 40.8% are men. Students come from 40 states and territories and 17 other countries. 36% are from Tennessee. 2.6% are international students. 70% returned for their sophomore year.

Facilities and Resources
The **library** has 78,727 books and 620 subscriptions.

Career Services
The career planning and placement office has 1 part-time staff member. Services include job fairs, resume preparation, career counseling, careers library, job bank, and job interviews.

Campus Life
There are 24 active organizations on campus, including a drama/theater group, newspaper, radio station, and choral group. No national or local **fraternities** or **sororities**. Milligan is a member of the NAIA. **Intercollegiate sports** (some offering scholarships) include baseball (m), basketball, cross-country running, golf (m), soccer, softball (w), tennis, volleyball (w).

Campus Safety
Student safety services include late-night transport/escort service and 24-hour patrols by trained security personnel.

Applying
Milligan requires an essay, SAT I or ACT, a high school transcript, 2 recommendations, and a minimum high school GPA of 2.0, and in some cases an interview. It recommends a minimum high school GPA of 3.0. Application deadline: rolling admissions; 3/1 priority date for financial aid. Deferred admission is possible. **Contact:** Mr. Michael A. Johnson, Vice President for Enrollment Management, PO Box 210, Milligan College, TN 37682, 423-461-8730 or toll-free 800-262-8337 (in-state); fax 423-461-8960.

GETTING IN LAST YEAR
762 applied
69% were accepted
214 enrolled (41%)
3.40 average high school GPA
29% had SAT verbal scores over 600
30% had SAT math scores over 600

53% had ACT scores over 24
7% had SAT verbal scores over 700
4% had SAT math scores over 700
3% had ACT scores over 30

COSTS AND FINANCIAL INFORMATION
$11,480 tuition and fees (1999–2000)
$4000 room and board

43% average percent of need met
$9896 average financial aid amount received per undergraduate (1998–99)

AFTER GRADUATION
10 organizations recruited on campus

MONTREAT COLLEGE
Montreat, North Carolina

http://www.montreat.edu/

Montreat College's beautiful mountain campus is located 15 miles east of Asheville, NC, in the heart of one of America's most spectacularly scenic areas—the Blue Ridge Mountains. With challenging programs and a favorable student/faculty ratio of 12:1, Montreat College enrollment is rapidly growing. The student body typically represents 35 states and 10 foreign countries. Students on the Montreat campus (the traditional program) may choose from more than 30 majors and minors. Montreat College's off-campus School of Professional and Adult Studies, which holds classes in Asheville, Charlotte, and various other NC locations, offers BBA and MBA degrees. Montreat College places great emphasis on the idea of servant leadership. Students are provided with numerous opportunities for practical leadership and service experience.

Academics
Montreat College awards associate, bachelor's, and master's **degrees**. Challenging opportunities include advanced placement, double majors, independent study, and a senior project. **Special programs** include cooperative education, internships, and off-campus study. A complete listing of majors at Montreat College appears in the Majors Index beginning on page 147. The **faculty** at Montreat College has 33 full-time members.

Students of Montreat College
The student body totals 1,054, of whom 992 are undergraduates. 56.9% are women and 43.1% are men. Students come from 30 states and territories and 9 other countries. 1% are international students. 81% returned for their sophomore year.

Facilities and Resources
The **library** has 67,378 books and 426 subscriptions.

Career Services
The career planning and placement office has 1 full-time staff member. Services include resume preparation, career counseling, and careers library.

Campus Life
There are 14 active organizations on campus, including a drama/theater group, newspaper, and choral group. No national or local **fraternities** or **sororities**. Montreat College is a member of the NAIA. **Intercollegiate sports** (some offering scholarships) include baseball (m), basketball, cross-country running, golf (m), soccer, softball (w), tennis, volleyball (w).

Campus Safety
Student safety services include 24-hour emergency telephone alarm devices, 24-hour patrols by trained security personnel, and electronically operated dormitory entrances.

Applying
Montreat College requires an essay, SAT I or ACT, a high school transcript, and 1 recommendation, and in some cases an interview. Application deadline: 8/20; 5/15 priority date for financial aid. Early and deferred admission are possible. **Contact:** Ms. Anita Darby, Director of Admissions, PO Box 1267, Montreat, NC 28757-1267, 828-669-8012 ext. 3784 or toll-free 800-622-6968 (in-state); fax 828-669-0120; e-mail admissions@montreat.edu.

GETTING IN LAST YEAR	9% had SAT math scores over 600	$9446 average financial aid amount received per undergraduate (1998–99)
382 applied	2% had SAT verbal scores over 700	
80% were accepted	2% had SAT math scores over 700	**AFTER GRADUATION**
10% from top tenth of their h.s. class		17% pursued further study
3.13 average high school GPA	**COSTS AND FINANCIAL INFORMATION**	70% had job offers within 6 months
17% had SAT verbal scores over 600	$10,862 tuition and fees (1999–2000)	17 organizations recruited on campus
	$4412 room and board	

MOUNT VERNON NAZARENE COLLEGE

Mount Vernon, Ohio

http://www.mvnc.edu/

At Mount Vernon Nazarene College you'll encounter a high-quality, higher education learning environment within a Christian worldview. Ours is a history of change and innovation; over the past three decades, we've become a leader in Christian higher education. Here you'll access more than 60 high-quality academic programs covering the full range of today's career fields, in-depth preprofessional preparation, and friends you will cherish the rest of your life—everything you need to build a successful future serving God and humanity in the 21st century!

Academics
MVNC awards associate, bachelor's, and master's **degrees**. Challenging opportunities include advanced placement, freshman honors college, an honors program, double majors, independent study, and a senior project. **Special programs** include internships, summer session for credit, off-campus study, and study-abroad. The most frequently chosen **baccalaureate** fields are business/marketing, education, and biological/life sciences. A complete listing of majors at MVNC appears in the Majors Index beginning on page 147. The **faculty** at MVNC has 69 full-time members. The student-faculty ratio is 17:1.

Students of MVNC
The student body totals 1,916, of whom 1,843 are undergraduates. 57.8% are women and 42.2% are men. Students come from 26 states and territories. 83% are from Ohio. 0.1% are international students. 75% returned for their sophomore year.

Facilities and Resources
The **library** has 90,045 books and 560 subscriptions.

Career Services
The career planning and placement office has 1 full-time, 1 part-time staff members. Services include job fairs, resume preparation, resume referral, career/interest testing, career counseling, careers library, job bank, and job interviews.

Campus Life
There are 36 active organizations on campus, including a drama/theater group, newspaper, radio station, and choral group. No national or local **fraternities** or **sororities**. MVNC is a member of the NAIA and NCCAA. **Intercollegiate sports** (some offering scholarships) include baseball (m), basketball, golf (m), soccer, softball (w), volleyball (w).

Campus Safety
Student safety services include late-night transport/escort service, 24-hour emergency telephone alarm devices, 24-hour patrols by trained security personnel, and electronically operated dormitory entrances.

Applying
MVNC requires an essay, ACT, a high school transcript, 2 recommendations, and a minimum high school GPA of 2.5. It recommends an interview. Application deadline: 5/30; 3/13 priority date for financial aid. Early and deferred admission are possible. **Contact:** 800 Martinsburg Road, Mount Vernon, OH 43050-9500, 740-397-9000 or toll-free 800-782-2435; e-mail admissions@mvnc.edu.

GETTING IN LAST YEAR
708 applied
89% were accepted
396 enrolled (63%)
18% from top tenth of their h.s. class
3.19 average high school GPA
41% had ACT scores over 24

7% had ACT scores over 30
1 National Merit Scholar
13 valedictorians

COSTS AND FINANCIAL INFORMATION
$11,926 tuition and fees (2000–2001)
$4203 room and board
85% average percent of need met

$5823 average financial aid amount received per undergraduate (1999–2000 estimated)

AFTER GRADUATION
Graduates pursuing further study: 5% arts and sciences, 4% business, 4% theology
73% had job offers within 6 months
28 organizations recruited on campus

NORTH GREENVILLE COLLEGE

Tigerville, South Carolina   *http://www.ngc.edu/*

Affiliated with, and committed to, the South Carolina Baptist Convention, North Greenville College is a small, coeducational liberal arts institution that provides opportunities for higher education in a Christian atmosphere. The college strives to prepare students to become better, contributing members of society by educating the whole person through an integration of academic discipline, a Christian lifestyle, and an enriched cultural experience while offering students the best opportunities for spiritual growth, academic training, and Christian service. Christ must be the center of the campus for the purpose of Christian education and Christian character-building.

Academics

NGC awards associate and bachelor's **degrees**. Challenging opportunities include advanced placement, accelerated degree programs, student-designed majors, freshman honors college, an honors program, double majors, independent study, and a senior project. **Special programs** include internships, summer session for credit, and Army ROTC. The most frequently chosen **baccalaureate** fields are philosophy, education, and business/marketing. A complete listing of majors at NGC appears in the Majors Index beginning on page 147. The **faculty** at NGC has 56 full-time members.

Students of NGC

The student body is made up of 1,220 undergraduates. 45.4% are women and 54.6% are men. Students come from 19 states and territories and 14 other countries. 89% are from South Carolina. 1.4% are international students. 65% returned for their sophomore year.

Facilities and Resources

The **library** has 46,870 books and 500 subscriptions.

Career Services

The career planning and placement office has 1 full-time staff member. Services include job fairs, resume preparation, interview workshops, resume referral, career counseling, careers library, job bank, and job interviews.

Campus Life

Active organizations on campus include a drama/theater group, newspaper, radio station, and choral group. No national or local **fraternities** or **sororities**. NGC is a member of the NAIA. **Intercollegiate sports** (some offering scholarships) include baseball (m), basketball, cross-country running, football (m), golf (m), soccer, softball (w), tennis, volleyball (w).

Campus Safety

Student safety services include 24-hour emergency telephone alarm devices, 24-hour patrols by trained security personnel, and electronically operated dormitory entrances.

Applying

NGC requires SAT I or ACT and a high school transcript, and in some cases CPT. It recommends CPT and a minimum high school GPA of 2.0. Application deadline: 8/24; 6/30 priority date for financial aid. Early and deferred admission are possible. **Contact:** Mr. Buddy Freeman, Executive Director of Admissions, PO Box 1892, Tigerville, SC 29688-1892, 864-977-7052 or toll-free 800-468-6642; fax 864-977-7177; e-mail bfreeman@ngc.edu.

GETTING IN LAST YEAR
963 applied
86% were accepted
348 enrolled (42%)
11% had SAT verbal scores over 600
11% had SAT math scores over 600
12% had ACT scores over 24

1% had SAT verbal scores over 700
1% had SAT math scores over 700
1% had ACT scores over 30

COSTS AND FINANCIAL INFORMATION
$7650 tuition and fees (1999–2000)
$4500 room and board
90% average percent of need met

$8100 average financial aid amount received per undergraduate (1999–2000)

AFTER GRADUATION
16% pursued further study
75% had job offers within 6 months
8 organizations recruited on campus

NORTH PARK UNIVERSITY

Chicago, Illinois   *http://www.northpark.edu/*

Founded in 1891 by the Evangelical Covenant Church, North Park is Chicago's inclusively Christian residential liberal arts university. Located in a park-like setting, North Park enrolls over 1,400 undergraduate and 400 graduate students from across the country (40 states) and around the world (22 countries). North Park, well-known for its small classes and personal attention from faculty, has repeatedly been named one of "America's Best Colleges" by *U.S. News & World Report.* The University provides over 40 majors, 20 urban ministry programs, 300 internship opportunities, and on-campus African American, Korean, Latino, Middle Eastern, and Scandinavian cultural study centers.

Academics

North Park awards bachelor's, master's, doctoral, and first-professional **degrees**. Challenging opportunities include advanced placement, accelerated degree programs, student-designed majors, freshman honors college, an honors program, and a senior project. **Special programs** include internships, summer session for credit, off-campus study, and study-abroad. The most frequently chosen **baccalaureate** fields are health professions and related sciences, social sciences and history, and business/marketing. A complete listing of majors at North Park appears in the Majors Index beginning on page 147. The **faculty** at North Park has 79 full-time members, 80% with terminal degrees. The student-faculty ratio is 16:1.

Students of North Park

The student body totals 2,154, of whom 1,619 are undergraduates. 61.4% are women and 38.6% are men. Students come from 36 states and territories and 29 other countries. 68% are from Illinois. 5.9% are international students. 70% returned for their sophomore year.

Facilities and Resources

The 5 **libraries** have 260,685 books and 1,178 subscriptions.

Career Services

The career planning and placement office has 1 full-time, 1 part-time staff members. Services include job fairs, resume preparation, resume referral, career counseling, careers library, job bank, and job interviews.

Campus Life

There are 10 active organizations on campus, including a drama/theater group, newspaper, and choral group. No national or local **fraternities** or **sororities**. North Park is a member of the NCAA (Division III). **Intercollegiate sports** include baseball (m), basketball, cross-country running, football (m), golf (m), soccer, softball (w), tennis (w), track and field, volleyball.

Campus Safety

Student safety services include late-night transport/escort service, 24-hour emergency telephone alarm devices, and 24-hour patrols by trained security personnel.

Applying

North Park requires an essay, SAT I or ACT, a high school transcript, 1 recommendation, and a minimum high school GPA of 2.0, and in some cases an interview. It recommends a minimum high school GPA of 3.0. Application deadline: rolling admissions; 5/1 priority date for financial aid. Early admission is possible. **Contact:** Office of Admissions, 3225 West Foster Avenue, Chicago, IL 60625-4895, 773-244-5500 or toll-free 800-888-NPC8; fax 773-583-0858; e-mail afao@northpark.edu.

GETTING IN LAST YEAR
1,049 applied
78% were accepted
487 enrolled (60%)
20% from top tenth of their h.s. class
38% had SAT verbal scores over 600
37% had SAT math scores over 600
36% had ACT scores over 24

6% had SAT verbal scores over 700
6% had SAT math scores over 700
3% had ACT scores over 30
5 National Merit Scholars

COSTS AND FINANCIAL INFORMATION
$16,180 tuition and fees (1999–2000)
$5570 room and board

AFTER GRADUATION
47% graduated in 4 years
11% graduated in 5 years
1% graduated in 6 years
20% pursued further study (10% arts and sciences, 4% theology, 3% medicine)
60% had job offers within 6 months
30 organizations recruited on campus

NORTHWEST CHRISTIAN COLLEGE

Eugene, Oregon   *http://www.nwcc.edu/*

For over 100 years, Northwest Christian College has provided a quality education in a vibrant and supportive academic community. Excellent programs of study linked to career preparation open doors in business, communications, counseling, ministry, teaching, and technology. Because the College is deliberately small, students receive personal attention every step of the way. Superb professors take a personal interest, not just in the classroom, but in every day settings where informal learning takes place. Students can expect an educational experience that develops their strengths, deepens their faith, and builds their professional potential.

Academics

NCC awards associate, bachelor's, and master's **degrees**. Challenging opportunities include advanced placement, accelerated degree programs, student-designed majors, double majors, independent study, and a senior project. **Special programs** include cooperative education, internships, off-campus study, study-abroad, and Army ROTC. The most frequently chosen **baccalaureate** fields are business/marketing, education, and philosophy. A complete listing of majors at NCC appears in the Majors Index beginning on page 147. The **faculty** at NCC has 19 full-time members, 63% with terminal degrees. The student-faculty ratio is 13:1.

Students of NCC

The student body totals 431, of whom 418 are undergraduates. 62% are women and 38% are men. Students come from 8 states and territories. 92% are from Oregon. 0.2% are international students. 65% returned for their sophomore year.

Facilities and Resources

The **library** has 60,247 books and 261 subscriptions.

Career Services

The career planning and placement office has 1 full-time, 1 part-time staff members. Services include job fairs, resume preparation, career counseling, careers library, and job bank.

Campus Life

There are 15 active organizations on campus, including a drama/theater group, newspaper, and choral group. No national or local **fraternities** or **sororities**. NCC is a member of the NSCAA and NCCAA. **Intercollegiate sports** (some offering scholarships) include basketball (m), softball (w).

Campus Safety

Student safety services include late-night patrols by trained security personnel, late-night transport/escort service, 24-hour emergency telephone alarm devices, and electronically operated dormitory entrances.

Applying

NCC requires an essay, SAT I or ACT, a high school transcript, 2 recommendations, and a minimum high school GPA of 2.5, and in some cases SAT II Subject Tests. It recommends an interview. Application deadline: rolling admissions; 3/1 priority date for financial aid. Deferred admission is possible. **Contact:** Mr. Bill Stenberg, Director of Admissions, 828 East 11th Avenue, Eugene, OR 97401-3727, 541-684-7209 or toll-free 877-463-6622; fax 541-684-7317; e-mail admissions@nwcc.edu.

GETTING IN LAST YEAR		COSTS AND FINANCIAL INFORMATION
156 applied	18% had SAT verbal scores over 600	$13,905 tuition and fees (2000–2001)
100% were accepted	6% had SAT math scores over 600	$5157 room and board
69 enrolled (44%)	34% had ACT scores over 24	
8% from top tenth of their h.s. class	6% had SAT verbal scores over 700	**AFTER GRADUATION**
3.17 average high school GPA	6% had ACT scores over 30	10% pursued further study
	3 class presidents	20 organizations recruited on campus

NORTHWEST COLLEGE

Kirkland, Washington

http://www.nwcollege.edu/

Since 1934, Northwest College has successfully prepared students for quality service and leadership. Situated on 65 beautiful acres, the campus overlooks the splendor of Lake Washington and is located just 10 miles east of Seattle. Approximately 1,000 students have the opportunity to select from nearly 45 academic programs, including education, behavioral sciences, church ministries, nursing, religion and philosophy, music, business management and administration, psychology, and teaching English as a second language. Athletics include basketball, volleyball, soccer, and cross-country, along with track and field. Student ministries provide a range of options including music and drama, as well as opportunities to serve children, prisoners, and the inner city populations. Northwest College offers you an opportunity to "Carry the Call." The environment is distinctly Christian and intensely academic.

Academics
NC awards associate and bachelor's **degrees**. Challenging opportunities include advanced placement, accelerated degree programs, student-designed majors, double majors, independent study, and a senior project. **Special programs** include internships, summer session for credit, and study-abroad. The most frequently chosen **baccalaureate** fields are business/marketing, philosophy, and education. A complete listing of majors at NC appears in the Majors Index beginning on page 147. The **faculty** at NC has 45 full-time members, 49% with terminal degrees. The student-faculty ratio is 17:1.

Students of NC
The student body is made up of 972 undergraduates. 55.7% are women and 44.3% are men. Students come from 26 states and territories and 15 other countries. 76% are from Washington. 3.1% are international students. 65% returned for their sophomore year.

Facilities and Resources
The **library** has 61,334 books and 1,007 subscriptions.

Career Services
The career planning and placement office has 1 full-time staff member. Services include job fairs, resume preparation, interview workshops, resume referral, career/interest testing, career counseling, careers library, job bank, and job interviews.

Campus Life
There are 10 active organizations on campus, including a drama/theater group, newspaper, radio station, and choral group. No national or local **fraternities** or **sororities**. NC is a member of the NAIA and NCCAA. **Intercollegiate sports** (some offering scholarships) include basketball, cross-country running, soccer (m), track and field, volleyball (w).

Campus Safety
Student safety services include late-night transport/escort service, 24-hour emergency telephone alarm devices, 24-hour patrols by trained security personnel, and electronically operated dormitory entrances.

Applying
NC requires an essay, SAT I or ACT, a high school transcript, 2 recommendations, and a minimum high school GPA of 2.3, and in some cases an interview. Application deadline: 8/1; 3/1 priority date for financial aid. Early and deferred admission are possible. **Contact:** Mr. Myles Corrigan, Director of Enrollment Services, PO Box 579, Kirkland, WA 98083-0579, 425-889-5209 or toll-free 800-669-3781; fax 425-425-0148; e-mail admissions@ncag.edu.

GETTING IN LAST YEAR
199 applied
99% were accepted
210 enrolled (106%)
3.1 average high school GPA
20% had SAT verbal scores over 600
5% had SAT math scores over 600
23% had ACT scores over 24

1% had SAT verbal scores over 700
1% had ACT scores over 30
1 National Merit Scholar
10 class presidents

COSTS AND FINANCIAL INFORMATION
$9870 tuition and fees (1999–2000)
$5030 room and board
79% average percent of need met

$9996 average financial aid amount received per undergraduate (1999–2000 estimated)

AFTER GRADUATION
39% graduated in 4 years
6% graduated in 5 years
2% graduated in 6 years

NORTHWESTERN COLLEGE

Orange City, Iowa   *http://www.nwciowa.edu/*

During your college years, you'll change from a student into someone who's ready for a career—and for life. At Northwestern, you'll not only get a great education and be prepared for a great career, but you'll also develop lifelong friends and strengthen your faith. All this takes place on a campus on which nearly all the academic facilities have been built or renovated in the last 15 years, along with an award-winning chapel, intercollegiate athletic center, and cafeteria. A fiber-optic computer network connects every campus building, allowing you to explore the Internet from the comfort of your residence hall room—one of the reasons we've been named among America's "most wired colleges." You're in training for your whole life. Get a whole education at Northwestern.

Academics
Northwestern awards associate and bachelor's **degrees**. Challenging opportunities include advanced placement, accelerated degree programs, student-designed majors, freshman honors college, an honors program, double majors, independent study, and a senior project. **Special programs** include cooperative education, internships, summer session for credit, off-campus study, and study-abroad. The most frequently chosen **baccalaureate** fields are education, business/marketing, and biological/life sciences. A complete listing of majors at Northwestern appears in the Majors Index beginning on page 147. The **faculty** at Northwestern has 65 full-time members, 68% with terminal degrees. The student-faculty ratio is 16:1.

Students of Northwestern
The student body is made up of 1,219 undergraduates. 61% are women and 39% are men. Students come from 30 states and territories and 16 other countries. 64% are from Iowa. 2.8% are international students. 75% returned for their sophomore year.

Facilities and Resources
The 2 **libraries** have 107,567 books and 563 subscriptions.

Career Services
The career planning and placement office has 1 full-time, 1 part-time staff members. Services include job fairs, resume preparation, interview workshops, resume referral, career/interest testing, career counseling, careers library, job bank, and job interviews.

Campus Life
There are 28 active organizations on campus, including a drama/theater group, newspaper, radio station, and choral group. No national or local **fraternities** or **sororities**. Northwestern is a member of the NAIA. **Intercollegiate sports** (some offering scholarships) include baseball (m), basketball, cross-country running, football (m), golf, soccer, softball (w), tennis, track and field, volleyball (w), wrestling (m).

Campus Safety
Student safety services include 24-hour emergency telephone alarm devices and electronically operated dormitory entrances.

Applying
Northwestern requires an essay, SAT I or ACT, a high school transcript, 1 recommendation, and a minimum high school GPA of 2.0. It recommends an interview and a minimum high school GPA of 2.5. Application deadline: rolling admissions; 4/1 priority date for financial aid. Deferred admission is possible. **Contact:** Mr. Ronald K. DeJong, Director of Admissions, 101 College Lane, Orange City, IA 51041-1996, 712-737-7130 or toll-free 800-747-4757; fax 712-737-7164; e-mail markb@nwciowa.edu.

GETTING IN LAST YEAR
1,080 applied
92% were accepted
366 enrolled (37%)
28% from top tenth of their h.s. class
3.2 average high school GPA
17% had SAT verbal scores over 600
40% had SAT math scores over 600
56% had ACT scores over 24

6% had SAT verbal scores over 700
13% had SAT math scores over 700
8% had ACT scores over 30
2 National Merit Scholars
32 valedictorians

COSTS AND FINANCIAL INFORMATION
$12,270 tuition and fees (1999–2000)
$3500 room and board
92% average percent of need met

$13,471 average financial aid amount received per undergraduate (1999–2000)

AFTER GRADUATION
45% graduated in 4 years
10% graduated in 5 years
9% pursued further study (3% theology, 2% arts and sciences, 2% medicine)
90% had job offers within 6 months
30 organizations recruited on campus

NORTHWESTERN COLLEGE

St. Paul, Minnesota

http://www.nwc.edu/

Northwestern is an accredited, nondenominational Christian college with a unique curriculum. A student's choice of one of 38 academic majors is complemented by a built-in second major in Bible. This encourages students to see the influence of spiritual truth as it relates to intellectual and professional pursuits. The warm and friendly atmosphere, challenging academic programs, and superb facilities offer students an excellent environment in which to develop academically, socially, physically, and spiritually.

Academics

Northwestern awards associate and bachelor's **degrees**. Challenging opportunities include advanced placement, double majors, independent study, and a senior project. **Special programs** include internships, summer session for credit, off-campus study, study-abroad, and Army and Air Force ROTC. The most frequently chosen **baccalaureate** fields are business/marketing, education, and psychology. A complete listing of majors at Northwestern appears in the Majors Index beginning on page 147. The **faculty** at Northwestern has 65 full-time members, 71% with terminal degrees. The student-faculty ratio is 14:1.

Students of Northwestern

The student body is made up of 1,744 undergraduates. 61.1% are women and 38.9% are men. Students come from 35 states and territories and 22 other countries. 64% are from Minnesota. 1% are international students. 77% returned for their sophomore year.

Facilities and Resources

The **library** has 74,857 books and 1,695 subscriptions.

Career Services

The career planning and placement office has 2 full-time staff members. Services include job fairs, resume preparation, interview workshops, resume referral, career/interest testing, career counseling, careers library, job bank, and job interviews.

Campus Life

There are 25 active organizations on campus, including a drama/theater group, newspaper, radio station, and choral group. No national or local **fraternities** or **sororities**. Northwestern is a member of the NAIA and NCCAA. **Intercollegiate sports** include baseball (m), basketball, cross-country running, football (m), golf (m), soccer, softball (w), tennis, track and field, volleyball (w).

Campus Safety

Student safety services include late-night transport/escort service, 24-hour patrols by trained security personnel, and electronically operated dormitory entrances.

Applying

Northwestern requires an essay, SAT I or ACT, a high school transcript, 2 recommendations, lifestyle agreement, statement of Christian faith, and a minimum high school GPA of 2.0, and in some cases an interview. It recommends an interview and a minimum high school GPA of 3.0. Application deadline: 8/15; 3/1 priority date for financial aid. Early and deferred admission are possible. **Contact:** Mr. Kenneth K. Faffler, Director of Recruitment, 3003 Snelling Avenue North, St. Paul, MN 55113-1598, 651-631-5209 or toll-free 800-827-6827; fax 651-631-5680.

GETTING IN LAST YEAR
1,181 applied
71% were accepted
404 enrolled (48%)
25% from top tenth of their h.s. class
3.47 average high school GPA
48% had SAT verbal scores over 600
45% had SAT math scores over 600

50% had ACT scores over 24
18% had SAT verbal scores over 700
5% had SAT math scores over 700
6% had ACT scores over 30
19 valedictorians

COSTS AND FINANCIAL INFORMATION
$14,982 tuition and fees (2000–2001)
$4448 room and board

AFTER GRADUATION
39% graduated in 4 years
9% graduated in 5 years
4% graduated in 6 years
6% pursued further study (2% arts and sciences, 1% education, 1% law)
77% had job offers within 6 months
147 organizations recruited on campus

NORTHWEST NAZARENE UNIVERSITY

Nampa, Idaho

http://www.nnu.edu/

Northwest Nazarene University emphasizes development of the whole person. Spiritual, physical, intellectual, and emotional well-being are treated as important aspects of the educational process. The success of this integrative process is reflected by *U.S. News & World Report* consistently placing NNU among the top liberal arts colleges in the western United States. Numerous cocurricular programs involve students in community service as well as assistance programs in foreign countries. The college has an honors program, an outstanding undergraduate research program open to all departments, and internship programs in many departments. NNU athletics teams recently moved from NAIA to NCAA Division II.

Academics

Northwest Nazarene University awards bachelor's and master's **degrees**. Challenging opportunities include advanced placement, accelerated degree programs, student-designed majors, freshman honors college, an honors program, independent study, and a senior project. **Special programs** include cooperative education, internships, summer session for credit, off-campus study, study-abroad, and Army ROTC. The most frequently chosen **baccalaureate** fields are education, philosophy, and business/marketing. A complete listing of majors at Northwest Nazarene University appears in the Majors Index beginning on page 147. The **faculty** at Northwest Nazarene University has 83 full-time members, 77% with terminal degrees. The student-faculty ratio is 14:1.

Students of Northwest Nazarene University

The student body totals 1,843, of whom 1,114 are undergraduates. 57.3% are women and 42.7% are men. Students come from 22 states and territories. 32% are from Idaho. 0.5% are international students. 72% returned for their sophomore year.

Facilities and Resources

The **library** has 100,966 books and 821 subscriptions.

Career Services

Services include job fairs, resume preparation, interview workshops, resume referral, career/interest testing, career counseling, careers library, job bank, and job interviews.

Campus Life

Active organizations on campus include a drama/theater group, newspaper, and choral group. No national or local **fraternities** or **sororities**. Northwest Nazarene University is a member of the NAIA. **Intercollegiate sports** (some offering scholarships) include baseball (m), basketball, cross-country running, golf (m), soccer, tennis, track and field, volleyball.

Campus Safety

Student safety services include residence hall check-in system, late-night transport/escort service, 24-hour patrols by trained security personnel, student patrols, and electronically operated dormitory entrances.

Applying

Northwest Nazarene University requires a high school transcript, 2 recommendations, and a minimum high school GPA of 2.5, and in some cases ACT and an interview. It recommends ACT. Application deadline: 9/1; 3/1 priority date for financial aid. Early and deferred admission are possible. **Contact:** Mr. Jim Butkus, Director of Admissions, 623 Holly Street, Nampa, ID 83686, 208-467-8648 or toll-free 877-NNU-4YOU; fax 208-467-8645; e-mail admissions@nnu.edu.

GETTING IN LAST YEAR
731 applied
71% were accepted
310 enrolled (60%)
27% from top tenth of their h.s. class
3.33 average high school GPA
38% had ACT scores over 24

4% had ACT scores over 30
4 National Merit Scholars
13 valedictorians

COSTS AND FINANCIAL INFORMATION
$13,500 tuition and fees (2000–2001)
$4020 room and board
69% average percent of need met

$9759 average financial aid amount received
per undergraduate (1999–2000)

AFTER GRADUATION
Graduates pursuing further study: 6% medicine, 5% law, 3% business

---

NYACK COLLEGE
Nyack, New York

http://www.nyackcollege.edu/

Beautifully situated in a suburban community on the Hudson River, Nyack College partakes of the rich cultural and ethnic diversity of suburban New York. Founded in 1882 for missionaries and ministers, Nyack has a long tradition of providing education that blends scholarship and service. Though today's curriculum is more diverse, ranging from business to missiology to communications, a sound education and a thorough grounding in the faith still characterize the Nyack graduate.

Academics
Nyack awards associate, bachelor's, master's, and first-professional **degrees** and post-bachelor's certificates. Challenging opportunities include advanced placement, an honors program, double majors, independent study, and a senior project. **Special programs** include internships, summer session for credit, off-campus study, and study-abroad. The most frequently chosen **baccalaureate** fields are business/marketing, philosophy, and education. A complete listing of majors at Nyack appears in the Majors Index beginning on page 147.

Students of Nyack
The student body totals 1,814, of whom 1,424 are undergraduates. 56.5% are women and 43.5% are men. Students come from 41 states and territories and 38 other countries. 57% are from New York. 6.4% are international students. 64% returned for their sophomore year.

Facilities and Resources
The 2 **libraries** have 81,029 books and 874 subscriptions.

Career Services
The career planning and placement office has 1 full-time, 1 part-time staff members. Services include job fairs, resume preparation, interview workshops, career/interest testing, career counseling, careers library, job bank, and job interviews.

Campus Life
There are 20 active organizations on campus, including a drama/theater group, newspaper, radio station, and choral group. No national or local **fraternities** or **sororities**. Nyack is a member of the NAIA and NCCAA. **Intercollegiate sports** (some offering scholarships) include baseball (m), basketball, cross-country running, soccer, softball (w), volleyball.

Campus Safety
Student safety services include late-night transport/escort service, 24-hour emergency telephone alarm devices, 24-hour patrols by trained security personnel, and student patrols.

Applying
Nyack requires an essay, SAT I or ACT, a high school transcript, 3 recommendations, and a minimum high school GPA of 2.0, and in some cases an interview. Application deadline: 9/1; 3/1 priority date for financial aid. Early and deferred admission are possible. **Contact:** Miguel A. Sanchez, Director of Admissions, 1 South Boulevard, Nyack, NY 10960-3698, 914-358-1710 ext. 350 or toll-free 800-33-NYACK; fax 914-358-3047; e-mail enroll@nyack.edu.

GETTING IN LAST YEAR
330 enrolled
10% from top tenth of their h.s. class
2.87 average high school GPA
20% had SAT verbal scores over 600
12% had SAT math scores over 600

29% had ACT scores over 24
1% had SAT verbal scores over 700
1% had SAT math scores over 700
2% had ACT scores over 30

COSTS AND FINANCIAL INFORMATION
$12,740 tuition and fees (2000–2001)

$5800 room and board
71% average percent of need met
$13,073 average financial aid amount
received per undergraduate (1999–2000)

OKLAHOMA BAPTIST UNIVERSITY

Shawnee, Oklahoma   *http://www.okbu.edu/*

Unique academic programs and an emphasis on learning through doing are hallmarks of Oklahoma Baptist University. Growing from the vision of Baptists of the Oklahoma Territory, OBU is a leader in ministry training, premedicine, teacher education, nursing, international business, music, and many other fields. OBU's innovative Unified Studies program provides a carefully constructed common core that integrates what students learn in various academic disciplines, providing a well-rounded liberal arts and sciences foundation for living in a rapidly changing world. Students excel in national exams and competitions and in their commitment to international service. OBU is a leader among Christian colleges and universities in the number of mission volunteers. OBU is nationally competitive in athletics with 14 varsity sports.

Academics
OBU awards bachelor's and master's **degrees**. Challenging opportunities include advanced placement, student-designed majors, an honors program, double majors, independent study, and a senior project. **Special programs** include cooperative education, internships, summer session for credit, off-campus study, study-abroad, and Air Force ROTC. A complete listing of majors at OBU appears in the Majors Index beginning on page 147. The **faculty** at OBU has 110 full-time members, 72% with terminal degrees. The student-faculty ratio is 14:1.

Students of OBU
The student body totals 2,123, of whom 2,098 are undergraduates. 52.6% are women and 47.4% are men. Students come from 41 states and territories and 23 other countries. 61% are from Oklahoma. 1.3% are international students. 74% returned for their sophomore year.

Facilities and Resources
The **library** has 290,000 books and 2,000 subscriptions.

Career Services
The career planning and placement office has 2 full-time staff members. Services include job fairs, resume preparation, resume referral, career counseling, careers library, job bank, and job interviews.

Campus Life
There are 50 active organizations on campus, including a drama/theater group, newspaper, television station, and choral group. 10% of eligible men and 10% of eligible women are members of local **fraternities** and local **sororities**. OBU is a member of the NAIA. **Intercollegiate sports** (some offering scholarships) include baseball (m), basketball, cross-country running, golf, softball (w), tennis, track and field.

Campus Safety
Student safety services include late-night transport/escort service, 24-hour emergency telephone alarm devices, 24-hour patrols by trained security personnel, and electronically operated dormitory entrances.

Applying
OBU requires SAT I or ACT, a high school transcript, and a minimum high school GPA of 2.5, and in some cases an essay, an interview, and recommendations. Application deadline: 8/1; 3/1 priority date for financial aid. Early and deferred admission are possible. **Contact:** Mr. Michael Cappo, Dean of Admissions, Box 61174, Shawnee, OK 74804, 405-878-2033 or toll-free 800-654-3285; fax 405-878-2046; e-mail admissions@mail.okbu.edu.

GETTING IN LAST YEAR
854 applied
89% were accepted
36% from top tenth of their h.s. class
3.65 average high school GPA
40% had SAT verbal scores over 600
34% had SAT math scores over 600
52% had ACT scores over 24

9% had SAT verbal scores over 700
4% had SAT math scores over 700
13% had ACT scores over 30
5 National Merit Scholars
42 valedictorians

COSTS AND FINANCIAL INFORMATION
$9440 tuition and fees (2000–2001)
$3417 room and board

AFTER GRADUATION
35% graduated in 4 years
14% graduated in 5 years
4% graduated in 6 years
Graduates pursuing further study: 16% theology, 12% arts and sciences, 5% business
45 organizations recruited on campus

OKLAHOMA CHRISTIAN UNIVERSITY OF SCIENCE AND ARTS

Oklahoma City, Oklahoma

http://www.oc.edu/

Oklahoma Christian University is nationally recognized for its academic programs and for its mission to create students who have purposeful lives of leadership and service. *U.S. News & World Report* ranked Oklahoma Christian in the top ten in our region for its academic quality and the John Templeton Foundation recognized the university as a character-building college. Oklahoma Christian has degree programs in more than 70 fields of study in its colleges of biblical studies, business, education, liberal arts, and science and engineering. The university has a master's in ministry program and a master's in business administration. Demonstrating its commitment to equipping students with the latest technology, the university launched "myOC" in the fall of 2000. It is an extensive e-campus project that is unduplicated on any other college campus. MyOC helps students do everything from enroll in classes, check assignments, look up the cafeteria menu, or find out the latest news on campus and around the world. MyOC will also be provided to parents, future students, alumni, and others interested in the university. Located in Oklahoma City, most of Oklahoma Christian's 2,000 students live on campus and are involved in a variety of projects including athletics, social service clubs, student government, social service, theater, and academic clubs.

Academics

Oklahoma Christian awards bachelor's and master's **degrees**. Challenging opportunities include advanced placement, accelerated degree programs, an honors program, and a senior project. **Special programs** include internships, summer session for credit, off-campus study, study-abroad, and Army and Air Force ROTC. The most frequently chosen **baccalaureate** fields are communications/communication technologies, education, and engineering/engineering technologies. A complete listing of majors at Oklahoma Christian appears in the Majors Index beginning on page 147. The **faculty** at Oklahoma Christian has 84 full-time members, 67% with terminal degrees. The student-faculty ratio is 19:1.

Students of Oklahoma Christian

The student body totals 1,734, of whom 1,701 are undergraduates. 50% are women and 50% are men. Students come from 59 states and territories. 47% are from Oklahoma. 67% returned for their sophomore year.

Facilities and Resources

The **library** has 95,789 books and 415 subscriptions.

Career Services

The career planning and placement office has 1 full-time, 2 part-time staff members. Services include job fairs, resume preparation, resume referral, career counseling, careers library, job bank, and job interviews.

Campus Life

Active organizations on campus include a drama/theater group, newspaper, radio station, and choral group. No national or local **fraternities** or **sororities**. Oklahoma Christian is a member of the NAIA. **Intercollegiate sports** (some offering scholarships) include baseball (m), basketball, cross-country running, golf (m), soccer, softball (w), tennis, track and field.

Campus Safety

Student safety services include late-night transport/escort service, 24-hour emergency telephone alarm devices, and 24-hour patrols by trained security personnel.

Applying

Oklahoma Christian requires SAT I or ACT and a high school transcript. Application deadline: rolling admissions; 3/15 priority date for financial aid. Early and deferred admission are possible. **Contact:** Mr. Kyle Ray, Director of Admissions, Box 11000, Oklahoma City, OK 73136-1100, 405-425-5050 or toll-free 800-877-5010 (in-state); fax 405-425-5208; e-mail info@oc.edu.

GETTING IN LAST YEAR
1,097 applied
90% were accepted
18% had SAT verbal scores over 600
29% had SAT math scores over 600
50% had ACT scores over 24

5% had SAT verbal scores over 700
11% had SAT math scores over 700
9% had ACT scores over 30

COSTS AND FINANCIAL INFORMATION
$9590 tuition and fees (1999–2000)
$4100 room and board

83% average percent of need met
$8750 average financial aid amount received per undergraduate (1999–2000)

AFTER GRADUATION
82% had job offers within 6 months
75 organizations recruited on campus

OLIVET NAZARENE UNIVERSITY

Bourbonnais, Illinois   *http://www.olivet.edu/*

Olivet Nazarene University exists to provide the highest quality academic programs, a fully Christ-centered environment, and the most exciting and fulfilling campus life to students from around the country. Located one hour south of Chicago's Loop, the 168-acre campus offers a small-town setting with world-class access. The campus includes a 3,000-seat athletic center, WONU 89.7 (a top-ten Christian radio station nationally), a planetarium, fiber optic network, and more. Over 500 students participate in 20 intramural sports, while a similar number participate in countless music and theatre opportunities.

Academics

Olivet awards bachelor's and master's **degrees**. Challenging opportunities include advanced placement, double majors, independent study, and a senior project. **Special programs** include internships, summer session for credit, study-abroad, and Army ROTC. The most frequently chosen **baccalaureate** fields are health professions and related sciences, business/marketing, and biological/life sciences. A complete listing of majors at Olivet appears in the Majors Index beginning on page 147. The **faculty** at Olivet has 82 full-time members, 60% with terminal degrees. The student-faculty ratio is 18:1.

Students of Olivet

The student body totals 2,498, of whom 1,850 are undergraduates. 59.2% are women and 40.8% are men. Students come from 40 states and territories. 0.3% are international students. 72% returned for their sophomore year.

Facilities and Resources

The **library** has 140,000 books and 1,000 subscriptions.

Career Services

The career planning and placement office has 2 full-time, 1 part-time staff members. Services include job fairs, resume preparation, interview workshops, resume referral, career/interest testing, career counseling, careers library, job bank, and job interviews.

Campus Life

There are 30 active organizations on campus, including a drama/theater group, newspaper, radio station, and choral group. No national or local **fraternities** or **sororities**. Olivet is a member of the NAIA. **Intercollegiate sports** (some offering scholarships) include baseball (m), basketball, cross-country running, football (m), golf (m), soccer, softball (w), tennis, track and field, volleyball.

Campus Safety

Student safety services include late-night transport/escort service and 24-hour patrols by trained security personnel.

Applying

Olivet requires ACT, a high school transcript, 2 recommendations, and a minimum high school GPA of 2.0. It recommends an interview. Application deadline: rolling admissions; 3/1 priority date for financial aid. Deferred admission is possible. **Contact:** Mr. Brian Parker, Director of Admissions, One University Avenue, Bourbonnais, IL 60904-2271, 815-939-5203 or toll-free 800-648-1463; e-mail admissions@olivet.edu.

GETTING IN LAST YEAR
1,026 applied
92% were accepted
411 enrolled (43%)
25% from top tenth of their h.s. class
3.3 average high school GPA
35% had ACT scores over 24

7% had ACT scores over 30

COSTS AND FINANCIAL INFORMATION
$12,728 tuition and fees (2000–2001)
$4696 room and board
92% average percent of need met
$12,323 average financial aid amount
   received per undergraduate (1999–2000)

AFTER GRADUATION
33% graduated in 4 years
13% graduated in 5 years
2% graduated in 6 years
10% pursued further study
15 organizations recruited on campus

ORAL ROBERTS UNIVERSITY

Tulsa, Oklahoma   *http://www.oru.edu/*

Oral Roberts University is a unique concept in higher education—combining strong academics, physical discipline, and spiritual development. Established in 1965, ORU serves over 5,200 students from all 50 states, as well as 57 countries. More than 65 undergraduate majors, as well as 10 master's and 2 doctoral programs, all challenge students to reach for their God-intended potential as leaders in their fields and Christians who will boldly and uncompromisingly impact their world for Christ.

Academics
ORU awards bachelor's, master's, and doctoral **degrees**. Challenging opportunities include advanced placement, accelerated degree programs, student-designed majors, freshman honors college, an honors program, double majors, independent study, and a senior project. **Special programs** include internships, summer session for credit, off-campus study, and study-abroad. The most frequently chosen **baccalaureate** fields are business/marketing, education, and philosophy. A complete listing of majors at ORU appears in the Majors Index beginning on page 147. The **faculty** at ORU has 188 full-time members, 51% with terminal degrees. The student-faculty ratio is 17:1.

Students of ORU
The student body totals 3,552, of whom 3,064 are undergraduates. 58% are women and 42% are men. Students come from 52 states and territories and 41 other countries. 36% are from Oklahoma. 2.3% are international students. 77% returned for their sophomore year.

Facilities and Resources
The 2 **libraries** have 291,899 books.

Career Services
The career planning and placement office has 1 full-time, 2 part-time staff members. Services include job fairs, resume preparation, resume referral, career/interest testing, career counseling, careers library, job bank, and job interviews.

Campus Life
There are 37 active organizations on campus, including a drama/theater group, newspaper, radio station, and choral group. No national or local **fraternities** or **sororities**. ORU is a member of the NCAA (Division I). **Intercollegiate sports** (some offering scholarships) include baseball (m), basketball, cross-country running, golf, soccer, tennis, track and field, volleyball (w).

Campus Safety
Student safety services include late-night transport/escort service, 24-hour emergency telephone alarm devices, and 24-hour patrols by trained security personnel.

Applying
ORU requires an essay, SAT I or ACT, a high school transcript, 1 recommendation, proof of immunization, and a minimum high school GPA of 2.6, and in some cases an interview. Application deadline: rolling admissions; 3/15 priority date for financial aid. Early and deferred admission are possible. **Contact:** Mrs. LeAnne Langley, Director of Undergraduate Admissions, 7777 South Lewis Avenue, Tulsa, OK 74171-0001, 918-495-6518 or toll-free 800-678-8876; fax 918-495-6222; e-mail admissions@oru.edu.

GETTING IN LAST YEAR
1,248 applied
92% were accepted
780 enrolled (68%)
24% from top tenth of their h.s. class
3.41 average high school GPA
28% had SAT verbal scores over 600
25% had SAT math scores over 600
42% had ACT scores over 24

4% had SAT verbal scores over 700
3% had SAT math scores over 700
5% had ACT scores over 30
6 National Merit Scholars

COSTS AND FINANCIAL INFORMATION
$11,650 tuition and fees (2000–2001)
$5076 room and board
92% average percent of need met

$11,612 average financial aid amount received per undergraduate (1999–2000 estimated)

AFTER GRADUATION
33% graduated in 4 years
13% graduated in 5 years
4% graduated in 6 years
70 organizations recruited on campus

PALM BEACH ATLANTIC COLLEGE

West Palm Beach, Florida   *http://www.pbac.edu/*

Palm Beach Atlantic College offers a curriculum of studies and a program of student activities dedicated to the development of moral character, the enrichment of spiritual lives, and the perpetuation of growth in Christian ideals. PBA's modern campus is committed to 21st century technology. Every residence hall room is equipped with a new computer connected to PalmNET, a campus-wide fiber optic network that gives students access to e-mail, the Internet, World Wide Web, and numerous electronic databases. Academic and extracurricular opportunities range from internships and real-world projects at area businesses to mission efforts around the world to a variety of on- and off-campus ministry opportunities.

Academics
PBA awards associate, bachelor's, and master's **degrees**. Challenging opportunities include advanced placement, student-designed majors, freshman honors college, an honors program, double majors, independent study, and a senior project. **Special programs** include internships, summer session for credit, and study-abroad. The most frequently chosen **baccalaureate** fields are business/marketing, psychology, and education. A complete listing of majors at PBA appears in the Majors Index beginning on page 147. The **faculty** at PBA has 70 full-time members. The student-faculty ratio is 18:1.

Students of PBA
The student body totals 2,163, of whom 1,838 are undergraduates. 60% are women and 40% are men. Students come from 42 states and territories and 36 other countries. 76% are from Florida. 67% returned for their sophomore year.

Facilities and Resources
The **library** has 81,016 books and 2,144 subscriptions.

Career Services
The career planning and placement office has 1 full-time, 1 part-time staff members. Services include job fairs, resume preparation, resume referral, career/interest testing, career counseling, careers library, job bank, and job interviews.

Campus Life
Active organizations on campus include a drama/theater group, newspaper, and choral group. No national or local **fraternities** or **sororities**. PBA is a member of the NAIA. **Intercollegiate sports** (some offering scholarships) include baseball (m), basketball, cross-country running, golf, soccer, softball (w), tennis, volleyball (w).

Campus Safety
Student safety services include late-night transport/escort service, 24-hour emergency telephone alarm devices, 24-hour patrols by trained security personnel, and electronically operated dormitory entrances.

Applying
PBA requires an essay, SAT I or ACT, a high school transcript, 2 recommendations, and a minimum high school GPA of 2.0. It recommends an interview and a minimum high school GPA of 3.0. Application deadline: rolling admissions. Early and deferred admission are possible. **Contact:** Mr. Buck James, Dean of Enrollment Services, 901 South Flagler Dr, PO Box 24708, West Palm Beach, FL 33416-4708, 561-803-2100 or toll-free 800-238-3998; e-mail admit@pbac.edu.

GETTING IN LAST YEAR
1,490 applied
69% were accepted
389 enrolled (38%)

COSTS AND FINANCIAL INFORMATION
$11,120 tuition and fees (1999–2000)
$4470 room and board
85% average percent of need met

$10,152 average financial aid amount received per undergraduate (1999–2000)

AFTER GRADUATION
75 organizations recruited on campus

POINT LOMA NAZARENE UNIVERSITY

San Diego, California   http://www.ptloma.edu/

Let Point Loma Nazarene University (PLNU) open your mind to a second-to-none academic experience and your heart to a world of opportunities to nurture your Christian faith. Bordered on the blue horizon of the Pacific Ocean, the beauty of the 90-acre campus only underscores Point Loma's unique learning experience and vibrant Christian community. A Christian, liberal arts university, founded in 1902, Point Loma features a landscape that is rich in history and architecture furnished with the latest technology. Above all, PLNU is a university set within an environment of "Vital Christianity" which permeates everything we do. As University President, Dr. Bob Brower states, "We're very deliberate about things we do at Point Loma Nazarene University. We are committed to making a difference in the lives of our students, so that they are encouraged to live a life of service that demonstrates a true Christian ethic. We intend to have an impact on character and person." Point Loma Nazarene University—A Journey of the Mind and Soul.

Academics
PLNU awards bachelor's and master's **degrees** and post-bachelor's and post-master's certificates. Challenging opportunities include advanced placement, independent study, and a senior project. **Special programs** include internships, summer session for credit, off-campus study, study-abroad, and Army, Navy and Air Force ROTC. The most frequently chosen **baccalaureate** fields are education, business/marketing, and liberal arts/general studies. A complete listing of majors at PLNU appears in the Majors Index beginning on page 147. The **faculty** at PLNU has 141 full-time members, 64% with terminal degrees. The student-faculty ratio is 16:1.

Students of PLNU
The student body totals 2,711, of whom 2,350 are undergraduates. 60.8% are women and 39.2% are men. Students come from 34 states and territories and 21 other countries. 78% are from California. 1.1% are international students. 76% returned for their sophomore year.

Facilities and Resources
The **library** has 120,991 books.

Career Services
The career planning and placement office has 1 full-time staff member. Services include job fairs, resume preparation, interview workshops, resume referral, career/interest testing, career counseling, careers library, job bank, and job interviews.

Campus Life
There are 30 active organizations on campus, including a drama/theater group, newspaper, radio station, and choral group. 3% of eligible men and 5% of eligible women are members of national **sororities**, local **fraternities**, and local sororities. PLNU is a member of the NAIA. **Intercollegiate sports** (some offering scholarships) include baseball (m), basketball, cross-country running, golf (m), soccer (m), softball (w), tennis, track and field, volleyball (w).

Campus Safety
Student safety services include late-night transport/escort service, 24-hour patrols by trained security personnel, and student patrols.

Applying
PLNU requires an essay, SAT I or ACT, a high school transcript, 2 recommendations, and a minimum high school GPA of 2.8, and in some cases an interview. It recommends SAT I. Application deadline: 3/1; 3/15 priority date for financial aid. Deferred admission is possible. **Contact:** Mr. Scott Shoemaker, Director of Admissions, 3900 Lomaland Drive, San Diego, CA 92106-2899, 619-849-2225; fax 619-849-2579; e-mail discover@ptloma.edu.

GETTING IN LAST YEAR
1,681 applied
78% were accepted
554 enrolled (43%)
33% from top tenth of their h.s. class
3.65 average high school GPA
21% had SAT verbal scores over 600
24% had SAT math scores over 600
38% had ACT scores over 24
2% had SAT verbal scores over 700
4% had SAT math scores over 700
6% had ACT scores over 30
19 valedictorians

COSTS AND FINANCIAL INFORMATION
$13,626 tuition and fees (1999–2000)
$5480 room and board

76% average percent of need met
$11,493 average financial aid amount
   received per undergraduate (1998–99)

AFTER GRADUATION
28% graduated in 4 years
12% graduated in 5 years
20% graduated in 6 years
100 organizations recruited on campus

REDEEMER UNIVERSITY COLLEGE

Ancaster, Ontario, Canada

http://www.redeemer.on.ca/

Just an hour's drive from Buffalo and Toronto, Redeemer University College offers an undergraduate liberal arts and science university education that explores the relationship of faith to learning and serving. A unique housing arrangement that features furnished apartment and townhouse residences, a wide range of extracurricular and service opportunities, and the opportunity to work alongside skilled and committed faculty means that Redeemer students are part of a dynamic, Christian academic community. Work-study grants, scholarship programs based on community service as well as academic ability, and innovative financial aid programs make tuition surprisingly affordable, and the current exchange rate for the Canadian dollar can provide American applicants with an additional 30 to 40 percent savings.

Academics
Redeemer awards bachelor's **degrees** and post-bachelor's certificates. Challenging opportunities include an honors program, double majors, independent study, and a senior project. **Special programs** include cooperative education, internships, summer session for credit, off-campus study, and study-abroad. The most frequently chosen **baccalaureate** fields are education, social sciences and history, and English. A complete listing of majors at Redeemer appears in the Majors Index beginning on page 147. The **faculty** at Redeemer has 34 full-time members, 88% with terminal degrees. The student-faculty ratio is 15:1.

Students of Redeemer
The student body is made up of 605 undergraduates. 61.2% are women and 38.8% are men. Students come from 8 states and territories and 17 other countries. 82% returned for their sophomore year.

Facilities and Resources
The **library** has 93,500 books and 419 subscriptions.

Career Services
The career planning and placement office has 1 full-time staff member. Services include resume preparation, interview workshops, career/interest testing, career counseling, careers library, and job bank.

Campus Life
There are 28 active organizations on campus, including a drama/theater group, newspaper, and choral group. No national or local **fraternities** or **sororities**. **Intercollegiate sports** include basketball, golf, soccer, volleyball.

Campus Safety
Student safety services include late-night transport/escort service, 24-hour emergency telephone alarm devices, and student patrols.

Applying
Redeemer requires a high school transcript, 2 recommendations, and pastoral reference, and in some cases an essay, SAT I or ACT, and an interview. Application deadline: 8/1. Deferred admission is possible. **Contact:** Office of Admissions, 777 Garner Road East, Ancaster, ON L9K 1J4, Canada, 905-648-2131 ext. 4280 or toll-free 800-263-6467 ext. 4280 (in-state); fax 905-648-2134; e-mail adm@redeemer.on.ca.

GETTING IN LAST YEAR
424 applied
80% were accepted
207 enrolled (61%)
3.3 average high school GPA
64% had ACT scores over 24

COSTS AND FINANCIAL INFORMATION
$8963 tuition and fees (1999–2000)
$4360 room and board

AFTER GRADUATION
38% graduated in 4 years
14% graduated in 5 years

1% graduated in 6 years
19% pursued further study (11% education, 5% theology, 1% arts and sciences)
61% had job offers within 6 months
25 organizations recruited on campus

ROBERTS WESLEYAN COLLEGE

Rochester, New York   *http://www.roberts.edu/*

Roberts Wesleyan College, a preeminent Christian liberal arts college, is located just 8 miles from the center of Rochester, New York. The College's broadly-based curriculum of 40 majors and preprofessional programs includes 5 with national professional accreditation: art, music, nursing, social work, and business and accounting. Roberts Wesleyan is on the cutting-edge of technology and was recently named one of the "most wired colleges" in the U.S. by Yahoo!. We are also recognized on The John Templeton Foundation Honor Roll for Character-Building Colleges. Roberts Wesleyan is also proud to be the only institution in the Council for Christian Colleges & Universities offering a CSWE-accredited Master of Social Work program. At Roberts Wesleyan College, we deliver an educational experience that not only provides students with skills for achieving academic and professional success, but also prepares students for living a life of faith and character.

Academics

Roberts Wesleyan awards associate, bachelor's, and master's **degrees**. Challenging opportunities include advanced placement, freshman honors college, an honors program, double majors, independent study, and a senior project. **Special programs** include cooperative education, internships, summer session for credit, off-campus study, study-abroad, and Army and Air Force ROTC. The most frequently chosen **baccalaureate** fields are business/marketing, education, and health professions and related sciences. A complete listing of majors at Roberts Wesleyan appears in the Majors Index beginning on page 147. The **faculty** at Roberts Wesleyan has 76 full-time members. The student-faculty ratio is 14:1.

Students of Roberts Wesleyan

The student body totals 1,405, of whom 1,149 are undergraduates. 66.2% are women and 33.8% are men. 89% are from New York. 4.7% are international students. 78% returned for their sophomore year.

Facilities and Resources

The **library** has 106,970 books and 792 subscriptions.

Career Services

The career planning and placement office has 1 full-time staff member. Services include job fairs, resume preparation, interview workshops, career/interest testing, career counseling, careers library, job bank, and job interviews.

Campus Life

There are 25 active organizations on campus, including a drama/theater group, newspaper, radio station, and choral group. No national or local **fraternities** or **sororities**. Roberts Wesleyan is a member of the NCAA (Division II), NAIA, and NCCAA. **Intercollegiate sports** (some offering scholarships) include basketball, bowling (w), cross-country running, soccer, track and field, volleyball (w).

Campus Safety

Student safety services include 24-hour Resident Life staff on-call, late-night transport/escort service, 24-hour emergency telephone alarm devices, 24-hour patrols by trained security personnel, and electronically operated dormitory entrances.

Applying

Roberts Wesleyan requires an essay, SAT I and SAT II or ACT, a high school transcript, and 2 recommendations. It recommends an interview and a minimum high school GPA of 2.5. Application deadline: 2/1; 3/15 priority date for financial aid. Early and deferred admission are possible. **Contact:** Ms. Linda Kurtz, Director of Admissions, 2301 Westside Drive, Rochester, NY 14624-1997, 716-594-6400 or toll-free 800-777-4RWC; fax 716-594-6371.

GETTING IN LAST YEAR
522 applied
94% were accepted
272 enrolled (56%)
22% from top tenth of their h.s. class
3.1 average high school GPA
25% had SAT verbal scores over 600
19% had SAT math scores over 600

51% had ACT scores over 24
4% had SAT verbal scores over 700
2% had SAT math scores over 700
5% had ACT scores over 30
7 valedictorians

COSTS AND FINANCIAL INFORMATION
$13,614 tuition and fees (1999–2000)
$4614 room and board

87% average percent of need met
$12,503 average financial aid amount
  received per undergraduate (1998–99)

AFTER GRADUATION
19% pursued further study (6% business, 6% education, 4% theology)
80% had job offers within 6 months
90 organizations recruited on campus

SEATTLE PACIFIC UNIVERSITY

Seattle, Washington

http://www.spu.edu/

Seattle Pacific University

Located in the beautiful Pacific Northwest, Seattle Pacific University is a fully accredited, distinctly Christian university of arts, sciences, and professional studies. The University enjoys national accreditation in business, electrical engineering, music, nursing, and teacher education. Rated by *U.S. News & World Report* as one of America's best colleges, SPU has also been recognized by the Templeton Foundation as one of the nation's top character-building colleges. Just minutes from downtown Seattle, SPU is ideally located for internship, service-learning, and ministry opportunities. Overall, SPU graduates students of competence and character who go on to engage the culture and change the world within their chosen careers.

Academics

SPU awards bachelor's, master's, and doctoral **degrees** and post-master's certificates. Challenging opportunities include advanced placement, student-designed majors, an honors program, double majors, independent study, and a senior project. **Special programs** include cooperative education, internships, summer session for credit, off-campus study, study-abroad, and Army, Navy and Air Force ROTC. The most frequently chosen **baccalaureate** fields are business/marketing, psychology, and health professions and related sciences. A complete listing of majors at SPU appears in the Majors Index beginning on page 147. The **faculty** at SPU has 152 full-time members, 90% with terminal degrees. The student-faculty ratio is 16:1.

Students of SPU

The student body totals 3,427, of whom 2,636 are undergraduates. 65.7% are women and 34.3% are men. Students come from 39 states and territories and 34 other countries. 64% are from Washington. 3.1% are international students. 80% returned for their sophomore year.

Facilities and Resources

The **library** has 128,506 books and 1,356 subscriptions.

Career Services

The career planning and placement office has 4 full-time, 3 part-time staff members. Services include job fairs, resume preparation, career/interest testing, career counseling, careers library, job bank, and job interviews.

Campus Life

There are 50 active organizations on campus, including a drama/theater group, newspaper, and choral group. No national or local **fraternities** or **sororities**. SPU is a member of the NCAA (Division II). **Intercollegiate sports** (some offering scholarships) include basketball, crew, cross-country running, gymnastics (w), soccer, track and field, volleyball (w).

Campus Safety

Student safety services include closed circuit TV monitors, late-night transport/escort service, 24-hour emergency telephone alarm devices, 24-hour patrols by trained security personnel, and student patrols.

Applying

SPU requires an essay, SAT I or ACT, a high school transcript, 2 recommendations, and a minimum high school GPA of 2.5. It recommends SAT I. Application deadline: 6/1; 1/31 priority date for financial aid. Early admission is possible. **Contact:** Mr. Ken Cornell, Director of Admissions, 3307 Third Avenue West, Seattle, WA 98119-1997, 206-281-2021 or toll-free 800-366-3344; e-mail admissions@spu.edu.

GETTING IN LAST YEAR
1,442 applied
93% were accepted
571 enrolled (43%)
42% from top tenth of their h.s. class
3.58 average high school GPA
40% had SAT verbal scores over 600
35% had SAT math scores over 600
64% had ACT scores over 24
7% had SAT verbal scores over 700

4% had SAT math scores over 700
10% had ACT scores over 30
8 National Merit Scholars
41 valedictorians

COSTS AND FINANCIAL INFORMATION
$14,934 tuition and fees (1999–2000)
$5724 room and board
81% average percent of need met
$12,576 average financial aid amount received per undergraduate (1999–2000 estimated)

AFTER GRADUATION
26% graduated in 4 years
21% graduated in 5 years
5% graduated in 6 years
12% pursued further study
86% had job offers within 6 months
56 organizations recruited on campus

SIMPSON COLLEGE AND GRADUATE SCHOOL

Redding, California

http://www.simpsonca.edu/

Whatever else you many want in college, more than likely you want a place where you can feel comfortable. If you're serious about your Christian faith,that's exactly the way you'll feel at Simpson. One of the most affordable colleges in the nation, Simpson is priced less than many comparable Christian colleges; even when compared to public education, Simpson is competitive. At Simpson, the approach to spiritual formation is unique. The goal: To help you understand and develop what God is doing in your life. Every summer, you'll have opportunities to work with inner city missions or travel overseas to work in a wide range of settings, ministering to others and spreading the gospel. Our location offers numerous recreational benefits. In the midst of the Shasta Recreation Area with rivers, lakes, and caverns—surrounded by majestic, snow-capped mountains—this place is great for snow boarding, skiing, fishing, rock climbing, boating, water skiing, and more. But the best part of Simpson College is living in a community where people share common ideals and interests—where friendships are close and lasting. Simpson College—once you've experienced it, you may never be the same!

Academics

Simpson awards associate, bachelor's, and master's **degrees**. Challenging opportunities include advanced placement, accelerated degree programs, student-designed majors, double majors, independent study, and a senior project. **Special programs** include internships, summer session for credit, off-campus study, and study-abroad. The most frequently chosen **baccalaureate** fields are liberal arts/general studies, psychology, and business/marketing. A complete listing of majors at Simpson appears in the Majors Index beginning on page 147. The **faculty** at Simpson has 41 full-time members, 59% with terminal degrees. The student-faculty ratio is 17:1.

Students of Simpson

The student body totals 1,186, of whom 971 are undergraduates. 63.7% are women and 36.3% are men. Students come from 28 states and territories and 7 other countries. 75% are from California. 1.3% are international students. 65% returned for their sophomore year.

Facilities and Resources

The **library** has 66,103 books and 316 subscriptions.

Career Services

The career planning and placement office has 1 full-time staff member. Services include job fairs, resume preparation, interview workshops, career/interest testing, career counseling, and job bank.

Campus Life

There are 14 active organizations on campus, including a drama/theater group, newspaper, and choral group. 60% of eligible men and 50% of eligible women are members of men's and women's associations. Simpson is a member of the NAIA and NCCAA. **Intercollegiate sports** include baseball (m), basketball, soccer, softball (w), volleyball.

Campus Safety

Student safety services include late night security patrols by trained personnel, 24-hour emergency telephone alarm devices, student patrols, and electronically operated dormitory entrances.

Applying

Simpson requires an essay, SAT I or ACT, a high school transcript, 2 recommendations, Christian commitment, and a minimum high school GPA of 2, and in some cases an interview. Application deadline: rolling admissions; 3/2 priority date for financial aid. Deferred admission is possible. **Contact:** Mrs. Beth Spencer, Administrative Assistant to Vice President for Enrollment, 2211 College View Drive, Redding, CA 96003-8606, 530-224-5606 ext. 2602 or toll-free 800-598-2493; fax 530-224-5608; e-mail admissions@simpsonca.edu.

GETTING IN LAST YEAR	18% had SAT math scores over 600	$4680 room and board
885 applied	28% had ACT scores over 24	82% average percent of need met
55% were accepted	3% had SAT verbal scores over 700	$10,815 average financial aid amount
191 enrolled (39%)	1% had SAT math scores over 700	received per undergraduate (1999–2000)
16% from top tenth of their h.s. class		estimated)
3.33 average high school GPA	**COSTS AND FINANCIAL INFORMATION**	
22% had SAT verbal scores over 600	$10,540 tuition and fees (1999–2000)	

SOUTHERN NAZARENE UNIVERSITY

Bethany, Oklahoma

http://www.snu.edu/

Southern Nazarene University, founded in 1899, is educating for responsible, Christian living. Students from all over the United States and 24 countries come to SNU to receive excellent professional and academic preparation in the context of a warm, Christian community. SNU offers fully accredited programs in more than 60 major fields of study, with a national reputation for its programs in the sciences, premedicine, physics, fine arts, education, and business. The School of Business has won international business competitions in 3 of the last 5 years. Additional academic offerings include programs in Washington, DC; Cairo, Egypt; Los Angeles, California; San José, Costa Rica; Moscow, Russia; and Oxford, England. Southern Nazarene University helps students prepare for their future and a life of service.

Academics

SNU awards associate, bachelor's, and master's **degrees**. Challenging opportunities include advanced placement, accelerated degree programs, student-designed majors, an honors program, double majors, and a senior project. **Special programs** include internships, summer session for credit, off-campus study, study-abroad, and Army and Air Force ROTC. A complete listing of majors at SNU appears in the Majors Index beginning on page 147. The **faculty** at SNU has 137 members.

Students of SNU

The student body totals 1,950, of whom 1,652 are undergraduates. 56.2% are women and 43.8% are men. Students come from 41 states and territories. 53% are from Oklahoma. 1.3% are international students. 77% returned for their sophomore year.

Facilities and Resources

The **library** has 115,564 books.

Career Services

The career planning and placement office has 1 full-time, 2 part-time staff members. Services include job fairs, resume preparation, interview workshops, resume referral, career/interest testing, career counseling, careers library, job bank, and job interviews.

Campus Life

There are 30 active organizations on campus, including a drama/theater group, newspaper, television station, and choral group. No national or local **fraternities** or **sororities**. SNU is a member of the NAIA. **Intercollegiate sports** (some offering scholarships) include baseball (m), basketball, cross-country running, golf, soccer, softball (w), tennis, track and field, volleyball (w).

Campus Safety

Student safety services include 24-hour emergency telephone alarm devices and electronically operated dormitory entrances.

Applying

SNU requires SAT I or ACT and a high school transcript. It recommends an interview. Application deadline: 8/15; 3/1 priority date for financial aid. Deferred admission is possible. **Contact:** Mr. Brad Townley, Director of Admissions, 6729 Northwest 39th Expressway, Bethany, OK 73008, 405-491-6324 or toll-free 800-648-9899; fax 405-491-6381; e-mail admiss@snu.edu.

GETTING IN LAST YEAR		
600 applied	3.4 average high school GPA	$4316 room and board
100% were accepted	38% had ACT scores over 24	**AFTER GRADUATION**
332 enrolled (55%)	6% had ACT scores over 30	22% pursued further study (10% theology, 8%
23% from top tenth of their h.s. class	**COSTS AND FINANCIAL INFORMATION**	business, 2% medicine)
	$9380 tuition and fees (1999–2000)	

SOUTHERN WESLEYAN UNIVERSITY

Central, South Carolina

http://www.swu.edu/

SOUTHERN
WESLEYAN
UNIVERSITY

Southern Wesleyan University is committed to providing a high-quality education from a Christian perspective. The issues of faith are explored in each course of study and practiced in daily life. The faculty's personal dedication and skills enable it to serve students from a wide variety of backgrounds—ranging from those who might be underprepared to National Merit Finalists—by providing the right amount of support and the right amount of challenge. A cooperative program with nearby Clemson University allows Southern Wesleyan's students to experience the atmosphere and fellowship of a Christian campus and the academic diversity of a large university. Graduates have distinguished themselves in their careers while maintaining active involvement in service to their communities and churches. An education at Southern Wesleyan provides what's needed for a career and for a satisfying and balanced life.

Academics

SWU awards associate, bachelor's, and master's **degrees**. Challenging opportunities include advanced placement, accelerated degree programs, an honors program, double majors, independent study, and a senior project. **Special programs** include internships, summer session for credit, off-campus study, study-abroad, and Army and Air Force ROTC. The most frequently chosen **baccalaureate** fields are business/marketing, education, and psychology. A complete listing of majors at SWU appears in the Majors Index beginning on page 147. The **faculty** at SWU has 43 full-time members, 77% with terminal degrees. The student-faculty ratio is 14:1.

Students of SWU

The student body totals 1,527, of whom 1,472 are undergraduates. 61.5% are women and 38.5% are men. Students come from 32 states and territories and 7 other countries. 84% are from South Carolina. 0.6% are international students. 66% returned for their sophomore year.

Facilities and Resources

The **library** has 67,823 books and 440 subscriptions.

Career Services

The career planning and placement office has 1 full-time, 1 part-time staff members. Services include job fairs, resume preparation, resume referral, career counseling, careers library, and job bank.

Campus Life

There are 9 active organizations on campus, including a drama/theater group and choral group. No national or local **fraternities** or **sororities**. SWU is a member of the NAIA and NCCAA. **Intercollegiate sports** (some offering scholarships) include baseball (m), basketball, cross-country running, golf (m), soccer, softball (w), volleyball (w).

Campus Safety

Student safety services include late night security patrols and 24-hour emergency telephone alarm devices.

Applying

SWU requires SAT I or ACT, a high school transcript, 2 recommendations, lifestyle statement, and a minimum high school GPA of 2.0, and in some cases an interview. Application deadline: 8/10; 6/30 priority date for financial aid. Early and deferred admission are possible. **Contact:** Mrs. Joy Bryant, Director of Admissions, 907 Wesleyan Drive, PO Box 1020, Central, SC 29630-1020, 864-644-5550 or toll-free 800-CUATSWU; fax 864-639-0826 ext. 327; e-mail admissions@swu.edu.

GETTING IN LAST YEAR	9% had SAT verbal scores over 600	$3852 room and board
468 applied	9% had SAT math scores over 600	85% average percent of need met
34% were accepted	11% had ACT scores over 24	$9500 average financial aid amount received
102 enrolled (64%)	2% had SAT verbal scores over 700	per undergraduate (1999–2000 estimated)
12% from top tenth of their h.s. class		
3.00 average high school GPA	**COSTS AND FINANCIAL INFORMATION**	**AFTER GRADUATION**
	$11,498 tuition and fees (1999–2000)	11 organizations recruited on campus

SOUTHWEST BAPTIST UNIVERSITY

Bolivar, Missouri

http://www.sbuniv.edu/

Southwest Baptist University is a Christ-centered, caring academic community preparing students to be servant leaders in a global society. With a strong emphasis on integrating faith and values with a quality liberal arts education, SBU is a Christian university, not simply a university for Christians. SBU's learning environment is comprised of energetic students, passionate faculty, and caring staff who make SBU a recognized leader in higher education. SBU has been named to the *Student's Guide to America's 100 Best College Buys* since 1996.

Academics

SBU awards associate, bachelor's, and master's **degrees**. Challenging opportunities include advanced placement, accelerated degree programs, an honors program, double majors, independent study, and a senior project. **Special programs** include cooperative education, internships, summer session for credit, study-abroad, and Army ROTC. The most frequently chosen **baccalaureate** fields are education, business/marketing, and health professions and related sciences. A complete listing of majors at SBU appears in the Majors Index beginning on page 147. The **faculty** at SBU has 103 full-time members. The student-faculty ratio is 19:1.

Students of SBU

The student body totals 3,634, of whom 2,801 are undergraduates. 65.3% are women and 34.7% are men. Students come from 39 states and territories and 8 other countries. 82% are from Missouri. 0.6% are international students. 70% returned for their sophomore year.

Facilities and Resources

The **library** has 108,128 books and 2,518 subscriptions.

Career Services

The career planning and placement office has 2 full-time, 1 part-time staff members. Services include job fairs, resume preparation, interview workshops, resume referral, career/interest testing, career counseling, careers library, job bank, and job interviews.

Campus Life

There are 27 active organizations on campus, including a drama/theater group, newspaper, and choral group. No national or local **fraternities** or **sororities**. SBU is a member of the NCAA (Division II). **Intercollegiate sports** (some offering scholarships) include baseball (m), basketball, cross-country running, football (m), golf (m), soccer, softball (w), tennis, volleyball (w).

Campus Safety

Student safety services include 24-hour emergency telephone alarm devices and 24-hour patrols by trained security personnel.

Applying

SBU requires SAT I or ACT and a high school transcript. It recommends an interview. Application deadline: rolling admissions; 3/15 priority date for financial aid. **Contact:** Mr. Rob Harris, Director of Admissions, 1600 University Avenue, Bolivar, MO 65613-2597, 417-328-1809 or toll-free 800-526-5859; fax 417-328-1514; e-mail rharris@sbuniv.edu.

GETTING IN LAST YEAR
883 applied
86% were accepted
528 enrolled (70%)
23% from top tenth of their h.s. class
3.24 average high school GPA
28% had SAT verbal scores over 600

17% had SAT math scores over 600
45% had ACT scores over 24
8% had SAT verbal scores over 700
2% had SAT math scores over 700
8% had ACT scores over 30

COSTS AND FINANCIAL INFORMATION
$9290 tuition and fees (1999–2000)

$2830 room and board
55% average percent of need met
$7885 average financial aid amount received
  per undergraduate (1999–2000 estimated)

AFTER GRADUATION
80% had job offers within 6 months
630 organizations recruited on campus

SPRING ARBOR COLLEGE

Spring Arbor, Michigan

http://www.arbor.edu/

Spring Arbor College is a community of learners distinguished by our life-long involvement in the study and application of the liberal arts, total commitment to Jesus Christ as our perspective for learning, and critical participation in the contemporary world. We are committed to preparing thinking Christians to be redemptively involved in all aspects of culture, transforming it one life at a time. In short, our goal is to prepare our graduates for more than their first job or even a career—it is to equip them to excel as salt and light in all they do. Our students confirm that they are growing spiritually, that our cross-cultural requirement and missions trips are expanding their worldview and equipping them to transform lives.

Academics

Spring Arbor awards associate, bachelor's, and master's **degrees**. Challenging opportunities include advanced placement, accelerated degree programs, student-designed majors, an honors program, double majors, independent study, and a senior project. **Special programs** include internships, summer session for credit, and off-campus study. The most frequently chosen **baccalaureate** fields are business/marketing, education, and social sciences and history. A complete listing of majors at Spring Arbor appears in the Majors Index beginning on page 147. The **faculty** at Spring Arbor has 54 full-time members. The student-faculty ratio is 16:1.

Students of Spring Arbor

The student body totals 2,434, of whom 2,139 are undergraduates. 66.7% are women and 33.3% are men. 89% are from Michigan. 1.4% are international students. 80% returned for their sophomore year.

Facilities and Resources

The **library** has 84,225 books.

Career Services

The career planning and placement office has 2 full-time, 4 part-time staff members. Services include job fairs, resume preparation, career counseling, careers library, job bank, and job interviews.

Campus Life

Active organizations on campus include a drama/theater group, newspaper, radio station, and choral group. No national or local **fraternities** or **sororities**. Spring Arbor is a member of the NAIA. **Intercollegiate sports** (some offering scholarships) include baseball (m), basketball, cross-country running, golf (m), soccer, softball (w), tennis, track and field, volleyball (w).

Campus Safety

Student safety services include late-night transport/escort service.

Applying

Spring Arbor requires SAT I or ACT and a high school transcript, and in some cases recommendations. It recommends an essay, an interview, and guidance counselor's evaluation form. Application deadline: rolling admissions; 2/15 priority date for financial aid. Early and deferred admission are possible. **Contact:** Mr. Jim Weidman, Director of Admissions, 106 East Main Street, Spring Arbor, MI 49283-9799, 517-750-1200 ext. 1475 or toll-free 800-968-0011; fax 517-750-1604; e-mail shellya@admin.arbor.edu.

GETTING IN LAST YEAR
597 applied
88% were accepted
185 enrolled (35%)
19% from top tenth of their h.s. class
3.30 average high school GPA

36% had ACT scores over 24
4% had ACT scores over 30

COSTS AND FINANCIAL INFORMATION
$11,706 tuition and fees (1999–2000)
$4460 room and board

AFTER GRADUATION
29% graduated in 4 years
17% graduated in 5 years
2% graduated in 6 years
12% pursued further study

STERLING COLLEGE
Sterling, Kansas

http://www.sterling.edu/

Sterling College is nationally recognized for developing creative and thoughtful leaders who understand a maturing Christian faith. The reason for this reputation is simple— Sterling cares about people. Sterling cares how its students are developing academically, socially, physically, and spiritually. Sterling College is also noted for its servant leadership and social entrepreneurship programs. Top-quality faculty members teach students how to think, not what to think. Strong theater, music, and art programs stretch students artistically and creatively. Dedicated staff members provide active and enthusiastic student-life activities. Concerned coaches help students maintain a proper balance between athletics and academics. All this individual attention is directed toward one aim—helping each student to learn, to grow, and to excel.

Academics
Sterling College awards bachelor's **degrees**. Challenging opportunities include advanced placement, student-designed majors, an honors program, double majors, independent study, and a senior project. **Special programs** include internships, off-campus study, and study-abroad. The most frequently chosen **baccalaureate** fields are education, biological/life sciences, and business/marketing. A complete listing of majors at Sterling College appears in the Majors Index beginning on page 147. The **faculty** at Sterling College has 33 full-time members, 42% with terminal degrees. The student-faculty ratio is 12:1.

Students of Sterling College
The student body is made up of 424 undergraduates. 53.8% are women and 46.2% are men. Students come from 25 states and territories and 1 other country. 59% are from Kansas. 0.2% are international students. 50% returned for their sophomore year.

Facilities and Resources
The **library** has 85,484 books and 482 subscriptions.

Career Services
The career planning and placement office has 2 full-time staff members. Services include job fairs, resume preparation, interview workshops, resume referral, career/interest testing, career counseling, careers library, job bank, and job interviews.

Campus Life
There are 23 active organizations on campus, including a drama/theater group, newspaper, and choral group. No national or local **fraternities** or **sororities**. Sterling College is a member of the NAIA. **Intercollegiate sports** (some offering scholarships) include baseball (m), basketball, cross-country running, football (m), soccer, softball (w), tennis, track and field, volleyball (w).

Campus Safety
Student safety services include late night security patrol.

Applying
Sterling College requires SAT I or ACT, a high school transcript, and a minimum high school GPA of 2.2, and in some cases recommendations. It recommends an essay. Application deadline: rolling admissions; 3/15 priority date for financial aid. Deferred admission is possible. **Contact:** Susan Sankey, Director of Admissions, PO Box 98, Sterling, KS 67579-0098, 316-278-4364 ext. 364 or toll-free 800-346-1017; fax 316-278-3690; e-mail admissions@sterling.edu.

GETTING IN LAST YEAR
434 applied
73% were accepted
115 enrolled (37%)
18% from top tenth of their h.s. class
3.52 average high school GPA
33% had SAT verbal scores over 600

33% had SAT math scores over 600
43% had ACT scores over 24
8% had ACT scores over 30
9 valedictorians

COSTS AND FINANCIAL INFORMATION
$11,030 tuition and fees (1999–2000)
$4586 room and board

80% average percent of need met
$9000 average financial aid amount received
  per undergraduate (1998–99)

AFTER GRADUATION
28% graduated in 4 years
15% graduated in 5 years
2% graduated in 6 years

TABOR COLLEGE
Hillsboro, Kansas

http://www.tabor.edu/

Tabor's religious heritage places utmost importance on a voluntary, adult commitment to follow Christ. This includes a life of personal devotion and outer witness, serious corporate biblical study, and service to others, which is the foundation of Tabor's mission statement. The academic program, therefore, is designed to develop servants of Christ for all walks of life. This occurs in a Christian learning community, which emphasizes fellowship and mutual accountability. Themes of stewardship and service infuse the College's majors. The student development program stresses personal growth, self-discipline, acceptance of responsibility, and the development of decision-making skills. Tabor provides global travel/service experiences each Interterm and structured opportunities to serve others for Christ through a variety of local ministries.

Academics
Tabor awards associate and bachelor's **degrees**. Challenging opportunities include advanced placement, accelerated degree programs, student-designed majors, an honors program, double majors, independent study, and a senior project. **Special programs** include internships, summer session for credit, off-campus study, and study-abroad. The most frequently chosen **baccalaureate** fields are business/marketing, education, and philosophy. A complete listing of majors at Tabor appears in the Majors Index beginning on page 147. The **faculty** at Tabor has 34 full-time members, 47% with terminal degrees. The student-faculty ratio is 14:1.

Students of Tabor
The student body is made up of 538 undergraduates. 49.3% are women and 50.7% are men. Students come from 22 states and territories. 63% are from Kansas. 0.7% are international students. 63% returned for their sophomore year.

Facilities and Resources
The 3 **libraries** have 76,730 books and 298 subscriptions.

Career Services
The career planning and placement office has 1 full-time, 1 part-time staff members. Services include job fairs, resume preparation, resume referral, career counseling, careers library, job bank, and job interviews.

Campus Life
There are 27 active organizations on campus, including a drama/theater group, newspaper, and choral group. No national or local **fraternities** or **sororities**. Tabor is a member of the NAIA. **Intercollegiate sports** (some offering scholarships) include baseball (m), basketball, cross-country running, football (m), golf, soccer, softball (w), tennis, track and field, volleyball (w).

Campus Safety
Student safety services include student patrols and electronically operated dormitory entrances.

Applying
Tabor requires an essay, SAT I or ACT, a high school transcript, 2 recommendations, and a minimum high school GPA of 2.0. It recommends SAT II Subject Tests, SAT II: Writing Test, an interview, and a minimum high school GPA of 3.0. Application deadline: 8/1; 8/15 for financial aid, with a 3/1 priority date. Deferred admission is possible. **Contact:** Mr. Glenn Lygrisse, Vice President for Enrollment Management, 400 South Jefferson, Hillsboro, KS 67063, 316-947-3121 ext. 1723 or toll-free 800-822-6799; fax 316-947-2607; e-mail admissions@tcnet.tabor.edu.

GETTING IN LAST YEAR
363 applied
63% were accepted
138 enrolled (61%)
18% from top tenth of their h.s. class
3.34 average high school GPA
31% had ACT scores over 24

6% had ACT scores over 30

COSTS AND FINANCIAL INFORMATION
$12,410 tuition and fees (2000–2001)
$4480 room and board
87% average percent of need met
$11,260 average financial aid amount
  received per undergraduate (1999–2000)

AFTER GRADUATION
43% graduated in 4 years
14% graduated in 5 years
2% graduated in 6 years
20% pursued further study
40 organizations recruited on campus

TAYLOR UNIVERSITY
Upland, Indiana

http://www.tayloru.edu/

Taylor University seeks Christian scholars who wish to experience thoughtful and rigorous academic studies thoroughly integrated with biblical Christianity. It seeks students who will respond to a supportive campus community that expects responsible decision making in the context of Christian freedom. It seeks students who will endeavor to translate their 4-year experience into lifelong learning and ministering the redemptive love of Jesus Christ to a world in need. Taylor's President, Dr. David Gyertson, and outstanding Christian faculty invite students to consider the call to become a part of Taylor's exceptional student body and begin their own Taylor Tradition.

Academics
Taylor awards associate and bachelor's **degrees**. Challenging opportunities include advanced placement, accelerated degree programs, student-designed majors, an honors program, double majors, independent study, and a senior project. **Special programs** include internships, summer session for credit, off-campus study, and study-abroad. The most frequently chosen **baccalaureate** fields are education, business/marketing, and psychology. A complete listing of majors at Taylor appears in the Majors Index beginning on page 147. The **faculty** at Taylor has 113 full-time members, 72% with terminal degrees. The student-faculty ratio is 16:1.

Students of Taylor
The student body is made up of 1,897 undergraduates. 52.8% are women and 47.2% are men. Students come from 48 states and territories and 19 other countries. 27% are from Indiana. 2% are international students. 89% returned for their sophomore year.

Facilities and Resources
The **library** has 188,000 books and 737 subscriptions.

Career Services
The career planning and placement office has 1 full-time, 1 part-time staff members. Services include job fairs, resume preparation, resume referral, career/interest testing, career counseling, careers library, job bank, and job interviews.

Campus Life
There are 30 active organizations on campus, including a drama/theater group, newspaper, radio station, and choral group. No national or local **fraternities** or **sororities**. Taylor is a member of the NAIA and NCCAA. **Intercollegiate sports** (some offering scholarships) include baseball (m), basketball, cross-country running, equestrian sports, football (m), golf (m), lacrosse (m), soccer, softball (w), tennis, track and field, volleyball.

Campus Safety
Student safety services include late-night transport/escort service, 24-hour patrols by trained security personnel, and student patrols.

Applying
Taylor requires an essay, SAT I or ACT, a high school transcript, an interview, and 2 recommendations. It recommends a minimum high school GPA of 2.8. Application deadline: rolling admissions; 3/1 for financial aid. Deferred admission is possible. **Contact:** Mr. Stephen R. Mortland, Director of Admissions, 236 West Reade Avenue, Upland, IN 46989-1001, 765-998-5134 or toll-free 800-882-3456; fax 765-998-4925; e-mail admissions_u@tayloru.edu.

GETTING IN LAST YEAR
1,624 applied
78% were accepted
475 enrolled (37%)
42% from top tenth of their h.s. class
3.6 average high school GPA
48% had SAT verbal scores over 600
45% had SAT math scores over 600
75% had ACT scores over 24
13% had SAT verbal scores over 700
9% had SAT math scores over 700

18% had ACT scores over 30
8 National Merit Scholars
37 valedictorians

COSTS AND FINANCIAL INFORMATION
$15,118 tuition and fees (1999–2000)
$4630 room and board
82% average percent of need met
$11,273 average financial aid amount received per undergraduate (1999–2000 estimated)

AFTER GRADUATION
71% graduated in 4 years
3% graduated in 5 years
1% graduated in 6 years
Graduates pursuing further study: 6% arts and sciences, 3% theology, 1% business
48% had job offers within 6 months
125 organizations recruited on campus

TREVECCA NAZARENE UNIVERSITY

Nashville, Tennessee

http://www.trevecca.edu/

Trevecca Nazarene's goal is to prepare students for Christian service in all areas of life by providing an education that integrates faith and learning. The University seeks to combine the best in liberal arts as "preparation for life" and the best in career education as "preparation to earn a living." It also provides many opportunities for spiritual growth through chapel services, student organizations, convocations and revivals, and visiting lecturers. In addition, students are actively involved with the Nashville community through local churches and service clubs, which reflects Trevecca's service-oriented philosophy.

Academics

Trevecca awards associate, bachelor's, master's, and doctoral **degrees** and post-master's certificates. Challenging opportunities include advanced placement, accelerated degree programs, double majors, and a senior project. **Special programs** include internships, summer session for credit, and Army ROTC. The most frequently chosen **baccalaureate** fields are business/marketing, health professions and related sciences, and education. A complete listing of majors at Trevecca appears in the Majors Index beginning on page 147. The **faculty** at Trevecca has 64 full-time members. The student-faculty ratio is 13:1.

Students of Trevecca

The student body totals 1,615, of whom 1,004 are undergraduates. 57.4% are women and 42.6% are men. Students come from 36 states and territories. 59% are from Tennessee. 58% returned for their sophomore year.

Facilities and Resources

The **library** has 102,419 books and 2,353 subscriptions.

Career Services

The career planning and placement office has 3 full-time, 3 part-time staff members. Services include job fairs, resume preparation, interview workshops, resume referral, career counseling, careers library, job bank, and job interviews.

Campus Life

Active organizations on campus include a drama/theater group, newspaper, radio station, and choral group. No national or local **fraternities** or **sororities**. Trevecca is a member of the NAIA. **Intercollegiate sports** (some offering scholarships) include baseball (m), basketball, golf, softball (w), volleyball (w).

Campus Safety

Student safety services include late-night transport/escort service, 24-hour patrols by trained security personnel, and student patrols.

Applying

Trevecca requires SAT I or ACT, a high school transcript, medical history and immunization records, and a minimum high school GPA of 2.5. It recommends ACT and recommendations. Application deadline: rolling admissions; 3/1 priority date for financial aid. Early and deferred admission are possible. **Contact:** Ms. Patricia D. Cook, Director of Admissions, 333 Murfreesboro Road, Nashville, TN 37210-2834, 615-248-1320 or toll-free 888-210-4TNU; fax 615-248-7728; e-mail admissions_und@trevecca.edu.

GETTING IN LAST YEAR		
424 applied	28% had ACT scores over 24	83% average percent of need met
84% were accepted	5% had ACT scores over 30	$9584 average financial aid amount received
200 enrolled (56%)	2 valedictorians	per undergraduate (1999–2000)
13% from top tenth of their h.s. class	**COSTS AND FINANCIAL INFORMATION**	**AFTER GRADUATION**
3.07 average high school GPA	$10,656 tuition and fees (1999–2000)	22% pursued further study
	$4448 room and board	31 organizations recruited on campus

TRINITY CHRISTIAN COLLEGE
Palos Heights, Illinois

http://www.trnty.edu/

Although Trinity Christian College is nestled in Palos Heights, a suburb southwest of Chicago, its proximity to the city offers students access to exciting cultural, educational, and employment opportunities through the College-wide internships and the Chicago Metropolitan Studies Program. Trinity offers majors in 25 areas of study; in addition, there are more than 25 minor programs available. The business program is accredited by the ACBSP, and the nursing program is fully accredited by the National League for Nursing. Recent campus additions include a 1,200 seat chapel/auditorium and construction of a science/technology center. Trinity graduates enjoy the benefits of a solid, Christian, liberal arts education that provides excellent preparation for and acceptance into graduate programs in business, education, science, and medicine as well as great success in finding jobs in their chosen careers.

Academics
Trinity Christian College awards bachelor's **degrees**. Challenging opportunities include advanced placement, an honors program, double majors, independent study, and a senior project. **Special programs** include internships, off-campus study, and study-abroad. The most frequently chosen **baccalaureate** fields are education, health professions and related sciences, and business/marketing. A complete listing of majors at Trinity Christian College appears in the Majors Index beginning on page 147. The **faculty** at Trinity Christian College has 41 full-time members, 66% with terminal degrees. The student-faculty ratio is 10:1.

Students of Trinity Christian College
The student body is made up of 723 undergraduates. 65% are women and 35% are men. Students come from 29 states and territories and 5 other countries. 58% are from Illinois. 1.5% are international students. 76% returned for their sophomore year.

Facilities and Resources
The **library** has 55,020 books and 437 subscriptions.

Career Services
The career planning and placement office has 1 full-time, 1 part-time staff members. Services include job fairs, resume preparation, interview workshops, resume referral, career/interest testing, career counseling, careers library, job bank, and job interviews.

Campus Life
There are 15 active organizations on campus, including a drama/theater group, newspaper, and choral group. No national or local **fraternities** or **sororities**. Trinity Christian College is a member of the NAIA and NCCAA. **Intercollegiate sports** (some offering scholarships) include baseball (m), basketball, soccer, softball (w), track and field, volleyball.

Campus Safety
Student safety services include late-night transport/escort service and student patrols.

Applying
Trinity Christian College requires an essay, SAT I or ACT, a high school transcript, an interview, and a minimum high school GPA of 2.0, and in some cases 1 recommendation. Application deadline: rolling admissions; 2/15 priority date for financial aid. Deferred admission is possible. **Contact:** Mr. Peter Hamstra, Dean of Admissions, 6601 West College Drive, Palos Heights, IL 60463-0929, 708-239-4709 or toll-free 800-748-0085; fax 708-239-3995; e-mail admissions@trnty.edu.

GETTING IN LAST YEAR
504 applied
99% were accepted
182 enrolled (36%)
14% from top tenth of their h.s. class
3.22 average high school GPA
36% had ACT scores over 24
6% had ACT scores over 30

8 valedictorians

COSTS AND FINANCIAL INFORMATION
$12,730 tuition and fees (1999–2000)
$5010 room and board
75% average percent of need met
$10,251 average financial aid amount received per undergraduate (1999–2000 estimated)

AFTER GRADUATION
47% graduated in 4 years
6% graduated in 5 years
Graduates pursuing further study: 3% business, 3% theology, 2% arts and sciences
92% had job offers within 6 months

TRINITY INTERNATIONAL UNIVERSITY
Deerfield, Illinois

http://www.tiu.edu/

Trinity will expand your intellect, challenge your faith, and prepare you for life. With 28 majors, Trinity provides many options for motivated students to integrate Christianity with academics. While excellence in the classroom is crucial, Trinity also expands your education beyond four walls. You have opportunities to test your knowledge and gain practical experience through internships and ministry opportunities. Music groups, athletics, and numerous other activities help you develop leadership and communications skills essential for the workplace. Upon graduation, you are ready for your first job, graduate school, and to impact your world for Christ. Trinity: "Forming students to transform the world through Christ."

Academics
Trinity awards bachelor's, master's, doctoral, and first-professional **degrees**. Challenging opportunities include advanced placement, an honors program, double majors, independent study, and a senior project. **Special programs** include cooperative education, internships, summer session for credit, off-campus study, and study-abroad. A complete listing of majors at Trinity appears in the Majors Index beginning on page 147. The **faculty** at Trinity has 79 full-time members.

Students of Trinity
The student body totals 2,571, of whom 964 are undergraduates. Students come from 33 states and territories and 6 other countries. 88% returned for their sophomore year.

Facilities and Resources
The **library** has 157,000 books and 1,200 subscriptions.

Career Services
The career planning and placement office has 1 full-time staff member. Services include job fairs, resume preparation, interview workshops, resume referral, career/interest testing, career counseling, careers library, job bank, and job interviews.

Campus Life
There are 15 active organizations on campus, including a drama/theater group, newspaper, and choral group. No national or local **fraternities** or **sororities**. Trinity is a member of the NAIA. **Intercollegiate sports** (some offering scholarships) include baseball (m), basketball, cross-country running, football (m), golf (m), soccer, softball (w), tennis, track and field, volleyball.

Campus Safety
Student safety services include 24-hour patrols by trained security personnel and electronically operated dormitory entrances.

Applying
Trinity requires an essay, SAT I or ACT, a high school transcript, 1 recommendation, and a minimum high school GPA of 2.5, and in some cases an interview. It recommends a minimum high school GPA of 3.0. Application deadline: rolling admissions; 4/15 priority date for financial aid. **Contact:** Mr. Brian Pomeroy, Director of Undergraduate Admissions, 2065 Half Day Road, Deerfield, IL 60015-1284, 847-317-7000 or toll-free 800-822-3225 (out-of-state); fax 847-317-7081; e-mail tcdadm@tiu.edu.

GETTING IN LAST YEAR
744 applied
96% were accepted
9% from top tenth of their h.s. class
3.12 average high school GPA
18% had SAT verbal scores over 600
14% had SAT math scores over 600

35% had ACT scores over 24
5% had SAT verbal scores over 700
3% had SAT math scores over 700
5% had ACT scores over 30
2 valedictorians

COSTS AND FINANCIAL INFORMATION
$13,630 tuition and fees (1999–2000)

$4950 room and board

AFTER GRADUATION
17% pursued further study (12% arts and sciences, 2% medicine, 2% theology)
86% had job offers within 6 months
69 organizations recruited on campus

TRINITY WESTERN UNIVERSITY

Langley, British Columbia, Canada   *http://www.twu.ca/*

Located in British Columbia's beautiful Fraser Valley, next door to Vancouver and two and a half hours from Seattle, Trinity Western University is one of Canada's most respected Christian liberal arts institutions. A commitment to developing the whole student—academically, socially, physically, and spiritually—distinguishes Trinity Western as a premier institute for leadership development. Taught by some of North America's finest scholars who have thoroughly integrated their studies with their faith, Trinity Western students acquire the critical thinking and reasoning skills, expertise, professional abilities, and character qualities essential for today's world marketplace.

Academics

TWU awards bachelor's and master's **degrees**. Challenging opportunities include advanced placement, an honors program, double majors, independent study, and a senior project. **Special programs** include cooperative education, internships, summer session for credit, off-campus study, and study-abroad. The most frequently chosen **baccalaureate** fields are liberal arts/general studies, psychology, and biological/life sciences. A complete listing of majors at TWU appears in the Majors Index beginning on page 147. The **faculty** at TWU has 77 full-time members, 90% with terminal degrees. The student-faculty ratio is 18:1.

Students of TWU

The student body totals 2,775, of whom 2,379 are undergraduates. Students come from 10 states and territories and 29 other countries. 67% are from British Columbia. 80% returned for their sophomore year.

Facilities and Resources

The **library** has 115,626 books and 2,316 subscriptions.

Career Services

The career planning and placement office has 4 full-time, 1 part-time staff members. Services include job fairs, resume preparation, resume referral, career counseling, careers library, job bank, and job interviews.

Campus Life

There are 33 active organizations on campus, including a drama/theater group, newspaper, and choral group. No national or local **fraternities** or **sororities**. **Intercollegiate sports** include basketball, cross-country running, golf (m), ice hockey, rugby, soccer, track and field, volleyball.

Campus Safety

Student safety services include late-night transport/escort service, 24-hour emergency telephone alarm devices, 24-hour patrols by trained security personnel, and electronically operated dormitory entrances.

Applying

TWU requires an essay, a high school transcript, 2 recommendations, community standards document, and a minimum high school GPA of 2.5, and in some cases SAT I or ACT and an interview. Application deadline: 6/15; 3/15 priority date for financial aid. Deferred admission is possible. **Contact:** Mr. Cam Lee, Director of Admissions, 7600 Glover Road, Langley, BC V2Y 1Y1, Canada, 604-513-2019 ext. 3015 or toll-free 888-468-6898; fax 604-513-2061; e-mail admissions@twu.ca.

GETTING IN LAST YEAR
1,371 applied
78% were accepted
3.0 average high school GPA

COSTS AND FINANCIAL INFORMATION
$10,460 tuition and fees (2000–2001)
$5990 room and board

AFTER GRADUATION
15% pursued further study

UNION UNIVERSITY

Jackson, Tennessee

http://www.uu.edu/

Conscious of the changing global atmosphere awaiting today's generation of students, Union University is preparing leaders and change agents for the 21st century. High-quality classroom teaching is a Union trademark, as students are challenged to become impact players in their chosen field of study. An enduring faith in God and an unfaltering commitment to Christian values shape Union's vision and goals toward excellence in liberal arts education. Union is a place where students grow both in faith and vision, fulfilling their dreams, and impacting the world.

Academics

Union awards associate, bachelor's, and master's **degrees**. Challenging opportunities include advanced placement, accelerated degree programs, an honors program, double majors, independent study, and a senior project. **Special programs** include internships, summer session for credit, off-campus study, and study-abroad. The most frequently chosen **baccalaureate** fields are health professions and related sciences, education, and business/marketing. A complete listing of majors at Union appears in the Majors Index beginning on page 147. The **faculty** at Union has 126 full-time members, 63% with terminal degrees. The student-faculty ratio is 13:1.

Students of Union

The student body totals 2,297, of whom 1,931 are undergraduates. 59.3% are women and 40.7% are men. Students come from 40 states and territories and 26 other countries. 74% are from Tennessee. 1.9% are international students. 93% returned for their sophomore year.

Facilities and Resources

The **library** has 129,678 books and 2,653 subscriptions.

Career Services

The career planning and placement office has 2 full-time staff members. Services include job fairs, resume preparation, interview workshops, resume referral, career/interest testing, career counseling, careers library, job bank, and job interviews.

Campus Life

There are 73 active organizations on campus, including a drama/theater group, newspaper, and choral group. 26% of eligible men and 23% of eligible women are members of national **fraternities** and national **sororities**. Union is a member of the NAIA and NCCAA. **Intercollegiate sports** (some offering scholarships) include baseball (m), basketball, cross-country running (w), golf (m), soccer (m), softball (w), tennis, volleyball (w).

Campus Safety

Student safety services include late-night transport/escort service, 24-hour emergency telephone alarm devices, 24-hour patrols by trained security personnel, and student patrols.

Applying

Union requires SAT I or ACT, a high school transcript, and a minimum high school GPA of 2.5, and in some cases recommendations. It recommends an essay and an interview. Application deadline: rolling admissions; 2/15 priority date for financial aid. Early admission is possible. **Contact:** Mr. Robbie Graves, Director of Enrollment Services, 1050 Union University Drive, Jackson, TN 38305-3697, 901-661-5008 or toll-free 800-33-UNION; fax 901-661-5187; e-mail info@uu.edu.

GETTING IN LAST YEAR		AFTER GRADUATION
913 applied	4 National Merit Scholars	46% graduated in 4 years
85% were accepted	44 valedictorians	12% graduated in 5 years
424 enrolled (55%)		2% graduated in 6 years
36% from top tenth of their h.s. class	**COSTS AND FINANCIAL INFORMATION**	40% pursued further study
3.48 average high school GPA	$11,900 tuition and fees (2000–2001)	85 organizations recruited on campus
55% had ACT scores over 24	$3850 room and board	
16% had ACT scores over 30	80% average percent of need met	
	$7800 average financial aid amount received	
	per undergraduate (1999–2000 estimated)	

UNIVERSITY OF SIOUX FALLS

Sioux Falls, South Dakota

http://www.usiouxfalls.edu/

The University of Sioux Falls is a 4-year Christian liberal arts university affiliated with the American Baptist Church. More than 1,100 students from more than twenty-five states and several foreign countries attend classes on this 23-acre residential campus. In an environment that both challenges and supports, students are encouraged to develop knowledge and wisdom for discerning truth and meeting human needs, to build a value system in keeping with Christ's teachings, to achieve emotional maturity, to pursue physical fitness, and to gain interpersonal skills. Students develop close, caring relationships with professors in and out of the classroom. Beyond the classroom, there are numerous cocurricular activities important to a college education.

Academics

USF awards associate, bachelor's, and master's **degrees**. Challenging opportunities include advanced placement, accelerated degree programs, student-designed majors, an honors program, double majors, independent study, and a senior project. **Special programs** include internships, summer session for credit, and off-campus study. A complete listing of majors at USF appears in the Majors Index beginning on page 147. The **faculty** at USF has 36 full-time members, 83% with terminal degrees.

Students of USF

The student body totals 1,107, of whom 946 are undergraduates. 55.9% are women and 44.1% are men. Students come from 19 states and territories and 6 other countries. 74% are from South Dakota. 1.3% are international students. 64% returned for their sophomore year.

Facilities and Resources

The **library** has 57,399 books and 364 subscriptions.

Career Services

The career planning and placement office has 2 full-time, 1 part-time staff members. Services include job fairs, resume preparation, resume referral, career counseling, careers library, job bank, and job interviews.

Campus Life

There are 12 active organizations on campus, including a drama/theater group, newspaper, radio station, television station, and choral group. No national or local **fraternities** or **sororities**. USF is a member of the NAIA. **Intercollegiate sports** (some offering scholarships) include baseball (m), basketball, cross-country running, football (m), soccer, softball (w), tennis, track and field, volleyball (w).

Campus Safety

Student safety services include late-night transport/escort service and electronically operated dormitory entrances.

Applying

USF requires SAT I and SAT II or ACT and a high school transcript, and in some cases an interview and 2 recommendations. It recommends an essay and a minimum high school GPA of 2.0. Application deadline: rolling admissions; 3/1 priority date for financial aid. Early and deferred admission are possible. **Contact:** Ms. Kathleen Houseman, Director of Admissions, 1101 West 22nd Street, Sioux Falls, SD 57105-1699, 605-331-6600 or toll-free 800-888-1047 (out-of-state); fax 605-331-6615; e-mail admissions@usiouxfalls.edu.

GETTING IN LAST YEAR		AFTER GRADUATION
424 applied	26% had ACT scores over 24	31% graduated in 5 years
97% were accepted	2% had ACT scores over 30	9% graduated in 6 years
181 enrolled (44%)		17% pursued further study
13% from top tenth of their h.s. class	**COSTS AND FINANCIAL INFORMATION**	94% had job offers within 6 months
2.98 average high school GPA	$11,500 tuition and fees (1999–2000)	188 organizations recruited on campus
	$3700 room and board	

VANGUARD UNIVERSITY OF SOUTHERN CALIFORNIA

Costa Mesa, California

http://www.vanguard.edu/

Vanguard University of Southern California is located 5 miles from the Pacific Ocean in Costa Mesa, California. Founded in 1920 and affiliated with the Southern California Assemblies of God, VU is a comprehensive, Christian university offering 30 academic majors and concentrations, along with opportunities for off-campus study. The campus is located in Orange County, perfectly located for jobs, internships, multicultural experiences, and recreation. Vanguard University believes that a liberal arts education illuminated by Christian truth fosters intellectual and spiritual development that prepares and challenges students to take an active role in shaping their culture and their world.

Academics

VU awards bachelor's and master's **degrees**. Challenging opportunities include advanced placement, accelerated degree programs, double majors, independent study, and a senior project. **Special programs** include internships, summer session for credit, off-campus study, study-abroad, and Army, Navy and Air Force ROTC. The most frequently chosen **baccalaureate** fields are business/marketing, liberal arts/general studies, and philosophy. A complete listing of majors at VU appears in the Majors Index beginning on page 147. The **faculty** at VU has 58 full-time members, 83% with terminal degrees. The student-faculty ratio is 16:1.

Students of VU

The student body totals 1,440, of whom 1,289 are undergraduates. 62% are women and 38% are men. Students come from 39 states and territories. 76% are from California. 1% are international students. 71% returned for their sophomore year.

Facilities and Resources

The **library** has 121,000 books and 825 subscriptions.

Career Services

Services include job fairs, resume preparation, interview workshops, career counseling, and job interviews.

Campus Life

There are 55 active organizations on campus, including a drama/theater group, newspaper, and choral group. No national or local **fraternities** or **sororities**. VU is a member of the NAIA. **Intercollegiate sports** (some offering scholarships) include baseball (m), basketball, cross-country running, soccer, softball (w), tennis, track and field, volleyball (w).

Campus Safety

Student safety services include late-night transport/escort service, 24-hour emergency telephone alarm devices, and 24-hour patrols by trained security personnel.

Applying

VU requires an essay, SAT I or ACT, a high school transcript, 1 recommendation, and a minimum high school GPA of 2.5, and in some cases an interview. Application deadline: rolling admissions; 3/2 priority date for financial aid. Deferred admission is possible. **Contact:** Ms. Jessica Mireles, Associate Director of Admissions, 55 Fair Drive, Costa Mesa, CA 92626-6597, 714-556-3610 ext. 327 or toll-free 800-722-6279; fax 714-668-6194.

GETTING IN LAST YEAR		COSTS AND FINANCIAL INFORMATION
582 applied	18% had SAT verbal scores over 600	$13,778 tuition and fees (2000–2001
90% were accepted	16% had SAT math scores over 600	estimated)
330 enrolled (63%)	1% had SAT verbal scores over 700	$5060 room and board
17% from top tenth of their h.s. class	1% had SAT math scores over 700	
3.36 average high school GPA	1 National Merit Scholar	
	5 valedictorians	

WARNER PACIFIC COLLEGE

Portland, Oregon

http://www.warnerpacific.edu/

Warner Pacific College promotes excellence in its students and offers them an individualized education in a Christian context. To uphold this mission, the academic program provides experiences that integrate knowledge, attitude, and faith with meaningful relationships. The concept of a Christian liberal arts education does not discount the importance of practical experience or the need to translate theory into practice. In fact, as a Christ-centered college, Warner Pacific emphasizes careers and lifelong learning with faulty, staff, and administrators that seek to prepare men and women for Kingdom service in the next millennium. And unlike many colleges, Warner Pacific's graduates are distinguished not only by their academic prowess, but also by their exemplary character, a quality much sought after by prospective employers. Set in an urban neighborhood, Warner offers many opportunities for students to fulfill our mission of being an environment that allows faith and scholarship to lead to Christian service.

Academics

Warner Pacific awards associate, bachelor's, and master's **degrees** and first-professional certificates. Challenging opportunities include advanced placement, student-designed majors, an honors program, double majors, independent study, and a senior project. **Special programs** include cooperative education, internships, summer session for credit, off-campus study, study-abroad, and Army and Air Force ROTC. The most frequently chosen **baccalaureate** fields are psychology, business/marketing, and philosophy. A complete listing of majors at Warner Pacific appears in the Majors Index beginning on page 147. The **faculty** at Warner Pacific has 38 full-time members, 53% with terminal degrees. The student-faculty ratio is 14:1.

Students of Warner Pacific

The student body totals 650, of whom 645 are undergraduates. 66.4% are women and 33.6% are men. Students come from 17 states and territories and 7 other countries. 68% are from Oregon. 2.8% are international students. 76% returned for their sophomore year.

Facilities and Resources

The **library** has 54,000 books and 400 subscriptions.

Career Services

The career planning and placement office has 1 full-time staff member. Services include job fairs, resume preparation, resume referral, career counseling, careers library, job bank, and job interviews.

Campus Life

There are 10 active organizations on campus, including a drama/theater group, newspaper, and choral group. No national or local **fraternities** or **sororities**. Warner Pacific is a member of the NCCAA. **Intercollegiate sports** (some offering scholarships) include basketball, cross-country running, soccer (m), volleyball (w).

Campus Safety

Student safety services include 14-hour patrols by trained security personnel, late-night transport/escort service, 24-hour emergency telephone alarm devices, student patrols, and electronically operated dormitory entrances.

Applying

Warner Pacific requires an essay, SAT I or ACT, a high school transcript, 2 recommendations, and a minimum high school GPA of 2.5, and in some cases an interview. It recommends SAT II Subject Tests, SAT II: Writing Test, an interview, and a minimum high school GPA of 3.0. Application deadline: rolling admissions; 5/1 priority date for financial aid. **Contact:** Mr. Rick Johnsen, Director of Admissions and Financial Aid, 2219 Southeast 68th Avenue, Portland, OR 97215, 503-517-1020 or toll-free 800-582-7885; fax 503-788-7425; e-mail admiss@warnerpacific.edu.

GETTING IN LAST YEAR
159 applied
79% were accepted
72 enrolled (57%)
3.25 average high school GPA
17% had SAT verbal scores over 600

19% had SAT math scores over 600
31% had ACT scores over 24
4% had SAT verbal scores over 700
2% had SAT math scores over 700

COSTS AND FINANCIAL INFORMATION
74% average percent of need met

$9944 average financial aid amount received per undergraduate (1998–99)

AFTER GRADUATION
31% graduated in 4 years
8% graduated in 5 years
2% graduated in 6 years

WARNER SOUTHERN COLLEGE

Lake Wales, Florida

http://www.warner.edu/

Warner Southern College's 380-acre campus is located in central Florida. This four-year college fosters an environment that allows students to search for truth in the context of Christian faith and academic excellence. Students are a top priority. Administration, faculty, and staff members are all committed to helping students develop, excel, and become contributors to the betterment of their community. Students develop a close bond with their professors because of the low student-teacher ratio and with fellow students because of the friendly atmosphere. Students often remark that they enjoy the size of classes and the spiritual atmosphere on campus.

Academics

Warner Southern awards associate and bachelor's **degrees**. Challenging opportunities include advanced placement, double majors, independent study, and a senior project. **Special programs** include internships and summer session for credit. The most frequently chosen **baccalaureate** fields are business/marketing, education, and philosophy. A complete listing of majors at Warner Southern appears in the Majors Index beginning on page 147. The **faculty** at Warner Southern has 22 full-time members, 45% with terminal degrees. The student-faculty ratio is 14:1.

Students of Warner Southern

The student body is made up of 844 undergraduates. 60.1% are women and 39.9% are men. Students come from 23 states and territories and 5 other countries. 90% are from Florida. 0.8% are international students. 68% returned for their sophomore year.

Facilities and Resources

The 2 **libraries** have 56,419 books and 224 subscriptions.

Career Services

The career planning and placement office has 1 part-time staff member. Services include resume preparation, career counseling, and careers library.

Campus Life

There are 4 active organizations on campus, including a choral group. No national or local **fraternities** or **sororities**. Warner Southern is a member of the NAIA. **Intercollegiate sports** (some offering scholarships) include baseball (m), basketball, cross-country running, golf (m), softball (w), volleyball (w).

Campus Safety

Student safety services include late-night transport/escort service, 24-hour emergency telephone alarm devices, 24-hour patrols by trained security personnel, and electronically operated dormitory entrances.

Applying

Warner Southern requires SAT I or ACT, a high school transcript, 1 recommendation, and a minimum high school GPA of 2.25, and in some cases an interview. It recommends an essay. Application deadline: rolling admissions; 4/1 priority date for financial aid. Deferred admission is possible. **Contact:** Mr. Jason Roe, Director of Admissions, 5301 US Highway 27 South, Lake Wales, FL 33853-8725, 863-638-7212 ext. 7213 or toll-free 800-949-7248 (in-state).

GETTING IN LAST YEAR		AFTER GRADUATION
236 applied	8% had SAT verbal scores over 600	16% graduated in 4 years
59% were accepted	8% had SAT math scores over 600	2% graduated in 5 years
78 enrolled (56%)	9% had ACT scores over 24	2% graduated in 6 years
22% from top tenth of their h.s. class		5% pursued further study
3.32 average high school GPA	**COSTS AND FINANCIAL INFORMATION**	
	$8980 tuition and fees (1999–2000)	
	$4358 room and board	

WESTERN BAPTIST COLLEGE

Salem, Oregon   *http://www.wbc.edu/*

As soon as students step onto the beautiful 100-acre campus in Salem, Oregon, they discover the family atmosphere and caring community of professing Christians. Western provides a strong academic program in the liberal arts and professional studies that is Bible centered. The college's vision for all students is that they have a heartfelt desire to make a difference in the world for Jesus Christ. Academic advisors meet with freshmen—usually in their homes before they ever enroll—to schedule classes and talk about the transition to college life. The goal is to see all students thrive at Western.

Academics

Western awards associate and bachelor's **degrees**. Challenging opportunities include advanced placement, accelerated degree programs, freshman honors college, an honors program, double majors, and a senior project. **Special programs** include internships, summer session for credit, off-campus study, and Army and Air Force ROTC. The most frequently chosen **baccalaureate** fields are business/marketing, psychology, and education. A complete listing of majors at Western appears in the Majors Index beginning on page 147. The **faculty** at Western has 30 full-time members, 37% with terminal degrees. The student-faculty ratio is 17:1.

Students of Western

The student body is made up of 683 undergraduates. 57.2% are women and 42.8% are men. Students come from 16 states and territories. 71% are from Oregon. 0.6% are international students. 65% returned for their sophomore year.

Facilities and Resources

The **library** has 73,205 books.

Career Services

The career planning and placement office has 1 full-time, 1 part-time staff members. Services include job fairs, resume preparation, interview workshops, resume referral, career/interest testing, career counseling, careers library, job bank, and job interviews.

Campus Life

Active organizations on campus include a drama/theater group, newspaper, and choral group. No national or local **fraternities** or **sororities**. Western is a member of the NAIA and NCCAA. **Intercollegiate sports** (some offering scholarships) include baseball (m), basketball, soccer, softball (w), volleyball (w).

Campus Safety

Student safety services include late-night transport/escort service, 24-hour emergency telephone alarm devices, and student patrols.

Applying

Western requires an essay, SAT I or ACT, a high school transcript, 3 recommendations, and a minimum high school GPA of 2.5. Application deadline: 8/1; 2/15 priority date for financial aid. Early admission is possible. **Contact:** Mr. Daren Milionis, Dean of Admissions, 5000 Deer Park Drive, SE, Salem, OR 97301-9392, 503-375-7005 or toll-free 800-845-3005 (out-of-state); fax 503-585-4316; e-mail dmilionis@wbc.edu.

GETTING IN LAST YEAR
335 applied
95% were accepted
126 enrolled (40%)
17% from top tenth of their h.s. class
3.40 average high school GPA
14% had SAT verbal scores over 600

15% had SAT math scores over 600
39% had ACT scores over 24
1% had SAT verbal scores over 700
8% had ACT scores over 30

COSTS AND FINANCIAL INFORMATION
$13,690 tuition and fees (2000–2001)
$4940 room and board

80% average percent of need met
$10,354 average financial aid amount
  received per undergraduate (1999–2000
  estimated)

AFTER GRADUATION
35% graduated in 4 years
9% graduated in 5 years

WESTMONT COLLEGE
Santa Barbara, California

http://www.westmont.edu/

Recognized as among the nation's finest liberal arts colleges, Westmont blends a rigorous curriculum with enthusiastic, evangelical Christian faith and community. Highly qualified faculty members with degrees from prestigious universities give priority to teaching and working closely with undergraduates while conducting significant scholarly research. Innovative, semester-long study programs at home and abroad offer a global perspective and cross-cultural experiences. On campus, students participate in leadership studies, creative and performing arts, student-led outreach programs in the local community and beyond, internships, and practica, and intercollegiate and intramural sports. College regulations are minimal and encourage students to make responsible personal choices.

Academics
Westmont awards bachelor's **degrees**. Challenging opportunities include advanced placement, accelerated degree programs, student-designed majors, an honors program, double majors, independent study, and a senior project. **Special programs** include cooperative education, internships, summer session for credit, off-campus study, study-abroad, and Army and Air Force ROTC. The most frequently chosen **baccalaureate** fields are social sciences and history, biological/life sciences, and liberal arts/general studies. A complete listing of majors at Westmont appears in the Majors Index beginning on page 147. The **faculty** at Westmont has 85 full-time members, 88% with terminal degrees. The student-faculty ratio is 14:1.

Students of Westmont
The student body totals 1,335, of whom 1,323 are undergraduates. 60.8% are women and 39.2% are men. Students come from 41 states and territories and 12 other countries. 69% are from California. 0.8% are international students. 84% returned for their sophomore year.

Facilities and Resources
The **library** has 158,332 books and 29,218 subscriptions.

Career Services
The career planning and placement office has 4 full-time, 1 part-time staff members. Services include job fairs, resume preparation, resume referral, career/interest testing, career counseling, careers library, job bank, and job interviews.

Campus Life
There are 50 active organizations on campus, including a drama/theater group, newspaper, radio station, and choral group. No national or local **fraternities** or **sororities**. Westmont is a member of the NAIA. **Intercollegiate sports** (some offering scholarships) include baseball (m), basketball, cross-country running, lacrosse (w), rugby (m), soccer, tennis, track and field, volleyball.

Campus Safety
Student safety services include late-night transport/escort service, 24-hour emergency telephone alarm devices, 24-hour patrols by trained security personnel, and electronically operated dormitory entrances.

Applying
Westmont requires an essay, SAT I or ACT, and a high school transcript, and in some cases an interview and recommendations. It recommends an interview, recommendations, and a minimum high school GPA of 3.0. Application deadline: 3/1; 3/2 for financial aid, with a 3/1 priority date. Early and deferred admission are possible. **Contact:** Mrs. Joyce Luy, Director of Admissions, 955 La Paz Road, Santa Barbara, CA 93108, 805-565-6200 ext. 6005 or toll-free 800-777-9011; fax 805-565-6234; e-mail admissions@westmont.edu.

GETTING IN LAST YEAR
1,292 applied
71% were accepted
318 enrolled (35%)
43% from top tenth of their h.s. class
3.64 average high school GPA
50% had SAT verbal scores over 600
48% had SAT math scores over 600
74% had ACT scores over 24

12% had SAT verbal scores over 700
8% had SAT math scores over 700
14% had ACT scores over 30
7 National Merit Scholars
50 class presidents
50 valedictorians

COSTS AND FINANCIAL INFORMATION
$20,965 tuition and fees (2000–2001)
$7068 room and board

78% average percent of need met
$15,299 average financial aid amount
   received per undergraduate (1999–2000)

AFTER GRADUATION
56% graduated in 4 years
3% graduated in 5 years
1% graduated in 6 years
66 organizations recruited on campus

WHEATON COLLEGE
Wheaton, Illinois

http://www.wheaton.edu/

Convinced that "all truth is God's truth," Wheaton College actively pursues the integration of biblical Christianity with rigorous academic study in the liberal arts, with the goal of serving Christ in this world. Wheaton has a national reputation built upon a distinguished and dedicated faculty known for its outstanding teaching and scholarship and a student body committed to academic achievement, leadership, and Christian service. It offers students a wide range of overseas study programs and opportunities to engage in collaborative research. Outstanding athletic programs and a full calendar of student activities add to the friendly and supportive campus community.

Academics
Wheaton awards bachelor's, master's, and doctoral **degrees** and post-bachelor's certificates. Challenging opportunities include advanced placement, student-designed majors, double majors, independent study, and a senior project. **Special programs** include internships, summer session for credit, off-campus study, study-abroad, and Army and Air Force ROTC. The most frequently chosen **baccalaureate** fields are English, philosophy, and social sciences and history. A complete listing of majors at Wheaton appears in the Majors Index beginning on page 147. The **faculty** at Wheaton has 171 full-time members, 91% with terminal degrees. The student-faculty ratio is 12:1.

Students of Wheaton
The student body totals 2,732, of whom 2,338 are undergraduates. 52.5% are women and 47.5% are men. Students come from 50 states and territories and 13 other countries. 23% are from Illinois. 1% are international students. 92% returned for their sophomore year.

Facilities and Resources
The 2 **libraries** have 342,746 books and 3,264 subscriptions.

Career Services
The career planning and placement office has 3 full-time, 2 part-time staff members. Services include job fairs, resume preparation, interview workshops, resume referral, career/interest testing, career counseling, careers library, job bank, and job interviews.

Campus Life
There are 71 active organizations on campus, including a drama/theater group, newspaper, radio station, television station, and choral group. No national or local **fraternities** or **sororities**. Wheaton is a member of the NCAA (Division III). **Intercollegiate sports** include baseball (m), basketball, crew, cross-country running, field hockey (w), football (m), golf (m), ice hockey (m), lacrosse, soccer, softball (w), swimming, tennis, track and field, volleyball, wrestling (m).

Campus Safety
Student safety services include late-night transport/escort service, 24-hour patrols by trained security personnel, and electronically operated dormitory entrances.

Applying
Wheaton requires an essay, SAT I or ACT, a high school transcript, and 2 recommendations. It recommends SAT II: Writing Test and an interview. Application deadline: 1/15; 2/15 priority date for financial aid. Deferred admission is possible. **Contact:** Mr. Dan Crabtree, Director of Admissions, 501 East College Avenue, Wheaton, IL 60187-5593, 630-752-5011 or toll-free 800-222-2419 (out-of-state); fax 630-752-5285; e-mail admissions@wheaton.edu.

GETTING IN LAST YEAR	33% had SAT verbal scores over 700	$13,109 average financial aid amount received per undergraduate (1999–2000)
1,964 applied	27% had SAT math scores over 700	
53% were accepted	43% had ACT scores over 30	**AFTER GRADUATION**
583 enrolled (56%)	59 National Merit Scholars	72% graduated in 4 years
61% from top tenth of their h.s. class		10% graduated in 5 years
3.66 average high school GPA	**COSTS AND FINANCIAL INFORMATION**	2% graduated in 6 years
78% had SAT verbal scores over 600	$14,930 tuition and fees (1999–2000)	25% pursued further study
77% had SAT math scores over 600	$5080 room and board	179 organizations recruited on campus
95% had ACT scores over 24	80% average percent of need met	

WHITWORTH COLLEGE
Spokane, Washington

http://www.whitworth.edu/

For over a century, Whitworth has dedicated itself to a blend of educational components: an integration of faith and learning in the classroom featuring rigorous academics taught by Christian scholars, active residential life, and a commitment to fostering an understanding of other cultures within the nation and the world. Study tours and exchanges provide opportunities for students to experience countries throughout Europe, Asia, and Central America. Cooperative education experiences and internships, which allow students to gain experience and build contacts in the professional community, are encouraged. Whitworth's stated mission is to equip its graduates to honor God, follow Christ, and serve humanity.

Academics

Whitworth awards bachelor's and master's **degrees**. Challenging opportunities include advanced placement, student-designed majors, and a senior project. **Special programs** include cooperative education, internships, summer session for credit, off-campus study, study-abroad, and Army ROTC. The most frequently chosen **baccalaureate** fields are education, business/marketing, and visual/performing arts. A complete listing of majors at Whitworth appears in the Majors Index beginning on page 147. The **faculty** at Whitworth has 92 full-time members, 77% with terminal degrees. The student-faculty ratio is 15:1.

Students of Whitworth

The student body totals 2,034, of whom 1,780 are undergraduates. 60.7% are women and 39.3% are men. Students come from 27 states and territories and 26 other countries. 55% are from Washington. 2.2% are international students. 83% returned for their sophomore year.

Facilities and Resources

The **library** has 135,373 books and 725 subscriptions.

Career Services

The career planning and placement office has 3 full-time, 4 part-time staff members. Services include job fairs, resume preparation, resume referral, career counseling, careers library, job bank, and job interviews.

Campus Life

Active organizations on campus include a drama/theater group, newspaper, radio station, and choral group. No national or local **fraternities** or **sororities**. Whitworth is a member of the NCAA (Division III). **Intercollegiate sports** include baseball (m), basketball, cross-country running, football (m), soccer, swimming, tennis, track and field, volleyball (w).

Campus Safety

Student safety services include late-night transport/escort service, 24-hour emergency telephone alarm devices, and 24-hour patrols by trained security personnel.

Applying

Whitworth requires an essay, SAT I or ACT, a high school transcript, and recommendations, and in some cases an interview. Application deadline: 3/1; 3/1 priority date for financial aid. Early and deferred admission are possible. **Contact:** Mr. Fred Pfursich, Dean of Enrollment Services, 300 West Hawthorne Road, Spokane, WA 99251-0001, 509-777-4348 or toll-free 800-533-4668 (out-of-state); fax 509-777-3773; e-mail admission@whitworth.edu.

GETTING IN LAST YEAR
1,291 applied
86% were accepted
404 enrolled (37%)
44% from top tenth of their h.s. class
3.56 average high school GPA
15% had SAT verbal scores over 600
30% had SAT math scores over 600

3% had SAT verbal scores over 700
4% had SAT math scores over 700
30 valedictorians

COSTS AND FINANCIAL INFORMATION
$16,924 tuition and fees (2000–2001)
$5500 room and board
86% average percent of need met
$14,550 average financial aid amount
   received per undergraduate (1999–2000)

AFTER GRADUATION
42% graduated in 4 years
14% graduated in 5 years
4% graduated in 6 years
20% pursued further study
125 organizations recruited on campus

WILLIAMS BAPTIST COLLEGE

Walnut Ridge, Arkansas

http://wbcoll.edu/

Williams vision is to be an exemplary Christian college with an integrated curriculum of liberal arts and professional studies shaped by a caring people committed to biblical precepts and the highest educational standards.

Academics

Williams awards associate and bachelor's **degrees**. Challenging opportunities include advanced placement, student-designed majors, an honors program, double majors, independent study, and a senior project. **Special programs** include internships, summer session for credit, off-campus study, study-abroad, and Army ROTC. The most frequently chosen **baccalaureate** fields are education, psychology, and philosophy. A complete listing of majors at Williams appears in the Majors Index beginning on page 147. The **faculty** at Williams has 29 full-time members, 48% with terminal degrees. The student-faculty ratio is 16:1.

Students of Williams

The student body is made up of 637 undergraduates. 55.9% are women and 44.1% are men. Students come from 14 states and territories and 6 other countries. 78% are from Arkansas. 3% are international students. 51% returned for their sophomore year.

Facilities and Resources

The **library** has 57,321 books and 284 subscriptions.

Career Services

The career planning and placement office has 2 part-time staff members. Services include job fairs, resume preparation, career counseling, and job bank.

Campus Life

There are 26 active organizations on campus, including a drama/theater group and choral group. No national or local **fraternities** or **sororities**. Williams is a member of the NAIA and NCCAA. **Intercollegiate sports** (some offering scholarships) include baseball (m), basketball, golf (m), soccer (m), softball (w), volleyball (w).

Campus Safety

Student safety services include 24-hour emergency telephone alarm devices and student patrols.

Applying

Williams requires SAT I or ACT, a high school transcript, and a minimum high school GPA of 2.25. It recommends an essay and an interview. Application deadline: rolling admissions. Early and deferred admission are possible. **Contact:** Ms. Angela Flippo, Director of Admissions, 60 West Fulbright Avenue, Walnut Ridge, AR 72476, 870-886-6741 ext. 127 or toll-free 800-722-4434; e-mail admissions@wbcoll.edu.

GETTING IN LAST YEAR		COSTS AND FINANCIAL INFORMATION
516 applied	20% from top tenth of their h.s. class	$6270 tuition and fees (1999–2000)
80% were accepted	3.20 average high school GPA	$3200 room and board
160 enrolled (39%)	29% had ACT scores over 24	

WILLIAM TYNDALE COLLEGE

Farmington Hills, Michigan

http://www.tyndalecollege.edu/

Since its beginning in 1945, the mission of William Tyndale College has been to provide a Christ-centered education designed to produce effective Christian living and service. Tyndale provides an accredited, quality education in Christian studies, arts and sciences, and professional studies through small classes taught by highly qualified and caring faculty. The college strives to integrate all academic subjects and cocurricular experiences within a Christian world view so that graduates are prepared for Christian living and service in a variety of vocations and life-callings.

Academics
Tyndale awards associate and bachelor's **degrees**. Challenging opportunities include advanced placement, accelerated degree programs, double majors, independent study, and a senior project. **Special programs** include internships and summer session for credit. The most frequently chosen **baccalaureate** fields are business/marketing, philosophy, and psychology. A complete listing of majors at Tyndale appears in the Majors Index beginning on page 147. The **faculty** at Tyndale has 15 full-time members. The student-faculty ratio is 12:1.

Students of Tyndale
The student body is made up of 637 undergraduates. 52.6% are women and 47.4% are men. Students come from 6 states and territories and 10 other countries. 99% are from Michigan. 3.1% are international students. 70% returned for their sophomore year.

Facilities and Resources
The **library** has 63,500 books and 230 subscriptions.

Career Services
Services include resume preparation, interview workshops, resume referral, and career counseling.

Campus Life
Active organizations on campus include a drama/theater group and choral group. No national or local **fraternities** or **sororities**. **Intercollegiate sports** include soccer (m).

Applying
Tyndale requires SAT I or ACT, a high school transcript, and a minimum high school GPA of 2.25, and in some cases an essay, an interview, and recommendations. It recommends a minimum high school GPA of 3.0. Application deadline: rolling admissions; 6/30 for financial aid, with a 2/21 priority date. Early and deferred admission are possible. **Contact:** Ms. Dianne Larimer, Counselor, 37500 West Twelve Mile Road, Farmington Hills, MI 48331, 248-553-7200 or toll-free 800-483-0707; fax 248-553-5963.

GETTING IN LAST YEAR	40% had ACT scores over 24	$4782 average financial aid amount received
140 applied	1% had ACT scores over 30	per undergraduate (1999–2000)
86% were accepted		
90 enrolled (75%)	**COSTS AND FINANCIAL INFORMATION**	**AFTER GRADUATION**
2% from top tenth of their h.s. class	$7050 tuition and fees (2000–2001)	18% graduated in 4 years
3.14 average high school GPA	$2800 room and board	4% graduated in 5 years
	60% average percent of need met	2% graduated in 6 years

Affiliates

■   Affiliates may include institutions which do not fully meet the criteria for Council membership, are not primarily four-year undergraduate colleges, or are located outside of North America. These institutions may include graduate schools, two-year colleges, and seminaries.

Non-Member Affiliates

Atlantic Baptist University
333 Gorge Road
Moncton, New Brunswick
CANADA E1C 8K2
Web site: http://www.abu.nb.ca
Admission contact
Ms. Shawna Peverill, Admissions Officer
506-858-8970

Atlantic Baptist University, begun as a Bible School over 40 years ago, is a Christ-centered university committed to providing a high quality educational experience grounded in the preeminence of Jesus Christ. The university provides liberal arts education leading to undergraduate degrees, diplomas and certifications in a broad range of academic subjects. Although owned and operated by the United Baptist Convention of the Atlantic Provinces, a variety of evangelical denominations are represented in their student body.

Bethune-Cookman College
640 Dr. Mary McLeod Bethune Blvd.
Daytona Beach, FL 32114-3099
Web site: http://www.cookman.edu
Admission contact
Mr. William Byrd, Assistant VP, Enrollment Management
904-255-1401 Ext. 358

Founded by Dr. Mary McLeod Bethune in 1904, Bethune-Cookman College is a historically black, United Methodist Church-related college offering baccalaureate degrees. The mission is to serve in the Christian tradition the educational, social and cultural needs of its students—traditional and nontraditional—and to develop in them the desire and capacity for continuous intellectual and professional growth, leadership, and service to others. The College has deep roots in the social history of America and continues to provide services to the broader community through its on- and off-campus outreach programs.

Central Baptist College
1501 College Avenue
Conway, AR 72032-6470
Admission contact
Mr. Eric Etchison, Director of Admissions
501-329-6872 Ext. 153

Founded as a junior college in 1952, Central Baptist now offers a four-year program leading to a bachelor of arts degree in numerous vocational ministries, as well as associate degrees in such fields as music, business, mathematics and science. Its motto—A College with Christian Ideals—embodies the educational philosophy of the college and expresses the point of reference from which the college seeks to educate the whole person.

Chongshin University & Theological Seminary
31-3, Sadang-Dong
Dongjak-Ku
Seoul 156-763 KOREA
Web site: http://www.congshin.ac.kr
Admission contact
Mr. Tae-je Moon, Director of Admissions (University)
(011-82) 2-3479-0253

Chongshin University & Theological Seminary is an institution of Christian higher education built upon the foundation of reformed theology. The seminary has 2,500 students in an M.Div. equivalent program which trains pastoral candidates to work for approximately 5,600 churches under the supervision of the General Assembly of the Presbyterian Church in Korea.

Columbia International University
PO Box 3122
Columbia, SC 29230-3122
Web site: http://www.ciu.edu
Admission contact
Kandi Mulligan, Vice President for Admissions
800-777-2227

Columbia International University is a multi-denominational Christian higher educational institution dedicated to preparing world Christians to serve God with excellence. Degree programs ranging from Associate to Doctor of Ministry feature majors designed to prepare students for a wide variety of church and marketplace ministries. The University's educational philosophy and programs emphasize spiritual formation, academic excellence with Bible at the core, cultivation of a biblical world view, and ministry skills development through supervised field education and internship experiences. Founded in 1923, CIU hosts students from 15 foreign countries and 40 states on its 400-acre campus located in Columbia, South Carolina's state capital.

Crestmont College
30840 Hawthorne Boulevard
Rancho Palos Verdes, CA 90275

Admission contact
310-377-0481

Crestmont College is a Salvation Army College for Officer Training whose mission is to train and produce effective, enthusiastic, and faithful Salvation Army officers of such Blood and Fire spirit that they will be enabled to sustain and advance the mission of the Salvation Army. The college offers an associate degree in ministries.

The Criswell College
4010 Gaston Avenue
Dallas, TX 75246
Website: http://www.criswell.edu

Admission contact
Mr. Joel Wilson, VP for Enrollment & Student Services
214-818-1302

The Criswell College exists to provide biblical, theological and professional education on both the undergraduate and graduate levels, preparing men and women to serve in Christian ministry. The inerrant Word of God remains central to every facet of the program.

Crown College
6425 County Road 30
St. Bonifacius, MN 55375-9001
Web site: http://www.crown.edu

Admission contact
Mrs. Janelle Wood, Director of Admissions
612-446-4144

Crown College, situated on a 193-acre campus west of Minneapolis, is the Midwestern regional college of the C&MA. Crown's mission is to provide a biblically-based education for Christian leadership in the C&MA, the church-at-large, and the world. To accomplish this mission, Crown endeavors to prepare men and women for ministry, develop students as earnest Christians, facilitate students' intellectual, emotional, physical and social development, encourage the understanding and appreciation of cultural and ethnic diversity, and offer an education integrated with biblical studies.

Denver Seminary
PO Box 100,000
Denver, CO 80250-0100
Web site: http://www.gospelcom.net/densem/

Admission contact
Dr. Gary Huckabay, Director of Admissions
303-761-2482 Ext. 234

Denver Seminary was founded in 1950 with an emphasis on a vibrant evangelicalism—commitment with freedom to think within the limits laid down in Scripture. Under President Clyde B. McDowell, the seminary has entered a major re-engineering process for equipping leaders, embodied by its new vision—to glorify God in partnership with his church by equipping leaders to know the truth, practice godliness and mobilize ministry. This new paradigm emphasizes high standards for academic content but also requires the development of godly character and Spirit-led competency through intensive mentoring by local churches and ministries.

European Nazarene Bible College
Postfac 60, 8238 Busingen
Switzerland
Web site: http://www.enbc.edu

Admission contact
Phil Petrie, Registrar
(011-49) 7734-80922

European Nazarene Bible College is an educational institution in the Wesleyan tradition which exists to help develop healthy, growing, reproducing, local Churches of the Nazarene by training people for active involvement in pastoral and lay ministry in local, district, regional, and global contexts, addressing the corresponding needs of churches and districts at various stages of development. ENBC was founded in 1966 and has an affiliation with MidAmerica Nazarene University in Olathe, Kansas. The College offers a one-year Spiritual Formation Certificate, a two-year Christian Ministry Certificate, a three-year Diploma in Bible and Theology, and a Bachelor of Arts in Religion and Missions in conjunction with MNU.

Franciscan University of Steubenville
1235 University Blvd.
Steubenville, OH 43952-1763
Web site: http://www.franuniv.edu

Admission contact
Mrs. Margaret Weber, Director of Admissions
740-283-6226

Founded in 1946 by Franciscan Friars of the Third Order Regular, Franciscan University of Steubenville integrates strong academic programs with a lively faith environment. This attractive combination—termed "dynamic orthodoxy" by Boston's Cardinal Bernard Law—draws over 1,900 students from all 50 states and over 40 foreign countries.

In addition to over 30 undergraduate and six graduate degree programs, Franciscan University offers the country's only Human Life Studies minor, which prepares students to think, speak and act intelligently in the defense of life in contemporary culture. Our theology major program attracts more undergrads than any other Catholic university in the United States.

Fuller Theological Seminary
135 North Oakland Avenue
Pasadena, CA 91182
Web site: http://www.fuller.edu
Admission contact
Mr. Howard G. Wilson, Director of Admissions
626-584-5434
Fuller Theological Seminary is an evangelical, multidenominational, international and multi-ethnic community dedicated to the preparation of men and women for the manifold ministries of Christ and his Church. As an educational arm of the church, Fuller's three graduate schools—Theology, Psychology, and World Mission—seek to serve the body of Christ in worldwide ministry, offering varied academic programs in Christian leadership.

Hoseo University
29-1 Sechul-ri
Baebang-myun
Asan-Si Chungnam, Korea, 336-795
Admission contact
Mr. Jong, Il-Ryong, Director of Admission
(011-82) 41-540-5050
Established by Dr. Kang Suk-Kyu in 1978 with the motto "Honor God, Esteem Yourself, Love Your Neighbor and Country", Hoseo University's mission is to promote learning and serve society in the spirit of Christianity. Hoseo University pursues excellence in teaching, research, and social service. The educational goals of Hoseo University are to help students acquire practical knowledge and skills that enable them to be useful members of our global society. It also aims to educate its students so that they have a positive spirit, a broad perspective, and a sense of responsibility.

Institute for Christian Studies
229 College Street, Suite 200
Toronto, Ontario
CANADA M5T 1R4
Web site: http://www.icscanada.edu
Admission contact
Mrs. Pam Thompson, Director of Student Services
416-979-2331 Ext. 239

The Institute for Christian Studies seeks to honour and proclaim Jesus Christ as the Redeemer of life and the Renewer of thought and learning. To carry out this mission, ICS engages in scholarship that reveals the religious roots of all learning and contributes to a scripturally-directed understanding of our world, and equips men and women for scholarly and other vocations through unique programs of graduate level education.

The International University
Rennweg 1
A-1030 Vienna
AUSTRIA
Admission contact
Mrs. Ana Benassi, Admissions Officer
(011-43) 1-718-50-6813
To prepare students from around the world to serve in the world—that is the mission of The International University. Based in Vienna, IU offers its international students a globalized liberal arts curriculum, featuring international business, computer information systems, and international studies. IU has an extension in Kiev, in conjunction with the Kiev State Economic University, as well as Agreements of Cooperation offering student exchange in Amman, Bratislava, Osaka and Prague. IU-Kiev is the first non-Soviet university to receive full recognition from the Ministry of Education and contributes significantly to the re-development of Ukraine, both spiritually and economically.

Jerusalem University College
PO Box 1276, Mt. Zion
91012 Jerusalem
ISRAEL
Web site: http://www.juc.edu
Admission contact
Mrs. Janet DeWaal, Director of Student Services
(011-972) 2-671-8628
Jerusalem University College is an independent, degree-granting Christian institution of higher education located in Jerusalem, Israel, which seeks to enhance its students' understanding of the Bible and the cultures of the Middle East. JUC offers graduate and undergraduate programs of study in Biblical history, geography, archaeology, and languages, in related literature, and in various cultural, philosophical and religious expressions of peoples of the modern Middle East. The school emphasizes a maximal use of, and personal interaction with, the unique academic and cultural resources available both in the classroom and field work in Israel and other Middle Eastern and eastern Mediterranean regions. By formally cooperating with over 100

colleges, universities and seminaries, JUC is able to bring its strengths to students throughout the world.

Lithuania Christian Fund College
Kretingos Centre 36a
LT-5808 Klaipeda
LITHUANIA
Web site: http://www.lccbc.org

Admission contact
Ms. Alma Jankauskaite, Director of Admissions
(011-370) 6-310745

Lithuania Christian Fund College exists to provide recognized university education that integrates academic excellence with Christian character, world view, and service. LCFC offers a one-year English Language Institute and four-year programs of study in Bible and Religion, Business Administration, and English.

North Central University
910 Elliot Avenue
Minneapolis, MN 55404
Web site: http://www.ncbc.edu

Admission contact
Mr. James Hubert, Director of Admissions
612-343-4483

North Central University is a four-year residential college located in downtown Minneapolis, whose purpose is to build Pentecostal leaders to serve God in the Church and in the world. Founded in 1930, NCU maintains an urban and international focus in its curriculum and cocurricular activities. Students choose from more than 20 academic majors ranging from pastoral studies and youth and children's ministries to communications and broadcasting to elementary education. Through teaching and scholarship, the faculty demonstrate a tradition of academic excellence combined with a strong commitment to develop spiritually mature alumni who understand and experience the challenge of God's inerrant Word.

Norwegian Teacher Academy
Post Box 74
Amalie Skrams vei 3
5035 Bergen-Sandviken
NORWAY
Web site: http://www.nla.no/

Admission contact
Mr. Arnfinn Norheim, Chief Enrollment Officer
(011-47) 55 54 07 52

Norsk Lærerakademi (The Norwegian Teacher Academy) is a private University College jointly run by seven Christian organizations within the (Lutheran) Church of Norway. Established in 1966, the Academy aims at equipping high school teachers, Christian youth workers and others with a deeper understanding of educational science in general and Christian Education in particular. In 1996 a College of Teacher Education for elementary school teachers was added. The Academy has Departments of Education and Religion offering both basic and intermediate (undergraduate) and graduate courses.

Philadelphia College of Bible
200 Manor Avenue
Langhorne, PA 19047-2990
Web site: http://www.pcb.edu

Admission contact
Mrs. Fran Emmons, VP of Admission Services
215-702-4239

Since 1913, Philadelphia College of Bible has been committed to teaching God's Word and preparing men and women for Christian ministry. In the process, PCB has distinguished itself as the nation's most accredited Bible college. At PCB every student majors in Bible, with some pursuing a second degree simultaneously in music, social work, education or business. All students choose from one of 42 programs designed to provide specific professional skills needed in ministry today. PCB continues to develop for the Christian church and its related ministries qualified leaders who possess a foundational knowledge of the Scriptures and a biblical world and life view.

Providence College & Seminary
Otterburne, Manitoba
CANADA R0A 1G0
Web site: http://www.providence.mb.ca

Admission contact
Mr. Mark Little, Dean of Admissions and Records
204-433-7488

The mission of Providence College is to educate students at a university level to think, live, and serve effectively as Christians in the church and society. Providence College differs from many Christian colleges in its commitment to conduct all of its education at the academic level of accredited university studies. A large and growing number of Canadian and international universities are recognizing this dimension of the Providence College educational program by granting a growing amount of transfer credit to alumni.

Regent University
1000 Regent University Drive
Virginia Beach, VA 23464-9800
Web site: http://www.regent.edu

Admission contact
Central Admissions Office
800-373-5504

Founded in 1977 as CBN University, Regent is a graduate institution preparing Christian leaders for the challenge of representing Christ in their professions. Through its offering of graduate degrees in business, communication, counseling, education, law, government, divinity, and organizational leadership. Regent seeks to send Christians into all professional spheres and to be a leading center of Christian thought and action.

Russian-American Christian University
kvartal 29/30, korpus 5
Noviye Cheryomushky
117420 Moscow
RUSSIA
Web site: http://www.racu.com

Admission contact
Ms. Darya K. Checareva, Admissions Director
(011-7) 095-719-7818

The Russian-American Christian University, established in the Russian Republic, is a comprehensive liberal arts university grounded in historic Biblical Christianity. Through the combined efforts of Russian and American educators, RACU offers to Russian students an educational program which trains them to be agents of renewal and reconciliation in the university, church, society and the world of business.

Seoul Women's University
#126 Kongreung-2-Dong, Nowon-Ku
Seoul 139-774 SOUTH KOREA
Web site: http://www.swu.ac.kr
Admission contact
82-02-970-5114
Founded in 1961 by the Presbyterian church, Seoul Women's University's main goal is to nurture women leaders equipped with academic ability and global citizenship. In order to attain the best results, SWU offers practical programs based on Christian principles, which encourage students to actively and creatively pursue truth. With 6,000 students and 36 departments, SWU offers undergraduate, graduate, and postgraduate studies.

Southwestern Baptist Theological Seminary
P.O. Box 22000
Fort Worth, TX 76122-0418
Web site: http://www.swbts.edu

Admission contact
Ms. Judy Morris, Director of Admissions
817-923-1921 Ext. 2777
Southwestern Baptist Theological Seminary's balance of sound scholarship, spiritual vitality and practical ministry and its historic commitment to missions and evangelism have been evidenced in the lives and work of men and women around the world for most of this century. SWBTS is committed both to a renewed emphasis on the historic traditions of Southwestern and to bring a part of the fresh and exciting winds in theological education that God seems to be sending across our world today. Southern Baptists and students from 39 other denominations have come to study in the Schools of Theology, Educational Ministries, and Church Music. SWBTS is today the world's largest school for graduate theological training. Since 1908, over 60,000 SWBTS students have gone out to contribute immeasurably to the life and work of Christian organizations around the world.

Taylor University Fort Wayne
1025 West Rudisill Blvd.
Fort Wayne, IN 46807
Web site: http://www.tayloru.edu/fw
Admission contact
Mr. Leo G. Gonot, Director of Admission
219-456-2111 Ext. 32347
In 1992, Taylor University established a second campus in Fort Wayne as the result of a merger with Summit Christian College, previously known as Fort Wayne Bible College. The Fort Wayne campus is unique in that it implements the Taylor tradition of scholarship, leadership and Christian commitment within an urban environment. Taylor University is currently celebrating its 151st year of providing quality Christian higher education.

Tokyo Christian University
3-301-5-1 Uchino
Inzai City
Chiba 270-13 JAPAN
Web site: http://www.tci.ac.jp/english/index.html
Admission contact
Dr. Akio Ito, Director of Admissions
(011-81) 476-46-1131 Ext. 62/169
Tokyo Christian University is a four-year theological university rooted in the liberal arts. Its Division of Theological Studies educates future pastors, missionaries and other church leaders to be "messengers of God" for the 21st century; the Division of International Christian Studies prepares students to be ministers of reconciliation to the world by emphasizing a Christian response to global human

concerns. With the slogan "From Chiba to the World!" TCU is full of enthusiasm for global missions.

Tyndale College & Seminary
25 Ballyconnor Court
Toronto, Ontario
CANADA M2M 4B3
Web site: http://www.tyndale-canada.edu

Admission contact
Mr. Don Russell, Director of Admissions
416-226-6380 Ext. 2190

Tyndale College & Seminary, formerly Ontario Bible College and Ontario Theological Seminary, seeks to educate and equip Christians to serve the world with passion for Jesus Christ. Student bodies and faculties reflect the broad spectrum of evangelical denominations and the multicultural nature of Toronto. Degree programs are offered in a wide variety of formats so as to make Christian education available to both traditional and non-traditional students of every age and vocational group.

Uganda Christian University Partners
PO Box 4
Mukono, Uganda
Web site: http://www.ugandapartners.org

Admission contact
(011-25) 6-41-290231
Founded in 1913 by the Anglican communion as Bishop Tucker Theological College, Uganda Christian became a university in 1992, dedicated through teaching, scholarship, service, spiritual formation, student development, and social involvement to the preparation of students for thoughtful, productive lives of Christian faith and service in their respective professions and places. The college offers undergraduate, graduate, and postgraduate degrees.

Universidad Evangélica Boliviana
Casilla 4027
Barrio Cruz del Sur UV117
Santa Cruz BOLIVIA

Admission contact
Lic. Miriam Guzmán de Molina, Chief Enrollment Officer
(011-591) 3-560991

The Universidad Evangélica Boliviana is a ministry of the World Gospel Mission, Marion, Indiana, in conjunction with three other U.S.-based missions and eight Bolivian evangelical institutions. It is the only American-sponsored university recognized by the Bolivian government and the first evangelical university in Spanish-speaking South America.

Waynesburg College
51 West College Street
Waynesburg, PA 15370
Web site: http://www.waynesburg.edu
Admission contact
Mrs. Robin Moore, Director of Admissions
724-852-3333

Recognized for its institutional commitment to service-learning for all enrolled students, Waynesburg College provides educational opportunities for students through both traditional and professional programs based upon a liberal arts foundation. Students are challenged to pursue scholarship, leadership and service based upon Christian values. The College has established active partnerships with other international educational institutions, and emphasis on the educational uses of technology has placed the institution on the "cutting edge" of innovative educational ventures. Waynesburg pledges to provide the means and inspiration by which its students may pursue lives of purpose.

Wesley Institute for Ministry & the Arts
5 Mary Street
PO Box 534
Drummoyne, NSW, 1470 Australia
Web site: http://www.wima.edu.au
Admission contact
Ms. Jane Kelly, Assistant Registrar
(011-02) 9719-1711
Wesley Institute for Ministry & the Arts is Australia's premier Christian college of the arts and theology. The Institute, established in 1989, reflects an evangelical, multi-denominational, multi-cultural, and multi-disciplinary approach to education, offering accredited degrees in Graphic Design, Music, Dance, Drama, and Theology as well as postgraduate courses in Counselling, Education, and Dance Therapy. Our courses combine creativity and spirituality with practicality and professionalism and offers students stimulating opportunities for academic and personal development in a caring Christian environment. Under the authority of Scripture, it seeks to fulfill its commitment to ministry through tertiary education, professional development, and spiritual formation. In all of its activities, including instruction, nurture, worship, service, and research, Wesley Institute strives for excellence in the service of Jesus Christ, under the guidance and power of the Holy Spirit, to the glory of the Father.

Special Programs

■ If reviewing a script for a movie director in Hollywood, studying environmental problems in the rain forests of Costa Rica, or working with lobbyists on Capitol Hill sounds like an appealing way to get your college degree, an off-campus study program may be right for you. In the United States and abroad, hundreds of students each year from Christian colleges and universities decide to make the world their classroom and spend a semester away from their home campus. This section contains descriptions of special off-campus study programs available to students at member schools of the Council for Christian Colleges & Universities. The Council sponsors nine programs: the American Studies Program, the China Studies Program, the Latin American Studies Program, the Los Angeles Film Studies Center, the Middle East Studies Program, the Honours Programme—CMRS, Oxford, and the Russian Studies Program. It also coordinates the Summer Programme—CMRS, Oxford and the Summer Institute of Journalism in Washington, D.C. In addition, the Council endorses a number of programs. While these programs are not sponsored by the Council, oversight for each is guided by at least ten participating colleges within the Council membership.

American Studies Program

Students in today's complex, competitive world face many challenges: to expand their world, to gain the education and experience they need, to get perspective, and to put their beliefs into practice.

For over two decades, the Council's American Studies Program (ASP) has challenged students to integrate their faith with the realities of the marketplace and public life through a semester of experiential learning in Washington, D.C. In the ASP, students can gain the experience they need to live and work in a biblically faithful way in society and in their chosen field.

Students enrolled at any of the colleges listed in this guide are invited to participate in this unique work-study program. ASP students earn academic credit by working about 20 to 25 hours a week as an unpaid intern in their intended vocational field and by participating in interdisciplinary, issue-oriented seminar classes.

Washington, D.C. is a stimulating educational laboratory that offers on-the-job training to help ASP students build a solid foundation for their future. ASP students live and study in the Council's Dellenback Center on Capitol Hill, which includes student apartments, a library, dining facilities, and a classroom.

Designed for juniors and seniors with a wide range of academic majors and career interests, the ASP provides many types of internships, including those in executive and congressional offices; business and trade associations; the law and social services; radio, TV, and print media; and think tanks, cultural institutions, and inner-city ministries. The American Studies Program works with students to tailor internships to fit their unique talents and aspirations.

While participating in the contemporary, issue-oriented seminar program, students and faculty members analyze current topics in domestic and international policy through two public policy units. In addition, each term begins and ends with a two-week unit on the foundation of Christian public involvement.

Over the years, the ASP has provided almost 1,700 college students with real-world experiences that have helped them gain the critical knowledge and preparation they need to begin understanding their life's vocation.

Because of its unique location in Washington, D.C., the program has a special way of challenging students to consider the meaning of the lordship of Christ in all areas of life, including career choices, public policy issues, and personal relationships.

ASP has had life-changing impact on its participants. As one alumnus says:

I loved the program because it challenged me to look deeper into beliefs I already had and to explore beliefs I'd never considered, substantiating them through Scripture and faith. The responsibilities expected of me, combined with the job skills I learned in the internship, provided a smoother transition from college to the workplace.

Additional information on the American Studies Program is available from the academic dean's office at any of the colleges listed in this guide or by contacting:

American Studies Program
CCCU Student Programs
329 Eighth Street, NE
Washington, D.C. 20002
Telephone: 202-546-3086
E-mail: asp@cccu.org
World Wide Web: www.cccu.org/students/

China Studies Program

 China is going through monumental changes that encompass all aspects of life: economic, social, religious, and political. Students from Council member institutions now have the unprecedented opportunity to gain knowledge and understanding of China's people, culture, and language firsthand through the Council's China Studies Program (CSP).

The CSP, an interdisciplinary semester program available to upperclass students, takes advantage of formal classes, travel, meeting and interacting with Chinese people from various backgrounds. Under the leadership of CSP's North American director, the program takes advantage of a number of strategic settings. Home base is a leading university in Shanghai, where students live for approximately nine weeks. During each semester, CSP participants also spend significant time in Xi'an, Beijing, and Hong Kong, and visit other areas of this vast country as well.

The curriculum for the CSP is designed to maximize the educational and experiential dimensions of a cross-cultural program. Studies in the standard Chinese language run throughout the time in Shanghai. The course is designed to help students gain an appreciation and beginning usage of spoken Mandarin. Language acquisition also occurs as it is practiced during the semester with Chinese students, faculty members, and others whom participants meet during their time in China.

In addition to the 3-credit **Basic Conversational Chinese,** studies also include the following seminar courses, each worth 3 semester credits:

• **Geography and History** is an introductory overview that includes archaeological findings from the Stone and Bronze Age, study of the ancient dynasties, slavery and feudalism, the Opium War, and China in revolution (1919–1949).

• **Society and Culture** builds on the first seminar, with overviews of China's diverse ethnic groups, population, and China's population policy; the various religions found throughout China's history; and its education, literature, music and art.

• **Relations with the World** begins with China's relationship at home—mainland China, Taiwan, and Hong Kong. The study broadens to include its relations with the rest of Asia and the West Pacific, the U.S., and the Western World, especially focusing on the Chinese dispersion, international relations, and foreign investments in China.

• **China's Modern Development.** Shanghai is the setting for the study of China's modern development, including its financial situation, economic reform, telecommunication, transportation, and modern industrial development. Students address questions related to China's future—with its own people and the world around it.

The curriculum also includes a 1-credit special seminar on local folk art and customs in Shanghai.

Further information on the China Studies Program is available from the academic dean's office at any of the colleges listed in this guide or by contacting:

China Studies Program
CCCU Student Programs
329 Eighth Street, NE
Washington, DC 20002
Telephone: 202-546-8713
E-mail: student-programs@cccu.org
World Wide Web: www.cccu.org/students/

Honours Programme—CMRS, Oxford

The Honours Programme—CMRS, Oxford (HP-O) is a partnership program between the Council for Christian Colleges & Universities and the Centre for Medieval and Renaissance Studies, affiliated to Keble College of the University of Oxford.

Juniors and seniors at member institutions of the Council having a GPA of 3.5 or better have the opportunity to join 25 other students in the exploration of what it means to study "Oxford style." Under the guidance of the Council-appointed program director, participants take part in the following 4-credit study components:

• Two tutorials, each worth 4 credits, in areas of study individually chosen. Course options include architecture, art, art history, European history, Greek, Latin, European languages, literature, drama, classics, writing, law, philosophy, political science, and Biblical and religious studies. These British tutorials provide the opportunity to study closely under Oxford dons (professors), who guide their students through research and wrestling with the issues involved, taking full advantage of this individual attention and supervision.

• An interactive seminar exploring the great questions of life during the Medieval, Reformation, and Counter-Reformation periods and other subject areas. In these small classes (made up of approximately 5 students), participants are challenged by different world views presented by Oxford dons, tutors and other students, while having the opportunity to share their own Christian perspectives.

• A semester-long integrative course designed specifically to engage the interconnections of faith, living, and learning under the leadership of the HP-O director. This course covers such topics as the Renaissance and humanism, conflict between Church and State, and society in transformation. As part of the course, students create and present a major scholarly project/paper at a final symposium.

In addition to study at Oxford, students also travel to significant historic and cultural sites in England on four study tours included in the program. These include visits to Bath, Glastonbury Abbey/Wells Cathedral, The Cotswolds, Stratford-upon-Avon, and St. Augustine's Abbey and Canterbury.

The HP-O serves as the "Oxford campus" of participants' home institutions. They receive credit from their sending campus for participation in the program.

Additional information about the Honours Programme—CMRS, Oxford is available from the academic dean's office at any of the colleges listed in this guide or by contacting:

Honours Programme—CMRS, Oxford
CCCU Student Programs
329 Eighth Street, NE
Washington, DC 20002
Telephone: 202-546-8713
E-mail: student-programs@cccu.org
World Wide Web: www.cccu.org/students/

Latin American Studies Program

An opportunity to live and learn in Latin America is available to students from Council member colleges in their junior or senior year through the Latin American Studies Program (LASP). Since 1986, the LASP, headquartered in San José, Costa Rica, has been committed to helping students examine and live out the lordship of Jesus Christ in an international context.

Each semester, a group of 36 to 40 students is selected to participate in this seminar/service travel experience in Latin America. The academic program, for which credit is awarded by the student's home institution, involves a combination of learning, serving, and observing.

In addition to the regular LASP experience, several tracks are available for students with specific major fields of study: the Advanced Language & Literature track (offered both fall and spring semesters), the International Business: Management and Marketing track (offered each fall semester), and the Tropical Science and Global Sustainability track (offered each spring semester). Students participating in a track rather than the regular program take five weeks of the semester to focus on courses and experiential learning unique to their field.

All participants are involved in three full weeks of intensive language study at the beginning of each semester, in which class assignment is based on language proficiency. Students practice their language skills with local Costa Ricans, including the host families who provide a home away from home for

each LASP student. These families are chosen for their Christian commitment and their willingness to share their culture and their friendship. At the same time, students take part in seminars coordinated by the LASP staff that deal with such issues as Third World development, Latin American history and culture, and the role of the church. Conducted in English and in Spanish, these seminar sessions enable students to interact with outside speakers, who bring a rich variety of perspectives to current issues.

The serving component involves hands-on experience working in a "servant role" in the Third World through participation in a service "opportunity." In order to get a better understanding of the complexities of Latin society, students are placed in a variety of service activities. The service opportunities may involve working in an orphanage or in an agency with abused children. The activities may also involve the fields of agriculture, economic development, education, environmental stewardship, and health. Track participants use this time to do hands-on activities in their field throughout the region.

In addition to living with Costa Rican families, students also have the opportunity to observe by traveling to at least two other Central American countries. By visiting Latin American countries outside Costa Rica, including Guatemala, Honduras, and Nicaragua, students enjoy a rich diversity of cultures in the cities, villages, and countryside of those areas. After participating in the Council's Latin American Studies Program, one student had this to say of his experience:

I feel this semester has been one of the hardest, most fun, most worthwhile experiences of my whole life, and I know that what I have learned will affect me always.

Applicants are required to have a minimum 2.75 GPA and the equivalent of 1 year of college-level Spanish. Additional information on the Latin American Studies Program is available from the academic dean's office at any of the colleges listed in this guide or by contacting:

Latin American Studies Program
CCCU Student Programs
329 Eighth Street, NE
Washington, D.C. 20002
Telephone: 202-546-8713
E-mail: student-programs@cccu.org
World Wide Web: www.cccu.org/students/

Los Angeles Film Studies Center

In January 1991, the Council for Christian Colleges & Universities inaugurated the Los Angeles Film Studies Center (LAFSC). This unique program serves as an introduction to the work and workings of the mainstream Hollywood film industry.

The LAFSC is conveniently located in Los Angeles near several of the major film and television studios. Accommodations are provided nearby in a corporate apartment complex featuring exceptional recreational facilities and comfortably furnished units.

The program is designed to allow students exposure to the industry, to the many academic disciplines that might be appropriate to it, and to critical thinking and reflection on what it means to be a Christian in the film world. As such, the curriculum is balanced between courses of a theoretical nature and courses that offer students an applied introduction to the world of film. LAFSC students participate in two required seminar courses, two of three elective options, and an internship in the film or television industry, as described below:

• **Inside Hollywood** (1 semester credit): This seminar examines the creative and operational aspects of the Hollywood film business, including the Christian's role in working within the entertainment business.

• **Faith, Film, and Culture** (3 semester credits): This course studies the relationship between film and popular culture, with emphasis on Christianity's role in these arenas. The course examines how faith, film, and culture mutually influence one another. It includes an overview of the historical relationship between the church and the movies, an understanding of a theology of the arts, a cultural studies approach to the nature of the arts in popular culture, and the Christian's role in identifying, discerning, and ultimately influencing movie content.

• **Introduction to Filmmaking** (3-semester-credit elective): Students receive an introduction to the theory and practice of motion picture filmmaking. Topics include familiarity with filmmaking equipment, converting idea to image, the use of lighting, editing, and sound in film; and the role of acting, directing and good storytelling in the filmmaking process. Students make several short Super 8 mm films that manifest their faith in content and practice.

• **Screenwriting** (3-semester-credit elective): This course serves as an introduction to contemporary screenwriting, including an understanding of dramatic structure, character and dialogue development, and the writing process. Students complete a full-length screenplay for a feature film or "movie-of-the-week." Emphasis is given to the role of Christian faith and values as they relate to script content.

• **Seminar in Producing the Independent Film** (3-semester-credit elective): This is an introduction to the process of producing an independent feature film. Topics include legal structures, business plans, preproduction activities such as scheduling and budgeting, and an overview of the producer's role in production, postproduction, and distribution.

• **Internships:** All LAFSC students are assigned a nonpaid internship in some aspect of the Hollywood film or television industry as arranged by the LAFSC staff. These internships are primarily in an office setting such as development companies, agencies, personal management companies, production offices, etc. Students are expected to work 20–24 hours a week throughout the entire semester. The internship serves as a laboratory to provide students with real-life exposure to the industry and as a basis for discussion and reflection in the courses.

Here is how one student viewed her semester:

The LAFSC is a great opportunity to get a broad overview of the film industry. The best part was actually being involved in the industry through my internship. I learned more through 'hands on' experience at a production company than I would have in any classroom setting.

Students interested in the Los Angeles Film Studies Center are invited to request additional information from the academic dean's office at any of the colleges listed in this guide or to contact the LAFSC directly:

Los Angeles Film Studies Center
CCCU Student Programs
3800 Barham Boulevard, Suite 202
Los Angeles, CA 90068
Telephone 213-882-6224
E-mail: LAFSC@aol.com
World Wide Web: www.cccu.org/students/

Middle East Studies Program

The Middle East, often called "the cradle of civilization," has always been a fascinating and complex region. The Council for Christian Colleges & Universities' Middle East Studies Program (MESP), based in Cairo, Egypt, exists to help college students understand the history, peoples, and cultures of the Middle East. Upperclass students enrolled at any of the colleges listed in this guide are eligible to apply for this unique learning experience. There is no language prerequisite.

While living in Cairo, students study spoken Arabic and participate in three interdisciplinary seminar courses designed to provide insights into the historical, religious, political, and economic dimensions of life in the Middle East. Academic credit for participation in the Middle East Studies Program is awarded by the student's home institution.

• **Peoples and Cultures of the Middle East** introduces students to the many different societies and ways of life in the region.

• **Islam in the Modern World** explains the basic tenets of the Islamic faith and seeks to give students an understanding of how Christians relate to Muslim countries and individuals.

• **Conflict and Change in the Middle East Today** addresses the ongoing quest for peace in this region, identifying the obstacles and the triumphs.

In all three seminar classes, personal interaction with resident scholars, local business people, religious leaders, and government officials enhances the education experience and provides perspectives no textbook can equal.

MESP students study Arabic language, focusing on spoken Arabic and on Arabic literature throughout the semester. This course is taught by native speakers of Arabic trained at the American University in Cairo, the program director, and guest lecturers. Ample opportunities exist to practice conversational skills with Egyptian students, other teachers, business people, and friends of the MESP.

Each week, students participate in a service opportunity in cooperation with one of the many organizations in Cairo, gaining valuable hands-on work experience and interaction with local Egyptians.

Safe and comfortable housing is provided in the international dormitory of the American University in Cairo and in nearby furnished apartments. All students live close to the MESP Center located on Zamalek, a large island in the Nile River just minutes from downtown Cairo. Students have access to American University's library and computer facilities. During the semester, participants travel by bus to Israel/Palestine to see the historic land of the Bible and to explore the many dimensions of the ongoing efforts for peace between Arabs and Israelis. On free weekends, students are able to travel within Egypt to Sinai, Alexandria, and Giza as well as to other locations. Much of the seminar "Peoples and Cultures" is taught "on site" while traveling through the Sinai, Jordan, Syria, and Turkey.

Participants in the Middle East Studies Program have the opportunity to gather a wide array of experiences. Says one student:

The MESP has, above all else, exposed me to a culture whose basis is not in Christianity. I now have a good Muslim friend whose faith is as strong as mine. It's an interesting situation for me to be in, because whenever I've been with people of deep faith before, they've been Christian.

Additional information about the Middle East Studies Program is available from the academic dean's office at any of the colleges listed in this guide or by contacting:

Middle East Studies Program
CCCU Student Programs
329 Eighth Street, NE
Washington, D.C. 20002
Telephone: 202-546-8713
E-mail: mesp@intouch.com or
    student-programs@cccu.org
World Wide Web: www.cccu.org/students/

Russian Studies Program

Upperclass students enrolled at one of the colleges listed in this guide have the opportunity to discover firsthand the richness of the Russian language, culture, and history through the Russian Studies Program (RSP).

The RSP is unique in that it makes use of the excellent resources found in three distinct locations: Moscow, Nizhni Novgorod, and St. Petersburg. The first ten days of the semester are spent in Moscow, where students receive an orientation to life in Russia and take in the city's extraordinary museums, galleries, landmarks, and historical resources.

Students then travel to Nizhni Novgorod, formerly Gorky, which becomes home for the next twelve weeks. As the "test site" for many economic reforms, the city is an ideal learning environment. While there, they take part in both language classes and seminars that explore the country's history, cultural and religious life, and literature, as well as challenges facing Russians today.

• **History and Sociology of Religion in Russia** (3 credits) delves into the history of religion in Russia from the beginnings of Christianity in the tenth century to the present day. The course also looks at the current government regulations from various points of view. Included are visits to churches and cathedrals in Moscow, St. Petersburg and Nizhni Novgorod and guest lectures by representatives of Russian Orthodox, Protestant and other religious perspectives.

• **Russian Peoples, Culture, and Literature** (4 credits) covers Russian history and culture using the rich resources of the three RSP sites, studying Russian people and culture throughout history using well-known works of Russian literature such as Tolstoy and Dostoyevsky.

• **Russia in Transition** (3 credits) focuses on contemporary Russia and her struggle to rebuild society following the collapse of Communism. Students are introduced to the complexities of economic transition from a centrally planned to a free-market economy and study efforts to build democratic institutions in Russia. This seminar includes service projects in selected educational institutions, orphanages, businesses, and other organizations in the Nizhni region, as well as travel throughout western Russia.

• **Russian Language** In addition to seminar classes, RSP students receive Russian language instruction by qualified native Russian language teachers, choosing either a 4-credit (80 hours in-class instruction) or 6-credit (120 hours) option. Prior knowledge of the Russian language is not required and students are placed in courses that correspond to their level of proficiency, from beginning to advanced. Students choosing the 4-credit option also take a 2-credit seminar on **Russian Business and International Relations.** Contacts with Russian students, particularly in Nizhni Novgorod, and the opportunity to live with Russian families for six weeks facilitate language acquisition.

After twelve weeks in Nizhni Novgorod, the RSP moves to St. Petersburg, Russian's former capital and its most westernized city. The richness of the historical and cultural resources of this beautiful city provide a venue for additional study of Russian/ Soviet society and a fitting conclusion for the program.

One RSP student observed:

The thing that surprised me most about Russian culture is the existence of religious history. I had thought of Russia as an antireligious country, but not even seventy years of communism could break the power of their religious past.

Said another student:

What really amazed me was the genuine sense of caring radiating from the Russians.... It felt like home there.

Additional information about the Russian Studies Program is available from the academic dean's office at any of the colleges listed in this guide or by contacting:

Russian Studies Program
CCCU Student Programs
329 Eighth Street, NE
Washington, D.C. 20002
Telephone: 202-546-8713
E-mail: wagler@wagler.kis.nnov.su or
    student-programs@cccu.org
World Wide Web: www.cccu.org/students/

Summer Programs

The Summer Institute of Journalism

Students at the colleges and universities listed in this guide are eligible to apply for participation in the Summer Institute of Journalism, a summer program managed by the Council for Christian Colleges & Universities.

Held for the first time in 1995, each summer 15 journalism students travel to Washington, D.C. for a month-long program designed to support the journalism education offered at Christian colleges and help equip journalism students for future work in the profession. The program, sometimes referred to as "Capstone in the Capital," enables participating students to interact with professional journalists in Washington, D.C. through seminars with media personnel and hands-on projects. Over 20 journalists representing the national media, including ABC News, the *Washington Post*, the Associated Press and *U.S. News & World Report*, typically participate in the program.

"This program is all about helping Christians develop the skills to be valid journalists," says Terry Mattingly, syndicated columnist and co-director of the Institute. "It is not about Christian journalism. It's about Christians being in journalism."

In addition to interacting with leading journalists, students have the opportunity to experience Washington, D.C. by visiting museums, monuments and art galleries. Students are housed at The Dellenback Center, located just blocks from Capitol Hill.

The program has positively influenced the students who have participated in it. Comments one participant:

My experience here (at The Summer Institute of Journalism) has motivated me to pursue all kinds of things in journalism, like small-town reporting, magazine reporting, and newspaper design. I know now that whatever I am doing, I am called by God to be there. This workshop has been confirmation of that.

Further information is available from the academic dean's office at any of the colleges listed in this guide or by contacting:

The Summer Institute of Journalism
CCCU Student Programs
329 Eighth St., NE
Washington, DC 20002
Telephone: 202-546-8713
E-mail: student-programs@cccu.org
World Wide Web: www.cccu.org/students/

Summer Programme—CMRS, Oxford

Students at the colleges and universities listed in this guide are eligible to apply for admission to the Summer Programme—CMRS, Oxford (SP-O), a multi-disciplinary program of study of the events of the Renaissance and Reformation. Located in Oxford, England, the program is cosponsored by the Council for Christian Colleges & Universities and the Centre for Medieval and Renaissance Studies, which is affiliated to Oxford's Keble College.

Inaugurated in 1975, the six-week program explores the Renaissance and Reformation through the study of the philosophy, art, literature, science, music, politics, and religion of this era. Many classes are conducted by Oxford dons, who also meet with students in seminars and in tutorials that are typical of the Oxford method of education.

Lectures, classes, meals, and social activities are held in St. Michael's Hall, which also houses faculty offices and the Centre's library. Students take residence at St. Michael's or at Wycliffe Hall, located next to the University's beautiful park.

Weekly field trips to places of importance outside Oxford introduce students to great cathedrals, castles, and historic towns nearby. Special activities include chapel, a garden party and formal dinner at Keble College, the annual Carl F. H. Henry Lecture, a weekly colloquium on faith and learning, and an evening at Shakespeare's Stratford-upon-Avon. The resources of Oxford, such as the world-famous Bodleian Library, are also available to students.

Participants in the SP-O have commented on the excellent experience that they have had:

I would definitely suggest this program for all students, regardless of one's major. It is an excellent opportunity for students to grow intellectually, but more importantly, to grow in their personal faith.

Further information is available from the academic dean's office at any of the colleges listed in this guide or by contacting:

Summer Programme—CMRS, Oxford
CCCU Student Programs
329 Eighth Street, NE
Washington, D.C. 20002
Telephone: 202-546-8713
E-mail: student-programs@cccu.org
World Wide Web: www.cccu.org/students/

Registered Programs

■ The following programs are registered with the Council. While not sponsored by the Council, oversight for each is guided by at least ten "participating colleges" within the Council membership.

The **AuSable Institute of Environmental Studies,** located in Michigan's lower peninsula, is an environmental stewardship program whose mission is to bring healing and wholeness to the biosphere and the whole of Creation. Students participate for college credit during January terms, May terms and summer schools. For more information:

AuSable Institute of Environmental Studies
7526 Sunset Trail, NE
Mancelona, MI 49659
Telephone: 231-587-8686
E-mail: admissions@ausable.org
Director: Dr. Cal DeWitt
Associate Director: Dr. David Mahan (contact person)

The **Christian Center for Urban Studies** (formerly the Wesleyan Urban Council) in Chicago, Illinois offers weekend, three-week and semester programs. Classes are offered in urban anthropology, culture, leadership, art, mission and service. For more information:

Christian Center for Urban Studies
Olive Branch Mission
6310 S. Claremont
Chicago, IL 60636-2427
Telephone: 773-476-6200, Ext. 39; 800-986-5483
Director: Julia Sittig

The **Focus on the Family Institute** in Colorado Springs, Colorado offers a semester-long program of on-site instruction and field experiences aimed at addressing the causes and cures for fractured families, and helping students become equipped to reverse societal trends that cause harm to traditional family structures and beliefs.

Focus on the Family Institute
Focus on the Family
8605 Explorer Drive
Colorado Springs, CO 80920
Telephone: 719-548-4560
Director: Dr. Michael Rosebush

EduVenture is a semester study-abroad program combining college-level courses with the adventure of hands-on mission experience. The overarching purpose of EduVenture is spiritual formation. This is achieved by providing a life-changing educational experience for North American Christian college and university students and participating holistic community development in West Papua, Indonesia (formerly Irian Jaya). Students study six subjects and earn 18 credits. Adventure activities such as trekking, coastal water activities, and spelunking take students into remote areas where they learn about and participate in local tribal cultures in the interior of West Papua.

EduVenture
5254 E. Holmes
Tucson, AZ 85711
Telephone: 520-750-8857
E-mail: EduVenture@earthlink.net
Director: B. Scotty Wisley

The **Global Stewardship Study Program** is based at an environmental center in the jungle of Belize, Central America. Students take four courses: Global Stewardship, Sustainable Development in Third World Communities, Tropical Ecology, and Biblical Stewardship. Additional electives and practicums are available, as well as a summer school option.

Global Stewardship Study Program
Target Earth International

3015-P Hopyard Road
Pleasanton, CA 94588
Telephone: 925-462-2439
E-mail: globalssp@aol.com
Director: Dr. Christopher Elisara

The **International Business Institute** is designed to give students in economics, business, and related areas a distinctive opportunity for study that incorporates the international dimension in these fields. This summer program is ten weeks in length and includes periods of residence in key locations as well as coordinated visits and presentations in the major political and economic centers of Western and Eastern Europe, Scandinavia, Finland, and Russia.

International Business Institute
1350 King College Road
Bristol, TN 37620
Telephone: 423-652-4736
E-mail: jnbane@king.edu
Program Coordinator: J. M. Lucarelli II

The **Jerusalem University College** in Jerusalem, Israel, (formerly the Institute for Holy Land Studies) offers credit for semester and yearlong programs of study. Students study the history, language, culture, archaeology, geography, and literature of the region, with a focus on enhancing their understanding of the Scriptures.

Jerusalem University College
4249 East State Street, Suite 203
Rockford, IL 61108
Telephone: 800-891-9408
E-mail: admissions@juc.edu
President: Dr. Sidney DeWaal
VP for North America: Mr. Michael McDonald (contact)

The **Netherlandic Student Program in Contemporary Europe** provides the opportunity to live in Amsterdam, one of the centers of the Western European Community. Participants receive 16 semester credits from courses in language, literature, the arts, history, and politics.

Options also exist for individualized study in other disciplines.

Netherlandic-SPICE Program
Dordt College
498 4th Avenue, NE
Sioux Center, IA 51250-1697
Telephone: 712-722-6358
E-mail: kboersma@dordt.edu
Director: Kenneth Boersma

The **Romanian Studies Program** of Eastern Nazarene College provides an opportunity for students to study and serve the people of Romania. Participants may enroll in the program for the fall or spring semesters, January term, or part of the summer. Courses offered are: Crosscultural Service Learning, Romanian Language and Culture, Arts and Music, and Environmental Science and Hiking.

Romanian Studies Program
Eastern Nazarene College
23 East Elm Avenue
Quincy, MA 02170
Telephone: 617-745-3827
E-mail: Romania@enc.edu
Director: Dr. Edward Mann

The **San Francisco Urban Program** of Westmont College provides an opportunity for a semester of Christ-centered study in the unique context of this great city. Students study urbanization, working in a practicum related to their interests, and have opportunities for independent study.

San Francisco Urban Program
3016 Jackson Street
San Francisco, CA 94115-1021
Telephone: 800-61-URBAN
E-mail: urban@westmont.edu
Director: Steve Schultz

The Council for Christian Colleges & Universities assumes no responsibility for the ownership and management of these programs.

Majors Index by School

ABILENE CHRISTIAN UNIVERSITY

Accounting, advertising, agribusiness, animal sciences, architectural engineering technology, area studies, art, art education, biblical studies, biochemistry, biology, biology education, business administration, business education, business marketing and marketing management, chemistry, chemistry education, child care/development, computer education, computer/information sciences, computer science, construction technology, criminal justice/law enforcement administration, (pre)dentistry, dietetics, drafting, drama and dance education, electrical/electronics engineering, elementary education, engineering physics, engineering science, English, English education, environmental science, exercise sciences, fashion merchandising, finance, fine/studio arts, French, French language education, geology, graphic design/commercial art/illustration, health education, health/physical education, history, history education, home economics, home economics education, human resources management, individual/family development, industrial arts education, industrial technology, interdisciplinary studies, interior design, international relations, journalism, (pre)law, liberal arts and studies, management science, mathematics, mathematics education, (pre)medicine, missionary studies, music, music education, music (piano and organ performance), music (voice and choral/opera performance), nursing, organizational psychology, pastoral counseling, (pre)pharmacy studies, physical education, physics, physics education, political science, psychology, public administration, range management, reading education, science education, secondary education, social science education, social studies education, social work, sociology, Spanish, Spanish language education, special education, speech education, speech-language pathology/audiology, speech/rhetorical studies, theater arts/drama, (pre)veterinary studies.

ANDERSON UNIVERSITY

Accounting, art education, athletic training/sports medicine, biblical studies, biology, business, business administration, business economics, business marketing and marketing management, chemistry, computer science, criminal justice/law enforcement administration, (pre)dentistry, education, elementary education, (pre)engineering, English, English education, family studies, finance, fine/studio arts, French, French language education, general studies, German, German language education, graphic design/commercial art/illustration, health education, health/physical education, history, (pre)law, management information systems/business data processing, mass communications, mathematics, mathematics/computer science, mathematics education, medical technology, (pre)medicine, music business management and merchandising, music education, music (general performance), nursing, philosophy, physical education, physics, political science, psychology, religious studies, sacred music, science education, social studies education, social work, sociology, Spanish, Spanish language education, speech education, theater arts/drama, theology, (pre)veterinary studies.

ASBURY COLLEGE

Accounting, applied mathematics, art education, athletic training/sports medicine, biblical studies, biochemistry, biology, business, chemistry, classics, computer/information sciences, elementary education, English, fine/studio arts, French, Greek (Ancient and Medieval), health/physical education, history, journalism, Latin (Ancient and Medieval), mathematics, middle school education, missionary studies, music, music education, philosophy, physical education, physical sciences, psychology, radio/television broadcasting technology, recreation/leisure facilities management, religious education, social sciences, social work, sociology, Spanish, speech/rhetorical studies.

AZUSA PACIFIC UNIVERSITY

Accounting, applied art, art, athletic training/sports medicine, biblical studies, biochemistry, biology, business administration, business marketing and marketing management, chemistry, communications, computer science, cultural studies, divinity/ministry, (pre)engineering, English, health science, history, international relations, (pre)law, liberal arts and studies, management information systems/business data processing, mathematics, music, natural sciences, nursing, philosophy, physical education, physics, political science, psychology, religious studies, social sciences, social work, sociology, Spanish, theology.

BARTLESVILLE WESLEYAN COLLEGE

Accounting, athletic training/sports medicine, behavioral sciences, biological and physical sciences, biology, business administration, business education, chemistry, (pre)dentistry, divinity/ministry, education, elementary education, English, exercise sciences, history, information sciences/systems, (pre)law, liberal arts and studies, linguistics, mass communications, mathematics, (pre)medicine, music, music (general performance), natural sciences, nursing, physical education, physical therapy, political science, religious studies, science education, secondary education, secretarial science, social sciences, teaching English as a second language, theology, (pre)veterinary studies.

BELHAVEN COLLEGE

Accounting, art, athletic training/sports medicine, biblical studies, biology, business administration, chemistry, communications, computer science, dance, elementary education, English, history, humanities, information sciences/systems, mathematics, music, pastoral counseling, philosophy, psychology, sport/fitness administration, theater arts/drama.

BETHEL COLLEGE (IN)

Accounting, aerospace engineering, art, biblical studies, biological and physical sciences, biology, biology education, business administration, business education, chemical engineering, chemistry, chemistry education, civil engineering, communications, computer/information sciences, computer science, (pre)dentistry, divinity/ministry, early childhood education, education, electrical/electronics engineering, elementary education, engineering science, English, English education, environmental biology, health education, history, interior design, journalism, (pre)law, liberal arts and studies, mathematics, mathematics education, mechanical engineering, (pre)medicine, metallurgical engineering, music, music education, music (piano and organ performance), music (voice and choral/opera performance), nursing, philosophy, physical education, physics education, psychology, religious studies, sacred music, science education, secondary education, secretarial science, sign language interpretation, social sciences, social studies education, sociology, theater arts/drama.

BETHEL COLLEGE (KS)

Accounting, art, biology, business administration, chemistry, communications, elementary education, English, fine/studio arts, German, health/physical education, history, mathematics, music, natural sciences, nursing, physics, psychology, religious studies, social sciences, social work, Spanish.

BETHEL COLLEGE (MN)

Accounting, adult/continuing education, art, art education, art history, athletic training/sports medicine, biblical studies, biochemistry, biology, business administration, chemistry, child care/development, computer science, creative writing, cultural studies, (pre)dentistry, early childhood education, economics, education, elementary education, English, environmental

Bethel College (MN) (continued)

science, finance, fine/studio arts, health education, history, international relations, (pre)law, liberal arts and studies, literature, management information systems/business data processing, mass communications, mathematics, (pre)medicine, molecular biology, music, music education, nursing, philosophy, physical education, physics, political science, psychology, sacred music, science education, secondary education, social work, Spanish, speech/rhetorical studies, theater arts/drama, (pre)veterinary studies.

BIOLA UNIVERSITY

Adult/continuing education, anthropology, art, biblical studies, bilingual/bicultural education, biochemistry, biology, business administration, clinical psychology, communication disorders, computer/information sciences, divinity/ministry, drawing, education, elementary education, English, exercise sciences, fine/studio arts, graphic design/commercial art/illustration, history, humanities, (pre)law, mathematics, missionary studies, music, nursing, pastoral counseling, philosophy, physical education, physical sciences, psychology, radio/television broadcasting, religious education, religious studies, secondary education, social sciences, sociology, Spanish, theology.

BLUFFTON COLLEGE

Accounting, art, art education, biology, business administration, business economics, business education, chemistry, child care/development, clothing and textiles, computer science, criminal justice/law enforcement administration, developmental/child psychology, dietetics, divinity/ministry, early childhood education, economics, education, elementary education, English, exercise sciences, fashion design/illustration, fashion merchandising, graphic design/commercial art/illustration, health education, history, home economics, home economics education, humanities, (pre)law, liberal arts and studies, mass communications, mathematics, medical technology, (pre)medicine, music, music education, nutrition science, peace and conflict studies, philosophy, physical education, physics, political science, psychology, recreation and leisure studies, religious studies, retail management, secondary education, social sciences, social work, sociology, Spanish, special education, speech/rhetorical studies, sport/fitness administration.

BRYAN COLLEGE

Biblical studies, biology, business administration, computer science, early childhood education, education, elementary education, English, history, liberal arts and studies, literature, mass communications, mathematics, (pre)medicine, middle school education, music, music business management and merchandising, music education, music (piano and organ performance), music (voice and choral/opera performance), physical education, psychology, religious education, sacred music, science education, secondary education, wind and percussion instruments.

CALIFORNIA BAPTIST UNIVERSITY

Art, behavioral sciences, biology, business administration, criminal justice studies, English, exercise sciences, fine/studio arts, history, information sciences/systems, liberal arts and studies, mathematics, music, philosophy, physical education, physical sciences, political science, psychology, religious studies, social sciences, theater arts/drama.

CALVIN COLLEGE

Accounting, American history, art, art education, art history, athletic training/sports medicine, biblical studies, bilingual/bicultural education, biochemistry, biological and physical sciences, biology, business administration, business communications, chemical engineering, chemistry, civil engineering, classics, computer science, criminal justice/law enforcement administration, (pre)dentistry, economics, electrical/electronics engineering, elementary education, engineering, English, environmental science, European history, exercise sciences, film studies, fine/studio arts, French, geography, geology, German, Greek (Modern), history, interdisciplinary studies, international relations, Latin (Ancient and Medieval), (pre)law, mass communications, mathematics, mechanical engineering, medical technology, (pre)medicine, music, music conducting, music education, music (general performance), music history, music (piano and organ performance), music theory and

composition, music (voice and choral/opera performance), natural sciences, nursing, occupational therapy, philosophy, physical education, physical sciences, physics, political science, psychology, public administration, recreation and leisure studies, religious studies, sacred music, science education, secondary education, social sciences, social work, sociology, Spanish, special education, speech-language pathology/audiology, speech/rhetorical studies, teaching English as a second language, theater arts/drama, theology, (pre)veterinary studies.

CAMPBELLSVILLE UNIVERSITY

Accounting, art, art education, athletic training/sports medicine, biblical studies, biology, business administration, business economics, business education, business marketing and marketing management, chemistry, criminal justice/law enforcement administration, data processing technology, (pre)dentistry, divinity/ministry, economics, elementary education, English, health education, history, information sciences/systems, journalism, (pre)law, mass communications, mathematics, medical technology, (pre)medicine, music, music education, music (piano and organ performance), music (voice and choral/opera performance), pastoral counseling, physical education, physics, political science, psychology, recreation and leisure studies, religious education, religious studies, sacred music, science education, secondary education, secretarial science, social sciences, social work, sociology, (pre)veterinary studies.

CAMPBELL UNIVERSITY

Accounting, advertising, art, athletic training/sports medicine, biochemistry, biology, biology education, business, chemistry, communications, computer/information sciences, criminal justice/law enforcement administration, (pre)dentistry, economics, education, education administration, elementary education, elementary/middle/secondary education administration, (pre)engineering, English, finance, fine/studio arts, French, graphic design/commercial art/illustration, health aide, health/physical education, health science, history, home economics, home economics education, industrial design, international business, international relations, journalism, (pre)law, liberal arts and studies, mathematics, medical pharmacology and pharmaceutical sciences, (pre)medicine, middle school education, music, music education, music (piano and organ performance), music theory and composition, pharmacy, physical education, political science, psychology, public administration, public relations, radio/television broadcasting, religious studies, secondary education, social sciences, social work, Spanish, sport/fitness administration, theater arts/drama, (pre)veterinary studies.

CEDARVILLE UNIVERSITY

Accounting, American studies, athletic training/sports medicine, biblical studies, biological and physical sciences, biology, biology education, broadcast journalism, business administration, business marketing and marketing management, chemistry, communication equipment technology, communications, computer science, criminal justice/law enforcement administration, (pre)dentistry, early childhood education, education, electrical/electronics engineering, elementary education, English, English education, environmental biology, finance, health education, health/physical education, history, information sciences/systems, international business, international relations, (pre)law, mathematics, mathematics education, mechanical engineering, medical technology, (pre)medicine, missionary studies, music, music education, music (piano and organ performance), music (voice and choral/opera performance), nursing, pastoral counseling, philosophy, physical education, political science, psychology, public administration, radio/television broadcasting, sacred music, science education, secondary education, secretarial science, social sciences, social studies education, social work, sociology, Spanish, Spanish language education, special education, speech education, speech/rhetorical studies, technical writing, theater arts/drama, theology, (pre)veterinary studies.

COLLEGE OF THE OZARKS

Accounting, agribusiness, agricultural education, agricultural mechanization, agronomy/crop science, animal sciences, art education, aviation technology, biology, biology education, broadcast journalism, business administration, business education, business marketing and marketing management, chemistry, chemistry education, child care/development, child guidance, clothing/apparel/textile studies, computer/information sciences, computer science, consumer services, corrections, criminal justice/law enforcement administration, criminology, dietetics, education, elementary education, English, English education, fine/studio arts, forensic technology, French, German, gerontology, health/physical education, health science, history, history education, home economics, home economics education, horticulture science, hotel and restaurant management, industrial arts, industrial arts education, interdisciplinary studies, journalism, law enforcement/police science, mass communications, mathematics, mathematics education, medical technology, (pre)medicine, middle school education, music, music business management and merchandising, music education, nutrition science, (pre)pharmacy studies, philosophy, physical education, political science, poultry science, psychology, public relations, recreation/leisure facilities management, religious studies, sacred music, science education, secondary education, social work, sociology, Spanish, speech/rhetorical studies, theater arts/drama, (pre)veterinary studies.

COLORADO CHRISTIAN UNIVERSITY
Accounting, adult/continuing education, art, biblical studies, biology, broadcast journalism, business, business administration, communications, computer/information sciences, divinity/ministry, elementary education, English, English education, history, humanities, human resources management, information sciences/systems, liberal arts and studies, management information systems/business data processing, mathematics, mathematics education, music, music education, music (general performance), music (voice and choral/opera performance), pastoral counseling, political science, psychology, sacred music, science education, secondary education, social studies education, theater arts/drama, theology.

CORNERSTONE UNIVERSITY
Accounting, adult/continuing education, aircraft pilot (professional), biblical languages/literatures, biblical studies, biology, broadcast journalism, business administration, business education, business marketing and marketing management, (pre)dentistry, divinity/ministry, early childhood education, education, elementary education, English, history, information sciences/systems, interdisciplinary studies, (pre)law, mass communications, mathematics, (pre)medicine, music, music education, pastoral counseling, physical education, psychology, religious studies, religious studies, science education, secondary education, social work, sociology, Spanish, speech/rhetorical studies, sport/fitness administration, (pre)veterinary studies.

COVENANT COLLEGE
Biblical studies, biology, business administration, chemistry, computer science, economics, elementary education, (pre)engineering, English, health science, history, interdisciplinary studies, (pre)law, (pre)medicine, music, natural sciences, nursing, philosophy, psychology, sociology.

CRICHTON COLLEGE
Biblical studies, biology, biology education, business administration, chemistry, clinical psychology, communications, counseling psychology, elementary education, English, English education, history, (pre)law, liberal arts and studies, psychology, school psychology, secondary education.

DALLAS BAPTIST UNIVERSITY
Accounting, art, biblical studies, biology, business administration, business economics, business marketing and marketing management, computer/information sciences, computer science, criminal justice/law enforcement administration, early childhood education, education, elementary education, English, finance, health services administration, history, interdisciplinary studies, liberal arts and studies, management information systems/business data processing, mass communications, mathematics, music, music education, music (piano and organ performance), music theory and composition, music (voice and choral/opera performance), pastoral counseling, philosophy, physical education, political science, psychology, religious education, sacred music, science education, secondary education, sociology.

DAVID LIPSCOMB UNIVERSITY
Accounting, American government, American studies, art, athletic training/sports medicine, biblical languages/literatures, biblical studies, biochemistry,

biology, biology education, business administration, business economics, business marketing and marketing management, chemistry, computer science, (pre)dentistry, dietetics, divinity/ministry, education, elementary education, engineering science, English, environmental science, exercise sciences, family/consumer studies, fashion merchandising, finance, fine/studio arts, food products retailing, French, French language education, German, graphic design/commercial art/illustration, health education, history, home economics, information sciences/systems, (pre)law, liberal arts and studies, mass communications, mathematics, (pre)medicine, middle school education, music, music education, music (piano and organ performance), music (voice and choral/opera performance), nursing, philosophy, physical education, physics, political science, psychology, public administration, public relations, secondary education, social work, Spanish, speech/rhetorical studies, stringed instruments, theology, urban studies, (pre)veterinary studies, wind and percussion instruments.

DORDT COLLEGE
Accounting, agricultural business, agricultural sciences, animal sciences, art, biology, business administration, business education, chemistry, computer science, criminal justice/law enforcement administration, data processing technology, (pre)dentistry, education, electrical/electronics engineering, elementary education, engineering, engineering mechanics, English, environmental science, exercise sciences, German, graphic design/commercial art/illustration, history, journalism, management information systems/business data processing, mass communications, mathematics, medical technology, (pre)medicine, music, music education, natural sciences, pastoral counseling, philosophy, physical education, physics, political science, psychology, recreation and leisure studies, religious studies, secondary education, secretarial science, social sciences, social work, sociology, Spanish, teacher assistant/aide, theater arts/drama, theology, (pre)veterinary studies.

EASTERN COLLEGE
Accounting, art history, astronomy, biblical studies, biochemistry, biology, business marketing and marketing management, chemistry, communications, creative writing, elementary education, English, English education, environmental science, finance, French, health facilities administration, health/physical education, history, liberal arts and studies, management information systems/business data processing, management science, mathematics, missionary studies, multimedia, music, nursing, philosophy, political science, psychology, secondary education, social work, sociology, Spanish, theology, urban studies.

EASTERN MENNONITE UNIVERSITY
Accounting, agricultural sciences, art, biblical studies, biochemistry, biology, business administration, chemistry, communications, community services, computer programming, computer science, data processing technology, (pre)dentistry, development economics, divinity/ministry, early childhood education, economics, education, elementary education, (pre)engineering, English, environmental science, French, German, health education, history, information sciences/systems, international agriculture, international business, liberal arts and studies, mathematics, medical technology, (pre)medicine, middle school education, music, music education, nursing, pastoral counseling, peace and conflict studies, physical education, psychology, recreation and leisure studies, religious studies, science education, secondary education, social work, sociology, Spanish, special education, sport/fitness administration, teacher assistant/aide, theater arts/drama, theology, (pre)veterinary studies.

EASTERN NAZARENE COLLEGE
Accounting, advertising, aerospace engineering, athletic training/sports medicine, bilingual/bicultural education, bioengineering, biological and physical sciences, biology, business, business administration, business marketing and marketing management, chemistry, clinical psychology, computer engineering, computer science, (pre)dentistry, developmental/child psychology, divinity/ministry, early childhood education, education, electrical/electronics engineering, elementary education, engineering physics, English, environmental science, French, general studies, health science, history, industrial engineering, journalism, (pre)law, liberal arts and studies, literature, mass communications, mathematics, mechanical engineering, (pre)medicine,

Eastern Nazarene College (continued)

middle school education, music, music education, music (general performance), pastoral counseling, pharmacy, physical education, physical therapy, physics, psychology, radio/television broadcasting, religious education, religious studies, sacred music, secondary education, social sciences, social work, sociology, Spanish, special education, systems engineering, teaching English as a second language, theater arts/drama, (pre)veterinary studies.

EAST TEXAS BAPTIST UNIVERSITY

Accounting, behavioral sciences, biology, biology education, business, business administration, business education, business marketing and marketing management, chemistry, chemistry education, computer education, computer/information sciences, drama and dance education, early childhood education, education (multiple levels), elementary education, English, English education, health/physical education, history, history education, liberal arts and studies, mathematics, mathematics education, medical technology, music, music education, music (piano and organ performance), music (voice and choral/opera performance), nursing, pastoral counseling, physical education, psychology, religious education, religious studies, sacred music, science education, secondary education, social studies education, sociology, Spanish, Spanish language education, speech education, speech/rhetorical studies, theater arts/drama, theology.

ERSKINE COLLEGE

Accounting, American studies, athletic training/sports medicine, behavioral sciences, biblical studies, biological and physical sciences, biology, business administration, chemistry, early childhood education, elementary education, English, French, health science, history, mathematics, medical technology, music, music business management and merchandising, music education, music (piano and organ performance), music (voice and choral/opera performance), natural sciences, physical education, physics, psychology, religious education, religious studies, sacred music, social studies education, Spanish, special education, sport/fitness administration.

EVANGEL UNIVERSITY

Accounting, art, art education, behavioral sciences, biblical studies, biology, broadcast journalism, business administration, business education, business marketing and marketing management, chemistry, child care/development, computer science, criminal justice/law enforcement administration, (pre)dentistry, early childhood education, education, elementary education, English, history, journalism, (pre)law, mass communications, mathematics, medical laboratory technologies, medical technology, (pre)medicine, mental health/rehabilitation, music, music education, physical education, political science, psychology, public administration, radio/television broadcasting, recreation and leisure studies, sacred music, science education, secondary education, secretarial science, social sciences, social work, sociology, Spanish, special education, speech/rhetorical studies, (pre)veterinary studies.

FRESNO PACIFIC UNIVERSITY

Accounting, applied mathematics, athletic training/sports medicine, biblical studies, bilingual/bicultural education, biology, business administration, business marketing and marketing management, chemistry, computer/information sciences, developmental/child psychology, divinity/ministry, education, elementary education, English, finance, history, humanities, international business, (pre)law, liberal arts and studies, literature, mass communications, mathematics, (pre)medicine, music, music education, natural sciences, nonprofit/public management, pastoral counseling, physical education, political science, psychology, religious studies, sacred music, science education, secondary education, social sciences, social work, sociology, Spanish, sport/fitness administration.

GENEVA COLLEGE

Accounting, applied mathematics, aviation management, biblical studies, biology, business administration, business education, chemical engineering, chemistry, communications, computer science, creative writing, elementary education, engineering, English, history, human services,

individual/family development, mathematics education, music, music business management and merchandising, music education, music (general performance), philosophy, physics, political science, psychology, radio/television broadcasting, secondary education, sociology, Spanish, special education, speech-language pathology/audiology, speech/rhetorical studies, (pre)theology.

GEORGE FOX UNIVERSITY

Art, athletic training/sports medicine, biblical studies, biology, biology education, business administration, business economics, chemistry, chemistry education, clinical psychology, cognitive psychology and psycholinguistics, communications, computer/information sciences, counseling psychology, curriculum and instruction, divinity/ministry, education (multiple levels), elementary education, engineering, English, English education, family resource management studies, fashion merchandising, health education, history, home economics, home economics education, human resources management, interdisciplinary studies, international relations, management information systems/business data processing, mathematics, mathematics education, missionary studies, music, music education, pastoral counseling, physical education, psychology, radio/television broadcasting, religious education, religious studies, social studies education, social work, sociology, Spanish, sport/fitness administration, theology.

GORDON COLLEGE (MA)

Accounting, art, biblical studies, biology, business administration, chemistry, communications, computer science, early childhood education, economics, education, elementary education, English, exercise sciences, foreign languages/literatures, French, German, history, international relations, mass communications, mathematics, middle school education, modern languages, music, music education, music (general performance), philosophy, physics, political science, psychology, recreation and leisure studies, religious education, social work, sociology, Spanish, special education.

GOSHEN COLLEGE

Accounting, art, art education, art therapy, biblical studies, bilingual/bicultural education, biology, broadcast journalism, business administration, business education, chemistry, child care/development, computer science, (pre)dentistry, early childhood education, economics, education, elementary education, English, environmental science, family/community studies, German, Hispanic-American studies, history, information sciences/systems, journalism, (pre)law, liberal arts and studies, mass communications, mathematics, (pre)medicine, music, music education, natural sciences, nursing, peace and conflict studies, physical education, physical sciences, physics, political science, psychology, religious studies, science education, secondary education, social work, sociology, Spanish, teaching English as a second language, theater arts/drama, (pre)veterinary studies.

GRACE COLLEGE

Accounting, art, art education, biblical studies, biology, business, business administration, counseling psychology, criminal justice/law enforcement administration, divinity/ministry, drawing, elementary education, English, English education, French, French language education, German, German language education, graphic design/commercial art/illustration, international business, management information systems/business data processing, mass communications, mathematics, mathematics education, music education, music (piano and organ performance), painting, pastoral counseling, physical education, psychology, science education, secretarial science, social work, sociology, Spanish, Spanish language education.

GRAND CANYON UNIVERSITY

Accounting, art, art education, athletic training/sports medicine, biblical studies, biology, business administration, business economics, business education, business marketing and marketing management, chemistry, criminal justice/law enforcement administration, (pre)dentistry, divinity/ministry, economics, elementary education, English, environmental biology, exercise sciences, finance, fine/studio arts, graphic design/commercial art/illustration, history, human resources management, international business, international relations, (pre)law, liberal arts and studies, literature, mass communications, mathematics, (pre)medicine, music, music business management and merchandising, music education, music (piano and organ performance), music (voice and choral/opera performance), nursing, physical education, physical sciences, political science, psychology, religious studies, sacred music, science education, secondary education, social sciences, sociology, special education, speech/rhetorical studies, theater arts/drama, theology, (pre)veterinary studies, wildlife biology, wind and percussion instruments.

GREENVILLE COLLEGE
Accounting, art, art education, biology, biology education, business administration, business marketing and marketing management, chemistry, chemistry education, computer science, (pre)dentistry, divinity/ministry, drama and dance education, early childhood education, education, elementary education, English, English education, environmental biology, foreign languages education, French, history, (pre)law, liberal arts and studies, management information systems/business data processing, mass communications, mathematics, mathematics education, (pre)medicine, modern languages, music, music education, pastoral counseling, philosophy, physical education, physics, physics education, political science, psychology, public relations, recreation and leisure studies, religious studies, sacred music, science education, secondary education, social studies education, social work, sociology, Spanish, Spanish language education, special education, speech education, speech/rhetorical studies, theater arts/drama, theology, (pre)veterinary studies.

HOPE INTERNATIONAL UNIVERSITY
Athletic training/sports medicine, biblical studies, business administration, child care/development, early childhood education, elementary education, English education, general studies, individual/family development, interdisciplinary studies, missionary studies, music education, physical therapy, physiological psychology/psychobiology, psychology, sacred music, social science education, social sciences, social work.

HOUGHTON COLLEGE
Accounting, art, art education, biblical studies, biological and physical sciences, biology, business administration, chemistry, computer science, creative writing, (pre)dentistry, divinity/ministry, education, elementary education, English, French, history, humanities, international relations, (pre)law, literature, mass communications, mathematics, medical technology, (pre)medicine, music, music education, music (piano and organ performance), music (voice and choral/opera performance), natural sciences, pastoral counseling, philosophy, physical education, physical sciences, physics, political science, psychology, recreation and leisure studies, religious education, religious studies, sacred music, science education, secondary education, social sciences, sociology, Spanish, stringed instruments, (pre)veterinary studies, wind and percussion instruments.

HOUSTON BAPTIST UNIVERSITY
Accounting, art, art education, biblical studies, bilingual/bicultural education, biology, broadcast journalism, business administration, business economics, business marketing and marketing management, chemistry, computer science, counselor education/guidance, (pre)dentistry, developmental/child psychology, early childhood education, economics, education, elementary education, engineering, engineering physics, engineering science, English, exercise sciences, finance, French, history, information sciences/systems, interdisciplinary studies, journalism, (pre)law, liberal arts and studies, mass communications, mathematics, medical technology, (pre)medicine, music, music education, nuclear medical technology, nursing, physics, political science, psychology, recreation and leisure studies, religious studies, sacred music, secondary education, sociology, Spanish, special education, speech/rhetorical studies, (pre)veterinary studies.

HOWARD PAYNE UNIVERSITY
Accounting, American studies, applied art, art, art education, athletic training/sports medicine, behavioral sciences, biblical languages/literatures, biblical studies, biology, business administration, business education, business marketing and marketing management, chemistry, communications, criminal justice/law enforcement administration, early childhood education, education, education (multiple levels), elementary education, English, entrepreneurship, European studies, exercise sciences, finance, fine/studio

arts, general studies, health services administration, history, information sciences/systems, interdisciplinary studies, (pre)law, liberal arts and studies, mathematics, medical technology, (pre)medicine, modern languages, music, music education, music (piano and organ performance), music (voice and choral/opera performance), paralegal/legal assistant, philosophy, physical education, political science, psychology, public relations, recreation and leisure studies, religious education, religious studies, sacred music, science education, secondary education, social sciences, social work, sociology, Spanish, speech education, speech/rhetorical studies, stringed instruments, telecommunications, theater arts/drama, theology, wind and percussion instruments.

HUNTINGTON COLLEGE
Accounting, art, art education, biblical studies, biological and physical sciences, biology, broadcast journalism, business administration, business economics, business education, chemistry, computer science, (pre)dentistry, divinity/ministry, economics, education, elementary education, English, exercise sciences, graphic design/commercial art/illustration, history, (pre)law, mass communications, mathematics, (pre)medicine, music, music education, music (piano and organ performance), music (voice and choral/opera performance), natural resources management, philosophy, physical education, psychology, recreation and leisure studies, religious studies, science education, secondary education, sociology, special education, theater arts/drama, theology, (pre)veterinary studies.

INDIANA WESLEYAN UNIVERSITY
Accounting, alcohol/drug abuse counseling, art, art education, athletic training/sports medicine, biblical languages/literatures, biblical studies, biology, business administration, business marketing and marketing management, ceramic arts, chemistry, communications, computer graphics, computer/information sciences, creative writing, criminal justice studies, cultural studies, (pre)dentistry, divinity/ministry, economics, education, elementary education, English, English education, finance, general studies, history, (pre)law, mathematics, mathematics education, medical technology, (pre)medicine, middle school education, music, music education, music theory and composition, nursing, painting, pastoral counseling, philosophy, photography, physical education, political science, printmaking, psychology, recreation/leisure facilities management, religious education, sacred music, science education, secondary education, social sciences, social studies education, social work, sociology, Spanish, special education, sport/fitness administration, theology, (pre)veterinary studies.

JOHN BROWN UNIVERSITY
Accounting, art, athletic training/sports medicine, biblical studies, biochemistry, biology, broadcast journalism, business administration, business education, chemistry, computer graphics, construction engineering, construction management, divinity/ministry, early childhood education, education, electrical/electronics engineering, elementary education, engineering, engineering/industrial management, engineering technology, English, environmental science, exercise sciences, graphic design/commercial art/illustration, health education, health services administration, history, interdisciplinary studies, international business, international relations, journalism, (pre)law, liberal arts and studies, mass communications, mathematics, mechanical engineering, medical technology, (pre)medicine, middle school education, missionary studies, music, music education, music (piano and organ performance), music (voice and choral/opera performance), pastoral counseling, physical education, psychology, public relations, radio/television broadcasting, recreation/leisure facilities management, religious education, religious studies, secondary education, social sciences, special education, teaching English as a second language, theology, (pre)veterinary studies.

JUDSON COLLEGE (AL)
Art, biology, business, chemistry, criminal justice studies, education, elementary education, English, English education, environmental science, exercise sciences, fashion merchandising, history, information sciences/systems, interdisciplinary studies, mathematics, mathematics education, middle school education, modern languages, music, music education, psychology, religious studies, science education, secondary education, social science education.

JUDSON COLLEGE (IL)
Accounting, anthropology, architecture, art, biblical studies, biological and physical sciences, biology, business administration, chemistry, computer graphics, computer science, criminal justice studies, drawing, early childhood education, education, elementary education, English, fine/studio arts, graphic design/commercial art/illustration, history, human resources management, human services, information sciences/systems, international business, journalism, (pre)law, linguistics, literature, management information systems/business data processing, mass communications, mathematics, (pre)medicine, music, music education, music (voice and choral/opera performance), nursing, philosophy, physical education, physical sciences, psychology, religious studies, science education, secondary education, social sciences, sociology, speech/rhetorical studies, sport/fitness administration, theater arts/drama.

KENTUCKY CHRISTIAN COLLEGE
Biblical studies, business administration, elementary education, history, interdisciplinary studies, middle school education, music, music education, pastoral counseling, psychology, religious education, secretarial science, social work.

KING COLLEGE
Accounting, American studies, behavioral sciences, biblical studies, biochemistry, biological and physical sciences, biology, biology education, business administration, chemistry, chemistry education, early childhood education, economics, education, elementary education, English, English education, fine/studio arts, French, French language education, history, history education, information sciences/systems, (pre)law, mathematics, mathematics/computer science, mathematics education, medical technology, (pre)medicine, middle school education, modern languages, music, nursing, (pre)pharmacy studies, physics, physics education, political science, psychology, religious studies, secondary education, Spanish, Spanish language education, (pre)veterinary studies.

THE KING'S UNIVERSITY COLLEGE
Biology, business administration, chemistry, elementary education, English, environmental science, history, music, philosophy, psychology, social sciences, sociology.

LEE UNIVERSITY
Accounting, biblical studies, biological and physical sciences, biology, business administration, business education, chemistry, education, elementary education, English, health education, history, individual/family development, information sciences/systems, international relations, mass communications, mathematics, medical technology, modern languages, music, music education, music (piano and organ performance), music (voice and choral/opera performance), natural sciences, pastoral counseling, physical education, psychology, religious education, respiratory therapy, secondary education, secretarial science, social sciences, sociology, special education, theology.

LETOURNEAU UNIVERSITY
Accounting, aircraft mechanic/airframe, aircraft pilot (professional), aviation technology, biblical studies, biology, business administration, business marketing and marketing management, chemistry, computer engineering, computer engineering technology, computer science, (pre)dentistry, drafting, electrical/electronic engineering technology, electrical/electronics engineering, elementary education, engineering, engineering technology, English, history, information sciences/systems, interdisciplinary studies, (pre)law, management information systems/business data processing, mathematics, mechanical engineering, mechanical engineering technology, (pre)medicine, natural sciences, physical education, psychology, religious studies, secondary education, sport/fitness administration, (pre)veterinary studies, welding technology.

MALONE COLLEGE
Accounting, art, art education, biblical studies, biology, broadcast journalism, business administration, chemistry, communications, computer science, early childhood education, education of the specific learning disabled, elementary education, English, exercise sciences, health education, health/physical education, history, international relations, journalism, (pre)law, liberal arts and studies, mathematics, medical technology, middle school education, music, musical instrument technology, music education, nursing (public health), pastoral counseling, physical education, physics education, psychology, sacred music, science education, social sciences, social studies education, social work, Spanish, Spanish language education, speech education, theater arts/drama, urban studies.

THE MASTER'S COLLEGE AND SEMINARY
Accounting, actuarial science, American government, applied mathematics, biblical languages/literatures, biblical studies, biological and physical sciences, biology, broadcast journalism, business administration, divinity/ministry, education, elementary education, English, environmental biology, finance, history, home economics, liberal arts and studies, management information systems/business data processing, mass communications, mathematics, (pre)medicine, middle school education, music, music business management and merchandising, music education, music (piano and organ performance), music (voice and choral/opera performance), natural sciences, nutrition science, pastoral counseling, physical education, physical sciences, political science, public relations, radio/television broadcasting, religious education, religious studies, sacred music, science education, secondary education, special education, speech/rhetorical studies, theology.

MESSIAH COLLEGE
Accounting, adapted physical education, art education, art history, athletic training/sports medicine, biblical studies, biochemistry, biology, biology education, business administration, business economics, business marketing and marketing management, chemistry, chemistry education, civil engineering, communications, computer/information sciences, dietetics, early childhood education, economics, elementary education, engineering, English, English education, environmental science, exercise sciences, family/community studies, fine/studio arts, French, French language education, German, German language education, history, humanities, human resources management, information sciences/systems, international business, journalism, mathematics, mathematics education, music, music education, nursing, philosophy, physical education, physics, political science, psychology, radio/television broadcasting, recreation and leisure studies, religious education, religious studies, social studies education, social work, sociology, Spanish, Spanish language education, theater arts/drama.

MIDAMERICA NAZARENE UNIVERSITY
Accounting, agricultural business, athletic training/sports medicine, biology, business administration, business education, chemistry, chemistry education, computer science, criminal justice/law enforcement administration, divinity/ministry, elementary education, English, English education, exercise sciences, health education, history, human resources management, international agriculture, liberal arts and studies, mass communications, mathematics, mathematics education, middle school education, modern languages, music, music education, music (voice and choral/opera performance), nursing, physical education, physics, psychology, public relations, religious education, religious studies, sacred music, science education, secondary education, social studies education, sociology, Spanish, Spanish language education.

MILLIGAN COLLEGE
Accounting, adult/continuing education, advertising, art, biblical studies, biological and physical sciences, biology, broadcast journalism, business administration, business economics, chemistry, computer science, (pre)dentistry, early childhood education, education, elementary education, engineering, English, exercise sciences, health education, health science, health services administration, history, humanities, human services, journalism, liberal arts and studies, mass communications, mathematics, medical laboratory technician, (pre)medicine, mortuary science, music, music education, music (piano

and organ performance), music (voice and choral/opera performance), nursing, pastoral counseling, physical education, psychology, public relations, radio/television broadcasting, religious education, sacred music, science education, secondary education, sociology, special education, theater arts/drama, (pre)veterinary studies.

MONTREAT COLLEGE

Accounting, American studies, art, biblical studies, business administration, business economics, business marketing and marketing management, child care/development, (pre)dentistry, ecology, economics, education, elementary education, (pre)engineering, English, environmental science, history, human services, (pre)law, liberal arts and studies, literature, management information systems/business data processing, mass communications, mathematics, (pre)medicine, music, music business management and merchandising, music education, music (piano and organ performance), music (voice and choral/opera performance), physical education, religious studies, secondary education, social sciences, Spanish, sport/fitness administration.

MOUNT VERNON NAZARENE COLLEGE

Accounting, applied art, art, art education, athletic training/sports medicine, biblical studies, biochemistry, biological and physical sciences, biology, broadcast journalism, business administration, business education, business marketing and marketing management, chemistry, computer science, criminal justice/law enforcement administration, data processing technology, (pre)dentistry, early childhood education, education, elementary education, English, history, home economics, home economics education, human services, (pre)law, liberal arts and studies, literature, mass communications, mathematics, medical technology, (pre)medicine, modern languages, music, music education, music (piano and organ performance), music (voice and choral/opera performance), natural resources management, nursing, philosophy, physical education, psychology, religious education, religious studies, sacred music, science education, secondary education, secretarial science, social sciences, social work, sociology, Spanish, special education, sport/fitness administration, theater arts/drama, theology, (pre)veterinary studies, wind and percussion instruments.

NORTH GREENVILLE COLLEGE

Art, biblical languages/literatures, biblical studies, business administration, business economics, early childhood education, elementary education, humanities, interdisciplinary studies, journalism, liberal arts and studies, mass communications, music, music education, music history, music (piano and organ performance), music (voice and choral/opera performance), pastoral counseling, religious education, religious studies, sacred music, sport/fitness administration, theater arts/drama, theology.

NORTH PARK UNIVERSITY

Accounting, anthropology, art, art education, athletic training/sports medicine, biblical studies, biological and physical sciences, biology, business administration, business marketing and marketing management, chemistry, community services, (pre)dentistry, divinity/ministry, early childhood education, economics, education, elementary education, English, exercise sciences, finance, fine/studio arts, French, history, international business, international relations, (pre)law, literature, mass communications, mathematics, medical technology, (pre)medicine, modern languages, music, music business management and merchandising, music education, music (voice and choral/opera performance), natural sciences, nursing, philosophy, physical education, physics, political science, psychology, religious studies, sacred music, Scandinavian languages, secondary education, social sciences, sociology, Spanish, speech/rhetorical studies, theater arts/drama, theology, urban studies, (pre)veterinary studies.

NORTHWEST CHRISTIAN COLLEGE

Area studies, biblical studies, business administration, business communications, business marketing and marketing management, communication disorders, elementary education, general studies, history, humanities, interdisciplinary studies, mass communications, (pre)medicine, missionary studies, modern languages, music, psychology, social sciences, speech/rhetorical studies, (pre)theology.

NORTHWEST COLLEGE (WA)

Behavioral sciences, biblical studies, business administration, divinity/ministry, education, elementary education, English, English education, environmental biology, health science, history, history education, interdisciplinary studies, (pre)law, liberal arts and studies, management science, middle school education, music, music education, music (piano and organ performance), music (voice and choral/opera performance), pastoral counseling, philosophy, physical education, psychology, religious education, religious studies, sacred music, secondary education, social sciences, special education, teaching English as a second language, theater arts/drama, theology.

NORTHWESTERN COLLEGE (IA)

Accounting, art, art education, biology, business administration, business education, chemistry, computer science, economics, education, elementary education, English, environmental science, exercise sciences, history, humanities, mass communications, mathematics, medical technology, music, music education, philosophy, physical education, political science, psychology, religious education, religious studies, secondary education, secretarial science, social work, sociology, Spanish, speech/rhetorical studies, theater arts/drama, theology.

NORTHWESTERN COLLEGE (MN)

Accounting, art education, athletic training/sports medicine, biblical studies, biology, business administration, business marketing and marketing management, child care/development, communications, creative writing, criminal justice studies, elementary education, English, English education, finance, fine/studio arts, graphic design/commercial art/illustration, history, international business, journalism, liberal arts and studies, management information systems/business data processing, mathematics, mathematics education, missionary studies, music, music education, music (general performance), music (piano and organ performance), music (voice and choral/opera performance), office management, organizational behavior, pastoral counseling, physical education, psychology, public relations, radio/television broadcasting, religious education, secretarial science, social sciences, social studies education, Spanish, sport/fitness administration, teaching English as a second language, technical writing, theater arts/drama, (pre)theology.

NORTHWEST NAZARENE UNIVERSITY

Accounting, art, art education, athletic training/sports medicine, biblical languages/literatures, biological and physical sciences, biology, biology education, business administration, business marketing and marketing management, chemistry, chemistry education, computer science, (pre)dentistry, divinity/ministry, drawing, elementary education, engineering physics, English, English education, finance, graphic design/commercial art/illustration, health/physical education, history, history education, international business, international relations, (pre)law, liberal arts and studies, mathematics, mathematics education, (pre)medicine, missionary studies, music, music education, music (general performance), music theory and composition, nursing, pastoral counseling, philosophy, physical education, physical therapy, physics, political science, psychology, recreation and leisure studies, religious education, religious studies, sacred music, secondary education, social science education, social sciences, social work, speech education, speech-language pathology/audiology, speech/rhetorical studies, theology, (pre)veterinary studies.

NYACK COLLEGE

Accounting, biblical studies, business administration, communications, computer science, elementary education, English, general studies, history, interdisciplinary studies, liberal arts and studies, mathematics, missionary studies, music, music education, music (piano and organ performance), music theory and composition, music (voice and choral/opera performance), pastoral counseling, philosophy, psychology, religious education, religious studies, sacred music, secondary education, social sciences, teaching English as a second language, theology.

OKLAHOMA BAPTIST UNIVERSITY

Accounting, advertising, applied art, art, art education, athletic training/sports medicine, biblical languages/literatures, biblical studies, biological and physical sciences, biology, biology education, broadcast journalism, business administration, business computer programming, business marketing and marketing management, chemistry, chemistry education, child care/development, child guidance, computer/information sciences, computer management, computer science, computer systems analysis, (pre)dentistry, developmental/child psychology, divinity/ministry, drama and dance education, early childhood education, education, education of the emotionally handicapped, education of the mentally handicapped, education of the specific learning disabled, elementary education, English, English composition, English education, exercise sciences, finance, fine/studio arts, French, French language education, German, German language education, health/physical education, history, history education, humanities, human resources management, information sciences/systems, interdisciplinary studies, international business, international business marketing, journalism, (pre)law, management information systems/business data processing, marriage and family counseling, mass communications, mathematics, mathematics education, (pre)medicine, missionary studies, museum studies, music, music education, music (piano and organ performance), music theory and composition, music (voice and choral/opera performance), natural sciences, nursing, pastoral counseling, (pre)pharmacy studies, philosophy, physical education, physical sciences, physics, political science, psychology, public relations, radio/television broadcasting, recreation and leisure studies, religious education, religious studies, sacred music, science education, secondary education, social science education, social sciences, social studies education, social work, sociology, Spanish, Spanish language education, special education, speech education, speech/rhetorical studies, telecommunications, theater arts/drama, theology, (pre)veterinary studies, wind and percussion instruments.

OKLAHOMA CHRISTIAN UNIVERSITY OF SCIENCE AND ARTS

Accounting, advertising, art, art education, biblical studies, biochemistry, biological and physical sciences, biology, broadcast journalism, business administration, business marketing and marketing management, chemistry, child care/development, community services, computer engineering, computer science, creative writing, (pre)dentistry, divinity/ministry, early childhood education, electrical/electronics engineering, elementary education, emergency medical technology, engineering, engineering physics, English, family/community studies, graphic design/commercial art/illustration, history, information sciences/systems, interior design, journalism, (pre)law, liberal arts and studies, mass communications, mathematics, mechanical engineering, medical technology, (pre)medicine, music, music education, music (voice and choral/opera performance), pastoral counseling, physical education, psychology, public relations, radio/television broadcasting, religious education, religious studies, science education, secondary education, Spanish, special education, speech/rhetorical studies, teaching English as a second language, theater arts/drama, (pre)veterinary studies, wind and percussion instruments.

OLIVET NAZARENE UNIVERSITY

Accounting, art, art education, athletic training/sports medicine, biblical studies, biochemistry, biological and physical sciences, biology, broadcast journalism, business administration, business economics, business marketing and marketing management, chemistry, child care/development, clothing and textiles, computer science, criminal justice/law enforcement administration, (pre)dentistry, developmental/child psychology, dietetics, early childhood education, earth sciences, economics, education, elementary education, engineering, English, environmental science, family/community studies, fashion merchandising, film studies, finance, food sciences, French, geology, graphic design/commercial art/illustration, history, home economics, home economics education, human resources management, information sciences/systems, interdisciplinary studies, journalism, (pre)law, liberal arts and studies, literature, mass communications, mathematics, medical technology, (pre)medicine, modern languages, music, music education, music (piano and organ performance), music (voice and choral/opera

performance), natural sciences, nursing, philosophy, physical education, physical sciences, psychology, radio/television broadcasting, religious education, religious studies, Romance languages, sacred music, science education, secondary education, social sciences, Spanish, speech/rhetorical studies, stringed instruments, theology, (pre)veterinary studies, wind and percussion instruments, zoology.

ORAL ROBERTS UNIVERSITY

Accounting, art education, biblical studies, biochemistry, bioengineering, biology, biomedical engineering-related technology, British literature, business administration, business marketing and marketing management, chemistry, communications, computer engineering, computer science, (pre)dentistry, early childhood education, education, education administration, education (multiple levels), electrical/electronics engineering, elementary education, engineering mechanics, English education, exercise sciences, finance, fine/studio arts, French, French language education, German, German language education, graphic design/commercial art/illustration, history, international relations, journalism, liberal arts and studies, management information systems/business data processing, management science, mathematics, mathematics education, mechanical engineering, (pre)medicine, missionary studies, music, music education, music (general performance), music theory and composition, nursing, pastoral counseling, philosophy, physical education, physics, political science, psychology, public relations, radio/television broadcasting, religious studies, sacred music, science education, social studies education, social work, Spanish, Spanish language education, special education, teaching English as a second language, theater arts/drama, theology.

PALM BEACH ATLANTIC COLLEGE

Art, art education, biology, business administration, business marketing and marketing management, early childhood education, education, elementary education, English, finance, general studies, history, human resources management, information sciences/systems, international business, (pre)law, mathematics, (pre)medicine, music, music education, music (voice and choral/opera performance), philosophy, physical education, political science, psychology, religious studies, sacred music, secondary education, stringed instruments, theater arts/drama, wind and percussion instruments.

POINT LOMA NAZARENE UNIVERSITY

Accounting, art, biblical studies, biochemistry, biology, British literature, business administration, business communications, business home economics, chemistry, child care/development, communications, computer science, dietetics, economics, engineering physics, family studies, graphic design/commercial art/illustration, health/physical education, history, home economics, journalism, liberal arts and studies, management information systems/business data processing, mass communications, mathematics, music, music business management and merchandising, nursing, organizational psychology, philosophy, physics, political science, psychology, Romance languages, sacred music, social sciences, social work, sociology, Spanish, speech/rhetorical studies, theater arts/drama, theology.

REDEEMER UNIVERSITY COLLEGE

Accounting, art, behavioral sciences, biblical studies, biological and physical sciences, biology, business administration, clinical psychology, computer science, (pre)dentistry, education, elementary education, English, exercise sciences, experimental psychology, French, health/physical education, history, humanities, human resources management, (pre)law, liberal arts and studies, mathematics, (pre)medicine, modern languages, music, natural sciences, pastoral counseling, philosophy, political science, psychology, recreation and leisure studies, religious studies, Romance languages, secondary education, social work, sociology, theater arts/drama, theology, (pre)theology, (pre)veterinary studies.

ROBERTS WESLEYAN COLLEGE

Accounting, art, art education, biochemistry, biological and physical sciences, biology, business administration, chemistry, communications, computer science, criminal justice/law enforcement administration, (pre)dentistry, divinity/ministry, education, elementary education, (pre)engineering, English, fine/studio arts, graphic design/commercial art/illustration, history, humanities, human resources management, (pre)law, mathematics, medical technology, (pre)medicine, music, music education, music (piano and organ performance), music (voice and choral/opera performance), natural sciences, nursing, pastoral counseling, (pre)pharmacy studies, philosophy, physical sciences, physics, psychology, religious studies, secondary education, social sciences, social work, sociology, (pre)veterinary studies.

SEATTLE PACIFIC UNIVERSITY
Accounting, art, art education, biochemistry, biology, biology education, business administration, business computer facilities operator, business economics, business systems analysis and design, chemistry, classics, clothing/apparel/textile studies, communications, computer science, (pre)dentistry, electrical/electronics engineering, engineering science, English, English education, European studies, exercise sciences, family/consumer studies, French, general studies, German, history, home economics education, Latin American studies, Latin (Ancient and Medieval), (pre)law, mathematics, mathematics education, (pre)medicine, music, music education, nursing, nutrition science, philosophy, physical education, physics, political science, psychology, religious education, religious studies, Russian, science education, social science education, sociology, Spanish, special education, theater arts/drama.

SIMPSON COLLEGE AND GRADUATE SCHOOL
Accounting, biblical studies, business administration, communications, divinity/ministry, education, elementary education, English, English education, general studies, history, human resources management, liberal arts and studies, mathematics, missionary studies, music, music education, pastoral counseling, psychology, religious education, sacred music, secondary education, social science education, social sciences.

SOUTHERN NAZARENE UNIVERSITY
Accounting, American studies, art education, athletic training/sports medicine, aviation management, biblical studies, biological and physical sciences, biology, biology education, broadcast journalism, business, business administration, business education, business marketing and marketing management, chemistry, chemistry education, communications, computer science, criminal justice studies, (pre)dentistry, early childhood education, education, elementary education, English, English education, environmental science, exercise sciences, family/community studies, family studies, finance, general studies, health education, history, information sciences/systems, interdisciplinary studies, international relations, journalism, (pre)law, literature, management information systems/business data processing, management science, mass communications, mathematics, mathematics education, (pre)medicine, missionary studies, music business management and merchandising, music education, music (general performance), music (piano and organ performance), music (voice and choral/opera performance), natural sciences, nursing, (pre)pharmacy studies, philosophy, physical education, physics, political science, psychology, religious education, religious studies, sacred music, secondary education, social science education, social work, sociology, Spanish, Spanish language education, speech education, speech/rhetorical studies, sport/fitness administration.

SOUTHERN WESLEYAN UNIVERSITY
Accounting, biology, business administration, chemistry, criminal justice/law enforcement administration, divinity/ministry, early childhood education, education, elementary education, English, Greek (Modern), history, mathematics, medical technology, music, music education, physical education, psychology, recreation and leisure studies, religious studies, social sciences, special education.

SOUTHWEST BAPTIST UNIVERSITY
Accounting, art, art education, biblical studies, biology, business, business administration, business education, chemistry, communications, computer science, criminal justice/law enforcement administration, elementary education, emergency medical technology, English, English education, general studies, graphic design/commercial art/illustration, history, human services,

information sciences/systems, mathematics, medical technology, middle school education, music, music education, nursing, occupational safety/health technology, physical education, political science, psychology, recreation and leisure studies, religious studies, secondary education, secretarial science, social sciences, sociology, Spanish, sport/fitness administration, theater arts/drama.

SPRING ARBOR COLLEGE
Accounting, art, biochemistry, biology, business administration, business economics, chemistry, computer science, divinity/ministry, early childhood education, elementary education, English, French, history, liberal arts and studies, mass communications, mathematics, music, philosophy, physical education, physics, psychology, religious studies, secondary education, social sciences, social work, sociology, Spanish, speech/rhetorical studies.

STERLING COLLEGE (KS)
Art, behavioral sciences, biology, business administration, computer/information sciences, elementary education, English, history, interdisciplinary studies, mathematics, music, music education, philosophy, physical education, religious education, religious studies, theater arts/drama.

TABOR COLLEGE
Accounting, actuarial science, adult/continuing education, agricultural business, applied mathematics, art education, athletic training/sports medicine, biblical studies, biological and physical sciences, biology, business administration, business education, business marketing and marketing management, chemistry, communications, computer science, (pre)dentistry, divinity/ministry, early childhood education, education, elementary education, (pre)engineering, English, environmental biology, health education, history, humanities, interdisciplinary studies, international relations, journalism, (pre)law, legal administrative assistant, mass communications, mathematics, medical administrative assistant, medical technology, (pre)medicine, music, music business management and merchandising, music education, music (piano and organ performance), music (voice and choral/opera performance), natural sciences, pastoral counseling, philosophy, physical education, psychology, religious studies, science education, secondary education, secretarial science, social sciences, sociology, special education, theater design, (pre)veterinary studies, zoology.

TAYLOR UNIVERSITY
Accounting, art, art education, athletic training/sports medicine, biblical languages/literatures, biblical studies, biology, business administration, chemistry, computer engineering, computer programming, computer science, creative writing, (pre)dentistry, early childhood education, economics, education, elementary education, engineering physics, English, environmental biology, environmental science, French, graphic design/commercial art/illustration, history, information sciences/systems, international business, international economics, international relations, (pre)law, literature, management information systems/business data processing, mass communications, mathematics, medical technology, (pre)medicine, middle school education, music, music business management and merchandising, music education, music (piano and organ performance), music (voice and choral/opera performance), natural sciences, philosophy, physical education, physics, political science, psychology, recreation and leisure studies, religious education, religious studies, sacred music, science education, secondary education, social sciences, social work, sociology, Spanish, sport/fitness administration, theater arts/drama, theology, (pre)veterinary studies.

TREVECCA NAZARENE UNIVERSITY
Accounting, behavioral sciences, biological and physical sciences, biology, biology education, broadcast journalism, business administration, business marketing and marketing management, chemistry, chemistry education, child care/development, communications, early childhood education, economics, elementary education, English, English education, exercise sciences, general studies, history, history education, information sciences/systems, mass communications, mathematics, mathematics education, medical technology, music, music business management and merchandising, music education, physical education, physics, psychology, radio/television

Trevecca Nazarene University (continued)

broadcasting technology, religious studies, sacred music, sales operations, secondary education, social sciences, speech/rhetorical studies, theater arts/drama.

TRINITY CHRISTIAN COLLEGE
Accounting, art, art education, biology, biology education, business, business administration, business education, business marketing and marketing management, ceramic arts, chemistry, chemistry education, communications, computer science, (pre)dentistry, drawing, education, education of the emotionally handicapped, education of the mentally handicapped, education of the specific learning disabled, elementary education, English, English education, entrepreneurship, financial planning, graphic design/commercial art/illustration, history, history education, human resources management, information sciences/systems, management information systems/business data processing, mathematics, mathematics education, (pre)medicine, middle school education, music, music education, music (general performance), music (piano and organ performance), music (voice and choral/opera performance), nursing, painting, philosophy, photography, physical education, printmaking, psychology, public relations, religious education, religious studies, science education, sculpture, secondary education, sociology, Spanish, special education, theology, (pre)theology, (pre)veterinary studies.

TRINITY INTERNATIONAL UNIVERSITY
Accounting, athletic training/sports medicine, biblical studies, biology, business administration, business marketing and marketing management, chemistry, computer science, divinity/ministry, economics, education, elementary education, English, history, humanities, human resources management, information sciences/systems, liberal arts and studies, mass communications, mathematics, (pre)medicine, music, music education, philosophy, physical education, psychology, sacred music, secondary education, social sciences, sociology.

TRINITY WESTERN UNIVERSITY
Aircraft pilot (professional), applied mathematics, biblical studies, biological and physical sciences, biology, business administration, chemistry, communications, computer science, (pre)dentistry, divinity/ministry, education, elementary education, English, environmental biology, environmental science, general studies, geography, health/physical education, history, humanities, human services, international relations, (pre)law, liberal arts and studies, linguistics, mathematics, mathematics/computer science, (pre)medicine, missionary studies, music, natural sciences, nursing, philosophy, physical education, political science, psychology, religious studies, secondary education, social sciences, theater arts/drama, (pre)veterinary studies.

UNION UNIVERSITY
Accounting, advertising, art, art education, athletic training/sports medicine, biblical languages/literatures, biblical studies, biological and physical sciences, biology, broadcast journalism, business administration, business economics, business education, business marketing and marketing management, chemistry, computer science, (pre)dentistry, early childhood education, economics, education, elementary education, English, family/community studies, finance, foreign languages/literatures, French, history, information sciences/systems, journalism, (pre)law, mass communications, mathematics, medical technology, (pre)medicine, music, music business management and merchandising, music education, music (piano and organ performance), music (voice and choral/opera performance), nursing, (pre)pharmacy studies, philosophy, physical education, physics, political science, psychology, public relations, radio/television broadcasting, recreation/leisure facilities management, religious studies, sacred music, science education, secondary education, social work, sociology, Spanish, special education, speech/rhetorical studies, sport/fitness administration, teaching English as a second language, theater arts/drama, theology.

UNIVERSITY OF SIOUX FALLS
Accounting, applied art, applied mathematics, art education, behavioral sciences, biology, business administration, business marketing and market-

ing management, chemistry, computer science, (pre)dentistry, developmental/child psychology, early childhood education, economics, education, elementary education, (pre)engineering, English, exercise sciences, graphic design/commercial art/illustration, health education, history, humanities, industrial radiologic technology, information sciences/systems, interdisciplinary studies, (pre)law, liberal arts and studies, management information systems/business data processing, mass communications, mathematics, medical technology, (pre)medicine, middle school education, music, music business management and merchandising, music education, music (piano and organ performance), music (voice and choral/opera performance), pastoral counseling, philosophy, physical education, political science, psychology, public relations, radio/television broadcasting, religious studies, science education, secondary education, secretarial science, social sciences, social work, sociology, speech/rhetorical studies, theater arts/drama, (pre)veterinary studies, wind and percussion instruments.

VANGUARD UNIVERSITY OF SOUTHERN CALIFORNIA
Accounting, anthropology, biblical studies, biological and physical sciences, biology, business administration, business marketing and marketing management, chemistry, education, English, film/video production, finance, history, interdisciplinary studies, international business, (pre)law, management information systems/business data processing, mass communications, mathematics, music, pastoral counseling, physical education, physical therapy, political science, psychology, radio/television broadcasting, religious education, religious studies, secondary education, social sciences, sociology, Spanish, speech/rhetorical studies, theater arts/drama.

WARNER PACIFIC COLLEGE
American studies, biblical studies, biological and physical sciences, biology, business administration, divinity/ministry, early childhood education, education, elementary education, English, exercise sciences, health science, history, individual/family development, (pre)law, liberal arts and studies, mathematics, (pre)medicine, middle school education, music, music business management and merchandising, music education, nursing, pastoral counseling, physical education, physical sciences, psychology, religious education, religious studies, science education, secondary education, social sciences, social work, theology, (pre)veterinary studies.

WARNER SOUTHERN COLLEGE
Accounting, biblical studies, biology, business administration, business education, business marketing and marketing management, communications, elementary education, English, English education, exercise sciences, finance, general studies, history, (pre)law, music education, physical education, psychology, recreation and leisure studies, sacred music, science education, social science education, social sciences, social work, special education, sport/fitness administration, (pre)theology.

WESTERN BAPTIST COLLEGE
Accounting, biblical studies, business administration, community services, computer science, divinity/ministry, education, elementary education, English, finance, health science, humanities, interdisciplinary studies, (pre)law, liberal arts and studies, mathematics, music, music education, pastoral counseling, psychology, religious education, religious studies, secondary education, social sciences, sport/fitness administration, theology.

WESTMONT COLLEGE
Anthropology, art, art education, biology, business, business economics, chemistry, communications, computer science, dance, (pre)dentistry, economics, education, elementary education, engineering physics, English, English education, exercise sciences, French, history, (pre)law, liberal arts and studies, mathematics, mathematics education, (pre)medicine, modern languages, music, neuroscience, (pre)pharmacy studies, philosophy, physical education, physics, political science, psychology, religious studies, secondary education, social science education, social sciences, sociology, Spanish, theater arts/drama, (pre)theology, (pre)veterinary studies.

WHEATON COLLEGE (IL)

Anthropology, archaeology, art, art history, biblical languages/literatures, biblical studies, biology, business economics, chemistry, computer science, economics, elementary education, engineering, English, environmental science, exercise sciences, French, geology, German, Greek (Ancient and Medieval), Hebrew, history, interdisciplinary studies, Latin (Ancient and Medieval), mathematics, music, music business management and merchandising, music education, music history, music (piano and organ performance), music (voice and choral/opera performance), nursing, philosophy, physical education, physical sciences, physics, political science, psychology, religious education, religious studies, social studies education, sociology, Spanish, speech/rhetorical studies, stringed instruments, wind and percussion instruments.

WHITWORTH COLLEGE

Accounting, American studies, art, art education, art history, arts management, athletic training/sports medicine, biology, business administration, chemistry, computer science, (pre)dentistry, economics, elementary education, English, fine/studio arts, French, history, international business, international relations, journalism, (pre)law, mass communications, mathematics, (pre)medicine, music, music education, music (piano and organ performance), music (voice and choral/opera performance), nursing, peace and conflict studies, philosophy, physical education, physics, political science, psychology, religious studies, secondary education, sociology, Spanish, special education, speech/rhetorical studies, theater arts/drama, (pre)veterinary studies.

WILLIAMS BAPTIST COLLEGE

Art, art education, biology, business administration, computer/information sciences, (pre)dentistry, divinity/ministry, early childhood education, education, elementary education, English, fine/studio arts, history, (pre)law, liberal arts and studies, mathematics, (pre)medicine, music, music education, pastoral counseling, physical education, psychology, religious education, religious studies, sacred music, secretarial science, theology.

WILLIAM TYNDALE COLLEGE

Biblical studies, business administration, early childhood education, English, history, (pre)law, liberal arts and studies, mathematics, Middle Eastern studies, music, music (general performance), music (piano and organ performance), music (voice and choral/opera performance), pastoral counseling, psychology, religious education, sacred music, social sciences, theology.

Majors Index by Major

ACCOUNTING
Abilene Christian University, TX
Anderson University, IN
Asbury College, KY
Azusa Pacific University, CA
Bartlesville Wesleyan College, OK
Belhaven College, MS
Bethel College, IN
Bethel College, KS
Bethel College, MN
Bluffton College, OH
Calvin College, MI
Campbellsville University, KY
Campbell University, NC
Cedarville University, OH
College of the Ozarks, MO
Colorado Christian University, CO
Cornerstone University, MI
Dallas Baptist University, TX
David Lipscomb University, TN
Dordt College, IA
Eastern College, PA
Eastern Mennonite University, VA
Eastern Nazarene College, MA
East Texas Baptist University, TX
Erskine College, SC
Evangel University, MO
Fresno Pacific University, CA
Geneva College, PA
Gordon College, MA
Goshen College, IN
Grace College, IN
Grand Canyon University, AZ
Greenville College, IL
Houghton College, NY
Houston Baptist University, TX
Howard Payne University, TX
Huntington College, IN
Indiana Wesleyan University, IN
John Brown University, AR
Judson College, IL
King College, TN
Lee University, TN
LeTourneau University, TX
Malone College, OH
The Master's College and Seminary, CA
Messiah College, PA
MidAmerica Nazarene University, KS
Milligan College, TN
Montreat College, NC
Mount Vernon Nazarene College, OH
North Park University, IL
Northwestern College, IA
Northwestern College, MN
Northwest Nazarene University, ID
Nyack College, NY
Oklahoma Baptist University, OK
Oklahoma Christian University of Science and
    Arts, OK

Olivet Nazarene University, IL
Oral Roberts University, OK
Point Loma Nazarene University, CA
Redeemer University College, ON
Roberts Wesleyan College, NY
Seattle Pacific University, WA
Simpson College and Graduate School, CA
Southern Nazarene University, OK
Southern Wesleyan University, SC
Southwest Baptist University, MO
Spring Arbor College, MI
Tabor College, KS
Taylor University, IN
Trevecca Nazarene University, TN
Trinity Christian College, IL
Trinity International University, IL
Union University, TN
University of Sioux Falls, SD
Vanguard University of Southern California, CA
Warner Southern College, FL
Western Baptist College, OR
Whitworth College, WA

ACTUARIAL SCIENCE
The Master's College and Seminary, CA
Tabor College, KS

ADAPTED PHYSICAL EDUCATION
Messiah College, PA

ADULT/CONTINUING EDUCATION
Bethel College, MN
Biola University, CA
Colorado Christian University, CO
Cornerstone University, MI
Milligan College, TN
Tabor College, KS

ADVERTISING
Abilene Christian University, TX
Campbell University, NC
Eastern Nazarene College, MA
Milligan College, TN
Oklahoma Baptist University, OK
Oklahoma Christian University of Science and
    Arts, OK
Union University, TN

AEROSPACE ENGINEERING
Bethel College, IN
Eastern Nazarene College, MA

AGRIBUSINESS
Abilene Christian University, TX
College of the Ozarks, MO

AGRICULTURAL BUSINESS
Dordt College, IA
MidAmerica Nazarene University, KS
Tabor College, KS

AGRICULTURAL EDUCATION
College of the Ozarks, MO

AGRICULTURAL MECHANIZATION
College of the Ozarks, MO

AGRICULTURAL SCIENCES
Dordt College, IA
Eastern Mennonite University, VA

AGRONOMY/CROP SCIENCE
College of the Ozarks, MO

AIRCRAFT MECHANIC/AIRFRAME
LeTourneau University, TX

AIRCRAFT PILOT (PROFESSIONAL)
Cornerstone University, MI
LeTourneau University, TX
Trinity Western University, BC

ALCOHOL/DRUG ABUSE COUNSELING
Indiana Wesleyan University, IN

AMERICAN GOVERNMENT
David Lipscomb University, TN
The Master's College and Seminary, CA

AMERICAN HISTORY
Calvin College, MI

AMERICAN STUDIES
Cedarville University, OH
David Lipscomb University, TN
Erskine College, SC
Howard Payne University, TX
King College, TN
Montreat College, NC
Southern Nazarene University, OK
Warner Pacific College, OR
Whitworth College, WA

ANIMAL SCIENCES
Abilene Christian University, TX
College of the Ozarks, MO
Dordt College, IA

ANTHROPOLOGY
Biola University, CA
Judson College, IL
North Park University, IL
Vanguard University of Southern California, CA
Westmont College, CA
Wheaton College, IL

APPLIED ART
Azusa Pacific University, CA
Howard Payne University, TX
Mount Vernon Nazarene College, OH
Oklahoma Baptist University, OK
University of Sioux Falls, SD

APPLIED MATHEMATICS
Asbury College, KY
Fresno Pacific University, CA
Geneva College, PA
The Master's College and Seminary, CA
Tabor College, KS
Trinity Western University, BC
University of Sioux Falls, SD

ARCHAEOLOGY
Wheaton College, IL

ARCHITECTURAL ENGINEERING TECHNOLOGY
Abilene Christian University, TX

ARCHITECTURE
Judson College, IL

AREA STUDIES
Abilene Christian University, TX
Northwest Christian College, OR

ART
Abilene Christian University, TX
Azusa Pacific University, CA
Belhaven College, MS
Bethel College, IN
Bethel College, KS
Bethel College, MN
Biola University, CA
Bluffton College, OH
California Baptist University, CA
Calvin College, MI
Campbellsville University, KY
Campbell University, NC
Colorado Christian University, CO
Dallas Baptist University, TX
David Lipscomb University, TN
Dordt College, IA
Eastern Mennonite University, VA
Evangel University, MO
George Fox University, OR
Gordon College, MA
Goshen College, IN
Grace College, IN
Grand Canyon University, AZ
Greenville College, IL
Houghton College, NY
Houston Baptist University, TX
Howard Payne University, TX
Huntington College, IN
Indiana Wesleyan University, IN
John Brown University, AR
Judson College, AL
Judson College, IL
Malone College, OH
Milligan College, TN
Montreat College, NC
Mount Vernon Nazarene College, OH
North Greenville College, SC
North Park University, IL
Northwestern College, IA
Northwest Nazarene University, ID
Oklahoma Baptist University, OK
Oklahoma Christian University of Science and
    Arts, OK
Olivet Nazarene University, IL
Palm Beach Atlantic College, FL
Point Loma Nazarene University, CA

Redeemer University College, ON
Roberts Wesleyan College, NY
Seattle Pacific University, WA
Southwest Baptist University, MO
Spring Arbor College, MI
Sterling College, KS
Taylor University, IN
Trinity Christian College, IL
Union University, TN
Westmont College, CA
Wheaton College, IL
Whitworth College, WA
Williams Baptist College, AR

ART EDUCATION
Abilene Christian University, TX
Anderson University, IN
Asbury College, KY
Bethel College, MN
Bluffton College, OH
Calvin College, MI
Campbellsville University, KY
College of the Ozarks, MO
Evangel University, MO
Goshen College, IN
Grace College, IN
Grand Canyon University, AZ
Greenville College, IL
Houghton College, NY
Houston Baptist University, TX
Howard Payne University, TX
Huntington College, IN
Indiana Wesleyan University, IN
Malone College, OH
Messiah College, PA
Mount Vernon Nazarene College, OH
North Park University, IL
Northwestern College, IA
Northwestern College, MN
Northwest Nazarene University, ID
Oklahoma Baptist University, OK
Oklahoma Christian University of Science and
    Arts, OK
Olivet Nazarene University, IL
Oral Roberts University, OK
Palm Beach Atlantic College, FL
Roberts Wesleyan College, NY
Seattle Pacific University, WA
Southern Nazarene University, OK
Southwest Baptist University, MO
Tabor College, KS
Taylor University, IN
Trinity Christian College, IL
Union University, TN
University of Sioux Falls, SD
Westmont College, CA
Whitworth College, WA
Williams Baptist College, AR

ART HISTORY
Bethel College, MN
Calvin College, MI
Eastern College, PA
Messiah College, PA
Wheaton College, IL
Whitworth College, WA

ARTS MANAGEMENT
Whitworth College, WA

ART THERAPY
Goshen College, IN

ASTRONOMY
Eastern College, PA

ATHLETIC TRAINING/SPORTS MEDICINE
Anderson University, IN
Asbury College, KY
Azusa Pacific University, CA
Bartlesville Wesleyan College, OK
Belhaven College, MS
Bethel College, MN
Calvin College, MI
Campbellsville University, KY
Campbell University, NC
Cedarville University, OH
David Lipscomb University, TN
Eastern Nazarene College, MA
Erskine College, SC
Fresno Pacific University, CA
George Fox University, OR
Grand Canyon University, AZ
Hope International University, CA
Howard Payne University, TX
Indiana Wesleyan University, IN
John Brown University, AR
Messiah College, PA
MidAmerica Nazarene University, KS
Mount Vernon Nazarene College, OH
North Park University, IL
Northwestern College, MN
Northwest Nazarene University, ID
Oklahoma Baptist University, OK
Olivet Nazarene University, IL
Southern Nazarene University, OK
Tabor College, KS
Taylor University, IN
Trinity International University, IL
Union University, TN
Whitworth College, WA

AVIATION MANAGEMENT
Geneva College, PA
Southern Nazarene University, OK

AVIATION TECHNOLOGY
College of the Ozarks, MO
LeTourneau University, TX

BEHAVIORAL SCIENCES
Bartlesville Wesleyan College, OK
California Baptist University, CA
East Texas Baptist University, TX
Erskine College, SC
Evangel University, MO
Howard Payne University, TX
King College, TN
Northwest College, WA
Redeemer University College, ON
Sterling College, KS
Trevecca Nazarene University, TN
University of Sioux Falls, SD

BIBLICAL LANGUAGES/LITERATURES
Cornerstone University, MI
David Lipscomb University, TN
Howard Payne University, TX
Indiana Wesleyan University, IN
The Master's College and Seminary, CA

Majors Index by Major

Biblical languages/literatures (continued)

North Greenville College, SC
Northwest Nazarene University, ID
Oklahoma Baptist University, OK
Taylor University, IN
Union University, TN
Wheaton College, IL

BIBLICAL STUDIES
Abilene Christian University, TX
Anderson University, IN
Asbury College, KY
Azusa Pacific University, CA
Belhaven College, MS
Bethel College, IN
Bethel College, MN
Biola University, CA
Bryan College, TN
Calvin College, MI
Campbellsville University, KY
Cedarville University, OH
Colorado Christian University, CO
Cornerstone University, MI
Covenant College, GA
Crichton College, TN
Dallas Baptist University, TX
David Lipscomb University, TN
Eastern College, PA
Eastern Mennonite University, VA
Erskine College, SC
Evangel University, MO
Fresno Pacific University, CA
Geneva College, PA
George Fox University, OR
Gordon College, MA
Goshen College, IN
Grace College, IN
Grand Canyon University, AZ
Hope International University, CA
Houghton College, NY
Houston Baptist University, TX
Howard Payne University, TX
Huntington College, IN
Indiana Wesleyan University, IN
John Brown University, AR
Judson College, IL
Kentucky Christian College, KY
King College, TN
Lee University, TN
LeTourneau University, TX
Malone College, OH
The Master's College and Seminary, CA
Messiah College, PA
Milligan College, TN
Montreat College, NC
Mount Vernon Nazarene College, OH
North Greenville College, SC
North Park University, IL
Northwest Christian College, OR
Northwest College, WA
Northwestern College, MN
Nyack College, NY
Oklahoma Baptist University, OK
Oklahoma Christian University of Science and
Arts, OK
Olivet Nazarene University, IL
Oral Roberts University, OK
Point Loma Nazarene University, CA

Redeemer University College, ON
Simpson College and Graduate School, CA
Southern Nazarene University, OK
Southwest Baptist University, MO
Tabor College, KS
Taylor University, IN
Trinity International University, IL
Trinity Western University, BC
Union University, TN
Vanguard University of Southern California, CA
Warner Pacific College, OR
Warner Southern College, FL
Western Baptist College, OR
Wheaton College, IL
William Tyndale College, MI

**BILINGUAL/BICULTURAL
EDUCATION**
Biola University, CA
Calvin College, MI
Eastern Nazarene College, MA
Fresno Pacific University, CA
Goshen College, IN
Houston Baptist University, TX

BIOCHEMISTRY
Abilene Christian University, TX
Asbury College, KY
Azusa Pacific University, CA
Bethel College, MN
Biola University, CA
Calvin College, MI
Campbell University, NC
David Lipscomb University, TN
Eastern College, PA
Eastern Mennonite University, VA
John Brown University, AR
King College, TN
Messiah College, PA
Mount Vernon Nazarene College, OH
Oklahoma Christian University of Science and
Arts, OK
Olivet Nazarene University, IL
Oral Roberts University, OK
Point Loma Nazarene University, CA
Roberts Wesleyan College, NY
Seattle Pacific University, WA
Spring Arbor College, MI

BIOENGINEERING
Eastern Nazarene College, MA
Oral Roberts University, OK

**BIOLOGICAL AND PHYSICAL
SCIENCES**
Bartlesville Wesleyan College, OK
Bethel College, IN
Calvin College, MI
Cedarville University, OH
Eastern Nazarene College, MA
Erskine College, SC
Houghton College, NY
Huntington College, IN
Judson College, IL
King College, TN
Lee University, TN
The Master's College and Seminary, CA
Milligan College, TN
Mount Vernon Nazarene College, OH
North Park University, IL

Northwest Nazarene University, ID
Oklahoma Baptist University, OK
Oklahoma Christian University of Science and
Arts, OK
Olivet Nazarene University, IL
Redeemer University College, ON
Roberts Wesleyan College, NY
Southern Nazarene University, OK
Tabor College, KS
Trevecca Nazarene University, TN
Trinity Western University, BC
Union University, TN
Vanguard University of Southern California, CA
Warner Pacific College, OR

BIOLOGY
Abilene Christian University, TX
Anderson University, IN
Asbury College, KY
Azusa Pacific University, CA
Bartlesville Wesleyan College, OK
Belhaven College, MS
Bethel College, IN
Bethel College, KS
Bethel College, MN
Biola University, CA
Bluffton College, OH
Bryan College, TN
California Baptist University, CA
Calvin College, MI
Campbellsville University, KY
Campbell University, NC
Cedarville University, OH
College of the Ozarks, MO
Colorado Christian University, CO
Cornerstone University, MI
Covenant College, GA
Crichton College, TN
Dallas Baptist University, TX
David Lipscomb University, TN
Dordt College, IA
Eastern College, PA
Eastern Mennonite University, VA
Eastern Nazarene College, MA
East Texas Baptist University, TX
Erskine College, SC
Evangel University, MO
Fresno Pacific University, CA
Geneva College, PA
George Fox University, OR
Gordon College, MA
Goshen College, IN
Grace College, IN
Grand Canyon University, AZ
Greenville College, IL
Houghton College, NY
Houston Baptist University, TX
Howard Payne University, TX
Huntington College, IN
Indiana Wesleyan University, IN
John Brown University, AR
Judson College, AL
Judson College, IL
King College, TN
The King's University College, AB
Lee University, TN
LeTourneau University, TX
Malone College, OH
The Master's College and Seminary, CA

160

Peterson's Christian Colleges & Universities

Messiah College, PA
MidAmerica Nazarene University, KS
Milligan College, TN
Mount Vernon Nazarene College, OH
North Park University, IL
Northwestern College, IA
Northwestern College, MN
Northwest Nazarene University, ID
Oklahoma Baptist University, OK
Oklahoma Christian University of Science and
    Arts, OK
Olivet Nazarene University, IL
Oral Roberts University, OK
Palm Beach Atlantic College, FL
Point Loma Nazarene University, CA
Redeemer University College, ON
Roberts Wesleyan College, NY
Seattle Pacific University, WA
Southern Nazarene University, OK
Southern Wesleyan University, SC
Southwest Baptist University, MO
Spring Arbor College, MI
Sterling College, KS
Tabor College, KS
Taylor University, IN
Trevecca Nazarene University, TN
Trinity Christian College, IL
Trinity International University, IL
Trinity Western University, BC
Union University, TN
University of Sioux Falls, SD
Vanguard University of Southern California, CA
Warner Pacific College, OR
Warner Southern College, FL
Westmont College, CA
Wheaton College, IL
Whitworth College, WA
Williams Baptist College, AR

BIOLOGY EDUCATION
Abilene Christian University, TX
Bethel College, IN
Campbell University, NC
Cedarville University, OH
College of the Ozarks, MO
Crichton College, TN
David Lipscomb University, TN
East Texas Baptist University, TX
George Fox University, OR
Greenville College, IL
King College, TN
Messiah College, PA
Northwest Nazarene University, ID
Oklahoma Baptist University, OK
Seattle Pacific University, WA
Southern Nazarene University, OK
Trevecca Nazarene University, TN
Trinity Christian College, IL

BIOMEDICAL ENGINEERING-RELATED TECHNOLOGY
Oral Roberts University, OK

BRITISH LITERATURE
Oral Roberts University, OK
Point Loma Nazarene University, CA

BROADCAST JOURNALISM
Cedarville University, OH

College of the Ozarks, MO
Colorado Christian University, CO
Cornerstone University, MI
Evangel University, MO
Goshen College, IN
Houston Baptist University, TX
Huntington College, IN
John Brown University, AR
Malone College, OH
The Master's College and Seminary, CA
Milligan College, TN
Mount Vernon Nazarene College, OH
Oklahoma Baptist University, OK
Oklahoma Christian University of Science and
    Arts, OK
Olivet Nazarene University, IL
Southern Nazarene University, OK
Trevecca Nazarene University, TN
Union University, TN

BUSINESS
Anderson University, IN
Asbury College, KY
Campbell University, NC
Colorado Christian University, CO
Eastern Nazarene College, MA
East Texas Baptist University, TX
Grace College, IN
Judson College, AL
Southern Nazarene University, OK
Southwest Baptist University, MO
Trinity Christian College, IL
Westmont College, CA

BUSINESS ADMINISTRATION
Abilene Christian University, TX
Anderson University, IN
Azusa Pacific University, CA
Bartlesville Wesleyan College, OK
Belhaven College, MS
Bethel College, IN
Bethel College, KS
Bethel College, MN
Biola University, CA
Bluffton College, OH
Bryan College, TN
California Baptist University, CA
Calvin College, MI
Campbellsville University, KY
Cedarville University, OH
College of the Ozarks, MO
Colorado Christian University, CO
Cornerstone University, MI
Covenant College, GA
Crichton College, TN
Dallas Baptist University, TX
David Lipscomb University, TN
Dordt College, IA
Eastern Mennonite University, VA
Eastern Nazarene College, MA
East Texas Baptist University, TX
Erskine College, SC
Evangel University, MO
Fresno Pacific University, CA
Geneva College, PA
George Fox University, OR
Gordon College, MA
Goshen College, IN
Grace College, IN

Grand Canyon University, AZ
Greenville College, IL
Hope International University, CA
Houghton College, NY
Houston Baptist University, TX
Howard Payne University, TX
Huntington College, IN
Indiana Wesleyan University, IN
John Brown University, AR
Judson College, IL
Kentucky Christian College, KY
King College, TN
The King's University College, AB
Lee University, TN
LeTourneau University, TX
Malone College, OH
The Master's College and Seminary, CA
Messiah College, PA
MidAmerica Nazarene University, KS
Milligan College, TN
Montreat College, NC
Mount Vernon Nazarene College, OH
North Greenville College, SC
North Park University, IL
Northwest Christian College, OR
Northwest College, WA
Northwestern College, IA
Northwestern College, MN
Northwest Nazarene University, ID
Nyack College, NY
Oklahoma Baptist University, OK
Oklahoma Christian University of Science and
    Arts, OK
Olivet Nazarene University, IL
Oral Roberts University, OK
Palm Beach Atlantic College, FL
Point Loma Nazarene University, CA
Redeemer University College, ON
Roberts Wesleyan College, NY
Seattle Pacific University, WA
Simpson College and Graduate School, CA
Southern Nazarene University, OK
Southern Wesleyan University, SC
Southwest Baptist University, MO
Spring Arbor College, MI
Sterling College, KS
Tabor College, KS
Taylor University, IN
Trevecca Nazarene University, TN
Trinity Christian College, IL
Trinity International University, IL
Trinity Western University, BC
Union University, TN
University of Sioux Falls, SD
Vanguard University of Southern California, CA
Warner Pacific College, OR
Warner Southern College, FL
Western Baptist College, OR
Whitworth College, WA
Williams Baptist College, AR
William Tyndale College, MI

BUSINESS COMMUNICATIONS
Calvin College, MI
Northwest Christian College, OR
Point Loma Nazarene University, CA

BUSINESS COMPUTER FACILITIES OPERATOR
Seattle Pacific University, WA

BUSINESS COMPUTER PROGRAMMING
Oklahoma Baptist University, OK

BUSINESS ECONOMICS
Anderson University, IN
Bluffton College, OH
Campbellsville University, KY
Dallas Baptist University, TX
David Lipscomb University, TN
George Fox University, OR
Grand Canyon University, AZ
Houston Baptist University, TX
Huntington College, IN
Messiah College, PA
Milligan College, TN
Montreat College, NC
North Greenville College, SC
Olivet Nazarene University, IL
Seattle Pacific University, WA
Spring Arbor College, MI
Union University, TN
Westmont College, CA
Wheaton College, IL

BUSINESS EDUCATION
Abilene Christian University, TX
Bartlesville Wesleyan College, OK
Bethel College, IN
Bluffton College, OH
Campbellsville University, KY
College of the Ozarks, MO
Cornerstone University, MI
Dordt College, IA
East Texas Baptist University, TX
Evangel University, MO
Geneva College, PA
Goshen College, IN
Grand Canyon University, AZ
Howard Payne University, TX
Huntington College, IN
John Brown University, AR
Lee University, TN
MidAmerica Nazarene University, KS
Mount Vernon Nazarene College, OH
Northwestern College, IA
Southern Nazarene University, OK
Southwest Baptist University, MO
Tabor College, KS
Trinity Christian College, IL
Union University, TN
Warner Southern College, FL

BUSINESS HOME ECONOMICS
Point Loma Nazarene University, CA

BUSINESS MARKETING AND MARKETING MANAGEMENT
Abilene Christian University, TX
Anderson University, IN
Azusa Pacific University, CA
Campbellsville University, KY
Cedarville University, OH
College of the Ozarks, MO
Cornerstone University, MI
Dallas Baptist University, TX

David Lipscomb University, TN
Eastern College, PA
Eastern Nazarene College, MA
East Texas Baptist University, TX
Evangel University, MO
Fresno Pacific University, CA
Grand Canyon University, AZ
Greenville College, IL
Houston Baptist University, TX
Howard Payne University, TX
Indiana Wesleyan University, IN
LeTourneau University, TX
Messiah College, PA
Montreat College, NC
Mount Vernon Nazarene College, OH
North Park University, IL
Northwest Christian College, OR
Northwestern College, MN
Northwest Nazarene University, ID
Oklahoma Baptist University, OK
Oklahoma Christian University of Science and Arts, OK
Olivet Nazarene University, IL
Oral Roberts University, OK
Palm Beach Atlantic College, FL
Southern Nazarene University, OK
Tabor College, KS
Trevecca Nazarene University, TN
Trinity Christian College, IL
Trinity International University, IL
Union University, TN
University of Sioux Falls, SD
Vanguard University of Southern California, CA
Warner Southern College, FL

BUSINESS SYSTEMS ANALYSIS AND DESIGN
Seattle Pacific University, WA

CERAMIC ARTS
Indiana Wesleyan University, IN
Trinity Christian College, IL

CHEMICAL ENGINEERING
Bethel College, IN
Calvin College, MI
Geneva College, PA

CHEMISTRY
Abilene Christian University, TX
Anderson University, IN
Asbury College, KY
Azusa Pacific University, CA
Bartlesville Wesleyan College, OK
Belhaven College, MS
Bethel College, IN
Bethel College, KS
Bethel College, MN
Bluffton College, OH
Calvin College, MI
Campbellsville University, KY
Campbell University, NC
Cedarville University, OH
College of the Ozarks, MO
Covenant College, GA
Crichton College, TN
David Lipscomb University, TN
Dordt College, IA
Eastern College, PA
Eastern Mennonite University, VA

Eastern Nazarene College, MA
East Texas Baptist University, TX
Erskine College, SC
Evangel University, MO
Fresno Pacific University, CA
Geneva College, PA
George Fox University, OR
Gordon College, MA
Goshen College, IN
Grand Canyon University, AZ
Greenville College, IL
Houghton College, NY
Houston Baptist University, TX
Howard Payne University, TX
Huntington College, IN
Indiana Wesleyan University, IN
John Brown University, AR
Judson College, AL
Judson College, IL
King College, TN
The King's University College, AB
Lee University, TN
LeTourneau University, TX
Malone College, OH
Messiah College, PA
MidAmerica Nazarene University, KS
Milligan College, TN
Mount Vernon Nazarene College, OH
North Park University, IL
Northwestern College, IA
Northwest Nazarene University, ID
Oklahoma Baptist University, OK
Oklahoma Christian University of Science and Arts, OK
Olivet Nazarene University, IL
Oral Roberts University, OK
Point Loma Nazarene University, CA
Roberts Wesleyan College, NY
Seattle Pacific University, WA
Southern Nazarene University, OK
Southern Wesleyan University, SC
Southwest Baptist University, MO
Spring Arbor College, MI
Tabor College, KS
Taylor University, IN
Trevecca Nazarene University, TN
Trinity Christian College, IL
Trinity International University, IL
Trinity Western University, BC
Union University, TN
University of Sioux Falls, SD
Vanguard University of Southern California, CA
Westmont College, CA
Wheaton College, IL
Whitworth College, WA

CHEMISTRY EDUCATION
Abilene Christian University, TX
Bethel College, IN
College of the Ozarks, MO
East Texas Baptist University, TX
George Fox University, OR
Greenville College, IL
King College, TN
Messiah College, PA
MidAmerica Nazarene University, KS
Northwest Nazarene University, ID

Oklahoma Baptist University, OK
Southern Nazarene University, OK
Trevecca Nazarene University, TN
Trinity Christian College, IL

CHILD CARE/DEVELOPMENT
Abilene Christian University, TX
Bethel College, MN
Bluffton College, OH
College of the Ozarks, MO
Evangel University, MO
Goshen College, IN
Hope International University, CA
Montreat College, NC
Northwestern College, MN
Oklahoma Baptist University, OK
Oklahoma Christian University of Science and
    Arts, OK
Olivet Nazarene University, IL
Point Loma Nazarene University, CA
Trevecca Nazarene University, TN

CHILD GUIDANCE
College of the Ozarks, MO
Oklahoma Baptist University, OK

CIVIL ENGINEERING
Bethel College, IN
Calvin College, MI
Messiah College, PA

CLASSICS
Asbury College, KY
Calvin College, MI
Seattle Pacific University, WA

CLINICAL PSYCHOLOGY
Biola University, CA
Crichton College, TN
Eastern Nazarene College, MA
George Fox University, OR
Redeemer University College, ON

CLOTHING AND TEXTILES
Bluffton College, OH
Olivet Nazarene University, IL

CLOTHING/APPAREL/TEXTILE STUDIES
College of the Ozarks, MO
Seattle Pacific University, WA

COGNITIVE PSYCHOLOGY AND PSYCHOLINGUISTICS
George Fox University, OR

COMMUNICATION DISORDERS
Biola University, CA
Northwest Christian College, OR

COMMUNICATION EQUIPMENT TECHNOLOGY
Cedarville University, OH

COMMUNICATIONS
Azusa Pacific University, CA
Belhaven College, MS
Bethel College, IN
Bethel College, KS
Campbell University, NC
Cedarville University, OH
Colorado Christian University, CO
Crichton College, TN

Eastern College, PA
Eastern Mennonite University, VA
Geneva College, PA
George Fox University, OR
Gordon College, MA
Howard Payne University, TX
Indiana Wesleyan University, IN
Malone College, OH
Messiah College, PA
Northwestern College, MN
Nyack College, NY
Oral Roberts University, OK
Point Loma Nazarene University, CA
Roberts Wesleyan College, NY
Seattle Pacific University, WA
Simpson College and Graduate School, CA
Southern Nazarene University, OK
Southwest Baptist University, MO
Tabor College, KS
Trevecca Nazarene University, TN
Trinity Christian College, IL
Trinity Western University, BC
Warner Southern College, FL
Westmont College, CA

COMMUNITY SERVICES
Eastern Mennonite University, VA
North Park University, IL
Oklahoma Christian University of Science and
    Arts, OK
Western Baptist College, OR

COMPUTER EDUCATION
Abilene Christian University, TX
East Texas Baptist University, TX

COMPUTER ENGINEERING
Eastern Nazarene College, MA
LeTourneau University, TX
Oklahoma Christian University of Science and
    Arts, OK
Oral Roberts University, OK
Taylor University, IN

COMPUTER ENGINEERING TECHNOLOGY
LeTourneau University, TX

COMPUTER GRAPHICS
Indiana Wesleyan University, IN
John Brown University, AR
Judson College, IL

COMPUTER/INFORMATION SCIENCES
Abilene Christian University, TX
Asbury College, KY
Bethel College, IN
Biola University, CA
Campbell University, NC
College of the Ozarks, MO
Colorado Christian University, CO
Dallas Baptist University, TX
East Texas Baptist University, TX
Fresno Pacific University, CA
George Fox University, OR
Indiana Wesleyan University, IN
Messiah College, PA
Oklahoma Baptist University, OK
Sterling College, KS
Williams Baptist College, AR

COMPUTER MANAGEMENT
Oklahoma Baptist University, OK

COMPUTER PROGRAMMING
Eastern Mennonite University, VA
Taylor University, IN

COMPUTER SCIENCE
Abilene Christian University, TX
Anderson University, IN
Azusa Pacific University, CA
Belhaven College, MS
Bethel College, IN
Bethel College, MN
Bluffton College, OH
Bryan College, TN
Calvin College, MI
Cedarville University, OH
College of the Ozarks, MO
Covenant College, GA
Dallas Baptist University, TX
David Lipscomb University, TN
Dordt College, IA
Eastern Mennonite University, VA
Eastern Nazarene College, MA
Evangel University, MO
Geneva College, PA
Gordon College, MA
Goshen College, IN
Greenville College, IL
Houghton College, NY
Houston Baptist University, TX
Huntington College, IN
Judson College, IL
LeTourneau University, TX
Malone College, OH
MidAmerica Nazarene University, KS
Milligan College, TN
Mount Vernon Nazarene College, OH
Northwestern College, IA
Northwest Nazarene University, ID
Nyack College, NY
Oklahoma Baptist University, OK
Oklahoma Christian University of Science and
    Arts, OK
Olivet Nazarene University, IL
Oral Roberts University, OK
Point Loma Nazarene University, CA
Redeemer University College, ON
Roberts Wesleyan College, NY
Seattle Pacific University, WA
Southern Nazarene University, OK
Southwest Baptist University, MO
Spring Arbor College, MI
Tabor College, KS
Taylor University, IN
Trinity Christian College, IL
Trinity International University, IL
Trinity Western University, BC
Union University, TN
University of Sioux Falls, SD
Western Baptist College, OR
Westmont College, CA
Wheaton College, IL
Whitworth College, WA

COMPUTER SYSTEMS ANALYSIS
Oklahoma Baptist University, OK

CONSTRUCTION ENGINEERING
John Brown University, AR

CONSTRUCTION MANAGEMENT
John Brown University, AR

CONSTRUCTION TECHNOLOGY
Abilene Christian University, TX

CONSUMER SERVICES
College of the Ozarks, MO

CORRECTIONS
College of the Ozarks, MO

COUNSELING PSYCHOLOGY
Crichton College, TN
George Fox University, OR
Grace College, IN

COUNSELOR EDUCATION/ GUIDANCE
Houston Baptist University, TX

CREATIVE WRITING
Bethel College, MN
Eastern College, PA
Geneva College, PA
Houghton College, NY
Indiana Wesleyan University, IN
Northwestern College, MN
Oklahoma Christian University of Science and
    Arts, OK
Taylor University, IN

CRIMINAL JUSTICE/LAW ENFORCEMENT ADMINISTRATION
Abilene Christian University, TX
Anderson University, IN
Bluffton College, OH
Calvin College, MI
Campbellsville University, KY
Campbell University, NC
Cedarville University, OH
College of the Ozarks, MO
Dallas Baptist University, TX
Dordt College, IA
Evangel University, MO
Grace College, IN
Grand Canyon University, AZ
Howard Payne University, TX
MidAmerica Nazarene University, KS
Mount Vernon Nazarene College, OH
Olivet Nazarene University, IL
Roberts Wesleyan College, NY
Southern Wesleyan University, SC
Southwest Baptist University, MO

CRIMINAL JUSTICE STUDIES
California Baptist University, CA
Indiana Wesleyan University, IN
Judson College, AL
Judson College, IL
Northwestern College, MN
Southern Nazarene University, OK

CRIMINOLOGY
College of the Ozarks, MO

CULTURAL STUDIES
Azusa Pacific University, CA
Bethel College, MN
Indiana Wesleyan University, IN

CURRICULUM AND INSTRUCTION
George Fox University, OR

DANCE
Belhaven College, MS
Westmont College, CA

DATA PROCESSING TECHNOLOGY
Campbellsville University, KY
Dordt College, IA
Eastern Mennonite University, VA
Mount Vernon Nazarene College, OH

(PRE)DENTISTRY
Abilene Christian University, TX
Anderson University, IN
Bartlesville Wesleyan College, OK
Bethel College, IN
Bethel College, MN
Calvin College, MI
Campbellsville University, KY
Campbell University, NC
Cedarville University, OH
Cornerstone University, MI
David Lipscomb University, TN
Dordt College, IA
Eastern Mennonite University, VA
Eastern Nazarene College, MA
Evangel University, MO
Goshen College, IN
Grand Canyon University, AZ
Greenville College, IL
Houghton College, NY
Houston Baptist University, TX
Huntington College, IN
Indiana Wesleyan University, IN
LeTourneau University, TX
Milligan College, TN
Montreat College, NC
Mount Vernon Nazarene College, OH
North Park University, IL
Northwest Nazarene University, ID
Oklahoma Baptist University, OK
Oklahoma Christian University of Science and
    Arts, OK
Olivet Nazarene University, IL
Oral Roberts University, OK
Redeemer University College, ON
Roberts Wesleyan College, NY
Seattle Pacific University, WA
Southern Nazarene University, OK
Tabor College, KS
Taylor University, IN
Trinity Christian College, IL
Trinity Western University, BC
Union University, TN
University of Sioux Falls, SD
Westmont College, CA
Whitworth College, WA
Williams Baptist College, AR

DEVELOPMENTAL/CHILD PSYCHOLOGY
Bluffton College, OH
Eastern Nazarene College, MA
Fresno Pacific University, CA
Houston Baptist University, TX
Oklahoma Baptist University, OK
Olivet Nazarene University, IL
University of Sioux Falls, SD

DEVELOPMENT ECONOMICS
Eastern Mennonite University, VA

DIETETICS
Abilene Christian University, TX
Bluffton College, OH
College of the Ozarks, MO
David Lipscomb University, TN
Messiah College, PA
Olivet Nazarene University, IL
Point Loma Nazarene University, CA

DIVINITY/MINISTRY
Azusa Pacific University, CA
Bartlesville Wesleyan College, OK
Bethel College, IN
Biola University, CA
Bluffton College, OH
Campbellsville University, KY
Colorado Christian University, CO
Cornerstone University, MI
David Lipscomb University, TN
Eastern Mennonite University, VA
Eastern Nazarene College, MA
Fresno Pacific University, CA
George Fox University, OR
Grace College, IN
Grand Canyon University, AZ
Greenville College, IL
Houghton College, NY
Huntington College, IN
Indiana Wesleyan University, IN
John Brown University, AR
The Master's College and Seminary, CA
MidAmerica Nazarene University, KS
North Park University, IL
Northwest College, WA
Northwest Nazarene University, ID
Oklahoma Baptist University, OK
Oklahoma Christian University of Science and
    Arts, OK
Roberts Wesleyan College, NY
Simpson College and Graduate School, CA
Southern Wesleyan University, SC
Spring Arbor College, MI
Tabor College, KS
Trinity International University, IL
Trinity Western University, BC
Warner Pacific College, OR
Western Baptist College, OR
Williams Baptist College, AR

DRAFTING
Abilene Christian University, TX
LeTourneau University, TX

DRAMA AND DANCE EDUCATION
Abilene Christian University, TX
East Texas Baptist University, TX
Greenville College, IL
Oklahoma Baptist University, OK

DRAWING
Biola University, CA
Grace College, IN
Judson College, IL
Northwest Nazarene University, ID
Trinity Christian College, IL

EARLY CHILDHOOD EDUCATION
Bethel College, IN

Bethel College, MN
Bluffton College, OH
Bryan College, TN
Cedarville University, OH
Cornerstone University, MI
Dallas Baptist University, TX
Eastern Mennonite University, VA
Eastern Nazarene College, MA
East Texas Baptist University, TX
Erskine College, SC
Evangel University, MO
Gordon College, MA
Goshen College, IN
Greenville College, IL
Hope International University, CA
Houston Baptist University, TX
Howard Payne University, TX
John Brown University, AR
Judson College, IL
King College, TN
Malone College, OH
Messiah College, PA
Milligan College, TN
Mount Vernon Nazarene College, OH
North Greenville College, SC
North Park University, IL
Oklahoma Baptist University, OK
Oklahoma Christian University of Science and
    Arts, OK
Olivet Nazarene University, IL
Oral Roberts University, OK
Palm Beach Atlantic College, FL
Southern Nazarene University, OK
Southern Wesleyan University, SC
Spring Arbor College, MI
Tabor College, KS
Taylor University, IN
Trevecca Nazarene University, TN
Union University, TN
University of Sioux Falls, SD
Warner Pacific College, OR
Williams Baptist College, AR
William Tyndale College, MI

EARTH SCIENCES
Olivet Nazarene University, IL

ECOLOGY
Montreat College, NC

ECONOMICS
Bethel College, MN
Bluffton College, OH
Calvin College, MI
Campbellsville University, KY
Campbell University, NC
Covenant College, GA
Eastern Mennonite University, VA
Gordon College, MA
Goshen College, IN
Grand Canyon University, AZ
Houston Baptist University, TX
Huntington College, IN
Indiana Wesleyan University, IN
King College, TN
Messiah College, PA
Montreat College, NC
North Park University, IL
Northwestern College, IA

Olivet Nazarene University, IL
Point Loma Nazarene University, CA
Taylor University, IN
Trevecca Nazarene University, TN
Trinity International University, IL
Union University, TN
University of Sioux Falls, SD
Westmont College, CA
Wheaton College, IL
Whitworth College, WA

EDUCATION
Anderson University, IN
Bartlesville Wesleyan College, OK
Bethel College, IN
Bethel College, MN
Biola University, CA
Bluffton College, OH
Bryan College, TN
Campbell University, NC
Cedarville University, OH
College of the Ozarks, MO
Cornerstone University, MI
Dallas Baptist University, TX
David Lipscomb University, TN
Dordt College, IA
Eastern Mennonite University, VA
Eastern Nazarene College, MA
Evangel University, MO
Fresno Pacific University, CA
Gordon College, MA
Goshen College, IN
Greenville College, IL
Houghton College, NY
Houston Baptist University, TX
Howard Payne University, TX
Huntington College, IN
Indiana Wesleyan University, IN
John Brown University, AR
Judson College, AL
Judson College, IL
King College, TN
Lee University, TN
The Master's College and Seminary, CA
Milligan College, TN
Montreat College, NC
Mount Vernon Nazarene College, OH
North Park University, IL
Northwest College, WA
Northwestern College, IA
Oklahoma Baptist University, OK
Olivet Nazarene University, IL
Oral Roberts University, OK
Palm Beach Atlantic College, FL
Redeemer University College, ON
Roberts Wesleyan College, NY
Simpson College and Graduate School, CA
Southern Nazarene University, OK
Southern Wesleyan University, SC
Tabor College, KS
Taylor University, IN
Trinity Christian College, IL
Trinity International University, IL
Trinity Western University, BC
Union University, TN
University of Sioux Falls, SD
Vanguard University of Southern California, CA
Warner Pacific College, OR
Western Baptist College, OR

Westmont College, CA
Williams Baptist College, AR

EDUCATION ADMINISTRATION
Campbell University, NC
Oral Roberts University, OK

EDUCATION (MULTIPLE LEVELS)
East Texas Baptist University, TX
George Fox University, OR
Howard Payne University, TX
Oral Roberts University, OK

**EDUCATION OF THE EMOTIONALLY
HANDICAPPED**
Oklahoma Baptist University, OK
Trinity Christian College, IL

**EDUCATION OF THE MENTALLY
HANDICAPPED**
Oklahoma Baptist University, OK
Trinity Christian College, IL

**EDUCATION OF THE SPECIFIC
LEARNING DISABLED**
Malone College, OH
Oklahoma Baptist University, OK
Trinity Christian College, IL

**ELECTRICAL/ELECTRONIC
ENGINEERING TECHNOLOGY**
LeTourneau University, TX

**ELECTRICAL/ELECTRONICS
ENGINEERING**
Abilene Christian University, TX
Bethel College, IN
Calvin College, MI
Cedarville University, OH
Dordt College, IA
Eastern Nazarene College, MA
John Brown University, AR
LeTourneau University, TX
Oklahoma Christian University of Science and
    Arts, OK
Oral Roberts University, OK
Seattle Pacific University, WA

ELEMENTARY EDUCATION
Abilene Christian University, TX
Anderson University, IN
Asbury College, KY
Bartlesville Wesleyan College, OK
Belhaven College, MS
Bethel College, IN
Bethel College, KS
Bethel College, MN
Biola University, CA
Bluffton College, OH
Bryan College, TN
Calvin College, MI
Campbellsville University, KY
Campbell University, NC
Cedarville University, OH
College of the Ozarks, MO
Colorado Christian University, CO
Cornerstone University, MI
Covenant College, GA
Crichton College, TN
Dallas Baptist University, TX
David Lipscomb University, TN

Elementary education (continued)

Dordt College, IA
Eastern College, PA
Eastern Mennonite University, VA
Eastern Nazarene College, MA
East Texas Baptist University, TX
Erskine College, SC
Evangel University, MO
Fresno Pacific University, CA
Geneva College, PA
George Fox University, OR
Gordon College, MA
Goshen College, IN
Grace College, IN
Grand Canyon University, AZ
Greenville College, IL
Hope International University, CA
Houghton College, NY
Houston Baptist University, TX
Howard Payne University, TX
Huntington College, IN
Indiana Wesleyan University, IN
John Brown University, AR
Judson College, AL
Judson College, IL
Kentucky Christian College, KY
King College, TN
The King's University College, AB
Lee University, TN
LeTourneau University, TX
Malone College, OH
The Master's College and Seminary, CA
Messiah College, PA
MidAmerica Nazarene University, KS
Milligan College, TN
Montreat College, NC
Mount Vernon Nazarene College, OH
North Greenville College, SC
North Park University, IL
Northwest Christian College, OR
Northwest College, WA
Northwestern College, IA
Northwestern College, MN
Northwest Nazarene University, ID
Nyack College, NY
Oklahoma Baptist University, OK
Oklahoma Christian University of Science and Arts, OK
Olivet Nazarene University, IL
Oral Roberts University, OK
Palm Beach Atlantic College, FL
Redeemer University College, ON
Roberts Wesleyan College, NY
Simpson College and Graduate School, CA
Southern Nazarene University, OK
Southern Wesleyan University, SC
Southwest Baptist University, MO
Spring Arbor College, MI
Sterling College, KS
Tabor College, KS
Taylor University, IN
Trevecca Nazarene University, TN
Trinity Christian College, IL
Trinity International University, IL
Trinity Western University, BC
Union University, TN
University of Sioux Falls, SD

Warner Pacific College, OR
Warner Southern College, FL
Western Baptist College, OR
Westmont College, CA
Wheaton College, IL
Whitworth College, WA
Williams Baptist College, AR

ELEMENTARY/MIDDLE/SECONDARY EDUCATION ADMINISTRATION
Campbell University, NC

EMERGENCY MEDICAL TECHNOLOGY
Oklahoma Christian University of Science and Arts, OK
Southwest Baptist University, MO

ENGINEERING
Calvin College, MI
Dordt College, IA
Geneva College, PA
George Fox University, OR
Houston Baptist University, TX
John Brown University, AR
LeTourneau University, TX
Messiah College, PA
Milligan College, TN
Oklahoma Christian University of Science and Arts, OK
Olivet Nazarene University, IL
Wheaton College, IL

(PRE)ENGINEERING
Anderson University, IN
Azusa Pacific University, CA
Campbell University, NC
Covenant College, GA
Eastern Mennonite University, VA
Montreat College, NC
Roberts Wesleyan College, NY
Tabor College, KS
University of Sioux Falls, SD

ENGINEERING/INDUSTRIAL MANAGEMENT
John Brown University, AR

ENGINEERING MECHANICS
Dordt College, IA
Oral Roberts University, OK

ENGINEERING PHYSICS
Abilene Christian University, TX
Eastern Nazarene College, MA
Houston Baptist University, TX
Northwest Nazarene University, ID
Oklahoma Christian University of Science and Arts, OK
Point Loma Nazarene University, CA
Taylor University, IN
Westmont College, CA

ENGINEERING SCIENCE
Abilene Christian University, TX
Bethel College, IN
David Lipscomb University, TN
Houston Baptist University, TX
Seattle Pacific University, WA

ENGINEERING TECHNOLOGY
John Brown University, AR

LeTourneau University, TX

ENGLISH
Abilene Christian University, TX
Anderson University, IN
Asbury College, KY
Azusa Pacific University, CA
Bartlesville Wesleyan College, OK
Belhaven College, MS
Bethel College, IN
Bethel College, KS
Bethel College, MN
Biola University, CA
Bluffton College, OH
Bryan College, TN
California Baptist University, CA
Calvin College, MI
Campbellsville University, KY
Campbell University, NC
Cedarville University, OH
College of the Ozarks, MO
Colorado Christian University, CO
Cornerstone University, MI
Covenant College, GA
Crichton College, TN
Dallas Baptist University, TX
David Lipscomb University, TN
Dordt College, IA
Eastern College, PA
Eastern Mennonite University, VA
Eastern Nazarene College, MA
East Texas Baptist University, TX
Erskine College, SC
Evangel University, MO
Fresno Pacific University, CA
Geneva College, PA
George Fox University, OR
Gordon College, MA
Goshen College, IN
Grace College, IN
Grand Canyon University, AZ
Greenville College, IL
Houghton College, NY
Houston Baptist University, TX
Howard Payne University, TX
Huntington College, IN
Indiana Wesleyan University, IN
John Brown University, AR
Judson College, AL
Judson College, IL
King College, TN
The King's University College, AB
Lee University, TN
LeTourneau University, TX
Malone College, OH
The Master's College and Seminary, CA
Messiah College, PA
MidAmerica Nazarene University, KS
Milligan College, TN
Montreat College, NC
Mount Vernon Nazarene College, OH
North Park University, IL
Northwest College, WA
Northwestern College, IA
Northwestern College, MN
Northwest Nazarene University, ID
Nyack College, NY
Oklahoma Baptist University, OK

Oklahoma Christian University of Science and
  Arts, OK
Olivet Nazarene University, IL
Palm Beach Atlantic College, FL
Redeemer University College, ON
Roberts Wesleyan College, NY
Seattle Pacific University, WA
Simpson College and Graduate School, CA
Southern Nazarene University, OK
Southern Wesleyan University, SC
Southwest Baptist University, MO
Spring Arbor College, MI
Sterling College, KS
Tabor College, KS
Taylor University, IN
Trevecca Nazarene University, TN
Trinity Christian College, IL
Trinity International University, IL
Trinity Western University, BC
Union University, TN
University of Sioux Falls, SD
Vanguard University of Southern California, CA
Warner Pacific College, OR
Warner Southern College, FL
Western Baptist College, OR
Westmont College, CA
Wheaton College, IL
Whitworth College, WA
Williams Baptist College, AR
William Tyndale College, MI

ENGLISH COMPOSITION
Oklahoma Baptist University, OK

ENGLISH EDUCATION
Abilene Christian University, TX
Anderson University, IN
Bethel College, IN
Cedarville University, OH
College of the Ozarks, MO
Colorado Christian University, CO
Crichton College, TN
Eastern College, PA
East Texas Baptist University, TX
George Fox University, OR
Grace College, IN
Greenville College, IL
Hope International University, CA
Indiana Wesleyan University, IN
Judson College, AL
King College, TN
Messiah College, PA
MidAmerica Nazarene University, KS
Northwest College, WA
Northwestern College, MN
Northwest Nazarene University, ID
Oklahoma Baptist University, OK
Oral Roberts University, OK
Seattle Pacific University, WA
Simpson College and Graduate School, CA
Southern Nazarene University, OK
Southwest Baptist University, MO
Trevecca Nazarene University, TN
Trinity Christian College, IL
Warner Southern College, FL
Westmont College, CA

ENTREPRENEURSHIP
Howard Payne University, TX

Trinity Christian College, IL

ENVIRONMENTAL BIOLOGY
Bethel College, IN
Cedarville University, OH
Grand Canyon University, AZ
Greenville College, IL
The Master's College and Seminary, CA
Northwest College, WA
Tabor College, KS
Taylor University, IN
Trinity Western University, BC

ENVIRONMENTAL SCIENCE
Abilene Christian University, TX
Bethel College, MN
Calvin College, MI
David Lipscomb University, TN
Dordt College, IA
Eastern College, PA
Eastern Mennonite University, VA
Eastern Nazarene College, MA
Goshen College, IN
John Brown University, AR
Judson College, AL
The King's University College, AB
Messiah College, PA
Montreat College, NC
Northwestern College, IA
Olivet Nazarene University, IL
Southern Nazarene University, OK
Taylor University, IN
Trinity Western University, BC
Wheaton College, IL

EUROPEAN HISTORY
Calvin College, MI

EUROPEAN STUDIES
Howard Payne University, TX
Seattle Pacific University, WA

EXERCISE SCIENCES
Abilene Christian University, TX
Bartlesville Wesleyan College, OK
Biola University, CA
Bluffton College, OH
California Baptist University, CA
Calvin College, MI
David Lipscomb University, TN
Dordt College, IA
Gordon College, MA
Grand Canyon University, AZ
Houston Baptist University, TX
Howard Payne University, TX
Huntington College, IN
John Brown University, AR
Judson College, AL
Malone College, OH
Messiah College, PA
MidAmerica Nazarene University, KS
Milligan College, TN
North Park University, IL
Northwestern College, IA
Oklahoma Baptist University, OK
Oral Roberts University, OK
Redeemer University College, ON
Seattle Pacific University, WA
Southern Nazarene University, OK
Trevecca Nazarene University, TN

University of Sioux Falls, SD
Warner Pacific College, OR
Warner Southern College, FL
Westmont College, CA
Wheaton College, IL

EXPERIMENTAL PSYCHOLOGY
Redeemer University College, ON

FAMILY/COMMUNITY STUDIES
Goshen College, IN
Messiah College, PA
Oklahoma Christian University of Science and
  Arts, OK
Olivet Nazarene University, IL
Southern Nazarene University, OK
Union University, TN

FAMILY/CONSUMER STUDIES
David Lipscomb University, TN
Seattle Pacific University, WA

FAMILY RESOURCE MANAGEMENT STUDIES
George Fox University, OR

FAMILY STUDIES
Anderson University, IN
Point Loma Nazarene University, CA
Southern Nazarene University, OK

FASHION DESIGN/ILLUSTRATION
Bluffton College, OH

FASHION MERCHANDISING
Abilene Christian University, TX
Bluffton College, OH
David Lipscomb University, TN
George Fox University, OR
Judson College, AL
Olivet Nazarene University, IL

FILM STUDIES
Calvin College, MI
Olivet Nazarene University, IL

FILM/VIDEO PRODUCTION
Vanguard University of Southern California, CA

FINANCE
Abilene Christian University, TX
Anderson University, IN
Bethel College, MN
Campbell University, NC
Cedarville University, OH
Dallas Baptist University, TX
David Lipscomb University, TN
Eastern College, PA
Fresno Pacific University, CA
Grand Canyon University, AZ
Houston Baptist University, TX
Howard Payne University, TX
Indiana Wesleyan University, IN
The Master's College and Seminary, CA
North Park University, IL
Northwestern College, MN
Northwest Nazarene University, ID
Oklahoma Baptist University, OK
Olivet Nazarene University, IL
Oral Roberts University, OK
Palm Beach Atlantic College, FL
Southern Nazarene University, OK

Finance (continued)

Union University, TN
Vanguard University of Southern California, CA
Warner Southern College, FL
Western Baptist College, OR

FINANCIAL PLANNING
Trinity Christian College, IL

FINE/STUDIO ARTS
Abilene Christian University, TX
Anderson University, IN
Asbury College, KY
Bethel College, KS
Bethel College, MN
Biola University, CA
California Baptist University, CA
Calvin College, MI
Campbell University, NC
College of the Ozarks, MO
David Lipscomb University, TN
Grand Canyon University, AZ
Howard Payne University, TX
Judson College, IL
King College, TN
Messiah College, PA
North Park University, IL
Northwestern College, MN
Oklahoma Baptist University, OK
Oral Roberts University, OK
Roberts Wesleyan College, NY
Whitworth College, WA
Williams Baptist College, AR

FOOD PRODUCTS RETAILING
David Lipscomb University, TN

FOOD SCIENCES
Olivet Nazarene University, IL

FOREIGN LANGUAGES EDUCATION
Greenville College, IL

FOREIGN LANGUAGES/LITERATURES
Gordon College, MA
Union University, TN

FORENSIC TECHNOLOGY
College of the Ozarks, MO

FRENCH
Abilene Christian University, TX
Anderson University, IN
Asbury College, KY
Calvin College, MI
Campbell University, NC
College of the Ozarks, MO
David Lipscomb University, TN
Eastern College, PA
Eastern Mennonite University, VA
Eastern Nazarene College, MA
Erskine College, SC
Gordon College, MA
Grace College, IN
Greenville College, IL
Houghton College, NY
Houston Baptist University, TX
King College, TN
Messiah College, PA
North Park University, IL

Oklahoma Baptist University, OK
Olivet Nazarene University, IL
Oral Roberts University, OK
Redeemer University College, ON
Seattle Pacific University, WA
Spring Arbor College, MI
Taylor University, IN
Union University, TN
Westmont College, CA
Wheaton College, IL
Whitworth College, WA

FRENCH LANGUAGE EDUCATION
Abilene Christian University, TX
Anderson University, IN
David Lipscomb University, TN
Grace College, IN
King College, TN
Messiah College, PA
Oklahoma Baptist University, OK
Oral Roberts University, OK

GENERAL STUDIES
Anderson University, IN
Eastern Nazarene College, MA
Hope International University, CA
Howard Payne University, TX
Indiana Wesleyan University, IN
Northwest Christian College, OR
Nyack College, NY
Palm Beach Atlantic College, FL
Seattle Pacific University, WA
Simpson College and Graduate School, CA
Southern Nazarene University, OK
Southwest Baptist University, MO
Trevecca Nazarene University, TN
Trinity Western University, BC
Warner Southern College, FL

GEOGRAPHY
Calvin College, MI
Trinity Western University, BC

GEOLOGY
Abilene Christian University, TX
Calvin College, MI
Olivet Nazarene University, IL
Wheaton College, IL

GERMAN
Anderson University, IN
Bethel College, KS
Calvin College, MI
College of the Ozarks, MO
David Lipscomb University, TN
Dordt College, IA
Eastern Mennonite University, VA
Gordon College, MA
Goshen College, IN
Grace College, IN
Messiah College, PA
Oklahoma Baptist University, OK
Oral Roberts University, OK
Seattle Pacific University, WA
Wheaton College, IL

GERMAN LANGUAGE EDUCATION
Anderson University, IN
Grace College, IN
Messiah College, PA
Oklahoma Baptist University, OK

Oral Roberts University, OK

GERONTOLOGY
College of the Ozarks, MO

GRAPHIC DESIGN/COMMERCIAL ART/ILLUSTRATION
Abilene Christian University, TX
Anderson University, IN
Biola University, CA
Bluffton College, OH
Campbell University, NC
David Lipscomb University, TN
Dordt College, IA
Grace College, IN
Grand Canyon University, AZ
Huntington College, IN
John Brown University, AR
Judson College, IL
Northwestern College, MN
Northwest Nazarene University, ID
Oklahoma Christian University of Science and
    Arts, OK
Olivet Nazarene University, IL
Oral Roberts University, OK
Point Loma Nazarene University, CA
Roberts Wesleyan College, NY
Southwest Baptist University, MO
Taylor University, IN
Trinity Christian College, IL
University of Sioux Falls, SD

GREEK (ANCIENT AND MEDIEVAL)
Asbury College, KY
Wheaton College, IL

GREEK (MODERN)
Calvin College, MI
Southern Wesleyan University, SC

HEALTH AIDE
Campbell University, NC

HEALTH EDUCATION
Abilene Christian University, TX
Anderson University, IN
Bethel College, IN
Bethel College, MN
Bluffton College, OH
Campbellsville University, KY
Cedarville University, OH
David Lipscomb University, TN
Eastern Mennonite University, VA
George Fox University, OR
John Brown University, AR
Lee University, TN
Malone College, OH
MidAmerica Nazarene University, KS
Milligan College, TN
Southern Nazarene University, OK
Tabor College, KS
University of Sioux Falls, SD

HEALTH FACILITIES ADMINISTRATION
Eastern College, PA

HEALTH/PHYSICAL EDUCATION
Abilene Christian University, TX
Anderson University, IN
Asbury College, KY

Bethel College, KS
Campbell University, NC
Cedarville University, OH
College of the Ozarks, MO
Eastern College, PA
East Texas Baptist University, TX
Malone College, OH
Northwest Nazarene University, ID
Oklahoma Baptist University, OK
Point Loma Nazarene University, CA
Redeemer University College, ON
Trinity Western University, BC

HEALTH SCIENCE
Azusa Pacific University, CA
Campbell University, NC
College of the Ozarks, MO
Covenant College, GA
Eastern Nazarene College, MA
Erskine College, SC
Milligan College, TN
Northwest College, WA
Warner Pacific College, OR
Western Baptist College, OR

HEALTH SERVICES ADMINISTRATION
Dallas Baptist University, TX
Howard Payne University, TX
John Brown University, AR
Milligan College, TN

HEBREW
Wheaton College, IL

HISPANIC-AMERICAN STUDIES
Goshen College, IN

HISTORY
Abilene Christian University, TX
Anderson University, IN
Asbury College, KY
Azusa Pacific University, CA
Bartlesville Wesleyan College, OK
Belhaven College, MS
Bethel College, IN
Bethel College, KS
Bethel College, MN
Biola University, CA
Bluffton College, OH
Bryan College, TN
California Baptist University, CA
Calvin College, MI
Campbellsville University, KY
Campbell University, NC
Cedarville University, OH
College of the Ozarks, MO
Colorado Christian University, CO
Cornerstone University, MI
Covenant College, GA
Crichton College, TN
Dallas Baptist University, TX
David Lipscomb University, TN
Dordt College, IA
Eastern College, PA
Eastern Mennonite University, VA
Eastern Nazarene College, MA
East Texas Baptist University, TX
Erskine College, SC
Evangel University, MO
Fresno Pacific University, CA

Geneva College, PA
George Fox University, OR
Gordon College, MA
Goshen College, IN
Grand Canyon University, AZ
Greenville College, IL
Houghton College, NY
Houston Baptist University, TX
Howard Payne University, TX
Huntington College, IN
Indiana Wesleyan University, IN
John Brown University, AR
Judson College, AL
Judson College, IL
Kentucky Christian College, KY
King College, TN
The King's University College, AB
Lee University, TN
LeTourneau University, TX
Malone College, OH
The Master's College and Seminary, CA
Messiah College, PA
MidAmerica Nazarene University, KS
Milligan College, TN
Montreat College, NC
Mount Vernon Nazarene College, OH
North Park University, IL
Northwest Christian College, OR
Northwest College, WA
Northwestern College, IA
Northwestern College, MN
Northwest Nazarene University, ID
Nyack College, NY
Oklahoma Baptist University, OK
Oklahoma Christian University of Science and
    Arts, OK
Olivet Nazarene University, IL
Oral Roberts University, OK
Palm Beach Atlantic College, FL
Point Loma Nazarene University, CA
Redeemer University College, ON
Roberts Wesleyan College, NY
Seattle Pacific University, WA
Simpson College and Graduate School, CA
Southern Nazarene University, OK
Southern Wesleyan University, SC
Southwest Baptist University, MO
Spring Arbor College, MI
Sterling College, KS
Tabor College, KS
Taylor University, IN
Trevecca Nazarene University, TN
Trinity Christian College, IL
Trinity International University, IL
Trinity Western University, BC
Union University, TN
University of Sioux Falls, SD
Vanguard University of Southern California, CA
Warner Pacific College, OR
Warner Southern College, FL
Westmont College, CA
Wheaton College, IL
Whitworth College, WA
Williams Baptist College, AR
William Tyndale College, MI

HISTORY EDUCATION
Abilene Christian University, TX
College of the Ozarks, MO

East Texas Baptist University, TX
King College, TN
Northwest College, WA
Northwest Nazarene University, ID
Oklahoma Baptist University, OK
Trevecca Nazarene University, TN
Trinity Christian College, IL

HOME ECONOMICS
Abilene Christian University, TX
Bluffton College, OH
Campbell University, NC
College of the Ozarks, MO
David Lipscomb University, TN
George Fox University, OR
The Master's College and Seminary, CA
Mount Vernon Nazarene College, OH
Olivet Nazarene University, IL
Point Loma Nazarene University, CA

HOME ECONOMICS EDUCATION
Abilene Christian University, TX
Bluffton College, OH
Campbell University, NC
College of the Ozarks, MO
George Fox University, OR
Mount Vernon Nazarene College, OH
Olivet Nazarene University, IL
Seattle Pacific University, WA

HORTICULTURE SCIENCE
College of the Ozarks, MO

HOTEL AND RESTAURANT MANAGEMENT
College of the Ozarks, MO

HUMANITIES
Belhaven College, MS
Biola University, CA
Bluffton College, OH
Colorado Christian University, CO
Fresno Pacific University, CA
Houghton College, NY
Messiah College, PA
Milligan College, TN
North Greenville College, SC
Northwest Christian College, OR
Northwestern College, IA
Oklahoma Baptist University, OK
Redeemer University College, ON
Roberts Wesleyan College, NY
Tabor College, KS
Trinity International University, IL
Trinity Western University, BC
University of Sioux Falls, SD
Western Baptist College, OR

HUMAN RESOURCES MANAGEMENT
Abilene Christian University, TX
Colorado Christian University, CO
George Fox University, OR
Grand Canyon University, AZ
Judson College, IL
Messiah College, PA
MidAmerica Nazarene University, KS
Oklahoma Baptist University, OK
Olivet Nazarene University, IL
Palm Beach Atlantic College, FL
Redeemer University College, ON
Roberts Wesleyan College, NY

Human resources management (continued)

Simpson College and Graduate School, CA
Trinity Christian College, IL
Trinity International University, IL

HUMAN SERVICES
Geneva College, PA
Judson College, IL
Milligan College, TN
Montreat College, NC
Mount Vernon Nazarene College, OH
Southwest Baptist University, MO
Trinity Western University, BC

INDIVIDUAL/FAMILY DEVELOPMENT
Abilene Christian University, TX
Geneva College, PA
Hope International University, CA
Lee University, TN
Warner Pacific College, OR

INDUSTRIAL ARTS
College of the Ozarks, MO

INDUSTRIAL ARTS EDUCATION
Abilene Christian University, TX
College of the Ozarks, MO

INDUSTRIAL DESIGN
Campbell University, NC

INDUSTRIAL ENGINEERING
Eastern Nazarene College, MA

INDUSTRIAL RADIOLOGIC TECHNOLOGY
University of Sioux Falls, SD

INDUSTRIAL TECHNOLOGY
Abilene Christian University, TX

INFORMATION SCIENCES/SYSTEMS
Bartlesville Wesleyan College, OK
Belhaven College, MS
California Baptist University, CA
Campbellsville University, KY
Cedarville University, OH
Colorado Christian University, CO
Cornerstone University, MI
David Lipscomb University, TN
Eastern Mennonite University, VA
Goshen College, IN
Houston Baptist University, TX
Howard Payne University, TX
Judson College, AL
Judson College, IL
King College, TN
Lee University, TN
LeTourneau University, TX
Messiah College, PA
Oklahoma Baptist University, OK
Oklahoma Christian University of Science and
    Arts, OK
Olivet Nazarene University, IL
Palm Beach Atlantic College, FL
Southern Nazarene University, OK
Southwest Baptist University, MO
Taylor University, IN
Trevecca Nazarene University, TN
Trinity Christian College, IL
Trinity International University, IL

Union University, TN
University of Sioux Falls, SD

INTERDISCIPLINARY STUDIES
Abilene Christian University, TX
Calvin College, MI
College of the Ozarks, MO
Cornerstone University, MI
Covenant College, GA
Dallas Baptist University, TX
George Fox University, OR
Hope International University, CA
Houston Baptist University, TX
Howard Payne University, TX
John Brown University, AR
Judson College, AL
Kentucky Christian College, KY
LeTourneau University, TX
North Greenville College, SC
Northwest Christian College, OR
Northwest College, WA
Nyack College, NY
Oklahoma Baptist University, OK
Olivet Nazarene University, IL
Southern Nazarene University, OK
Sterling College, KS
Tabor College, KS
University of Sioux Falls, SD
Vanguard University of Southern California, CA
Western Baptist College, OR
Wheaton College, IL

INTERIOR DESIGN
Abilene Christian University, TX
Bethel College, IN
Oklahoma Christian University of Science and
    Arts, OK

INTERNATIONAL AGRICULTURE
Eastern Mennonite University, VA
MidAmerica Nazarene University, KS

INTERNATIONAL BUSINESS
Campbell University, NC
Cedarville University, OH
Eastern Mennonite University, VA
Fresno Pacific University, CA
Grace College, IN
Grand Canyon University, AZ
John Brown University, AR
Judson College, IL
Messiah College, PA
North Park University, IL
Northwestern College, MN
Northwest Nazarene University, ID
Oklahoma Baptist University, OK
Palm Beach Atlantic College, FL
Taylor University, IN
Vanguard University of Southern California, CA
Whitworth College, WA

INTERNATIONAL BUSINESS MARKETING
Oklahoma Baptist University, OK

INTERNATIONAL ECONOMICS
Taylor University, IN

INTERNATIONAL RELATIONS
Abilene Christian University, TX
Azusa Pacific University, CA

Bethel College, MN
Calvin College, MI
Campbell University, NC
Cedarville University, OH
George Fox University, OR
Gordon College, MA
Grand Canyon University, AZ
Houghton College, NY
John Brown University, AR
Lee University, TN
Malone College, OH
North Park University, IL
Northwest Nazarene University, ID
Oral Roberts University, OK
Southern Nazarene University, OK
Tabor College, KS
Taylor University, IN
Trinity Western University, BC
Whitworth College, WA

JOURNALISM
Abilene Christian University, TX
Asbury College, KY
Bethel College, IN
Campbellsville University, KY
Campbell University, NC
College of the Ozarks, MO
Dordt College, IA
Eastern Nazarene College, MA
Evangel University, MO
Goshen College, IN
Houston Baptist University, TX
John Brown University, AR
Judson College, IL
Malone College, OH
Messiah College, PA
Milligan College, TN
North Greenville College, SC
Northwestern College, MN
Oklahoma Baptist University, OK
Oklahoma Christian University of Science and
    Arts, OK
Olivet Nazarene University, IL
Oral Roberts University, OK
Point Loma Nazarene University, CA
Southern Nazarene University, OK
Tabor College, KS
Union University, TN
Whitworth College, WA

LATIN AMERICAN STUDIES
Seattle Pacific University, WA

LATIN (ANCIENT AND MEDIEVAL)
Asbury College, KY
Calvin College, MI
Seattle Pacific University, WA
Wheaton College, IL

(PRE)LAW
Abilene Christian University, TX
Anderson University, IN
Azusa Pacific University, CA
Bartlesville Wesleyan College, OK
Bethel College, IN
Bethel College, MN
Biola University, CA
Bluffton College, OH
Calvin College, MI
Campbellsville University, KY

Campbell University, NC
Cedarville University, OH
Cornerstone University, MI
Covenant College, GA
Crichton College, TN
David Lipscomb University, TN
Eastern Nazarene College, MA
Evangel University, MO
Fresno Pacific University, CA
Goshen College, IN
Grand Canyon University, AZ
Greenville College, IL
Houghton College, NY
Houston Baptist University, TX
Howard Payne University, TX
Huntington College, IN
Indiana Wesleyan University, IN
John Brown University, AR
Judson College, IL
King College, TN
LeTourneau University, TX
Malone College, OH
Montreat College, NC
Mount Vernon Nazarene College, OH
North Park University, IL
Northwest College, WA
Northwest Nazarene University, ID
Oklahoma Baptist University, OK
Oklahoma Christian University of Science and
    Arts, OK
Olivet Nazarene University, IL
Palm Beach Atlantic College, FL
Redeemer University College, ON
Roberts Wesleyan College, NY
Seattle Pacific University, WA
Southern Nazarene University, OK
Tabor College, KS
Taylor University, IN
Trinity Western University, BC
Union University, TN
University of Sioux Falls, SD
Vanguard University of Southern California, CA
Warner Pacific College, OR
Warner Southern College, FL
Western Baptist College, OR
Westmont College, CA
Whitworth College, WA
Williams Baptist College, AR
William Tyndale College, MI

LAW ENFORCEMENT/POLICE SCIENCE
College of the Ozarks, MO

LEGAL ADMINISTRATIVE ASSISTANT
Tabor College, KS

LIBERAL ARTS AND STUDIES
Abilene Christian University, TX
Azusa Pacific University, CA
Bartlesville Wesleyan College, OK
Bethel College, IN
Bethel College, MN
Bluffton College, OH
Bryan College, TN
California Baptist University, CA
Campbell University, NC
Colorado Christian University, CO
Crichton College, TN

Dallas Baptist University, TX
David Lipscomb University, TN
Eastern College, PA
Eastern Mennonite University, VA
Eastern Nazarene College, MA
East Texas Baptist University, TX
Fresno Pacific University, CA
Goshen College, IN
Grand Canyon University, AZ
Greenville College, IL
Houston Baptist University, TX
Howard Payne University, TX
John Brown University, AR
Malone College, OH
The Master's College and Seminary, CA
MidAmerica Nazarene University, KS
Milligan College, TN
Montreat College, NC
Mount Vernon Nazarene College, OH
North Greenville College, SC
Northwest College, WA
Northwestern College, MN
Northwest Nazarene University, ID
Nyack College, NY
Oklahoma Christian University of Science and
    Arts, OK
Olivet Nazarene University, IL
Oral Roberts University, OK
Point Loma Nazarene University, CA
Redeemer University College, ON
Simpson College and Graduate School, CA
Spring Arbor College, MI
Trinity International University, IL
Trinity Western University, BC
University of Sioux Falls, SD
Warner Pacific College, OR
Western Baptist College, OR
Westmont College, CA
Williams Baptist College, AR
William Tyndale College, MI

LINGUISTICS
Bartlesville Wesleyan College, OK
Judson College, IL
Trinity Western University, BC

LITERATURE
Bethel College, MN
Bryan College, TN
Eastern Nazarene College, MA
Fresno Pacific University, CA
Grand Canyon University, AZ
Houghton College, NY
Judson College, IL
Montreat College, NC
Mount Vernon Nazarene College, OH
North Park University, IL
Olivet Nazarene University, IL
Southern Nazarene University, OK
Taylor University, IN

MANAGEMENT INFORMATION SYSTEMS/BUSINESS DATA PROCESSING
Anderson University, IN
Azusa Pacific University, CA
Bethel College, MN
Colorado Christian University, CO
Dallas Baptist University, TX

Dordt College, IA
Eastern College, PA
George Fox University, OR
Grace College, IN
Greenville College, IL
Judson College, IL
LeTourneau University, TX
The Master's College and Seminary, CA
Montreat College, NC
Northwestern College, MN
Oklahoma Baptist University, OK
Oral Roberts University, OK
Point Loma Nazarene University, CA
Southern Nazarene University, OK
Taylor University, IN
Trinity Christian College, IL
University of Sioux Falls, SD
Vanguard University of Southern California, CA

MANAGEMENT SCIENCE
Abilene Christian University, TX
Eastern College, PA
Northwest College, WA
Oral Roberts University, OK
Southern Nazarene University, OK

MARRIAGE AND FAMILY COUNSELING
Oklahoma Baptist University, OK

MASS COMMUNICATIONS
Anderson University, IN
Bartlesville Wesleyan College, OK
Bethel College, MN
Bluffton College, OH
Bryan College, TN
Calvin College, MI
Campbellsville University, KY
College of the Ozarks, MO
Colorado Christian University, CO
Cornerstone University, MI
Dallas Baptist University, TX
David Lipscomb University, TN
Dordt College, IA
Eastern Nazarene College, MA
Evangel University, MO
Fresno Pacific University, CA
Gordon College, MA
Goshen College, IN
Grace College, IN
Grand Canyon University, AZ
Greenville College, IL
Houghton College, NY
Houston Baptist University, TX
Huntington College, IN
John Brown University, AR
Judson College, IL
Lee University, TN
The Master's College and Seminary, CA
MidAmerica Nazarene University, KS
Milligan College, TN
Montreat College, NC
Mount Vernon Nazarene College, OH
North Greenville College, SC
North Park University, IL
Northwest Christian College, OR
Northwestern College, IA
Oklahoma Baptist University, OK
Oklahoma Christian University of Science and
    Arts, OK

Mass communications (continued)

Mass communications (continued)

Olivet Nazarene University, IL
Point Loma Nazarene University, CA
Southern Nazarene University, OK
Spring Arbor College, MI
Tabor College, KS
Taylor University, IN
Trevecca Nazarene University, TN
Trinity International University, IL
Union University, TN
University of Sioux Falls, SD
Vanguard University of Southern California, CA
Whitworth College, WA

MATHEMATICS
Abilene Christian University, TX
Anderson University, IN
Asbury College, KY
Azusa Pacific University, CA
Bartlesville Wesleyan College, OK
Belhaven College, MS
Bethel College, IN
Bethel College, KS
Bethel College, MN
Biola University, CA
Bluffton College, OH
Bryan College, TN
California Baptist University, CA
Calvin College, MI
Campbellsville University, KY
Campbell University, NC
Cedarville University, OH
College of the Ozarks, MO
Colorado Christian University, CO
Cornerstone University, MI
Dallas Baptist University, TX
David Lipscomb University, TN
Dordt College, IA
Eastern College, PA
Eastern Mennonite University, VA
Eastern Nazarene College, MA
East Texas Baptist University, TX
Erskine College, SC
Evangel University, MO
Fresno Pacific University, CA
George Fox University, OR
Gordon College, MA
Goshen College, IN
Grace College, IN
Grand Canyon University, AZ
Greenville College, IL
Houghton College, NY
Houston Baptist University, TX
Howard Payne University, TX
Huntington College, IN
Indiana Wesleyan University, IN
John Brown University, AR
Judson College, AL
Judson College, IL
King College, TN
Lee University, TN
LeTourneau University, TX
Malone College, OH
The Master's College and Seminary, CA
Messiah College, PA
MidAmerica Nazarene University, KS
Milligan College, TN
Montreat College, NC

Mount Vernon Nazarene College, OH
North Park University, IL
Northwestern College, IA
Northwestern College, MN
Northwest Nazarene University, ID
Nyack College, NY
Oklahoma Baptist University, OK
Oklahoma Christian University of Science and Arts, OK
Olivet Nazarene University, IL
Oral Roberts University, OK
Palm Beach Atlantic College, FL
Point Loma Nazarene University, CA
Redeemer University College, ON
Roberts Wesleyan College, NY
Seattle Pacific University, WA
Simpson College and Graduate School, CA
Southern Nazarene University, OK
Southern Wesleyan University, SC
Southwest Baptist University, MO
Spring Arbor College, MI
Sterling College, KS
Tabor College, KS
Taylor University, IN
Trevecca Nazarene University, TN
Trinity Christian College, IL
Trinity International University, IL
Trinity Western University, BC
Union University, TN
University of Sioux Falls, SD
Vanguard University of Southern California, CA
Warner Pacific College, OR
Western Baptist College, OR
Westmont College, CA
Wheaton College, IL
Whitworth College, WA
William Tyndale College, MI

MATHEMATICS/COMPUTER SCIENCE
Anderson University, IN
King College, TN
Trinity Western University, BC

MATHEMATICS EDUCATION
Abilene Christian University, TX
Anderson University, IN
Bethel College, IN
Cedarville University, OH
College of the Ozarks, MO
Colorado Christian University, CO
East Texas Baptist University, TX
Geneva College, PA
George Fox University, OR
Grace College, IN
Greenville College, IL
Indiana Wesleyan University, IN
Judson College, AL
King College, TN
Messiah College, PA
MidAmerica Nazarene University, KS
Northwestern College, MN
Northwest Nazarene University, ID
Oklahoma Baptist University, OK
Oral Roberts University, OK
Seattle Pacific University, WA
Southern Nazarene University, OK
Trevecca Nazarene University, TN
Trinity Christian College, IL
Westmont College, CA

MECHANICAL ENGINEERING
Bethel College, IN
Calvin College, MI
Cedarville University, OH
Eastern Nazarene College, MA
John Brown University, AR
LeTourneau University, TX
Oklahoma Christian University of Science and Arts, OK
Oral Roberts University, OK

MECHANICAL ENGINEERING TECHNOLOGY
LeTourneau University, TX

MEDICAL ADMINISTRATIVE ASSISTANT
Tabor College, KS

MEDICAL LABORATORY TECHNICIAN
Milligan College, TN

MEDICAL LABORATORY TECHNOLOGIES
Evangel University, MO

MEDICAL PHARMACOLOGY AND PHARMACEUTICAL SCIENCES
Campbell University, NC

MEDICAL TECHNOLOGY
Anderson University, IN
Bluffton College, OH
Calvin College, MI
Campbellsville University, KY
Cedarville University, OH
College of the Ozarks, MO
Dordt College, IA
Eastern Mennonite University, VA
East Texas Baptist University, TX
Erskine College, SC
Evangel University, MO
Houghton College, NY
Houston Baptist University, TX
Howard Payne University, TX
Indiana Wesleyan University, IN
John Brown University, AR
King College, TN
Lee University, TN
Malone College, OH
Mount Vernon Nazarene College, OH
North Park University, IL
Northwestern College, IA
Oklahoma Christian University of Science and Arts, OK
Olivet Nazarene University, IL
Roberts Wesleyan College, NY
Southern Wesleyan University, SC
Southwest Baptist University, MO
Tabor College, KS
Taylor University, IN
Trevecca Nazarene University, TN
Union University, TN
University of Sioux Falls, SD

(PRE)MEDICINE
Abilene Christian University, TX
Anderson University, IN
Bartlesville Wesleyan College, OK
Bethel College, IN
Bethel College, MN

Bluffton College, OH
Bryan College, TN
Calvin College, MI
Campbellsville University, KY
Campbell University, NC
Cedarville University, OH
College of the Ozarks, MO
Cornerstone University, MI
Covenant College, GA
David Lipscomb University, TN
Dordt College, IA
Eastern Mennonite University, VA
Eastern Nazarene College, MA
Evangel University, MO
Fresno Pacific University, CA
Goshen College, IN
Grand Canyon University, AZ
Greenville College, IL
Houghton College, NY
Houston Baptist University, TX
Howard Payne University, TX
Huntington College, IN
Indiana Wesleyan University, IN
John Brown University, AR
Judson College, IL
King College, TN
LeTourneau University, TX
The Master's College and Seminary, CA
Milligan College, TN
Montreat College, NC
Mount Vernon Nazarene College, OH
North Park University, IL
Northwest Christian College, OR
Northwest Nazarene University, ID
Oklahoma Baptist University, OK
Oklahoma Christian University of Science and
    Arts, OK
Olivet Nazarene University, IL
Oral Roberts University, OK
Palm Beach Atlantic College, FL
Redeemer University College, ON
Roberts Wesleyan College, NY
Seattle Pacific University, WA
Southern Nazarene University, OK
Tabor College, KS
Taylor University, IN
Trinity Christian College, IL
Trinity International University, IL
Trinity Western University, BC
Union University, TN
University of Sioux Falls, SD
Warner Pacific College, OR
Westmont College, CA
Whitworth College, WA
Williams Baptist College, AR

MENTAL HEALTH/REHABILITATION
Evangel University, MO

METALLURGICAL ENGINEERING
Bethel College, IN

MIDDLE EASTERN STUDIES
William Tyndale College, MI

MIDDLE SCHOOL EDUCATION
Asbury College, KY
Bryan College, TN
Campbell University, NC
College of the Ozarks, MO

David Lipscomb University, TN
Eastern Mennonite University, VA
Eastern Nazarene College, MA
Gordon College, MA
Indiana Wesleyan University, IN
John Brown University, AR
Judson College, AL
Kentucky Christian College, KY
King College, TN
Malone College, OH
The Master's College and Seminary, CA
MidAmerica Nazarene University, KS
Northwest College, WA
Southwest Baptist University, MO
Taylor University, IN
Trinity Christian College, IL
University of Sioux Falls, SD
Warner Pacific College, OR

MISSIONARY STUDIES
Abilene Christian University, TX
Asbury College, KY
Biola University, CA
Cedarville University, OH
Eastern College, PA
George Fox University, OR
Hope International University, CA
John Brown University, AR
Northwest Christian College, OR
Northwestern College, MN
Northwest Nazarene University, ID
Nyack College, NY
Oklahoma Baptist University, OK
Oral Roberts University, OK
Simpson College and Graduate School, CA
Southern Nazarene University, OK
Trinity Western University, BC

MODERN LANGUAGES
Gordon College, MA
Greenville College, IL
Howard Payne University, TX
Judson College, AL
King College, TN
Lee University, TN
MidAmerica Nazarene University, KS
Mount Vernon Nazarene College, OH
North Park University, IL
Northwest Christian College, OR
Olivet Nazarene University, IL
Redeemer University College, ON
Westmont College, CA

MOLECULAR BIOLOGY
Bethel College, MN

MORTUARY SCIENCE
Milligan College, TN

MULTIMEDIA
Eastern College, PA

MUSEUM STUDIES
Oklahoma Baptist University, OK

MUSIC
Abilene Christian University, TX
Asbury College, KY
Azusa Pacific University, CA
Bartlesville Wesleyan College, OK
Belhaven College, MS

Bethel College, IN
Bethel College, KS
Bethel College, MN
Biola University, CA
Bluffton College, OH
Bryan College, TN
California Baptist University, CA
Calvin College, MI
Campbellsville University, KY
Campbell University, NC
Cedarville University, OH
College of the Ozarks, MO
Colorado Christian University, CO
Cornerstone University, MI
Covenant College, GA
Dallas Baptist University, TX
David Lipscomb University, TN
Dordt College, IA
Eastern College, PA
Eastern Mennonite University, VA
Eastern Nazarene College, MA
East Texas Baptist University, TX
Erskine College, SC
Evangel University, MO
Fresno Pacific University, CA
Geneva College, PA
George Fox University, OR
Gordon College, MA
Goshen College, IN
Grand Canyon University, AZ
Greenville College, IL
Houghton College, NY
Houston Baptist University, TX
Howard Payne University, TX
Huntington College, IN
Indiana Wesleyan University, IN
John Brown University, AR
Judson College, AL
Judson College, IL
Kentucky Christian College, KY
King College, TN
The King's University College, AB
Lee University, TN
Malone College, OH
The Master's College and Seminary, CA
Messiah College, PA
MidAmerica Nazarene University, KS
Milligan College, TN
Montreat College, NC
Mount Vernon Nazarene College, OH
North Greenville College, SC
North Park University, IL
Northwest Christian College, OR
Northwest College, WA
Northwestern College, IA
Northwestern College, MN
Northwest Nazarene University, ID
Nyack College, NY
Oklahoma Baptist University, OK
Oklahoma Christian University of Science and
    Arts, OK
Olivet Nazarene University, IL
Oral Roberts University, OK
Palm Beach Atlantic College, FL
Point Loma Nazarene University, CA
Redeemer University College, ON
Roberts Wesleyan College, NY
Seattle Pacific University, WA

Music (continued)

Simpson College and Graduate School, CA
Southern Wesleyan University, SC
Southwest Baptist University, MO
Spring Arbor College, MI
Sterling College, KS
Tabor College, KS
Taylor University, IN
Trevecca Nazarene University, TN
Trinity Christian College, IL
Trinity International University, IL
Trinity Western University, BC
Union University, TN
University of Sioux Falls, SD
Vanguard University of Southern California, CA
Warner Pacific College, OR
Western Baptist College, OR
Westmont College, CA
Wheaton College, IL
Whitworth College, WA
Williams Baptist College, AR
William Tyndale College, MI

MUSICAL INSTRUMENT TECHNOLOGY
Malone College, OH

MUSIC BUSINESS MANAGEMENT AND MERCHANDISING
Anderson University, IN
Bryan College, TN
College of the Ozarks, MO
Erskine College, SC
Geneva College, PA
Grand Canyon University, AZ
The Master's College and Seminary, CA
Montreat College, NC
North Park University, IL
Point Loma Nazarene University, CA
Southern Nazarene University, OK
Tabor College, KS
Taylor University, IN
Trevecca Nazarene University, TN
Union University, TN
University of Sioux Falls, SD
Warner Pacific College, OR
Wheaton College, IL

MUSIC CONDUCTING
Calvin College, MI

MUSIC EDUCATION
Abilene Christian University, TX
Anderson University, IN
Asbury College, KY
Bethel College, IN
Bethel College, MN
Bluffton College, OH
Bryan College, TN
Calvin College, MI
Campbellsville University, KY
Campbell University, NC
Cedarville University, OH
College of the Ozarks, MO
Colorado Christian University, CO
Cornerstone University, MI
Dallas Baptist University, TX
David Lipscomb University, TN

Dordt College, IA
Eastern Mennonite University, VA
Eastern Nazarene College, MA
East Texas Baptist University, TX
Erskine College, SC
Evangel University, MO
Fresno Pacific University, CA
Geneva College, PA
George Fox University, OR
Gordon College, MA
Goshen College, IN
Grace College, IN
Grand Canyon University, AZ
Greenville College, IL
Hope International University, CA
Houghton College, NY
Houston Baptist University, TX
Howard Payne University, TX
Huntington College, IN
Indiana Wesleyan University, IN
John Brown University, AR
Judson College, AL
Judson College, IL
Kentucky Christian College, KY
Lee University, TN
Malone College, OH
The Master's College and Seminary, CA
Messiah College, PA
MidAmerica Nazarene University, KS
Milligan College, TN
Montreat College, NC
Mount Vernon Nazarene College, OH
North Greenville College, SC
North Park University, IL
Northwest College, WA
Northwestern College, IA
Northwestern College, MN
Northwest Nazarene University, ID
Nyack College, NY
Oklahoma Baptist University, OK
Oklahoma Christian University of Science and Arts, OK
Olivet Nazarene University, IL
Oral Roberts University, OK
Palm Beach Atlantic College, FL
Roberts Wesleyan College, NY
Seattle Pacific University, WA
Simpson College and Graduate School, CA
Southern Nazarene University, OK
Southern Wesleyan University, SC
Southwest Baptist University, MO
Sterling College, KS
Tabor College, KS
Taylor University, IN
Trevecca Nazarene University, TN
Trinity Christian College, IL
Trinity International University, IL
Union University, TN
University of Sioux Falls, SD
Warner Pacific College, OR
Warner Southern College, FL
Western Baptist College, OR
Wheaton College, IL
Whitworth College, WA
Williams Baptist College, AR

MUSIC (GENERAL PERFORMANCE)
Anderson University, IN
Bartlesville Wesleyan College, OK

Calvin College, MI
Colorado Christian University, CO
Eastern Nazarene College, MA
Geneva College, PA
Gordon College, MA
Northwestern College, MN
Northwest Nazarene University, ID
Oral Roberts University, OK
Southern Nazarene University, OK
Trinity Christian College, IL
William Tyndale College, MI

MUSIC HISTORY
Calvin College, MI
North Greenville College, SC
Wheaton College, IL

MUSIC (PIANO AND ORGAN PERFORMANCE)
Abilene Christian University, TX
Bethel College, IN
Bryan College, TN
Calvin College, MI
Campbellsville University, KY
Campbell University, NC
Cedarville University, OH
Dallas Baptist University, TX
David Lipscomb University, TN
East Texas Baptist University, TX
Erskine College, SC
Grace College, IN
Grand Canyon University, AZ
Houghton College, NY
Howard Payne University, TX
Huntington College, IN
John Brown University, AR
Lee University, TN
The Master's College and Seminary, CA
Milligan College, TN
Montreat College, NC
Mount Vernon Nazarene College, OH
North Greenville College, SC
Northwest College, WA
Northwestern College, MN
Nyack College, NY
Oklahoma Baptist University, OK
Olivet Nazarene University, IL
Roberts Wesleyan College, NY
Southern Nazarene University, OK
Tabor College, KS
Taylor University, IN
Trinity Christian College, IL
Union University, TN
University of Sioux Falls, SD
Wheaton College, IL
Whitworth College, WA
William Tyndale College, MI

MUSIC THEORY AND COMPOSITION
Calvin College, MI
Campbell University, NC
Dallas Baptist University, TX
Indiana Wesleyan University, IN
Northwest Nazarene University, ID
Nyack College, NY
Oklahoma Baptist University, OK
Oral Roberts University, OK

MUSIC (VOICE AND CHORAL/OPERA PERFORMANCE)
Abilene Christian University, TX

Bethel College, IN
Bryan College, TN
Calvin College, MI
Campbellsville University, KY
Cedarville University, OH
Colorado Christian University, CO
Dallas Baptist University, TX
David Lipscomb University, TN
East Texas Baptist University, TX
Erskine College, SC
Grand Canyon University, AZ
Houghton College, NY
Howard Payne University, TX
Huntington College, IN
John Brown University, AR
Judson College, IL
Lee University, TN
The Master's College and Seminary, CA
MidAmerica Nazarene University, KS
Milligan College, TN
Montreat College, NC
Mount Vernon Nazarene College, OH
North Greenville College, SC
North Park University, IL
Northwest College, WA
Northwestern College, MN
Nyack College, NY
Oklahoma Baptist University, OK
Oklahoma Christian University of Science and
  Arts, OK
Olivet Nazarene University, IL
Palm Beach Atlantic College, FL
Roberts Wesleyan College, NY
Southern Nazarene University, OK
Tabor College, KS
Taylor University, IN
Trinity Christian College, IL
Union University, TN
University of Sioux Falls, SD
Wheaton College, IL
Whitworth College, WA
William Tyndale College, MI

NATURAL RESOURCES MANAGEMENT
Huntington College, IN
Mount Vernon Nazarene College, OH

NATURAL SCIENCES
Azusa Pacific University, CA
Bartlesville Wesleyan College, OK
Bethel College, KS
Calvin College, MI
Covenant College, GA
Dordt College, IA
Erskine College, SC
Fresno Pacific University, CA
Goshen College, IN
Houghton College, NY
Lee University, TN
LeTourneau University, TX
The Master's College and Seminary, CA
North Park University, IL
Oklahoma Baptist University, OK
Olivet Nazarene University, IL
Redeemer University College, ON
Roberts Wesleyan College, NY
Southern Nazarene University, OK
Tabor College, KS

Taylor University, IN
Trinity Western University, BC

NEUROSCIENCE
Westmont College, CA

NONPROFIT/PUBLIC MANAGEMENT
Fresno Pacific University, CA

NUCLEAR MEDICAL TECHNOLOGY
Houston Baptist University, TX

NURSING
Abilene Christian University, TX
Anderson University, IN
Azusa Pacific University, CA
Bartlesville Wesleyan College, OK
Bethel College, IN
Bethel College, KS
Bethel College, MN
Biola University, CA
Calvin College, MI
Cedarville University, OH
Covenant College, GA
David Lipscomb University, TN
Eastern College, PA
Eastern Mennonite University, VA
East Texas Baptist University, TX
Goshen College, IN
Grand Canyon University, AZ
Houston Baptist University, TX
Indiana Wesleyan University, IN
Judson College, IL
King College, TN
Messiah College, PA
MidAmerica Nazarene University, KS
Milligan College, TN
Mount Vernon Nazarene College, OH
North Park University, IL
Northwest Nazarene University, ID
Oklahoma Baptist University, OK
Olivet Nazarene University, IL
Oral Roberts University, OK
Point Loma Nazarene University, CA
Roberts Wesleyan College, NY
Seattle Pacific University, WA
Southern Nazarene University, OK
Southwest Baptist University, MO
Trinity Christian College, IL
Trinity Western University, BC
Union University, TN
Warner Pacific College, OR
Wheaton College, IL
Whitworth College, WA

NURSING (PUBLIC HEALTH)
Malone College, OH

NUTRITION SCIENCE
Bluffton College, OH
College of the Ozarks, MO
The Master's College and Seminary, CA
Seattle Pacific University, WA

OCCUPATIONAL SAFETY/HEALTH TECHNOLOGY
Southwest Baptist University, MO

OCCUPATIONAL THERAPY
Calvin College, MI

OFFICE MANAGEMENT
Northwestern College, MN

ORGANIZATIONAL BEHAVIOR
Northwestern College, MN

ORGANIZATIONAL PSYCHOLOGY
Abilene Christian University, TX
Point Loma Nazarene University, CA

PAINTING
Grace College, IN
Indiana Wesleyan University, IN
Trinity Christian College, IL

PARALEGAL/LEGAL ASSISTANT
Howard Payne University, TX

PASTORAL COUNSELING
Abilene Christian University, TX
Belhaven College, MS
Biola University, CA
Campbellsville University, KY
Cedarville University, OH
Colorado Christian University, CO
Cornerstone University, MI
Dallas Baptist University, TX
Dordt College, IA
Eastern Mennonite University, VA
Eastern Nazarene College, MA
East Texas Baptist University, TX
Fresno Pacific University, CA
George Fox University, OR
Grace College, IN
Greenville College, IL
Houghton College, NY
Indiana Wesleyan University, IN
John Brown University, AR
Kentucky Christian College, KY
Lee University, TN
Malone College, OH
The Master's College and Seminary, CA
Milligan College, TN
North Greenville College, SC
Northwest College, WA
Northwestern College, MN
Northwest Nazarene University, ID
Nyack College, NY
Oklahoma Baptist University, OK
Oklahoma Christian University of Science and
  Arts, OK
Oral Roberts University, OK
Redeemer University College, ON
Roberts Wesleyan College, NY
Simpson College and Graduate School, CA
Tabor College, KS
University of Sioux Falls, SD
Vanguard University of Southern California, CA
Warner Pacific College, OR
Western Baptist College, OR
Williams Baptist College, AR
William Tyndale College, MI

PEACE AND CONFLICT STUDIES
Bluffton College, OH
Eastern Mennonite University, VA
Goshen College, IN
Whitworth College, WA

PHARMACY
Campbell University, NC

Pharmacy (continued)

Eastern Nazarene College, MA

(PRE)PHARMACY STUDIES
Abilene Christian University, TX
College of the Ozarks, MO
King College, TN
Oklahoma Baptist University, OK
Roberts Wesleyan College, NY
Southern Nazarene University, OK
Union University, TN
Westmont College, CA

PHILOSOPHY
Anderson University, IN
Asbury College, KY
Azusa Pacific University, CA
Belhaven College, MS
Bethel College, IN
Bethel College, MN
Biola University, CA
Bluffton College, OH
California Baptist University, CA
Calvin College, MI
Cedarville University, OH
College of the Ozarks, MO
Covenant College, GA
Dallas Baptist University, TX
David Lipscomb University, TN
Dordt College, IA
Eastern College, PA
Geneva College, PA
Gordon College, MA
Greenville College, IL
Houghton College, NY
Howard Payne University, TX
Huntington College, IN
Indiana Wesleyan University, IN
Judson College, IL
The King's University College, AB
Messiah College, PA
Mount Vernon Nazarene College, OH
North Park University, IL
Northwest College, WA
Northwestern College, IA
Northwest Nazarene University, ID
Nyack College, NY
Oklahoma Baptist University, OK
Olivet Nazarene University, IL
Oral Roberts University, OK
Palm Beach Atlantic College, FL
Point Loma Nazarene University, CA
Redeemer University College, ON
Roberts Wesleyan College, NY
Seattle Pacific University, WA
Southern Nazarene University, OK
Spring Arbor College, MI
Sterling College, KS
Tabor College, KS
Taylor University, IN
Trinity Christian College, IL
Trinity International University, IL
Trinity Western University, BC
Union University, TN
University of Sioux Falls, SD
Westmont College, CA
Wheaton College, IL
Whitworth College, WA

PHOTOGRAPHY
Indiana Wesleyan University, IN
Trinity Christian College, IL

PHYSICAL EDUCATION
Abilene Christian University, TX
Anderson University, IN
Asbury College, KY
Azusa Pacific University, CA
Bartlesville Wesleyan College, OK
Bethel College, IN
Bethel College, MN
Biola University, CA
Bluffton College, OH
Bryan College, TN
California Baptist University, CA
Calvin College, MI
Campbellsville University, KY
Campbell University, NC
Cedarville University, OH
College of the Ozarks, MO
Cornerstone University, MI
Dallas Baptist University, TX
David Lipscomb University, TN
Dordt College, IA
Eastern Mennonite University, VA
Eastern Nazarene College, MA
East Texas Baptist University, TX
Erskine College, SC
Evangel University, MO
Fresno Pacific University, CA
George Fox University, OR
Goshen College, IN
Grace College, IN
Grand Canyon University, AZ
Greenville College, IL
Houghton College, NY
Howard Payne University, TX
Huntington College, IN
Indiana Wesleyan University, IN
John Brown University, AR
Judson College, IL
Lee University, TN
LeTourneau University, TX
Malone College, OH
The Master's College and Seminary, CA
Messiah College, PA
MidAmerica Nazarene University, KS
Milligan College, TN
Montreat College, NC
Mount Vernon Nazarene College, OH
North Park University, IL
Northwest College, WA
Northwestern College, IA
Northwestern College, MN
Northwest Nazarene University, ID
Oklahoma Baptist University, OK
Oklahoma Christian University of Science and
  Arts, OK
Olivet Nazarene University, IL
Oral Roberts University, OK
Palm Beach Atlantic College, FL
Seattle Pacific University, WA
Southern Nazarene University, OK
Southern Wesleyan University, SC
Southwest Baptist University, MO
Spring Arbor College, MI
Sterling College, KS
Tabor College, KS

Taylor University, IN
Trevecca Nazarene University, TN
Trinity Christian College, IL
Trinity International University, IL
Trinity Western University, BC
Union University, TN
University of Sioux Falls, SD
Vanguard University of Southern California, CA
Warner Pacific College, OR
Warner Southern College, FL
Westmont College, CA
Wheaton College, IL
Whitworth College, WA
Williams Baptist College, AR

PHYSICAL SCIENCES
Asbury College, KY
Biola University, CA
California Baptist University, CA
Calvin College, MI
Goshen College, IN
Grand Canyon University, AZ
Houghton College, NY
Judson College, IL
The Master's College and Seminary, CA
Oklahoma Baptist University, OK
Olivet Nazarene University, IL
Roberts Wesleyan College, NY
Warner Pacific College, OR
Wheaton College, IL

PHYSICAL THERAPY
Bartlesville Wesleyan College, OK
Eastern Nazarene College, MA
Hope International University, CA
Northwest Nazarene University, ID
Vanguard University of Southern California, CA

PHYSICS
Abilene Christian University, TX
Anderson University, IN
Azusa Pacific University, CA
Bethel College, KS
Bethel College, MN
Bluffton College, OH
Calvin College, MI
Campbellsville University, KY
David Lipscomb University, TN
Dordt College, IA
Eastern Nazarene College, MA
Erskine College, SC
Geneva College, PA
Gordon College, MA
Goshen College, IN
Greenville College, IL
Houghton College, NY
Houston Baptist University, TX
King College, TN
Messiah College, PA
MidAmerica Nazarene University, KS
North Park University, IL
Northwest Nazarene University, ID
Oklahoma Baptist University, OK
Oral Roberts University, OK
Point Loma Nazarene University, CA
Roberts Wesleyan College, NY
Seattle Pacific University, WA
Southern Nazarene University, OK
Spring Arbor College, MI

Taylor University, IN
Trevecca Nazarene University, TN
Union University, TN
Westmont College, CA
Wheaton College, IL
Whitworth College, WA

PHYSICS EDUCATION
Abilene Christian University, TX
Bethel College, IN
Greenville College, IL
King College, TN
Malone College, OH

PHYSIOLOGICAL PSYCHOLOGY/ PSYCHOBIOLOGY
Hope International University, CA

POLITICAL SCIENCE
Abilene Christian University, TX
Anderson University, IN
Azusa Pacific University, CA
Bartlesville Wesleyan College, OK
Bethel College, MN
Bluffton College, OH
California Baptist University, CA
Calvin College, MI
Campbellsville University, KY
Campbell University, NC
Cedarville University, OH
College of the Ozarks, MO
Colorado Christian University, CO
Dallas Baptist University, TX
David Lipscomb University, TN
Dordt College, IA
Eastern College, PA
Evangel University, MO
Fresno Pacific University, CA
Geneva College, PA
Gordon College, MA
Goshen College, IN
Grand Canyon University, AZ
Greenville College, IL
Houghton College, NY
Houston Baptist University, TX
Howard Payne University, TX
Indiana Wesleyan University, IN
King College, TN
The Master's College and Seminary, CA
Messiah College, PA
North Park University, IL
Northwestern College, IA
Northwest Nazarene University, ID
Oklahoma Baptist University, OK
Oral Roberts University, OK
Palm Beach Atlantic College, FL
Point Loma Nazarene University, CA
Redeemer University College, ON
Seattle Pacific University, WA
Southern Nazarene University, OK
Southwest Baptist University, MO
Taylor University, IN
Trinity Western University, BC
Union University, TN
University of Sioux Falls, SD
Vanguard University of Southern California, CA
Westmont College, CA
Wheaton College, IL
Whitworth College, WA

POULTRY SCIENCE
College of the Ozarks, MO

PRINTMAKING
Indiana Wesleyan University, IN
Trinity Christian College, IL

PSYCHOLOGY
Abilene Christian University, TX
Anderson University, IN
Asbury College, KY
Azusa Pacific University, CA
Belhaven College, MS
Bethel College, IN
Bethel College, KS
Bethel College, MN
Biola University, CA
Bluffton College, OH
Bryan College, TN
California Baptist University, CA
Calvin College, MI
Campbellsville University, KY
Campbell University, NC
Cedarville University, OH
College of the Ozarks, MO
Colorado Christian University, CO
Cornerstone University, MI
Covenant College, GA
Crichton College, TN
Dallas Baptist University, TX
David Lipscomb University, TN
Dordt College, IA
Eastern College, PA
Eastern Mennonite University, VA
Eastern Nazarene College, MA
East Texas Baptist University, TX
Erskine College, SC
Evangel University, MO
Fresno Pacific University, CA
Geneva College, PA
George Fox University, OR
Gordon College, MA
Goshen College, IN
Grace College, IN
Grand Canyon University, AZ
Greenville College, IL
Hope International University, CA
Houghton College, NY
Houston Baptist University, TX
Howard Payne University, TX
Huntington College, IN
Indiana Wesleyan University, IN
John Brown University, AR
Judson College, AL
Judson College, IL
Kentucky Christian College, KY
King College, TN
The King's University College, AB
Lee University, TN
LeTourneau University, TX
Malone College, OH
Messiah College, PA
MidAmerica Nazarene University, KS
Milligan College, TN
Mount Vernon Nazarene College, OH
North Park University, IL
Northwest Christian College, OR
Northwest College, WA
Northwestern College, IA

Northwestern College, MN
Northwest Nazarene University, ID
Nyack College, NY
Oklahoma Baptist University, OK
Oklahoma Christian University of Science and Arts, OK
Olivet Nazarene University, IL
Oral Roberts University, OK
Palm Beach Atlantic College, FL
Point Loma Nazarene University, CA
Redeemer University College, ON
Roberts Wesleyan College, NY
Seattle Pacific University, WA
Simpson College and Graduate School, CA
Southern Nazarene University, OK
Southern Wesleyan University, SC
Southwest Baptist University, MO
Spring Arbor College, MI
Tabor College, KS
Taylor University, IN
Trevecca Nazarene University, TN
Trinity Christian College, IL
Trinity International University, IL
Trinity Western University, BC
Union University, TN
University of Sioux Falls, SD
Vanguard University of Southern California, CA
Warner Pacific College, OR
Warner Southern College, FL
Western Baptist College, OR
Westmont College, CA
Wheaton College, IL
Whitworth College, WA
Williams Baptist College, AR
William Tyndale College, MI

PUBLIC ADMINISTRATION
Abilene Christian University, TX
Calvin College, MI
Campbell University, NC
Cedarville University, OH
David Lipscomb University, TN
Evangel University, MO

PUBLIC RELATIONS
Campbell University, NC
College of the Ozarks, MO
David Lipscomb University, TN
Greenville College, IL
Howard Payne University, TX
John Brown University, AR
The Master's College and Seminary, CA
MidAmerica Nazarene University, KS
Milligan College, TN
Northwestern College, MN
Oklahoma Baptist University, OK
Oklahoma Christian University of Science and Arts, OK
Oral Roberts University, OK
Trinity Christian College, IL
Union University, TN
University of Sioux Falls, SD

RADIO/TELEVISION BROADCASTING
Biola University, CA
Campbell University, NC
Cedarville University, OH
Eastern Nazarene College, MA
Evangel University, MO

Radio/television broadcasting (continued)

Geneva College, PA
George Fox University, OR
John Brown University, AR
The Master's College and Seminary, CA
Messiah College, PA
Milligan College, TN
Northwestern College, MN
Oklahoma Baptist University, OK
Oklahoma Christian University of Science and
    Arts, OK
Olivet Nazarene University, IL
Oral Roberts University, OK
Union University, TN
University of Sioux Falls, SD
Vanguard University of Southern California, CA

RADIO/TELEVISION BROADCASTING TECHNOLOGY
Asbury College, KY
Trevecca Nazarene University, TN

RANGE MANAGEMENT
Abilene Christian University, TX

READING EDUCATION
Abilene Christian University, TX

RECREATION AND LEISURE STUDIES
Bluffton College, OH
Calvin College, MI
Campbellsville University, KY
Dordt College, IA
Eastern Mennonite University, VA
Evangel University, MO
Gordon College, MA
Greenville College, IL
Houghton College, NY
Houston Baptist University, TX
Howard Payne University, TX
Huntington College, IN
Messiah College, PA
Northwest Nazarene University, ID
Oklahoma Baptist University, OK
Redeemer University College, ON
Southern Wesleyan University, SC
Southwest Baptist University, MO
Taylor University, IN
Warner Southern College, FL

RECREATION/LEISURE FACILITIES MANAGEMENT
Asbury College, KY
College of the Ozarks, MO
Indiana Wesleyan University, IN
John Brown University, AR
Union University, TN

RELIGIOUS EDUCATION
Asbury College, KY
Biola University, CA
Bryan College, TN
Campbellsville University, KY
Cornerstone University, MI
Dallas Baptist University, TX
Eastern Nazarene College, MA
East Texas Baptist University, TX
Erskine College, SC
George Fox University, OR

Gordon College, MA
Houghton College, NY
Howard Payne University, TX
Indiana Wesleyan University, IN
John Brown University, AR
Kentucky Christian College, KY
Lee University, TN
The Master's College and Seminary, CA
Messiah College, PA
MidAmerica Nazarene University, KS
Milligan College, TN
Mount Vernon Nazarene College, OH
North Greenville College, SC
Northwest College, WA
Northwestern College, IA
Northwestern College, MN
Northwest Nazarene University, ID
Nyack College, NY
Oklahoma Baptist University, OK
Oklahoma Christian University of Science and
    Arts, OK
Olivet Nazarene University, IL
Seattle Pacific University, WA
Simpson College and Graduate School, CA
Southern Nazarene University, OK
Sterling College, KS
Taylor University, IN
Trinity Christian College, IL
Vanguard University of Southern California, CA
Warner Pacific College, OR
Western Baptist College, OR
Wheaton College, IL
Williams Baptist College, AR
William Tyndale College, MI

RELIGIOUS STUDIES
Anderson University, IN
Azusa Pacific University, CA
Bartlesville Wesleyan College, OK
Bethel College, IN
Bethel College, KS
Biola University, CA
Bluffton College, OH
California Baptist University, CA
Calvin College, MI
Campbellsville University, KY
Campbell University, NC
College of the Ozarks, MO
Cornerstone University, MI
Dordt College, IA
Eastern Mennonite University, VA
Eastern Nazarene College, MA
East Texas Baptist University, TX
Erskine College, SC
Fresno Pacific University, CA
George Fox University, OR
Goshen College, IN
Grand Canyon University, AZ
Greenville College, IL
Houghton College, NY
Houston Baptist University, TX
Howard Payne University, TX
Huntington College, IN
John Brown University, AR
Judson College, AL
Judson College, IL
King College, TN
LeTourneau University, TX
The Master's College and Seminary, CA

Messiah College, PA
MidAmerica Nazarene University, KS
Montreat College, NC
Mount Vernon Nazarene College, OH
North Greenville College, SC
North Park University, IL
Northwest College, WA
Northwestern College, IA
Northwest Nazarene University, ID
Nyack College, NY
Oklahoma Baptist University, OK
Oklahoma Christian University of Science and
    Arts, OK
Olivet Nazarene University, IL
Oral Roberts University, OK
Palm Beach Atlantic College, FL
Redeemer University College, ON
Roberts Wesleyan College, NY
Seattle Pacific University, WA
Southern Nazarene University, OK
Southern Wesleyan University, SC
Southwest Baptist University, MO
Spring Arbor College, MI
Sterling College, KS
Tabor College, KS
Taylor University, IN
Trevecca Nazarene University, TN
Trinity Christian College, IL
Trinity Western University, BC
Union University, TN
University of Sioux Falls, SD
Vanguard University of Southern California, CA
Warner Pacific College, OR
Western Baptist College, OR
Westmont College, CA
Wheaton College, IL
Whitworth College, WA
Williams Baptist College, AR

RESPIRATORY THERAPY
Lee University, TN

RETAIL MANAGEMENT
Bluffton College, OH

ROMANCE LANGUAGES
Olivet Nazarene University, IL
Point Loma Nazarene University, CA
Redeemer University College, ON

RUSSIAN
Seattle Pacific University, WA

SACRED MUSIC
Anderson University, IN
Bethel College, IN
Bethel College, MN
Bryan College, TN
Calvin College, MI
Campbellsville University, KY
Cedarville University, OH
College of the Ozarks, MO
Colorado Christian University, CO
Dallas Baptist University, TX
Eastern Nazarene College, MA
East Texas Baptist University, TX
Erskine College, SC
Evangel University, MO
Fresno Pacific University, CA
Grand Canyon University, AZ

Greenville College, IL
Hope International University, CA
Houghton College, NY
Houston Baptist University, TX
Howard Payne University, TX
Indiana Wesleyan University, IN
Malone College, OH
The Master's College and Seminary, CA
MidAmerica Nazarene University, KS
Milligan College, TN
Mount Vernon Nazarene College, OH
North Greenville College, SC
North Park University, IL
Northwest College, WA
Northwest Nazarene University, ID
Nyack College, NY
Oklahoma Baptist University, OK
Olivet Nazarene University, IL
Oral Roberts University, OK
Palm Beach Atlantic College, FL
Point Loma Nazarene University, CA
Simpson College and Graduate School, CA
Southern Nazarene University, OK
Taylor University, IN
Trevecca Nazarene University, TN
Trinity International University, IL
Union University, TN
Warner Southern College, FL
Williams Baptist College, AR
William Tyndale College, MI

SALES OPERATIONS
Trevecca Nazarene University, TN

SCANDINAVIAN LANGUAGES
North Park University, IL

SCHOOL PSYCHOLOGY
Crichton College, TN

SCIENCE EDUCATION
Abilene Christian University, TX
Anderson University, IN
Bartlesville Wesleyan College, OK
Bethel College, IN
Bethel College, MN
Bryan College, TN
Calvin College, MI
Campbellsville University, KY
Cedarville University, OH
College of the Ozarks, MO
Colorado Christian University, CO
Cornerstone University, MI
Dallas Baptist University, TX
Eastern Mennonite University, VA
East Texas Baptist University, TX
Evangel University, MO
Fresno Pacific University, CA
Goshen College, IN
Grace College, IN
Grand Canyon University, AZ
Greenville College, IL
Houghton College, NY
Howard Payne University, TX
Huntington College, IN
Indiana Wesleyan University, IN
Judson College, AL
Judson College, IL
Malone College, OH
The Master's College and Seminary, CA

MidAmerica Nazarene University, KS
Milligan College, TN
Mount Vernon Nazarene College, OH
Oklahoma Baptist University, OK
Oklahoma Christian University of Science and Arts, OK
Olivet Nazarene University, IL
Oral Roberts University, OK
Seattle Pacific University, WA
Tabor College, KS
Taylor University, IN
Trinity Christian College, IL
Union University, TN
University of Sioux Falls, SD
Warner Pacific College, OR
Warner Southern College, FL

SCULPTURE
Trinity Christian College, IL

SECONDARY EDUCATION
Abilene Christian University, TX
Bartlesville Wesleyan College, OK
Bethel College, IN
Bethel College, MN
Biola University, CA
Bluffton College, OH
Bryan College, TN
Calvin College, MI
Campbellsville University, KY
Campbell University, NC
Cedarville University, OH
College of the Ozarks, MO
Colorado Christian University, CO
Cornerstone University, MI
Crichton College, TN
Dallas Baptist University, TX
David Lipscomb University, TN
Dordt College, IA
Eastern College, PA
Eastern Mennonite University, VA
Eastern Nazarene College, MA
East Texas Baptist University, TX
Evangel University, MO
Fresno Pacific University, CA
Geneva College, PA
Goshen College, IN
Grand Canyon University, AZ
Greenville College, IL
Houghton College, NY
Houston Baptist University, TX
Howard Payne University, TX
Huntington College, IN
Indiana Wesleyan University, IN
John Brown University, AR
Judson College, AL
Judson College, IL
King College, TN
Lee University, TN
LeTourneau University, TX
The Master's College and Seminary, CA
MidAmerica Nazarene University, KS
Milligan College, TN
Montreat College, NC
Mount Vernon Nazarene College, OH
North Park University, IL
Northwest College, WA
Northwestern College, IA
Northwest Nazarene University, ID

Nyack College, NY
Oklahoma Baptist University, OK
Oklahoma Christian University of Science and Arts, OK
Olivet Nazarene University, IL
Palm Beach Atlantic College, FL
Redeemer University College, ON
Roberts Wesleyan College, NY
Simpson College and Graduate School, CA
Southern Nazarene University, OK
Southwest Baptist University, MO
Spring Arbor College, MI
Tabor College, KS
Taylor University, IN
Trevecca Nazarene University, TN
Trinity Christian College, IL
Trinity International University, IL
Trinity Western University, BC
Union University, TN
University of Sioux Falls, SD
Vanguard University of Southern California, CA
Warner Pacific College, OR
Western Baptist College, OR
Westmont College, CA
Whitworth College, WA

SECRETARIAL SCIENCE
Bartlesville Wesleyan College, OK
Bethel College, IN
Campbellsville University, KY
Cedarville University, OH
Dordt College, IA
Evangel University, MO
Grace College, IN
Kentucky Christian College, KY
Lee University, TN
Mount Vernon Nazarene College, OH
Northwestern College, IA
Northwestern College, MN
Southwest Baptist University, MO
Tabor College, KS
University of Sioux Falls, SD
Williams Baptist College, AR

SIGN LANGUAGE INTERPRETATION
Bethel College, IN

SOCIAL SCIENCE EDUCATION
Abilene Christian University, TX
Hope International University, CA
Judson College, AL
Northwest Nazarene University, ID
Oklahoma Baptist University, OK
Seattle Pacific University, WA
Simpson College and Graduate School, CA
Southern Nazarene University, OK
Warner Southern College, FL
Westmont College, CA

SOCIAL SCIENCES
Asbury College, KY
Azusa Pacific University, CA
Bartlesville Wesleyan College, OK
Bethel College, IN
Bethel College, KS
Biola University, CA
Bluffton College, OH
California Baptist University, CA
Calvin College, MI
Campbellsville University, KY

Social sciences (continued)

Campbell University, NC
Cedarville University, OH
Dordt College, IA
Eastern Nazarene College, MA
Evangel University, MO
Fresno Pacific University, CA
Grand Canyon University, AZ
Hope International University, CA
Houghton College, NY
Howard Payne University, TX
Indiana Wesleyan University, IN
John Brown University, AR
Judson College, IL
The King's University College, AB
Lee University, TN
Malone College, OH
Montreat College, NC
Mount Vernon Nazarene College, OH
North Park University, IL
Northwest Christian College, OR
Northwest College, WA
Northwestern College, MN
Northwest Nazarene University, ID
Nyack College, NY
Oklahoma Baptist University, OK
Olivet Nazarene University, IL
Point Loma Nazarene University, CA
Roberts Wesleyan College, NY
Simpson College and Graduate School, CA
Southern Wesleyan University, SC
Southwest Baptist University, MO
Spring Arbor College, MI
Tabor College, KS
Taylor University, IN
Trevecca Nazarene University, TN
Trinity International University, IL
Trinity Western University, BC
University of Sioux Falls, SD
Vanguard University of Southern California, CA
Warner Pacific College, OR
Warner Southern College, FL
Western Baptist College, OR
Westmont College, CA
William Tyndale College, MI

SOCIAL STUDIES EDUCATION
Abilene Christian University, TX
Anderson University, IN
Bethel College, IN
Cedarville University, OH
Colorado Christian University, CO
East Texas Baptist University, TX
Erskine College, SC
George Fox University, OR
Greenville College, IL
Indiana Wesleyan University, IN
Malone College, OH
Messiah College, PA
MidAmerica Nazarene University, KS
Northwestern College, MN
Oklahoma Baptist University, OK
Oral Roberts University, OK
Wheaton College, IL

SOCIAL WORK
Abilene Christian University, TX
Anderson University, IN

Asbury College, KY
Azusa Pacific University, CA
Bethel College, KS
Bethel College, MN
Bluffton College, OH
Calvin College, MI
Campbellsville University, KY
Campbell University, NC
Cedarville University, OH
College of the Ozarks, MO
Cornerstone University, MI
David Lipscomb University, TN
Dordt College, IA
Eastern College, PA
Eastern Mennonite University, VA
Eastern Nazarene College, MA
Evangel University, MO
Fresno Pacific University, CA
George Fox University, OR
Gordon College, MA
Goshen College, IN
Grace College, IN
Greenville College, IL
Hope International University, CA
Howard Payne University, TX
Indiana Wesleyan University, IN
Kentucky Christian College, KY
Malone College, OH
Messiah College, PA
Mount Vernon Nazarene College, OH
Northwestern College, IA
Northwest Nazarene University, ID
Oklahoma Baptist University, OK
Oral Roberts University, OK
Point Loma Nazarene University, CA
Redeemer University College, ON
Roberts Wesleyan College, NY
Southern Nazarene University, OK
Spring Arbor College, MI
Taylor University, IN
Union University, TN
University of Sioux Falls, SD
Warner Pacific College, OR
Warner Southern College, FL

SOCIOLOGY
Abilene Christian University, TX
Anderson University, IN
Asbury College, KY
Azusa Pacific University, CA
Bethel College, IN
Biola University, CA
Bluffton College, OH
Calvin College, MI
Campbellsville University, KY
Cedarville University, OH
College of the Ozarks, MO
Cornerstone University, MI
Covenant College, GA
Dallas Baptist University, TX
Dordt College, IA
Eastern College, PA
Eastern Mennonite University, VA
Eastern Nazarene College, MA
East Texas Baptist University, TX
Evangel University, MO
Fresno Pacific University, CA
Geneva College, PA
George Fox University, OR

Gordon College, MA
Goshen College, IN
Grace College, IN
Grand Canyon University, AZ
Greenville College, IL
Houghton College, NY
Houston Baptist University, TX
Howard Payne University, TX
Huntington College, IN
Indiana Wesleyan University, IN
Judson College, IL
The King's University College, AB
Lee University, TN
Messiah College, PA
MidAmerica Nazarene University, KS
Milligan College, TN
Mount Vernon Nazarene College, OH
North Park University, IL
Northwestern College, IA
Oklahoma Baptist University, OK
Point Loma Nazarene University, CA
Redeemer University College, ON
Roberts Wesleyan College, NY
Seattle Pacific University, WA
Southern Nazarene University, OK
Southwest Baptist University, MO
Spring Arbor College, MI
Tabor College, KS
Taylor University, IN
Trinity Christian College, IL
Trinity International University, IL
Union University, TN
University of Sioux Falls, SD
Vanguard University of Southern California, CA
Westmont College, CA
Wheaton College, IL
Whitworth College, WA

SPANISH
Abilene Christian University, TX
Anderson University, IN
Asbury College, KY
Azusa Pacific University, CA
Bethel College, KS
Bethel College, MN
Biola University, CA
Bluffton College, OH
Calvin College, MI
Campbell University, NC
Cedarville University, OH
College of the Ozarks, MO
Cornerstone University, MI
David Lipscomb University, TN
Dordt College, IA
Eastern College, PA
Eastern Mennonite University, VA
Eastern Nazarene College, MA
East Texas Baptist University, TX
Erskine College, SC
Evangel University, MO
Fresno Pacific University, CA
Geneva College, PA
George Fox University, OR
Gordon College, MA
Goshen College, IN
Grace College, IN
Greenville College, IL
Houghton College, NY
Houston Baptist University, TX

Howard Payne University, TX
Indiana Wesleyan University, IN
King College, TN
Malone College, OH
Messiah College, PA
MidAmerica Nazarene University, KS
Montreat College, NC
Mount Vernon Nazarene College, OH
North Park University, IL
Northwestern College, IA
Northwestern College, MN
Oklahoma Baptist University, OK
Oklahoma Christian University of Science and
  Arts, OK
Olivet Nazarene University, IL
Oral Roberts University, OK
Point Loma Nazarene University, CA
Seattle Pacific University, WA
Southern Nazarene University, OK
Southwest Baptist University, MO
Spring Arbor College, MI
Taylor University, IN
Trinity Christian College, IL
Union University, TN
Vanguard University of Southern California, CA
Westmont College, CA
Wheaton College, IL
Whitworth College, WA

SPANISH LANGUAGE EDUCATION
Abilene Christian University, TX
Anderson University, IN
Cedarville University, OH
East Texas Baptist University, TX
Grace College, IN
Greenville College, IL
King College, TN
Malone College, OH
Messiah College, PA
MidAmerica Nazarene University, KS
Oklahoma Baptist University, OK
Oral Roberts University, OK
Southern Nazarene University, OK

SPECIAL EDUCATION
Abilene Christian University, TX
Bluffton College, OH
Calvin College, MI
Cedarville University, OH
Eastern Mennonite University, VA
Eastern Nazarene College, MA
Erskine College, SC
Evangel University, MO
Geneva College, PA
Gordon College, MA
Grand Canyon University, AZ
Greenville College, IL
Houston Baptist University, TX
Huntington College, IN
Indiana Wesleyan University, IN
John Brown University, AR
Lee University, TN
The Master's College and Seminary, CA
Milligan College, TN
Mount Vernon Nazarene College, OH
Northwest College, WA
Oklahoma Baptist University, OK
Oklahoma Christian University of Science and
  Arts, OK

Oral Roberts University, OK
Seattle Pacific University, WA
Southern Wesleyan University, SC
Tabor College, KS
Trinity Christian College, IL
Union University, TN
Warner Southern College, FL
Whitworth College, WA

SPEECH EDUCATION
Abilene Christian University, TX
Anderson University, IN
Cedarville University, OH
East Texas Baptist University, TX
Greenville College, IL
Howard Payne University, TX
Malone College, OH
Northwest Nazarene University, ID
Oklahoma Baptist University, OK
Southern Nazarene University, OK

SPEECH-LANGUAGE PATHOLOGY/
AUDIOLOGY
Abilene Christian University, TX
Calvin College, MI
Geneva College, PA
Northwest Nazarene University, ID

SPEECH/RHETORICAL STUDIES
Abilene Christian University, TX
Asbury College, KY
Bethel College, MN
Bluffton College, OH
Calvin College, MI
Cedarville University, OH
College of the Ozarks, MO
Cornerstone University, MI
David Lipscomb University, TN
East Texas Baptist University, TX
Evangel University, MO
Geneva College, PA
Grand Canyon University, AZ
Greenville College, IL
Houston Baptist University, TX
Howard Payne University, TX
Judson College, IL
The Master's College and Seminary, CA
North Park University, IL
Northwest Christian College, OR
Northwestern College, IA
Northwest Nazarene University, ID
Oklahoma Baptist University, OK
Oklahoma Christian University of Science and
  Arts, OK
Olivet Nazarene University, IL
Point Loma Nazarene University, CA
Southern Nazarene University, OK
Spring Arbor College, MI
Trevecca Nazarene University, TN
Union University, TN
University of Sioux Falls, SD
Vanguard University of Southern California, CA
Wheaton College, IL
Whitworth College, WA

SPORT/FITNESS ADMINISTRATION
Belhaven College, MS
Bluffton College, OH
Campbell University, NC
Cornerstone University, MI

Eastern Mennonite University, VA
Erskine College, SC
Fresno Pacific University, CA
George Fox University, OR
Indiana Wesleyan University, IN
Judson College, IL
LeTourneau University, TX
Montreat College, NC
Mount Vernon Nazarene College, OH
North Greenville College, SC
Northwestern College, MN
Southern Nazarene University, OK
Southwest Baptist University, MO
Taylor University, IN
Union University, TN
Warner Southern College, FL
Western Baptist College, OR

STRINGED INSTRUMENTS
David Lipscomb University, TN
Houghton College, NY
Howard Payne University, TX
Olivet Nazarene University, IL
Palm Beach Atlantic College, FL
Wheaton College, IL

SYSTEMS ENGINEERING
Eastern Nazarene College, MA

TEACHER ASSISTANT/AIDE
Dordt College, IA
Eastern Mennonite University, VA

TEACHING ENGLISH AS A SECOND
LANGUAGE
Bartlesville Wesleyan College, OK
Calvin College, MI
Eastern Nazarene College, MA
Goshen College, IN
John Brown University, AR
Northwest College, WA
Northwestern College, MN
Nyack College, NY
Oklahoma Christian University of Science and
  Arts, OK
Oral Roberts University, OK
Union University, TN

TECHNICAL WRITING
Cedarville University, OH
Northwestern College, MN

TELECOMMUNICATIONS
Howard Payne University, TX
Oklahoma Baptist University, OK

THEATER ARTS/DRAMA
Abilene Christian University, TX
Anderson University, IN
Belhaven College, MS
Bethel College, IN
Bethel College, MN
California Baptist University, CA
Calvin College, MI
Campbell University, NC
Cedarville University, OH
College of the Ozarks, MO
Colorado Christian University, CO
Dordt College, IA
Eastern Mennonite University, VA
Eastern Nazarene College, MA

Majors Index by Major

Theater arts/drama (continued)

East Texas Baptist University, TX
Goshen College, IN
Grand Canyon University, AZ
Greenville College, IL
Howard Payne University, TX
Huntington College, IN
Judson College, IL
Malone College, OH
Messiah College, PA
Milligan College, TN
Mount Vernon Nazarene College, OH
North Greenville College, SC
North Park University, IL
Northwest College, WA
Northwestern College, IA
Northwestern College, MN
Oklahoma Baptist University, OK
Oklahoma Christian University of Science and
    Arts, OK
Oral Roberts University, OK
Palm Beach Atlantic College, FL
Point Loma Nazarene University, CA
Redeemer University College, ON
Seattle Pacific University, WA
Southwest Baptist University, MO
Sterling College, KS
Taylor University, IN
Trevecca Nazarene University, TN
Trinity Western University, BC
Union University, TN
University of Sioux Falls, SD
Vanguard University of Southern California, CA
Westmont College, CA
Whitworth College, WA

THEATER DESIGN
Tabor College, KS

THEOLOGY
Anderson University, IN
Azusa Pacific University, CA
Bartlesville Wesleyan College, OK
Biola University, CA
Calvin College, MI
Cedarville University, OH
Colorado Christian University, CO
David Lipscomb University, TN
Dordt College, IA
Eastern College, PA
Eastern Mennonite University, VA
East Texas Baptist University, TX
George Fox University, OR
Grand Canyon University, AZ

Greenville College, IL
Howard Payne University, TX
Huntington College, IN
Indiana Wesleyan University, IN
John Brown University, AR
Lee University, TN
The Master's College and Seminary, CA
Mount Vernon Nazarene College, OH
North Greenville College, SC
North Park University, IL
Northwest College, WA
Northwestern College, IA
Northwest Nazarene University, ID
Nyack College, NY
Oklahoma Baptist University, OK
Olivet Nazarene University, IL
Oral Roberts University, OK
Point Loma Nazarene University, CA
Redeemer University College, ON
Taylor University, IN
Trinity Christian College, IL
Union University, TN
Warner Pacific College, OR
Western Baptist College, OR
Williams Baptist College, AR
William Tyndale College, MI

(PRE)THEOLOGY
Geneva College, PA
Northwest Christian College, OR
Northwestern College, MN
Redeemer University College, ON
Trinity Christian College, IL
Warner Southern College, FL
Westmont College, CA

URBAN STUDIES
David Lipscomb University, TN
Eastern College, PA
Malone College, OH
North Park University, IL

(PRE)VETERINARY STUDIES
Abilene Christian University, TX
Anderson University, IN
Bartlesville Wesleyan College, OK
Bethel College, MN
Calvin College, MI
Campbellsville University, KY
Campbell University, NC
Cedarville University, OH
College of the Ozarks, MO
Cornerstone University, MI
David Lipscomb University, TN
Dordt College, IA

Eastern Mennonite University, VA
Eastern Nazarene College, MA
Evangel University, MO
Goshen College, IN
Grand Canyon University, AZ
Greenville College, IL
Houghton College, NY
Houston Baptist University, TX
Huntington College, IN
Indiana Wesleyan University, IN
John Brown University, AR
King College, TN
LeTourneau University, TX
Milligan College, TN
Mount Vernon Nazarene College, OH
North Park University, IL
Northwest Nazarene University, ID
Oklahoma Baptist University, OK
Oklahoma Christian University of Science and
    Arts, OK
Olivet Nazarene University, IL
Redeemer University College, ON
Roberts Wesleyan College, NY
Tabor College, KS
Taylor University, IN
Trinity Christian College, IL
Trinity Western University, BC
University of Sioux Falls, SD
Warner Pacific College, OR
Westmont College, CA
Whitworth College, WA

WELDING TECHNOLOGY
LeTourneau University, TX

WILDLIFE BIOLOGY
Grand Canyon University, AZ

WIND AND PERCUSSION INSTRUMENTS
Bryan College, TN
David Lipscomb University, TN
Grand Canyon University, AZ
Houghton College, NY
Howard Payne University, TX
Mount Vernon Nazarene College, OH
Oklahoma Baptist University, OK
Oklahoma Christian University of Science and
    Arts, OK
Olivet Nazarene University, IL
Palm Beach Atlantic College, FL
University of Sioux Falls, SD
Wheaton College, IL

ZOOLOGY
Olivet Nazarene University, IL
Tabor College, KS

Athletic Index

BASEBALL

Abilene Christian University, TX	M(s)
Anderson University, IN	M
Asbury College, KY	M
Azusa Pacific University, CA	M(s)
Bartlesville Wesleyan College, OK	M(s)
Belhaven College, MS	M(s)
Bethel College, IN	M(s)
Bethel College, KS	M
Bethel College, MN	M
Biola University, CA	M(s)
Bluffton College, OH	M
California Baptist University, CA	M(s)
Calvin College, MI	M
Campbellsville University, KY	M(s)
Campbell University, NC	M(s)
Cedarville University, OH	M(s)
College of the Ozarks, MO	M(s)
Crichton College, TN	M
Dallas Baptist University, TX	M(s)
David Lipscomb University, TN	M(s)
Eastern College, PA	M
Eastern Mennonite University, VA	M
Eastern Nazarene College, MA	M
East Texas Baptist University, TX	M
Erskine College, SC	M(s)
Evangel University, MO	M(s)
Geneva College, PA	M(s)
George Fox University, OR	M
Gordon College, MA	M
Goshen College, IN	M(s)
Grace College, IN	M(s)
Grand Canyon University, AZ	M(s)
Greenville College, IL	M
Houston Baptist University, TX	M(s)
Howard Payne University, TX	M
Huntington College, IN	M(s)
Indiana Wesleyan University, IN	M(s)
Judson College, IL	M(s)
King College, TN	M(s)
LeTourneau University, TX	M
Malone College, OH	M(s)
The Master's College and Seminary, CA	M(s)
Messiah College, PA	M
MidAmerica Nazarene University, KS	M(s)
Milligan College, TN	M(s)
Montreat College, NC	M(s)
Mount Vernon Nazarene College, OH	M(s)
North Greenville College, SC	M(s)
North Park University, IL	M
Northwestern College, IA	M(s)
Northwestern College, MN	M
Northwest Nazarene University, ID	M(s)
Nyack College, NY	M
Oklahoma Baptist University, OK	M(s)
Oklahoma Christian University of Science and Arts, OK	M(s)
Olivet Nazarene University, IL	M(s)
Oral Roberts University, OK	M(s)
Palm Beach Atlantic College, FL	M(s)
Point Loma Nazarene University, CA	M(s)
Simpson College and Graduate School, CA	M
Southern Nazarene University, OK	M(s)

Southern Wesleyan University, SC	M(s)
Southwest Baptist University, MO	M(s)
Spring Arbor College, MI	M(s)
Sterling College, KS	M(s)
Tabor College, KS	M(s)
Taylor University, IN	M(s)
Trevecca Nazarene University, TN	M(s)
Trinity Christian College, IL	M(s)
Trinity International University, IL	M
Union University, TN	M(s)
University of Sioux Falls, SD	M(s)
Vanguard University of Southern California, CA	M(s)
Warner Southern College, FL	M(s)
Western Baptist College, OR	M(s)
Westmont College, CA	M(s)
Wheaton College, IL	M
Whitworth College, WA	M
Williams Baptist College, AR	M(s)

BASKETBALL

Abilene Christian University, TX	M(s), W(s)
Anderson University, IN	M, W
Asbury College, KY	M, W
Azusa Pacific University, CA	M(s), W(s)
Bartlesville Wesleyan College, OK	M(s), W(s)
Belhaven College, MS	M(s), W(s)
Bethel College, IN	M(s), W(s)
Bethel College, KS	M(s), W(s)
Bethel College, MN	M, W
Biola University, CA	M(s), W(s)
Bluffton College, OH	M, W
Bryan College, TN	M(s), W(s)
California Baptist University, CA	M(s), W(s)
Calvin College, MI	M, W
Campbellsville University, KY	M(s), W(s)
Campbell University, NC	M(s), W(s)
Cedarville University, OH	M(s), W(s)
College of the Ozarks, MO	M(s), W(s)
Colorado Christian University, CO	M(s), W(s)
Cornerstone University, MI	M(s), W(s)
Covenant College, GA	M(s), W(s)
David Lipscomb University, TN	M(s), W(s)
Dordt College, IA	M(s), W(s)
Eastern College, PA	M, W
Eastern Mennonite University, VA	M, W
Eastern Nazarene College, MA	M, W
East Texas Baptist University, TX	M, W
Erskine College, SC	M(s), W(s)
Evangel University, MO	M(s), W(s)
Fresno Pacific University, CA	M(s), W(s)
Geneva College, PA	M(s), W(s)
George Fox University, OR	M, W
Gordon College, MA	M, W
Goshen College, IN	M(s), W(s)
Grace College, IN	M(s), W(s)
Grand Canyon University, AZ	M(s), W(s)
Greenville College, IL	M, W
Hope International University, CA	M(s), W(s)
Houghton College, NY	M(s), W(s)
Houston Baptist University, TX	M(s), W(s)
Howard Payne University, TX	M, W
Huntington College, IN	M(s), W(s)

Indiana Wesleyan University, IN	M(s), W(s)
John Brown University, AR	M(s), W(s)
Judson College, AL	W(s)
Judson College, IL	M(s), W(s)
Kentucky Christian College, KY	M, W
King College, TN	M(s), W(s)
The King's University College, AB	M(s), W(s)
Lee University, TN	M(s), W(s)
LeTourneau University, TX	M, W
Malone College, OH	M(s), W(s)
The Master's College and Seminary, CA	M(s), W(s)
Messiah College, PA	M, W
MidAmerica Nazarene University, KS	M(s), W(s)
Milligan College, TN	M(s), W(s)
Montreat College, NC	M(s), W(s)
Mount Vernon Nazarene College, OH	M(s), W(s)
North Greenville College, SC	M(s), W(s)
North Park University, IL	M, W
Northwest Christian College, OR	M(s)
Northwest College, WA	M(s), W(s)
Northwestern College, IA	M(s), W(s)
Northwestern College, MN	M, W
Northwest Nazarene University, ID	M(s), W(s)
Nyack College, NY	M(s), W(s)
Oklahoma Baptist University, OK	M(s), W(s)
Oklahoma Christian University of Science and Arts, OK	M(s), W(s)
Olivet Nazarene University, IL	M(s), W(s)
Oral Roberts University, OK	M(s), W(s)
Palm Beach Atlantic College, FL	M(s), W(s)
Point Loma Nazarene University, CA	M(s), W(s)
Redeemer University College, ON	M, W
Roberts Wesleyan College, NY	M(s), W(s)
Seattle Pacific University, WA	M(s), W(s)
Simpson College and Graduate School, CA	M, W
Southern Nazarene University, OK	M(s), W(s)
Southern Wesleyan University, SC	M(s), W(s)
Southwest Baptist University, MO	M(s), W(s)
Spring Arbor College, MI	M(s), W(s)
Sterling College, KS	M(s), W(s)
Tabor College, KS	M(s), W(s)
Taylor University, IN	M(s), W(s)
Trevecca Nazarene University, TN	M(s), W(s)
Trinity Christian College, IL	M(s), W(s)
Trinity International University, IL	M(s), W(s)
Trinity Western University, BC	M, W
Union University, TN	M(s), W(s)
University of Sioux Falls, SD	M(s), W(s)
Vanguard University of Southern California, CA	M(s), W(s)
Warner Pacific College, OR	M(s), W(s)
Warner Southern College, FL	M(s), W(s)
Western Baptist College, OR	M(s), W(s)
Westmont College, CA	M(s), W(s)
Wheaton College, IL	M, W
Whitworth College, WA	M, W
Williams Baptist College, AR	M(s), W(s)

BOWLING

Roberts Wesleyan College, NY	W

CREW

Seattle Pacific University, WA	M, W
Wheaton College, IL	M, W

CROSS-COUNTRY RUNNING

Abilene Christian University, TX	M(s), W(s)
Anderson University, IN	M, W
Asbury College, KY	M, W
Azusa Pacific University, CA	M(s), W(s)
Belhaven College, MS	M(s), W(s)
Bethel College, IN	M(s), W(s)
Bethel College, MN	M, W
Biola University, CA	M(s), W(s)
Bluffton College, OH	M, W
California Baptist University, CA	M(s), W(s)
Calvin College, MI	M, W
Campbellsville University, KY	M(s), W(s)
Campbell University, NC	M(s), W(s)
Cedarville University, OH	M(s), W(s)
Colorado Christian University, CO	M, W
Cornerstone University, MI	M(s), W(s)
Covenant College, GA	M(s), W(s)
Dallas Baptist University, TX	M, W(s)
David Lipscomb University, TN	M(s), W(s)
Dordt College, IA	M(s), W(s)
Eastern Mennonite University, VA	M, W
Eastern Nazarene College, MA	M, W
Erskine College, SC	M(s), W(s)
Evangel University, MO	M(s), W(s)
Fresno Pacific University, CA	M(s), W(s)
Geneva College, PA	M(s), W(s)
George Fox University, OR	M, W
Gordon College, MA	M, W
Goshen College, IN	M(s), W(s)
Grace College, IN	M(s), W(s)
Greenville College, IL	M, W
Houghton College, NY	M(s), W(s)
Howard Payne University, TX	M, W
Huntington College, IN	M(s), W(s)
Indiana Wesleyan University, IN	M(s), W(s)
Judson College, IL	M(s), W(s)
Kentucky Christian College, KY	M, W
Lee University, TN	M(s), W(s)
LeTourneau University, TX	M, W
Malone College, OH	M(s), W(s)
The Master's College and Seminary, CA	M(s), W(s)
Messiah College, PA	M, W
MidAmerica Nazarene University, KS	M(s), W(s)
Milligan College, TN	M(s), W(s)
Montreat College, NC	M(s), W(s)
North Greenville College, SC	M(s), W(s)
North Park University, IL	M, W
Northwest College, WA	M(s), W(s)
Northwestern College, IA	M(s), W(s)
Northwestern College, MN	M, W
Northwest Nazarene University, ID	M(s), W(s)
Nyack College, NY	M, W
Oklahoma Baptist University, OK	M(s), W(s)
Oklahoma Christian University of Science and Arts, OK	M(s), W(s)
Olivet Nazarene University, IL	M(s), W(s)
Oral Roberts University, OK	M(s), W(s)
Palm Beach Atlantic College, FL	M(s), W(s)
Point Loma Nazarene University, CA	M(s), W(s)
Roberts Wesleyan College, NY	M(s), W(s)
Seattle Pacific University, WA	M(s), W(s)
Southern Nazarene University, OK	M(s), W(s)
Southern Wesleyan University, SC	M(s), W(s)
Southwest Baptist University, MO	M(s), W(s)
Spring Arbor College, MI	M(s), W(s)
Sterling College, KS	M(s), W(s)
Tabor College, KS	M(s), W(s)
Taylor University, IN	M(s), W(s)
Trinity International University, IL	M, W
Trinity Western University, BC	M, W
Union University, TN	W(s)
University of Sioux Falls, SD	M(s), W(s)
Vanguard University of Southern California, CA	M(s), W(s)
Warner Pacific College, OR	M(s), W(s)
Warner Southern College, FL	M(s), W(s)
Westmont College, CA	M(s), W(s)
Wheaton College, IL	M, W
Whitworth College, WA	M, W

EQUESTRIAN SPORTS

Erskine College, SC	M, W
Judson College, AL	W
Taylor University, IN	M, W

FIELD HOCKEY

Eastern College, PA	W
Eastern Mennonite University, VA	W
Gordon College, MA	W
Houghton College, NY	W(s)
Messiah College, PA	W
Wheaton College, IL	W

FOOTBALL

Abilene Christian University, TX	M(s)
Anderson University, IN	M
Azusa Pacific University, CA	M(s)
Belhaven College, MS	M(s)
Bethel College, KS	M(s)
Bethel College, MN	M
Bluffton College, OH	M
Campbellsville University, KY	M(s)
East Texas Baptist University, TX	M
Evangel University, MO	M(s)
Geneva College, PA	M(s)
Greenville College, IL	M
Howard Payne University, TX	M
Malone College, OH	M(s)
MidAmerica Nazarene University, KS	M(s)
North Greenville College, SC	M(s)
North Park University, IL	M
Northwestern College, IA	M(s)
Northwestern College, MN	M
Olivet Nazarene University, IL	M(s)
Southwest Baptist University, MO	M(s)
Sterling College, KS	M(s)
Tabor College, KS	M(s)
Taylor University, IN	M(s)
Trinity International University, IL	M(s)
University of Sioux Falls, SD	M(s)
Wheaton College, IL	M
Whitworth College, WA	M

GOLF

Abilene Christian University, TX	M(s)
Anderson University, IN	M, W
Azusa Pacific University, CA	M(s)
Bartlesville Wesleyan College, OK	M(s)
Belhaven College, MS	M(s), W(s)
Bethel College, IN	M(s)
Bethel College, MN	M

Bluffton College, OH	M
California Baptist University, CA	M(s)
Calvin College, MI	M, W
Campbellsville University, KY	M(s), W(s)
Campbell University, NC	M(s), W(s)
Cedarville University, OH	M(s)
Colorado Christian University, CO	M(s)
Cornerstone University, MI	M(s)
David Lipscomb University, TN	M(s), W(s)
Dordt College, IA	M(s)
East Texas Baptist University, TX	M, W
Evangel University, MO	M(s), W(s)
Goshen College, IN	M(s)
Grace College, IN	M(s)
Grand Canyon University, AZ	M(s)
Greenville College, IL	M
Howard Payne University, TX	M, W
Huntington College, IN	M(s), W(s)
Indiana Wesleyan University, IN	M(s)
King College, TN	M(s)
Lee University, TN	M(s)
LeTourneau University, TX	M, W
Malone College, OH	M(s), W(s)
Messiah College, PA	M
Milligan College, TN	M(s)
Montreat College, NC	M(s)
Mount Vernon Nazarene College, OH	M(s)
North Greenville College, SC	M(s)
North Park University, IL	M
Northwestern College, IA	M(s), W(s)
Northwestern College, MN	M
Northwest Nazarene University, ID	M(s)
Oklahoma Baptist University, OK	M(s), W(s)
Oklahoma Christian University of Science and Arts, OK	M(s)
Olivet Nazarene University, IL	M(s)
Oral Roberts University, OK	M(s), W(s)
Palm Beach Atlantic College, FL	M(s), W
Point Loma Nazarene University, CA	M(s)
Redeemer University College, ON	M, W
Southern Nazarene University, OK	M(s), W(s)
Southern Wesleyan University, SC	M(s)
Southwest Baptist University, MO	M(s)
Spring Arbor College, MI	M(s)
Tabor College, KS	M(s), W(s)
Taylor University, IN	M(s)
Trevecca Nazarene University, TN	M, W
Trinity International University, IL	M(s)
Trinity Western University, BC	M
Union University, TN	M(s)
Warner Southern College, FL	M(s)
Wheaton College, IL	M
Williams Baptist College, AR	M(s)

GYMNASTICS

Seattle Pacific University, WA	W(s)

ICE HOCKEY

Bethel College, MN	M, W
Calvin College, MI	M
Dordt College, IA	M
Trinity Western University, BC	M, W
Wheaton College, IL	M

LACROSSE

Calvin College, MI	M, W

Eastern College, PA	M, W
Eastern Nazarene College, MA	M
Gordon College, MA	M, W
Messiah College, PA	M, W
Taylor University, IN	M
Westmont College, CA	W
Wheaton College, IL	M, W

RUGBY

Trinity Western University, BC	M, W
Westmont College, CA	M

SOCCER

Abilene Christian University, TX	M, W
Anderson University, IN	M, W
Asbury College, KY	M
Azusa Pacific University, CA	M(s), W(s)
Bartlesville Wesleyan College, OK	M(s), W(s)
Belhaven College, MS	M(s), W(s)
Bethel College, IN	M(s), W(s)
Bethel College, KS	M(s), W(s)
Bethel College, MN	M, W
Biola University, CA	M(s), W(s)
Bluffton College, OH	M, W
Bryan College, TN	M(s), W(s)
California Baptist University, CA	M(s), W(s)
Calvin College, MI	M, W
Campbellsville University, KY	M(s), W(s)
Campbell University, NC	M(s), W(s)
Cedarville University, OH	M(s), W(s)
Colorado Christian University, CO	M(s), W(s)
Cornerstone University, MI	M(s), W(s)
Covenant College, GA	M(s), W(s)
Dallas Baptist University, TX	M, W(s)
David Lipscomb University, TN	M(s), W(s)
Dordt College, IA	M(s), W(s)
Eastern College, PA	M, W
Eastern Mennonite University, VA	M, W
Eastern Nazarene College, MA	M, W
East Texas Baptist University, TX	M, W
Erskine College, SC	M(s), W(s)
Fresno Pacific University, CA	M(s)
Geneva College, PA	M(s), W(s)
George Fox University, OR	M, W
Gordon College, MA	M, W
Goshen College, IN	M(s), W(s)
Grace College, IN	M(s), W(s)
Grand Canyon University, AZ	M(s), W(s)
Greenville College, IL	M, W
Hope International University, CA	M(s), W(s)
Houghton College, NY	M(s), W(s)
Howard Payne University, TX	M
Huntington College, IN	M(s)
Indiana Wesleyan University, IN	M(s), W(s)
John Brown University, AR	M(s)
Judson College, IL	M(s), W(s)
Kentucky Christian College, KY	M
King College, TN	M(s), W(s)
The King's University College, AB	M, W
Lee University, TN	M(s), W(s)
LeTourneau University, TX	M, W
Malone College, OH	M(s), W(s)
The Master's College and Seminary, CA	M(s), W(s)
Messiah College, PA	M, W
Milligan College, TN	M(s), W(s)
Montreat College, NC	M(s), W(s)

Mount Vernon Nazarene College, OH	M(s), W(s)
North Greenville College, SC	M(s), W(s)
North Park University, IL	M, W
Northwest College, WA	M(s)
Northwestern College, IA	M(s), W(s)
Northwestern College, MN	M, W
Northwest Nazarene University, ID	M(s), W(s)
Nyack College, NY	M(s), W(s)
Oklahoma Christian University of Science and Arts, OK	M(s), W(s)
Olivet Nazarene University, IL	M(s), W(s)
Oral Roberts University, OK	M(s), W(s)
Palm Beach Atlantic College, FL	M(s), W(s)
Point Loma Nazarene University, CA	M(s)
Redeemer University College, ON	M, W
Roberts Wesleyan College, NY	M(s), W(s)
Seattle Pacific University, WA	M(s), W
Simpson College and Graduate School, CA	M, W
Southern Nazarene University, OK	M(s), W(s)
Southern Wesleyan University, SC	M(s), W(s)
Southwest Baptist University, MO	M(s), W(s)
Spring Arbor College, MI	M(s), W(s)
Sterling College, KS	M(s), W(s)
Tabor College, KS	M(s), W(s)
Taylor University, IN	M(s), W(s)
Trinity Christian College, IL	M(s), W(s)
Trinity International University, IL	M(s), W(s)
Trinity Western University, BC	M, W
Union University, TN	M(s)
University of Sioux Falls, SD	M(s), W(s)
Vanguard University of Southern California, CA	M(s), W(s)
Warner Pacific College, OR	M(s)
Western Baptist College, OR	M(s), W(s)
Westmont College, CA	M(s), W(s)
Wheaton College, IL	M, W
Whitworth College, WA	M, W
Williams Baptist College, AR	M(s)
William Tyndale College, MI	M

SOFTBALL

Abilene Christian University, TX	W(s)
Anderson University, IN	W
Asbury College, KY	W
Azusa Pacific University, CA	W(s)
Bartlesville Wesleyan College, OK	W(s)
Belhaven College, MS	W(s)
Bethel College, IN	W(s)
Bethel College, MN	W
Biola University, CA	W(s)
Bluffton College, OH	W
California Baptist University, CA	W(s)
Calvin College, MI	W
Campbellsville University, KY	W(s)
Campbell University, NC	W(s)
Cedarville University, OH	W(s)
Cornerstone University, MI	W(s)
David Lipscomb University, TN	W(s)
Dordt College, IA	W(s)
Eastern College, PA	W
Eastern Mennonite University, VA	W
Eastern Nazarene College, MA	W
East Texas Baptist University, TX	W
Erskine College, SC	W(s)
Evangel University, MO	W(s)
Geneva College, PA	W(s)

George Fox University, OR	W
Gordon College, MA	W
Goshen College, IN	W(s)
Grace College, IN	W(s)
Greenville College, IL	W
Hope International University, CA	W(s)
Houston Baptist University, TX	W(s)
Howard Payne University, TX	W
Huntington College, IN	W(s)
Indiana Wesleyan University, IN	W(s)
Judson College, AL	W(s)
Judson College, IL	W(s)
Lee University, TN	W(s)
LeTourneau University, TX	W
Malone College, OH	W(s)
Messiah College, PA	W
MidAmerica Nazarene University, KS	W(s)
Milligan College, TN	W(s)
Montreat College, NC	W(s)
Mount Vernon Nazarene College, OH	W(s)
North Greenville College, SC	W(s)
North Park University, IL	W
Northwest Christian College, OR	W
Northwestern College, IA	W(s)
Northwestern College, MN	W
Nyack College, NY	W
Oklahoma Baptist University, OK	W(s)
Oklahoma Christian University of Science and Arts, OK	W(s)
Olivet Nazarene University, IL	W
Palm Beach Atlantic College, FL	W
Point Loma Nazarene University, CA	W(s)
Simpson College and Graduate School, CA	W
Southern Nazarene University, OK	W(s)
Southern Wesleyan University, SC	W(s)
Southwest Baptist University, MO	W(s)
Spring Arbor College, MI	W(s)
Sterling College, KS	W(s)
Tabor College, KS	W(s)
Taylor University, IN	W(s)
Trevecca Nazarene University, TN	W(s)
Trinity Christian College, IL	W(s)
Trinity International University, IL	W(s)
Union University, TN	W(s)
University of Sioux Falls, SD	W(s)
Vanguard University of Southern California, CA	W(s)
Warner Southern College, FL	W(s)
Western Baptist College, OR	W
Wheaton College, IL	W
Williams Baptist College, AR	W(s)

SWIMMING

Asbury College, KY	M, W
Biola University, CA	M(s), W(s)
California Baptist University, CA	M(s), W(s)
Calvin College, MI	M, W
Campbellsville University, KY	M(s), W(s)
Gordon College, MA	M, W
John Brown University, AR	M(s), W(s)
Wheaton College, IL	M, W
Whitworth College, WA	M, W

TENNIS

Abilene Christian University, TX	M(s), W(s)
Anderson University, IN	M, W
Asbury College, KY	M, W
Azusa Pacific University, CA	M(s)

Southwest Baptist University, MO	W(s)	University of Sioux Falls, SD	W(s)
Spring Arbor College, MI	W(s)	Vanguard University of Southern California,	
Sterling College, KS	W(s)	CA	W(s)
Tabor College, KS	W(s)	Warner Pacific College, OR	W(s)
Taylor University, IN	M, W(s)	Warner Southern College, FL	W(s)
Trevecca Nazarene University, TN	W(s)	Western Baptist College, OR	W(s)
Trinity Christian College, IL	M(s), W(s)	Westmont College, CA	M, W(s)
Trinity International University, IL	M, W(s)	Wheaton College, IL	M, W
Trinity Western University, BC	M, W	Whitworth College, WA	W
Union University, TN	W(s)	Williams Baptist College, AR	W(s)

WATER POLO

California Baptist University, CA	M(s), W(s)

WRESTLING

Campbell University, NC	M(s)
Evangel University, MO	W
Messiah College, PA	M
Northwestern College, IA	M(s)
Wheaton College, IL	M

Graduate Majors Index

ACCOUNTING
Abilene Christian University	M
Dallas Baptist University	M
Eastern College	M
Houston Baptist University	M
Oral Roberts University	M
Southwest Baptist University	M

ADVANCED PRACTICE NURSING
Houston Baptist University	M
Seattle Pacific University	O

AMERICAN STUDIES
Wheaton College	M

ARCHAEOLOGY
Wheaton College	M

BIOETHICS
Trinity International University	P,M,D,O

BUSINESS ADMINISTRATION AND MANAGEMENT—GENERAL
Abilene Christian University	M
Azusa Pacific University	M
Belhaven College	M
Bethel College (IN)	M
California Baptist University	M
Campbell University	M
Colorado Christian University	M
Dallas Baptist University	M
David Lipscomb University	M
Eastern College	M
Eastern Mennonite University	M
Fresno Pacific University	M
George Fox University	M
Grand Canyon University	M
Hope International University	M
Houston Baptist University	M
Indiana Wesleyan University	M
John Brown University	M
LeTourneau University	M
Malone College	M
MidAmerica Nazarene University	M
Montreat College	M
North Park University	M
Northwest Nazarene University	M
Olivet Nazarene University	M
Oral Roberts University	M
Palm Beach Atlantic College	M
Roberts Wesleyan College	M
Seattle Pacific University	M
Southern Nazarene University	M
Southern Wesleyan University	M
Southwest Baptist University	M
Spring Arbor College	M
Trevecca Nazarene University	M
Union University	M
University of Sioux Falls	M
Whitworth College	M

CHILD AND FAMILY STUDIES
Abilene Christian University	M
Roberts Wesleyan College	M

CITY AND REGIONAL PLANNING
North Park University	M

CLINICAL PSYCHOLOGY
Abilene Christian University	M
Azusa Pacific University	M,D
Evangel University	M
George Fox University	M,D
Seattle Pacific University	D
Wheaton College	M,D

COMMUNICATION—GENERAL
Abilene Christian University	M
Bethel College (MN)	M

COMPUTER SCIENCE
Azusa Pacific University	M,O

CONFLICT RESOLUTION AND MEDIATION/PEACE STUDIES
Dallas Baptist University	M
Eastern Mennonite University	M
Fresno Pacific University	M

COUNSELING PSYCHOLOGY
Abilene Christian University	M
Bethel College (IN)	M
Eastern College	M
Eastern Nazarene College	M
Geneva College	M
Hope International University	M
Lee University	M
Palm Beach Atlantic College	M
Southern Nazarene University	M
Trevecca Nazarene University	M
Trinity International University	M
Trinity Western University	M

COUNSELOR EDUCATION
Abilene Christian University	M
Campbell University	M
Dallas Baptist University	M
Eastern College	M
Evangel University	M
Fresno Pacific University	M
Houston Baptist University	M
Indiana Wesleyan University	M
John Brown University	M
Malone College	M
Northwest Nazarene University	M
Palm Beach Atlantic College	M
Seattle Pacific University	M
Trevecca Nazarene University	M
Whitworth College	M

CURRICULUM AND INSTRUCTION
Azusa Pacific University	M
California Baptist University	M

EARLY CHILDHOOD EDUCATION
Calvin College	M
Campbellsville University	M
Colorado Christian University	M
Fresno Pacific University	M
Indiana Wesleyan University	M
Malone College	M
MidAmerica Nazarene University	M
Northwest Nazarene University	M
Olivet Nazarene University	M
Oral Roberts University	M
Simpson College and Graduate School	M
Trevecca Nazarene University	M

EARLY CHILDHOOD EDUCATION
Dallas Baptist University	M
Eastern Nazarene College	M,O
Oral Roberts University	M

ECONOMICS
Eastern College	M
Seattle Pacific University	M

EDUCATION—GENERAL
Abilene Christian University	M
Azusa Pacific University	M,D
Bethel College (MN)	M
Biola University	M
Bluffton College	M
California Baptist University	M
Calvin College	M
Campbellsville University	M
Campbell University	M
Colorado Christian University	M
Covenant College	M
Dallas Baptist University	M
David Lipscomb University	M
Dordt College	M
Eastern College	M,O
Eastern Mennonite University	M
Eastern Nazarene College	M,O
Evangel University	M
Fresno Pacific University	M
Geneva College	M
George Fox University	M,D
Gordon College	M
Grand Canyon University	M
Hope International University	M
Houston Baptist University	M
Indiana Wesleyan University	M
Lee University	M
Malone College	M
MidAmerica Nazarene University	M
Milligan College	M
Mount Vernon Nazarene College	M
North Park University	M
Northwest Nazarene University	M
Olivet Nazarene University	M
Oral Roberts University	M
Palm Beach Atlantic College	M
Point Loma Nazarene University	M,O

Roberts Wesleyan College	M
Seattle Pacific University	M,D,O
Southern Nazarene University	M
Southwest Baptist University	M
Spring Arbor College	M
Trevecca Nazarene University	M,D
Union University	M
University of Sioux Falls	M
Vanguard University of Southern California	M
Wheaton College	M
Whitworth College	M

EDUCATIONAL ADMINISTRATION

Abilene Christian University	M
Azusa Pacific University	M,D
California Baptist University	M
Campbell University	M
Dallas Baptist University	M
Eastern Nazarene College	M,O
Fresno Pacific University	M
Geneva College	M
Houston Baptist University	M
Northwest Nazarene University	M
Oral Roberts University	M
Seattle Pacific University	M,D
Southwest Baptist University	M
Trevecca Nazarene University	M
University of Sioux Falls	M
Whitworth College	M

EDUCATIONAL MEASUREMENT AND EVALUATION

Abilene Christian University	M
Houston Baptist University	M

EDUCATIONAL MEDIA/ INSTRUCTIONAL TECHNOLOGY

Azusa Pacific University	M
Fresno Pacific University	M
Malone College	M
University of Sioux Falls	M

EDUCATIONAL PSYCHOLOGY

Eastern College	M

EDUCATION OF THE GIFTED

Whitworth College	M

EDUCATION OF THE MULTIPLY HANDICAPPED

Fresno Pacific University	M

ELEMENTARY EDUCATION

Abilene Christian University	M
Campbell University	M
Dallas Baptist University	M
Eastern Nazarene College	M,O
Evangel University	M
Grand Canyon University	M
Houston Baptist University	M
Olivet Nazarene University	M
Palm Beach Atlantic College	M
Trevecca Nazarene University	M

ENGLISH

Abilene Christian University	M

ENGLISH AS A SECOND LANGUAGE

Azusa Pacific University	M,O
Biola University	M,D,O
Eastern College	O
Eastern Nazarene College	M,O

Fresno Pacific University	M
Grand Canyon University	M
Oral Roberts University	M
Seattle Pacific University	M
Wheaton College	M,O
Whitworth College	M

ENGLISH EDUCATION

California Baptist University	M
Campbell University	M

ETHICS

Biola University	P,M,D

EXERCISE AND SPORTS SCIENCE

California Baptist University	M

FINANCE AND BANKING

Dallas Baptist University	M
Eastern College	M
Houston Baptist University	M
Oral Roberts University	M

GERONTOLOGY

Abilene Christian University	M

HEALTH EDUCATION

Eastern College	M

HEALTH SERVICES MANAGEMENT AND HOSPITAL ADMINISTRATION

Houston Baptist University	M
Southwest Baptist University	M

HIGHER EDUCATION

Azusa Pacific University	M
Dallas Baptist University	M
Geneva College	M

HISTORY

Abilene Christian University	M

HUMAN RESOURCES DEVELOPMENT

Abilene Christian University	M
Azusa Pacific University	M
Palm Beach Atlantic College	M

HUMAN RESOURCES MANAGEMENT

Dallas Baptist University	M
Houston Baptist University	M

HUMAN SERVICES

Abilene Christian University	M
Roberts Wesleyan College	M

INTERDISCIPLINARY STUDIES

Fresno Pacific University	M
Trinity International University	M
Wheaton College	M

INTERNATIONAL BUSINESS

Azusa Pacific University	M
Dallas Baptist University	M
Hope International University	M
Oral Roberts University	M
Whitworth College	M

JOURNALISM

Abilene Christian University	M

LAW

Campbell University	P
Trinity International University	P

LIBERAL STUDIES

Abilene Christian University	M
Dallas Baptist University	M
Houston Baptist University	M
Lee University	M

LINGUISTICS

Biola University	M,D,O

MANAGEMENT INFORMATION SYSTEMS

Dallas Baptist University	M
Houston Baptist University	M
Seattle Pacific University	M

MANAGEMENT STRATEGY AND POLICY

Azusa Pacific University	M

MARKETING

Dallas Baptist University	M
Eastern College	M
Houston Baptist University	M
Oral Roberts University	M

MARRIAGE AND FAMILY THERAPY

Abilene Christian University	M
Bethel College (IN)	M
California Baptist University	M
Eastern Nazarene College	M
Geneva College	M
George Fox University	P,M
Hope International University	M
John Brown University	M
Northwest Christian College	M,O
Oklahoma Baptist University	M
Palm Beach Atlantic College	M
Seattle Pacific University	M
Trevecca Nazarene University	M
Vanguard University of Southern California	M

MASS COMMUNICATION

Abilene Christian University	M

MATHEMATICS EDUCATION

Campbell University	M
Fresno Pacific University	M

MIDDLE SCHOOL EDUCATION

Campbell University	M
Eastern Nazarene College	M,O
Evangel University	M

MISSIONS AND MISSIOLOGY

Abilene Christian University	M
Biola University	M,D,O
Oral Roberts University	P,M,D
Simpson College and Graduate School	M
Trinity International University	P,M,D,O
Wheaton College	M,O

MULTILINGUAL AND MULTICULTURAL EDUCATION

Azusa Pacific University	M
California Baptist University	M
Eastern College	M
Eastern Nazarene College	M,O
Fresno Pacific University	M
Houston Baptist University	M

MUSIC

Azusa Pacific University	M
Hope International University	M

Music (continued)

Lee University .... M

MUSIC EDUCATION
Azusa Pacific University .... M
Campbellsville University .... M
Eastern Nazarene College .... M,O

NONPROFIT MANAGEMENT
Eastern College .... M
Hope International University .... M

NURSING—GENERAL
Abilene Christian University .... M
Azusa Pacific University .... M
Bethel College (MN) .... M
Houston Baptist University .... M
Indiana Wesleyan University .... M
North Park University .... M
Seattle Pacific University .... M,O

NURSING EDUCATION
Indiana Wesleyan University .... M

OCCUPATIONAL THERAPY
Milligan College .... M

ORGANIZATIONAL BEHAVIOR
Bethel College (MN) .... M
Dallas Baptist University .... M
Geneva College .... M
Spring Arbor College .... M
Trevecca Nazarene University .... M

PASTORAL MINISTRY AND COUNSELING
Abilene Christian University .... M,D
Azusa Pacific University .... P,M,D
Bethel College (IN) .... M
Colorado Christian University .... M
Eastern Mennonite University .... P,M
George Fox University .... P,M
Hope International University .... M
Huntington College .... M
Malone College .... M
Oklahoma Christian University of Science and
  Arts .... M
Olivet Nazarene University .... M
Oral Roberts University .... P,M,D
Southern Wesleyan University .... M
Trinity International University .... P,M,D,O

PHARMACY
Campbell University .... P

PHYSICAL EDUCATION
Azusa Pacific University .... M
Campbell University .... M
Eastern Nazarene College .... M,O
Seattle Pacific University .... M
Whitworth College .... M

PHYSICAL THERAPY
Azusa Pacific University .... M
Southwest Baptist University .... M

PHYSICIAN ASSISTANT STUDIES
Trevecca Nazarene University .... M

PSYCHOLOGY—GENERAL
Abilene Christian University .... M
Azusa Pacific University .... M,D
Bethel College (MN) .... M
Biola University .... M,D
Evangel University .... M
George Fox University .... M,D
Grace College .... M
Hope International University .... M
Houston Baptist University .... M
Southern Nazarene University .... M
Wheaton College .... M,D

PUBLIC HEALTH NURSING
Indiana Wesleyan University .... M

READING EDUCATION
Abilene Christian University .... M
California Baptist University .... M
Dallas Baptist University .... M
Eastern Nazarene College .... M,O
Evangel University .... M
Fresno Pacific University .... M
Grand Canyon University .... M
Houston Baptist University .... M
Malone College .... M
Seattle Pacific University .... M
University of Sioux Falls .... M
Whitworth College .... M

RELIGION
Azusa Pacific University .... P,M,D
Biola University .... P,M,D
Colorado Christian University .... M
David Lipscomb University .... P,M
Eastern Mennonite University .... P,M
Hope International University .... M
Northwest Nazarene University .... M
Olivet Nazarene University .... M
Point Loma Nazarene University .... M
Southern Nazarene University .... M
Trevecca Nazarene University .... M
Trinity International University .... P,M,D,O
Trinity Western University .... M
Vanguard University of Southern California .... M
Warner Pacific College .... M
Wheaton College .... M

RELIGIOUS EDUCATION
Abilene Christian University .... P,M,D
Biola University .... P,M,D
Campbell University .... P,M
George Fox University .... P,M
Huntington College .... M
Oral Roberts University .... P,M,D
Trinity International University .... P,M,D,O
Wheaton College .... M

SCHOOL PSYCHOLOGY
Abilene Christian University .... M
Fresno Pacific University .... M
Seattle Pacific University .... O

SCIENCE EDUCATION
Fresno Pacific University .... M

SECONDARY EDUCATION
Abilene Christian University .... M
Campbell University .... M
Eastern Nazarene College .... M,O
Grand Canyon University .... M
Houston Baptist University .... M
Olivet Nazarene University .... M
Seattle Pacific University .... M
Wheaton College .... M

SOCIAL SCIENCES EDUCATION
Campbell University .... M

SOCIAL WORK
Roberts Wesleyan College .... M

SOFTWARE ENGINEERING
Azusa Pacific University .... M,O

SPECIAL EDUCATION
Azusa Pacific University .... M
California Baptist University .... M
Calvin College .... M
Eastern Nazarene College .... M,O
Fresno Pacific University .... M
Houston Baptist University .... M
Malone College .... M
Northwest Nazarene University .... M
Whitworth College .... M

SPEECH AND INTERPERSONAL COMMUNICATION
Abilene Christian University .... M

SPORTS ADMINISTRATION
Whitworth College .... M

TELECOMMUNICATIONS
Azusa Pacific University .... M,O

THEOLOGY
Abilene Christian University .... P,M
Anderson University .... P,M,D
Azusa Pacific University .... P,M,D
Biola University .... P,M,D
Campbell University .... P,M
David Lipscomb University .... P,M
Eastern Mennonite University .... P,M
George Fox University .... P,M
Houston Baptist University .... M
Indiana Wesleyan University .... M
The Master's College and Seminary .... P,M
Mount Vernon Nazarene College .... M
Oklahoma Christian University of Science and
  Arts .... M
Olivet Nazarene University .... M
Oral Roberts University .... P,M,D
Palm Beach Atlantic College .... M
Simpson College and Graduate School .... M
Southern Nazarene University .... M
Trinity International University .... P,M,D,O
Trinity Western University .... P,M,D
Vanguard University of Southern California .... M
Wheaton College .... M,O

VOCATIONAL AND TECHNICAL EDUCATION
California Baptist University .... M

WRITING
Abilene Christian University .... M